AF333434

The Definitive Guide to the C&A Transformation

The First Publication of a Comprehensive View of the C&A Transformation

PN #	Item ID	Alibris ID	Media Type	Title / Author	Seller List Price	Order Date
76524116-36	SKU1013773	B083663626	BOOK	The Definitive Guide to the C&a Transformation Julie E Mehan; Waylon Krush	$19.00	Jul, 6 2026

alibris

CALLIOPEBOOKS
9824 GLENOLDEN DR
ROCKVILLE, MD 20854
UNITED STATES

**To: ALIBRIS APEX DC 76524116-36
APEX
800 AVONDALE AVE.
GRANDVIEW HEIGHTS, OH 43212-3473**

Shipping Instructions for EMILYANN

Print this Packing Slip and enclose inside the front cover of the book.

Please ship this item no later than Thu Jul 16, 2026.

Ship to:

ALIBRIS APEX DC 76524116-36
APEX
800 AVONDALE AVE.
GRANDVIEW HEIGHTS, OH 43212-3473
UNITED STATES

The Definitive Guide to the C&A Transformation

The First Publication of a Comprehensive View of the C&A Transformation

DR JULIE E. MEHAN, PHD, CISSP

WAYLON KRUSH, CISSP, CISA, CAP

IT Governance Publishing

Every possible effort has been made to ensure that the information contained in this book is accurate at the time of going to press, and the publisher and the authors cannot accept responsibility for any errors or omissions, however caused. No responsibility for loss or damage occasioned to any person acting, or refraining from action, as a result of the material in this publication can be accepted by the publisher or the authors.

The publisher and authors have taken all reasonable care to ensure that all material in this book is original, is in the public domain, or is used with the permission of the original copyright owner. However, if any person believes that material for which they own the copyright has found its way into this book without permission, please contact the publisher who will investigate and remedy any inadvertent infringement.

Apart from any fair dealing for the purposes of research or private study, or criticism or review, as permitted under the Copyright, Designs and Patents Act 1988, this publication may only be reproduced, stored or transmitted, in any form, or by any means, with the prior permission in writing of the publisher or, in the case of reprographic reproduction, in accordance with the terms of licences issued by the Copyright Licensing Agency. Enquiries concerning reproduction outside those terms should be sent to the publisher at the following address:

IT Governance Publishing
IT Governance Limited
Unit 3, Clive Court
Bartholomew's Walk
Cambridgeshire Business Park
Ely
Cambridgeshire
CB7 4EH
United Kingdom

www.itgovernance.co.uk

© J. E. Mehan & W. Krush 2009

The authors have asserted the rights of the authors under the Copyright, Designs and Patents Act, 1988, to be identified as the authors of this work.

First published in the United Kingdom in 2009 by IT Governance Publishing.

ISBN 978-1-84928-006-8

PREFACE

War is always a product of its age. And information systems are one of the primary drivers of war in the age of information. The tools and tactics used to fight the information war have evolved with advances in technology. So, it is no wonder that the tools and tactics needed to defend critical information systems must also evolve.

One of the tools in the defense toolkit is the process known as Certification and Accreditation (C&A) or authorization. At its best, C&A can be extremely effective in ensuring the implementation of the measures necessary to protect the information network. At its worst, it can be cumbersome, laborious, and costly without providing any real security value.

The challenges of effectively executing C&A – or authorization as it has most recently been termed – within an agency or large enterprise have been staggering and often cost-prohibitive, primarily because traditionally the implementation of C&A[1] varied not only from site to site or from agency to agency, but even within a single agency or organization.

Between them, the authors of this book have over 35 years' experience in information systems security – including C&A. We have witnessed firsthand the costs and effort required to execute what has often been – at best – a time-consuming, costly, complex and often inaccurate process.

We recognized early that in the current environment, with its declining monetary and personnel resources, linked with the increasingly rapid advances in technology, an integrated, cost-effective authorization process is necessary. We also know that there is a dynamic threat environment, which necessitates a

---

[1] The term Certification & Accreditation (C&A) is used here because of its historical reference. Although "Authorization to Operate" is the emerging terminology, many organizations hold to the traditional term of C&A. As a result, both terms are used interchangeably within this book.

transformation to more efficient and integrated processes to ensure that C&A (or authorization) represents a truly relevant part of an information systems security program. We have been a part of this transformation.

It may be months, or even years, before the final chapter on C&A transformation will be written. This book has been written to help prepare organizations for the journey that will take them through the C&A transformation. This is the first book that describes the transformation and provides guidance that reflects the emerging requirements. There are hundreds of documents – laws, regulations, policies, and guidance – that state the requirement for C&A, but few provide a step-by-step guide to a required process in a changing environment. In this book, we provide an overview of the challenges of today's information systems security environment and convey how the existing requirements and best practices can actually be effective in protecting information systems and their associated software. The Department of Defense's DIACAP and the federal government's NIST processes are highlighted, and we provide a step-by step approach to executing the authorization process to meet the demands of each; not only to achieve legally-mandated compliance under FISMA, but more importantly, to securely acquire, develop, deploy, and sustain an organization's information systems. We have written this book for two main reasons. The first is the desire to debunk three prevailing concepts about information system (IS) security authorization:

- Authorization is an exercise focused primarily on the production of massive amounts of documentation.
- Authorization is costly and time-consuming, but has no real relevance to true information systems security.
- Authorization is only about compliance and compliance is impossible to achieve.

The second reason is an underlying conviction that the authorization process – ***properly executed*** – constitutes one of the most critical components of an effective information systems security program. In order to be relevant, authorization – like all elements of a successful security program – must be focused on ***Security beyond Compliance***!

We seek to provide a comprehensive handbook so that planning, executing, managing and tracking authorization is no longer just a labor intensive, complex, costly process that challenges even the most efficient organization. By the time you reach the end, we hope to have presented methods and best practices for an efficient, cost effective, and relevant process that makes a tangible contribution to the overall security posture of the organization – without losing your mind or your budget!

Each chapter provides a list of related references, as well as recommendations for additional reading. Each section will refer to relevant templates and references that will be included in a usable format on the accompanying CD. The book, together with the CD, provides a useful authorization-process hands-on reference for security practitioners, system administrators, managers, standards developers, evaluators, testers, and those just wanting to be knowledgeable about the establishment and sustainment of a secure information environment. The following URL links to the website product page for this book which includes further information about the accompanying CD-ROM and supplementary product-related information (including updates):
http://www.itgovernanceusa.com/information-assurance.aspx.

NOTE: ***Most of our readers will be familiar with the use of the term C&A and some will be aware of the proposed change in terminology to authorization. In order to avoid confusion, and to ensure that this book represents the most current concepts and use of lexicons, we will use the term authorization throughout the book, with the exception of those sections specific to the DOD and IC, and to those uses where it is historically relevant, where we will refer to the process as C&A.***

Dr Julie E. Mehan, PhD, CISSP
Waylon Krush, CISSP, CISA, CAP

ABOUT THE AUTHORS

Dr Julie E. Mehan, PhD, CISSP

Dr Julie Mehan is President/CEO of JEMStone Strategies and a Principal Analyst for a strategic consulting firm in the State of Virginia. She has been a career Government Service employee, a strategic consultant, and an entrepreneur – which either demonstrates her flexibility or inability to hold on to a steady job! She has led business operations, as well as information technology governance and information assurance-related services, including certification and accreditation, systems security engineering process improvement, and information assurance strategic planning and programme management. During previous years, she delivered information assurance and security-related privacy services to senior Department of Defense, federal government, and commercial clients working in Italy, Australia, Canada, Belgium, and the United States.

She served on the President's Partnership for Critical Infrastructure Security, Task Force on Interdependency and Vulnerability Assessments. Dr Mehan is on the SANS Advisory Board, a voting board member for the International Systems Security Professional Certification Scheme (ISSPCS), and chair of the Systems Certification Working Group of the International Systems Security Engineers Association. Dr Mehan also serves as an Associate Professor at the University of Maryland University College, specializing in courses in Information Technology and Organizational Structure, and Ethics in Information Technology.

Dr Mehan graduated *summa cum laude* with a PhD from Capella University in Organization and Management, focusing her research into challenges facing Chief Security Officers in large government and commercial organizations and the development of a dynamic model of Chief Security Officer leadership. She holds a Master of Arts with honours in International Relations and Law from Boston

University and a Bachelor of Science degree in History and Languages from the University of New York.

Dr Mehan was awarded the Meritorious Civilian Service Award for her actions in Bosnia and the Commander's Award for Civilian Service for her initiatives in establishing the Army's first Red and Blue Team capability. Dr Mehan was elected 2003 Woman of Distinction by the Women of Greater Washington. In April 2008, Dr Mehan's book *CyberWar, CyberTerror, CyberCrime: A Guide to the Role of Standards in an Environment of Change and Danger* was published through IT Governance Publishing. She has also published numerous articles, including, *Framework for Reasoning About Security – A Comparison of the Concepts of Immunology and Security; System Dynamics, Criminal Behavior Theory and Computer-Enabled Crime*; and *The Value of Information-Based Warfare To Affect Adversary Decision Cycles*. Dr Mehan is fluent in German and has conversational skills in French and Italian.

She can be contacted at *je.mehan@JEMStoneStrategies.com*

Waylon Krush, CISSP, CISA, CAP

Waylon Krush is currently the Chief Executive Officer (CEO) of Lunarline, Inc, a successful privately held information security (IS)/information assurance (IA) company that provides secure solutions for the federal government, Department of Defense (DOD), Intelligence Community (IC), and Fortune 500 companies worldwide. Mr Krush provides subject matter expertise in identification and authentication (I&A), encryption, secure system design, software assurance, medical device, embedded/wireless device security, and certification and accreditation (C&A) for the Department of Transportation (DOT), DOD and commercial companies.

Prior to becoming the CEO of Lunarline, Inc, Waylon was a senior information security engineer in AT&T's Advanced Systems Division (ASD), and Chief of the Information Assurance (IA) group for GRC-TSC. At AT&T Mr Krush developed solutions (software and hardware) and provided consulting in DOD and Intelligence Community (IC) architecture, identity management, public key infrastructure, secure knowledge management/sharing and critical infrastructure protection, and intrusion protection.

Mr Krush proudly served seven years in the United States Army in various intelligence/information operation (IO) and security related technical and leadership roles throughout the world. Mr Krush was the lead technical member of the Land and Information Warfare Activity (LIWA) Red Team (US Army Red Team) and developed systems for RF/signal monitoring and analysis systems for various customers worldwide. Mr Krush also served as the technical lead for the Information Systems Security Monitoring (ISSM) group in the US Army.   Mr Krush won many military awards and recognition related to computer network operations (CNO) and information operations (IO).

Waylon holds a BS in Computer Information Science from the University of Maryland University College, and is a Certified Information Systems Security Professional (CISSP), Certified Certification and Accreditation Professional (CAP), and Certified

Information Security Auditor (CISA). Mr Krush also has over 3000 hours of training from the National Security Agency (NSA) National Cryptologic School (NCS).

Mr Krush has been an active participant in the development of information security and information assurance guidelines and standards to include: NIST SP 800-53A (Identification and Authentication Family), and is currently working with Dr Scott Bernard and Dr Ron Ross on the CIO Counsel Enterprise Architecture (EA) Security and Privacy Profile (SPP) version 3.0.

Waylon is a recipient of the Knowlton Award, DOT Cyber Security Excellence Award, United States Marine Corp Scholastic Leadership Award, Air Force Advanced Signals Award, 718th Military Intelligence (MI) Soldier of the Year, NSA Professional of the Quarter, Voice of America Award, American Legion Award (2 years), and various military/technical awards and honors.

ACKNOWLEDGEMENTS

An outstanding team of dedicated professionals at IT Governance Publishing has made the creation of this book a pleasure and not a task.

We appreciate the contributions of all who supported us and participated in the content of the book or provided useful suggestions:

To Jack:

I, Julie, am forever indebted to my partner and best friend, Jack, for believing in me and never allowing me to falter in my belief in myself. A simple thank you will never be enough.

To Angela:

For your unfailing professionalism and responsiveness — this constant connection gave us encouragement and support.

CONTENTS

Contents

INTRODUCTION

For over three decades, the authors of this book have been deeply involved in developing C&A policy, but more importantly in actually providing hands-on help to organizations, ranging from large federal agencies to commercial entities, to successfully navigate the C&A process. We continue to be directly and intensely involved in the C&A transformation, including the transition in terminology from C&A to authorization. We share a driving thought: to do whatever is necessary to protect the information systems of our clients.

Purpose and scope

This basic purpose of this book is to provide a definitive guide to authorization for persons with knowledge of information systems and/or information systems security, but not necessarily the same level of expertise with certification and accreditation (C&A) standards and best practices; it points to references for further knowledge.

It is scoped to present the information needed to meaningfully recognize, implement, and manage authorization requirements and achieve compliance with federal, local and agency laws and policies.

This book cannot, of course, enumerate all of the knowledge needed in order to secure information systems against all threats. Nor does it seek to do so. Our real motivation is more clearly defined below.

According to OMB's March 2004 report to Congress, funding for IT security ... increased from $2.7B in 2002 to $4.2B in 2004. Nevertheless, a total of 18 agencies identified funding as a challenge to performing their certifications and accreditations.
GAO Report 04-376

Motivation – what do we hope to accomplish with this book?

It has been 20+ years since certification and accreditation (C&A) – referred to as authorization by the National Institute of Standards and Technology (NIST) — has been part of the regulatory landscape. In this time the federal government – which includes the US Department of Defense (DOD) – has easily spent billions (that's right – billions) of dollars in meeting compliance requirements. The demonstrated return on investment, however, has been less than encouraging. Richard Bejtlick, President & CEO of TaoSecurity stated: "Millions of dollars and thousands of hours are spent on C&A … In reality, C&A is a 20-year old paperwork exercise which does not yield improved security."

Historically, the C&A process was introduced as a means to ensure the information systems security posture of information technology (IT). In fact, under FISMA, C&A evolved into one of the primary measures used to evaluate the success of an organization's information systems security posture. Properly executed, C&A can actually go a very long way towards improving and maintaining a high standard of information systems security.

But, over the years, the C&A process has become "bureaucratized." It has manifested itself as cumbersome, laborious, and costly – with the final output consisting of thousands of pages of documentation and often little else. Some have even termed it a mind-numbing, picayune process generating reams of security documentation on an agency's IT systems and infrastructure with little real relevance to the true state of the organization's information system security. The true value of C&A will only be realized when both organizations and individuals focus the process on more directly addressing security concerns, while concurrently minimizing complexity and redundancy – and unnecessary paperwork.

Today's information environment demands a workforce skilled in the implementation and management of a secure information systems environment. Vulnerabilities[2] in our information systems are open to discovery – and potential exploitation – by unauthorized, unethical, criminal, or even uneducated individuals. While an information systems security incident can have a serious impact upon an organization's ability to process essential information, the effects can also be seen in the form of heavy costs for recovery and remediation and a negative impact on the organization's reputation.[3]

The optimal approach to addressing the challenges of this environment and obtaining a real return on investment from authorization is a re-evaluation of the way in which the authorization process is addressed. The most effective approach to authorization involves standardization and simplification, resulting in a tailorable, repeatable, and cost-efficient process. The second requirement is a trained and experienced work force. And there are efforts in the US federal government and the DOD to make this a reality.

In a best case scenario, there would be one single standard that would apply to all federal agencies, the DOD, and the Intelligence Community (IC). But this is unfortunately not yet the case – although it is the goal of the ongoing effort across the federal government to revitalize the C&A process. Until that wondrous day finally arrives, however, this book seeks to provide readers with a comprehensive handbook for authorization across the US federal government and DOD – as well as for commercial entities – that is focused on practical and proven solutions that are both cost and time efficient.

While the content of this guide provides broad coverage of the authorization landscape, readers interested in gaining an even

---

[2] 'Vulnerability: Weakness in an information system, system security procedures, internal controls, or implementation that could be exploited or triggered by a threat source.' [NIST FIPS 200].

[3] A study in the *Journal of Computer Security* measured the results of security breaches in several ways. The results indicated that relying only on an analysis of the cash cost can be misleading; rather, the impact on their reputation can be even more devastating. Additional information on this study can be obtained at:
http://brief.weburb.dk/archive/00000130/01/2003-costs-security-on-stockvalue-9972866.pdf.

deeper knowledge of security laws, standards, requirements, and best practices are encouraged to read the references provided throughout this document and to refer to documents on the accompanying CD.

Who is the target audience?

Simply stated, the target audience is anyone concerned with, responsible for, or associated with the security of information systems. We intend this book to benefit the senior leadership chartered with making difficult security decisions, as well as the systems administrators responsible for implementing and managing many of the security measures needed to protect the operation of the information system. And the audience is not limited to those within the US federal government – commercial entities who want to sell to the government or who just want more secure information systems – can also benefit from an understanding of the authorization process.

C&A does not apply only to the federal government. Approximately 90 percent of the nation's critical infrastructure is on private networks that are not part of any US federal department or agency. The nation's critical infrastructure includes information technology systems that run electrical systems, chemical systems, nuclear systems, transportation systems, telecommunication systems, banking and financial systems, and agricultural and food and water supply systems. These private organizations can also take advantage of these same methodologies to mitigate risks on their information systems and networks.

We have personally witnessed a definite increase in non-government interest in the authorization process, either because commercial entities see it as a value-added process for security, or because they have a desire to add the US government to their existing client base.

Terminology

In any work of this nature, it is important to establish a context and a vocabulary. Like most environments, an entire vernacular has evolved in the field of security. So, in order to ensure clarity, we would like to establish a few definitions and the specific terminology we will be using.

Several terms are used interchangeably to refer to the security requirements specific to automated information systems (AIS): INFOSEC, computer security, information assurance, and information systems security.[4] For the purposes of this book, we will use the term "information systems security," since we feel that it is much more comprehensive and best expresses the goals of the authorization process.

Three other terms are directly relevant to the context of this book: certification and accreditation. *The National Information Assurance Glossary, CNSS Instruction 4009,* provides the following definitions:

- **Certification:** Comprehensive evaluation of the technical and nontechnical security safeguards of an IS to support the accreditation process that establishes the extent to which a particular design and implementation meets a set of specified security requirements. The terminology is changing to "Security Controls Assessment" in some of the recent doctrinal releases; but we will continue to use certification in this book.

- **Accreditation**[5]: Formal declaration by an authorizing official or designated accrediting authority (DAA)[6] that an IS is approved to operate at an acceptable level of risk, based on the implementation of an approved set of technical, managerial, and procedural safeguards. Although the terms certification and accreditation have been traditionally used to refer to this process, we have chosen to use the term "Authorization" in the book

---

[4] See the glossary for definitions of each of these terms.
[5] Most recently referred to as "authorization" by NIST.
[6] Senior official executive with the authority to formally accept responsibility for operating an information system at an acceptable level of risk.

except for those cases where the term C&A is still a part of the official designation.

- **Authorization**[7]: The official management decision given by a senior organizational official to authorize operation of an information system and to explicitly accept the risk to organizational operations and assets, individuals, other organizations, and the Nation based on the implementation of an agreed-upon set of security controls. Under the C&A transition, "authorization" will be the term used to refer to this official decision.

Certification is still a critical part of the authorization process. Certification provides the needed level of assurance to the decision making authorizing official that the technical and non-technical security features of an information system meet a set of specified security requirements or controls. It standardizes the activities leading to an authorization to operate.

But someone has to make the final decision to accept the risk and allow an information system to operate – and that individual – the authorizing official or designated accrediting authority (DAA) – makes the authorization decision. Without the foundation of a solid certification process, the DAA would not have the essential understanding of the real security of an IS and would not be able to realistically make a risk-based decision.

Overview of the contents

Chapter 1 provides a quick outline of the evolution of information technology from the mainframe to today's global network of interconnected systems and considers how technological progress was accompanied by a co-evolution in security policy. We take a deep dive into the most influential legislation, regulations, policy and guidance in the information systems security landscape. There

---

[7] This definition is taken from NIST SP 800-37, Rev 1.

is a focus on those documents that have a close or direct relationship to the authorization process.

Chapter 2 introduces an authorization framework, based on a consistent set of processes that emphasizes the value of standardization in the authorization process.

We really start to discuss the "how" of authorization in **Chapter 3**. Here, the activities – such as establishing an information systems security program – that are necessary for establishing the foundation for a successful authorization process are discussed in detail.

Chapter 4 looks at essential pre-authorization activities, such as establishing your security authorization team, determining the authorization boundary, and training.

Chapters 5 through 8 present a "deep dive" into an authorization approach that will meet the needs of any organization, whether a federal agency, a DOD component, or an industry partner.

In **Chapter 9**, we address the authorization package and its required contents. In addition, we provide extensive guidance to the preparation of supporting evidence, such as configuration management, contingency planning, incident response, etc.

Chapters 10 and 11 present the C&A/authorization processes currently in use in the Department of Defense (DOD) and the federal government agencies. These processes have been the most influential; consequently, we do not have a specific chapter on the processes used by the US Intelligence Community.

The Federal Information Security Management Act (FISMA) has had a major influence on information systems security, and most specifically, the C&A/authorization process. **Chapter 12** provides an overview of FISMA and how organizations might move from understanding to compliance.

Integration of security into the system (development) life cycle (SLC) has been a resounding cry across the federal government. In **Chapter 13**, we take a quick look at C&A/authorization and the SLC.

Chapter 14 looks at current initiatives to formalize requirements for information systems security training, education and certification. In particular, we look at the DOD's efforts as published in the DOD 8570.1-M, which provides DOD requirements for information assurance (IA) workforce training and certification.

Last, but certainly not least, we introduce the ongoing effort to revitalize C&A/authorization across the federal government in **Chapter 15**. The results of this effort will have far-reaching effects and we are enthusiastic to continue to be contributing members of the revitalization process.

In addition to the above chapters, we have also produced a companion CD to this book. This CD is a valuable reference tool and a resource. It contains the documents referenced in this text, as well as templates and samples of the documentation required as part of the C&A process. There is an index to the contents of the CD at the end of this book.

CHAPTER 1: AN ABRIDGED HISTORY OF INFORMATION TECHNOLOGY AND INFORMATION SYSTEMS SECURITY

Security can be achieved only through constant change, through discarding old ideas outliving their usefulness, and adapting others to current facts.

William O. Douglas, US Supreme Court Justice
(1898-1980)

In this chapter:

An abridged history of information technology

Information systems and information systems security – merging concerns

Information security[8] itself is not a new concept – decision makers have taken steps to protect critical information since the emergence of governments and supporting infrastructures. New technologies, however, have forever changed the way information is developed, stored, published, and shared. In order to help you to understand the value of information today and the role of information systems security authorization in its protection, we need to take a walk back in time and engage in a short retrospective of information, information systems, and information systems security.

From physical to virtual – a highly abridged history of information technology

Until the relatively recent emergence of information systems (otherwise known as computers), information[9] was held largely in physical form – as documents, manuscripts, and books – starting with etchings in stone and ending with mass-printed materials. So, here's a very abridged history of the evolution of information management from the physical to the virtual.

At some point around 20,000 years ago, mankind invented the means to store data (e.g. information) in pictures or symbols. The use of these pictures and symbols, later alphabets and words, gradually evolved to create powerful information content, which now required decisions on how to store the information and who should be allowed access to it.

Over time, the storage of information evolved into paper form, which then led to the emergence of mass printing, in turn rendering the information increasingly easy to reproduce and distribute. New

---

[8] Information security is defined by Carnegie Mellon University Software Engineering Institute as "the concepts, techniques, technical measures, and administrative measures used to protect information assets from deliberate or inadvertent unauthorized acquisition, damage, disclosure, manipulation, modification, loss, or use." [See presentation with the definition by *McDaniel 94*]
[9] There have been many attempts to define information over the generations. One of the primary constructs is that information consists of multiple elements of data, each of which may not be useful on its own. Over time, these individual points of data evolve into more sophisticated content.

methods for storing different forms of information evolved, such as recordings and film.

Since that long ago date, the developers and distributors of information recognized that the information itself possessed a level of value and, as such, deserved protection. Protection of this information was done almost exclusively through physical means, such as fences, guards, secure containers, and access-control to buildings.

In the last few decades, and certainly within the memory of most of us today, information and its production, storage and sharing has undergone radical change brought about by the development of the computer. Many claim that the first computer was the Abacus developed centuries ago by the Chinese, largely as a device to count money.

For over a thousand years after this first computing device, there was little progress made in designing an automated means to count and solve number-related problems. The next advance was brought about by Blaise Pascal and his design of the first mechanical adding machine in 1642. His device proved so successful that history also tells of the first wave of "technophobia"[10] among mathematicians who feared the device would render them unnecessary.

Charles Babbage caused the next leap forward in computing technology in 1822, when he first produced the "difference engine."[11] He followed this in 1833 with the "analytic engine," the first real parallel decimal computer using instructions stored on punched cards. This device reflected virtually every aspect of computing as we know it today.

---

[10] Merriam Webster's Online Dictionary defines technophobia as "fear or dislike of advanced technology or complex devices and especially computers." (*http://www.merriam-webster.com/dictionary/technophobia*)

[11] The difference engine was a fully automatic, steam-powered device commanded by a fixed instruction program. (*http://www.computerhistory.org/babbage/*)

Punch-card computing machines remained the mainstay until the mid-1900s. These progressed through the Harvard Mark I[12] to the breakthrough ENIAC[13] machine. In the mid-1950s, the ENIAC gave way to the EDVAC, the first computer to use binary rather than decimal units. 1958 saw the breakthrough invention of the computer chip by Texas Instruments, opening the way to replace inefficient vacuum tubes and to begin the process of "miniaturizing" the computer.

The first microprocessor was released in 1971 by Intel. This was the turning point, after which the path to today's computing environment became irreversible.

Computers had been almost exclusively the legion of the military, universities, and very large corporations simply because they were extremely expensive and maintenance was complex. In 1975, the cover of Popular Electronics featured a story on the world's first minicomputer kit to rival commercial models – the Altair 8800 – which was produced by a company called Micro Instrumentation and Telementry Systems (MITS). The Altair retailed for $397, finally making computing affordable for the masses, including a small but growing hacker community.

Since the Altair hit the market, there has been a veritable explosion of mass market computing devices. Today, most individuals have their own desktop computers – each of which has more processing power than the entire suite of computers powering the first NASA excursions into space.

---

[12] The Mark I was constructed by Howard Aiken in combination with engineers from IBM and was the first of a series of computers that were fully automatic and could execute long calculations largely without human intervention.

[13] ENIAC stands for Electrical Numerical Integrator and Calculator and was a giant computing machine developed at the University of Pittsburgh. ENIAC was kept in use successfully from 1946 to 1955.

Information systems and information systems security – merging concerns

The Internet, personal computers, laptops, and other mobile computing devices are so pervasive in today's society that it is hard to remember that just 40 years ago they didn't exist. Considering the sheer volume of security laws and regulations today, it is also difficult to believe that the concepts of information systems security are a relatively recent development.

40 years ago: The Dinosaur Age – the mainframe

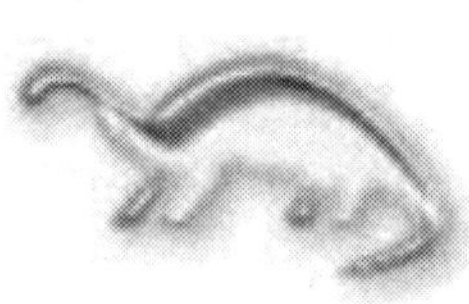

The Internet, or the web of individual computing devices, came about in the early 1960s as the consequence of a group of visionary thinkers who saw value in developing a capability to share research and development information.

The Internet Age of the Dinosaur was populated by mainframe computers – large, unwieldy machines occupying entire rooms. Scientists and engineers interacted one-on-one with the systems, continuously rewiring their circuits to perform specific functions and managing the processes through the use of punch cards. Each mainframe was isolated and the only way to communicate between machines was to share punch tape or cards, and later through huge magnetic tapes. Physical protections and access restrictions were the primary means of security during the Dinosaur Age.

30 years ago: The caveman and the wheel – ftp, email, and telnet

In the 1970s, the ARPANET became the DARPANET or Defense Advanced Research Project Network under the US Department of Defense (DOD). Now, a large percentage of universities were connected to the DARPANET and – of course – they were much more interested in the free sharing of information than in access restriction.

Email, ftp, and telnet commands were standardized, making it significantly easier for non-technical individuals to use the network. By today's standards, it was not simple, but these protocols opened up use of the network to more people, who made use of the net to communicate and more quickly and easily share files and resources.

As the use of the network grew, so did the need for security. More attention was being paid to security, largely as a result of a report authored for the US DOD by Rand, entitled *Security Controls for Computer Systems*.[14] This paper is regarded as a seminal work in the study of computer security. For the first time, there was an explicit call for a shift away from thinking about the protection of computers solely in terms of physical and hardware protection to a concept of security expressed in terms of data, users, and infrastructure. The Rand Report called for the recognition of the data itself as a commodity, with credentials for users needed in order to keep the commodity safe. It also recognized the need for security of specific types of systems, especially those processing critical national security information.

---

[14] Available at *http://www.rand.org/pubs/reports/R609-1/R609.1.html*.

20 years ago: The automobile meets the road – rise of the personal computer

As the 1970s moved into the 1980s, there was a quantum leap in information systems technology. During the space of just a few years, the trend evolved away from mainframe computers and the personal computer literally exploded on to the scene. By 1977, personal computers were crowding the store shelves. All of this occurred despite Ken Olson's[15] prediction in 1972: "There's no reason anyone would want a computer in their home."

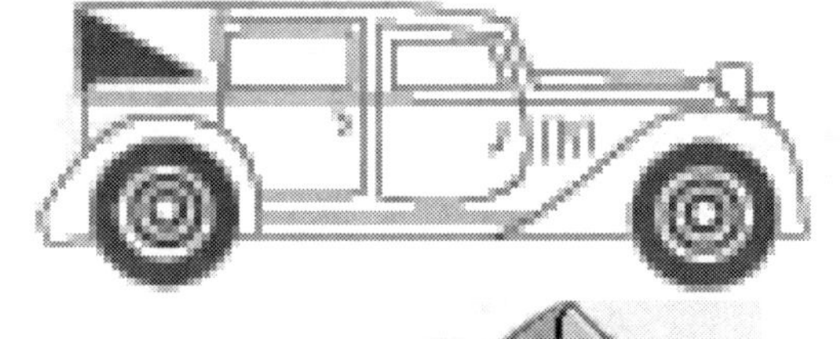

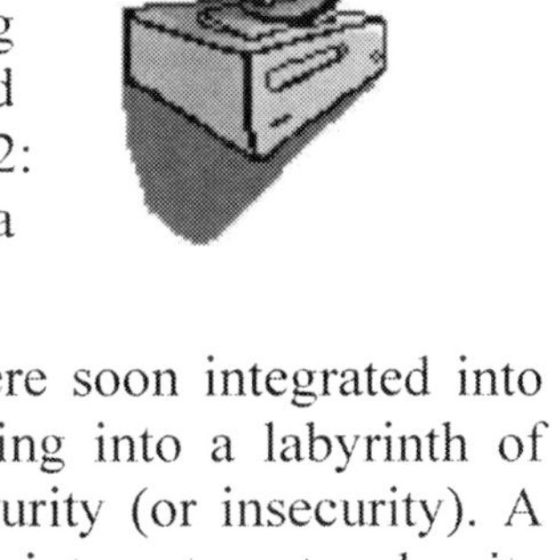

Individual personal computers (or PCs) were soon integrated into small local area networks, gradually forming into a labyrinth of networks each with varying degrees of security (or insecurity). A simple common network system called the internet protocol suite allowed the network to be separated from its physical implementation forming a global inter-network that would be called the Internet. The Internet began to penetrate into the world as it became the de-facto international standard and global network.

As the network expanded, so did attacks on computer systems. Organizations began to invest in preliminary efforts towards a security infrastructure. DOD and the National Computer Security Center collaborated on the Rainbow Series.[16] The Rainbow Series

---

[15] Kenneth Olson was the founder of the Digital Equipment Corporation (DEC). Although there were many voices within DEC seeking to influence Olson to produce a single-user, desktop style of computer, he was dead-set against the idea. This led ultimately to the demise of the company.

[16] The Rainbow Series (also called the Rainbow Books) is a comprehensive series of computer security standards published by the US government during the 1980s and 1990s. They were originally published by the US DOD Computer Security Center, and then later by the National Computer Security Center (NCSC). The term Rainbow Series comes from the fact that each book was a different color. They can be found and downloaded from *http://csrc.nist.gov/publications/secpubs/rainbow/*.

documents are still referenced today. The series consists of approximately 37 volumes, each in a different color and each addressing a specific information systems security need. The primary document of the set was known as the *Trusted Computer System Evaluation Criteria (5200.28-STD,* known as the Orange Book) published in 1985.

Using the Rainbow Series of regulations, US government entities (as well as private firms) now required formal certification[17] of computer technology and its security using these processes as part of their criteria.

10 years ago: The Autobahn – the information super-highway

Throughout the 1990s and early 2000s, the Internet grew beyond all previous imagination into a massive and largely uncontrolled network.

Throughout the 1990s, wave after wave of enthusiasm about new Internet and information technologies deluged the marketplace. But now the innovation was not limited to finding new ways to employ information systems – it now extended into new attacks and new protection technologies: firewalls, encryption, virtual private networks, intrusion detection, and the public key infrastructure.

Today: The sky is the limit – networking without boundaries!

After the unprecedented growth of the Internet during the previous decade – one that continues unabated – the world is continuing to see new trends in information technology.

---

[17] The same document describes certification as "The technical evaluation of a system's security features, made as part of and in support of the approval/accreditation process, which establishes the extent to which a particular computer system's design and implementation meet a set of specified security requirements."

 The growth of the Internet has also spawned a massive on-line marketplace and business environment. Consumers can do almost everything through their computers – from purchasing a home, scheduling a vacation, to paying their taxes.

Computing mobility has also untethered us from the office and has allowed us to take advantage of communications from just about anywhere – from the local Starbucks to the waiting rooms at the airport. Traditional concepts of securing the network were based on the ability to protect a boundary through a layered series of assurance devices, such as firewalls, proxy servers, intrusion detection systems, and corporate anti-virus systems. The problem has become how to extend these same protections where there are no defined boundaries.

As a result of these and other trends influenced by the unprecedented level of information gathering, storing, and sharing through the use of information technology, these past 10 years have also seen a dramatic increase in legislation addressing information systems security.

The following chapter will therefore attempt to review the most significant information systems security regulations in today's certification and accreditation field.

Further reading

De Leeuw, Karl and Bergstra, Jan. *The History of Information Security,* Elsevier Publishing, August 2007.

Hoyle, Michelle. *The History of Computing Science,* *http://lecture.eingang.org/toc.html.*

Khosrow-Pour, Mehdi. *Emerging Trends and Challenges in Information Technology Management,* IGI Global Publishing, May 2006.

References

Berkus, David. *Ten Trends in Technology*. A Presentation at the 2005 Harvard Business Conference, Anaheim, California.

Elon University/Pew Internet Project. *Imagining the Internet: A History and Forecast*. "Imagining the Internet: A Quick Look at the Early History of the Internet." Elon University/Pew Internet Project. Available at: *http://www.elon.edu/predictions*.

Hauben, Michael. *Behind the Net: The Untold History of the ARPANET*. Available at: *http://www.dei.isep.ipp.pt/~acc/docs/arpa.html*.

Kanellos, Michael. *Gordon Moore on 40 Years of His Processor Law*. Available on: *http://news.cnet.com/Gordon-Moore-on-40-years-of-his-processor-law/2008-1006_3-5657677.html*

Leiner, Barry M; Cerf, Vinton G; Clark, David D; Kahn, Robert E; Kleinrock, Leonard; Lynch, Daniel C; Postel, Jon; Roberts, Larry G; Wolff, Stephen. *A Brief History of the Internet*. Available at: *http://www.isoc.org/internet/history/brief.shtml*.

Moor, James H. *What is Computer Ethics?* Available at: *http://www.southernct.edu/organizations/rccs/resources/teaching/teaching_mono/moor/moor_definition.html*.

CHAPTER 2: THE ESSENTIAL INFORMATION SYSTEMS SECURITY REGULATIONS

Liberty is the chief cornerstone of the American system of government and provisions for its security are embedded in the written charter and interwoven in the moral fabric of its laws.[18]

Thomas Y. Bayard, 30th US Secretary of State

In this chapter:

Information systems security regulations you need to know

---

[18] OMB – US Office of Management and Budget: OMB is the official conduit by which the US White House oversees the activities of all federal agencies, including management, legislative, regulatory, and budgetary issues.

Information systems security regulations you need to know

The events of 11 September 2001 changed the security landscape in many visible and long-lasting ways. While the terrorist attacks of that date were not directly targeted against information systems, there were nevertheless several security related lessons learned. Businesses and other agencies developed a heightened awareness of the vulnerability of information systems in the event of disaster and the costs of recovery. But the primary result was a flood of security related legislation, much of it focused on information systems security.

The field of security is now awash in laws, regulations, and guidance. As you read through the abstracts to follow, please note that these are only the tip of the iceberg. There are many, many more pieces of important security requirements not discussed here — but here we present those laws, policies, regulations and guidance documents that have the most relevance to the world of certification and accreditation today (at least in the opinion of the authors).

Each of the laws, regulations, or other policy documents discussed in the next sections are included on the accompanying CD. These references are current as of the time of writing. The CD also includes a full set of security references beyond those discussed here, but that may be useful to you as security professionals.

Remember, however, that requirements can change over time. Be sure to check the status of the requirements document prior to use.

Executive orders, laws, regulations, and standards

Information system security requirements can take many forms. Understanding who issues the requirement, how it is issued, what it requires, and who it covers, as well the implications of compliance and non-compliance, is essential to keeping your sanity in a world gone completely berserk with regulation and oversight. In this chapter, we introduce each of the different types of compliance mechanisms — laws, regulations, and guidance or standards —

focusing on those that have a direct or indirect relationship with the authorization process.

First, we will start with laws. After all, this is where compliance begins.

Laws

At their most elemental, laws are specific rules established by a governing authority (e.g. Congress) to institute and maintain an orderly co-existence within the nation. Law is also a piece of "enacted legislation."[19]

So, what exactly is a law? In the US, Federal Laws are bills passed by Congress and signed into law by the President; they are characterized by the following statements:

- Laws specify the requirements, but do not dictate how an activity must be accomplished.
- Laws generally specify which entity within the Executive Branch is responsible for drafting the regulations to implement the law.
- Laws can be vague and ambiguous, and thus often require interpretation in order to advance from requirement to implementation.

In the past decade, lawmakers have been very active in drafting new computer or information systems security-related laws and updating older ones. For many years, legislators had little interest in what the "computer geeks" were up to or how their activities would eventually affect the policy landscape. Today, many of these same members of Congress wouldn't be seen without their cell phones, BlackBerries, or other personal communications/computing devices. And this is reflected in the amount of legislation issued in recent years. This is a relatively new legal field, and the legal establishment is still struggling to arrive at even a broad agreement

---

[19] Answers.com *http://www.answers.com/law*.

on many key issues. In this still-evolving environment, even basic vocabulary can be the subject of contention.

Let's now take a look at the most relevant information systems security laws:

The Privacy Act of 1974: If we were to discuss the emergence of information systems security laws in chronological order, we would start with the *Privacy Act of 1974* (PL 93-579). The Privacy Act is a law, which means that it is bound with compliance requirements and the potential for legal, punitive measures for non-compliance.

The Act's importance lies in the fact that it imposes a wholly new set of requirements on how the federal government is authorized to handle information about private individuals. The Act includes a complex set of definitions and exceptions, but it also limits the unnecessary accumulation of personal, private information by the federal government, precludes the unauthorized or improper disclosure of such information, and gives individuals a mechanism to discover what information the government is holding about them and the right and means to correct errors in the records.

It roots really lay in a series of hearings held by the House of Representatives Subcommittee on Invasion of Privacy. To put it into historical context, in 1974, nearing the end of the Vietnam War and in the grips of Watergate, Congress was concerned with curbing the illegal surveillance and investigation of individuals by federal agencies exposed during the Watergate scandal.

This legislation was also the first to recognize that information collection and retention by government agencies should be narrowly confined to explicit operational needs, and that individuals must be provided with the means to determine this information and to compel the correction of any inaccuracies. This was an important new concept, since this represented recognition of the unprecedented ability of information systems to collect and store information – which could be of critical importance to individuals seeking government benefits, licenses, or employment – yet could often contain serious errors.

While there are situations in which access to personal, private information is essential to the efficient operation of the government, proponents argued that there were too many situations in which the information was wrongly handled or disclosed.

There were other requirements in the Act specifically focusing on the security of computers – for the first time. These included:

- Mandatory, periodic computer security awareness and acceptable use training for all employees designed to:

  - enhance awareness of vulnerabilities of and threats to information systems;
  - encourage the use of appropriate security practices.

- Establishment of a plan for the security and privacy of federal information systems commensurate with the risk and magnitude of potential harm resulting from the loss, misuse, or unauthorized access to and/or modification of information within the system.

The Computer Fraud and Abuse Act of 1986: The *Computer Fraud and Abuse Act of 1986* was voted into law by Congress as a consequence of the exploits of Ian Murphy, also known as "Captain Zap." Murphy broke into military computers, stole information from corporate merchandise databases, and tapped into restricted government telephone switchboards to make illegal phone calls.

The Act amended Title 18, United Stated Code (USC) Section 1030 to introduce penalties of six types of criminal activities: (1) unauthorized access to a computer to obtain protected financial or credit information; (2) unauthorized access into a federal government computer; (3) unauthorized interstate or foreign access of a computer system with intent to defraud; (4) fraudulent trafficking in computer passwords affecting interstate commerce; (5) unauthorized interstate or foreign access to computer systems resulting in a minimum of $1000 aggregate damage; and (6) the unauthorized access to a computer to obtain national security information with intent to injure the US or to provide an advantage to a foreign nation. Robert Morris, the graduate student who unleashed the now-infamous Morris worm, was prosecuted and convicted under this Act.

The Act remains in effect today, but was amended in 1994, 1996 and in 2001 by the USA Patriot Act.

Office of Management & Budget (OMB) Circular A-130: *OMB Circular A-130, Management of Federal Information Resources,* is considered one of the most critical and influential pieces of legislature in the history of information systems security law. It laid out broad security guidance for federal information systems by establishing "a mandate for agencies to perform their information resource management activities in an efficient, effective and economical manner."

Considered the most critical component, Appendix III, *Security of Federal Automated Resources,* establishes a minimum set of information security controls[20], assigns agency responsibility for the security of federal information, and links agency information systems security programs to management control systems (established under OMB Circular A-123). OMB Circular A-130 was the first law to introduce the concept of "authorizing" an information system to operate. It further assigned the responsibility for accepting the risk of operating an information system to the manager who authorizes its operation.

Other important new information system security requirements established under this Act include:

- The requirement for an information system security plan (SSP), which must include rules of secure system operation, training, personnel controls, incident response capability, continuity of operations, technical security, and system interconnection.
- Mandatory review of the security controls when significant modifications are made to the system, but no later than every three years.

---

[20] The concept of security controls, or specific security requirements implemented to mitigate risk, introduced by OMB A-130 remains in use today. They are often categorized as operational, technical, and managerial.

Since its passage in 1986, the Circular has undergone numerous revisions and updates.

National Security Directive (NSD) 42: The roles and responsibilities associated with security of national security systems are established in *NSD-42* signed into effect in July 1990 by President George H. W. Bush. NSD-42 created the Committee on National Security Systems (CNSS) and directs the organization to:

- provide information systems security guidance for national security systems to federal departments and agencies; and
- submit an annual report on the security status of national security systems to the executive agent[21].

NSD-42 also designates the director of the National Security Agency (NSA) as the National Manager for National Security Telecommunications and Information Systems Security.

Clinger Cohen Act of 1996: Following the Computer Security Act of 1987, there was a period of relative calm until the *Clinger Cohen Act* (CCA) of 1996[22] once again opened the policy floodgates. This single piece of legislation introduced dramatic changes into the landscape of federal IT.

The Act was primarily intended to remedy steadily growing deficiencies in the world of federal IT. Notable issues included cost overruns, system abuses, poor accountability, and a noticeable lack of attention to critical business processes that should form the foundation for sound IT investments. One of the primary results of the Act was that it finally gave federal CIOs a seat at the management table.

By ensuring a reporting chain to the agency heads, the CCA practically catapulted federal CIOs to the executive ranks. They rather suddenly became visible and influential members of the organization. CCA also forced the creation of the Federal CIO

---

[21] The executive agent for the federal government is the Secretary of Defense.
[22] Also known as the Information Technology Management Reform Act.

Council, which remains an important forum for promoting government-wide IT policies, standards and programs.

The Act addressed a remarkable spectrum of IT issues, from information systems security, architecture and acquisition, to IT workforce issues, capital planning and performance-based management. As a result, CCA forcibly broadened the IT perspectives of federal CIOs and their executive colleagues.

Finally, CCA was influential in efforts to reform IT acquisition. It decentralized federal acquisition control from the General Services Administration to individual agencies, in turn making them more accountable for their IT investment decisions.

Here are some of the most important provisions of the CCA:

- Decentralization of procurement authority: Under the CCA, agencies are able purchase their own IT without having to go through the General Services Administration (GSA). OMB was given oversight control over agency IT spending through a robust budgeting process.
- Capital planning and investment control: Agencies must make IT investment decisions on the basis of measurable criteria linked to a calculated return on investment, to present alternative solutions, to determine means to share benefits or costs with other agencies, and to provide evidence of verifiable progress in meeting mission schedule, quality, and cost goals.
- Performance and results-based management: Strategic performance goals have to be developed for any IT that supports the agency. Agencies are mandated to quantitatively assess federal performance improvement against comparable private or public sector best practice benchmarks. These assessments include calculations on cost, schedule, productivity, and quality of results. Organizations must analyze progress in meeting strategic goals, and adjust budget and acquisition processes as needed prior to making significant IT.
- Accountability: Agencies must be accountable for implementing IT accounting, financial, and asset management, and other

systems to provide reliable, consistent, and timely performance data.

- Standards and guidelines: Agencies must establish, maintain, and follow prescribed standards and guidelines for efficiency, security, and privacy of federal IT systems.

- Five-year IT cost and performance goals: Each year, agencies must develop plans for attaining at least a 5 percent decrease in cost incurred to operate and maintain IT systems, concurrently with a 5 percent increase in agency operational efficiency as a result of IT investments.

- Procurement procedures: Federal agencies must implement an IT acquisition process that is simple, clear, and understandable. To the maximum extent practicable, agencies must capitalize on available commercial IT and employ incremental (modular) acquisition practices, with a goal for vendors to deliver system modules within 18 months of contract award. Delivery, implementation, and testing of each IT increment shall be independent of subsequent deliveries to permit the employment of evolving technologies unavailable in earlier increments.

Homeland Security Act (HSA) of 2002, Critical Infrastructure Information Act: The *Homeland Security Act of 2002*, PL 107-296, was one of the first pieces of significant security legislation issued in the aftermath of September 11. Signed into effect by President Bush on 25 November 2002, this Act generated one of the biggest changes in the federal government in over 50 years: the consolidation of over 20 existing federal agencies into a single Department of Homeland Security (DHS). Not since the Department of Defense was created by President Truman in 1947 had the US government undergone such a radical restructuring.

The Act also transferred federal responsibility for cybersecurity (e.g. information systems security) to DHS and described several infrastructure protection responsibilities related to DHS' cybersecurity mission. Responsibility for cybersecurity was centralized in its National Cyber Security Division (NCSD), which evolved out of the transfer of several existing high-level federal information systems security programs to DHS, including:

- National Infrastructure Protection Center (from the Federal Bureau of Investigation);
- National Communication System (an interagency group formerly supported by the Department of Defense);
- Critical Infrastructure Assurance Office (from the Department of Commerce);
- National Infrastructure Simulation and Analysis Center (a partnership between Sandia and Los Alamos National Laboratories, supported by the Department of Energy); and
- Federal Computer Incident Response Center (from the General Services Administration).

Despite, or perhaps because of its broad charter, NCSD has been afflicted with leadership problems. In the first years of its existence, NCSD had multiple directors, each resigning after serving only short, and often – in their own words – frustrating terms. Richard Clarke, who had already made a reputation in cybersecurity, was the first candidate offered the position of director of the NCSD; however, he refused the position based on his unease that there were too many bureaucratic layers between him and the Secretary of Homeland Security, Thomas Ridge.

Robert Liscouski took the position temporarily while a permanent director was sought and he later remained as assistant director until February 2005. In September 2003, Amit Yoran was named director of NCSD and had some success with the establishment of a cybersecurity alert system. After only a year in the job, however, Amit left abruptly in October 2004 – reportedly with only one day's notice – citing frustration with the limitations placed upon the division, despite its critical charter of responsibility.

Amit Yoran was succeeded by one of NCSD's deputies, Andy Purdy, who assumed the role of interim director shortly after Amit's departure. Unfortunately, the position was once again associated with unwanted publicity. The Washington Post reported that Purdy, who worked for NCSD under a contract from Carnegie Mellon University, "…drew congressional scrutiny after The Associated Press reported in June that Purdy's cybersecurity division has paid Carnegie Mellon $19 million in contracts this year, almost one-fifth of the unit's total budget."[23] Shortly after the release of this story, Andy Purdy also stepped down from the position.

Following yet another rather unexpected and rapid loss of an NCSD director, Jerry Dixon took the acting director position until he was officially appointed to the position of executive director in January 2007. He left the position in September of 2007, leaving Cheri McGuire to take the position of acting director until March of 2008, at which time Cornelius Tate became the current director of NCSD.

The leadership turmoil has had its effects. Inspector General (IG) audits and Government Accounting Office (GAO) reports have reported negatively on some aspects of NCSD's performance, such as its failures to set priorities, develop strategic plans, and provide effective leadership in national cybersecurity issues. Nevertheless, there are also several successes on NCSD's report card, including the formation of the US Computer Emergency Readiness Team (US-CERT) and its cyber alert system.

Federal Information Security Act (FISMA) of 2002: *FISMA* was enacted in 2002 as Title III of the E-Government Act of 2002 (PL. 107-347, 116 Stat. 2899). It replaced GISRA and made the information systems security requirements permanent with an immediate and very tangible focus. In 2003, more than 1.4 million information systems security incidents were reported at federal agencies – a more than threefold increase over 2002.

As a result of the concerns prompted by this increase, the requirements of FISMA go far beyond preceding legislation on key issues, such as accountability, implementation of security controls, and annual testing and reporting. Central to FISMA, is the requirement for each federal agency to submit annual reports, including an evaluation of the effectiveness of their information systems security programs, from the agency CIO and agency head to the Office of Management and Budget (OMB) and Congress.

---

[23] Retrieved from *http://www.washingtonpost.com/wp-dyn/content/article/2006/06/28/AR2006062801903.html*

Under FISMA, federal agencies, including DOD, must meet and report on eight broad requirements:

- Perform risk assessments at least annually to estimate the amount of damage that would be caused by a disruption of services.
- Formulate policies and procedures designed to cost-effectively mitigate the risks identified in the risk assessment.
- Implement security plans describing tangible security measures, or controls, to address specific system or operational requirements and ensure compliance with policy and procedures.
- Conduct initial and refresher security awareness training for all users of the information systems, including contractors.
- Execute security testing at least annually of all security controls, including technical, managerial, and operational controls.
- Implement remediation procedures on identified security deficiencies and track the remediation throughout the system life cycle.
- Develop incident response procedures that enable sufficient capability to detect and respond to information security incidents.
- Document and test contingency plans and the ability to restore continuity of operations in the event of a disruption at least annually.

FISMA also gave several federal agencies expanded information system security charters and authorizes the:

- National Institute of Standards and Technology (NIST) to develop federal information systems security standards and guidelines for IS;
- Secretary of Commerce to decide which standards should be promulgated;
- Director of OMB to oversee the development and implementation of the standards including:
    - requiring agencies to follow the NIST standards and guidelines;
    - annually reviewing and evaluating agency information systems security programs;

- summarizing the results of the evaluations in an annual report to Congress.

FISMA has brought about a number of positive cultural changes in thinking about information systems security by forcing:

- Standardization: Federal agencies had long relied on their own, often highly disparate, information systems security practices and policies. FISMA has clearly demonstrated that standard practices and measures are essential resulting in an ever-increasing push for standardization across the federal government.
- Accountability: FISMA linked information systems security with budget and raised the visibility of vulnerabilities by exposing federal agencies to public scrutiny.
- Transparency: In order to meet FISMA compliance requirements, agencies must clearly demonstrate how their overall information systems security strategy and budget support the mission and goals of their agency.

The original language in FISMA excluded its application for National Security Systems as defined in NSD-42. Supplementary instructions, however, amended this statement and required their inclusion, resulting in more comprehensive federal accountability and transparency.

FISMA under fire: The effectiveness of FISMA has been hotly debated. Despite the fact that this Act has opened up information systems security to congressional and public scrutiny since 2002, security analysts and federal information technology managers alike have complained that FISMA has not met its goal of making federal information systems more secure. The reason, they claim, lies in the fact that FISMA has simply become a reporting exercise on whether federal agencies are following certain specified security processes, such as certifying and accrediting systems.

If for some reason an organization fails to meet the FISMA requirements, or gets a low grade, it instantly becomes public knowledge. In recent years, the media covering government IT affairs has developed a fondness for reporting on agency FISMA grades. The annual evaluations were intended to show how effectively federal agencies are managing security year by year. And consistently, the scores have reflected serious deficiencies in meeting the FISMA goals. The good grades of a few federal agencies have consistently been offset by the poor performance of some of the largest and most visible government organizations. In the report of May 2008, DHS earned a D, a minor improvement for the nation's primary security agency from their prior three Fs in a row. The US DOD has been given a failing score for several years in a row.[24] In 2005, one federal agency with a failing FISMA grade suffered a major security breach, resulting in the theft of personal identity information from millions of US citizens.

Can an increased security budget lead to better FISMA scores? Evaluations indicate that there may not necessarily be a clear correlation between information systems security spending and good security compliance scores.

The US DOD, for example, has consistently budgeted well over $1B annually for information systems security — and still has a failing FISMA score. So, what's the problem? Basically, the DOD is such a huge, sprawling and diverse organization that achieving any kind of consistent information systems security reporting process across all of its estimated 2.7 million employees and widely dispersed organizations may be virtually impossible.

Federal Information Processing Standard (FIPS) 199, *Standards for Security Categorization of Federal Information and Information Systems*: <u>FIPS 199</u>, published in February 2004, is a critical element in the suite of NIST standards and guidelines designed to improve the security of federal information systems, including information systems contributing to the support of the nation's critical infrastructure.

The publication of FIPS 199 was based on a simple concept – defining a process for assigning appropriate priorities for federal agency information systems and subsequently applying the

---

[24] See <u>*http://republicans.oversight.house.gov/FISMA/*</u> for the 2007 FISMA Scorecard.

necessary information systems security measures to protect those systems. Security controls for a federal IS should be commensurate with the system's criticality and sensitivity.

FIPS 199 calls this process "security categorization," and bases the security controls selection on the potential impact (defined as low (L), moderate (M), or high (H)) on agency operations (mission, functions, image, or reputation), agency assets, or individuals in the event of a security incident caused by the loss of confidentiality (i.e. unauthorized disclosure of information), integrity (i.e. unauthorized modification of information), or availability (i.e. denial of service).

Federal Information Processing Standard (FIPS) 200, *Minimum Security Requirements for Federal Information and Information Systems***:** Effective 31 March 2006, the Secretary of Commerce approved *FIPS 200*. FIPS 200 and its requirements are considered compulsory and binding on federal agencies for:

- all information within the federal government other than that information that has been determined pursuant to Executive Order 12958, as amended by Executive Order 13292, or any predecessor order, or by the Atomic Energy Act of 1954, as amended, to require protection against unauthorized disclosure and is marked to indicate its classified status; and
- all federal information systems other than those information systems designated as national security systems. FIPS 200 was developed to complement similar standards for national security systems.

FIPS 200 is the second standard specified by FISMA as an integral part of the NIST's overall risk management framework. This framework was developed to aid federal agencies in determining appropriate requirements for information systems security based on levels of risk. The provisions of FIPS 200 require federal agencies to categorize their systems as required by FIPS 199, and then identify and implement the essential set of security controls derived from NIST SP 800-53 sufficient to satisfy minimum security requirements.

FIPS 200 identifies 17 security controls that agencies can use to protect their information and information systems, including access controls, security awareness and training, and configuration management. Federal agencies were directed to comply with FIPS 200 by March 2007.

Like so many compliance-related standards, FIPS 200 has attracted criticism from security experts, who claim it will not result in better information systems security because there is still too much variation regarding how agencies implement security controls and audit their information systems. Other security experts have labeled FIPS 200 as the most complete information systems security standard available to date. Clint Kreitner, President and CEO of the Center for Internet Security (CIS), portrayed FIPS 200 as "the most comprehensive work available in the area of information security management – public or private."

So, love it or hate it, FIPS 200 is the law.

Executive orders

An executive order is defined as a "President's or Governor's declaration, which has the force of law, usually based on existing statutory powers, and requiring no action by Congress or state legislature."[25] Executive orders have the same compliance mandate as law if they are based either on the President's constitutional powers or laws already passed by Congress.

In short, executive orders are directions from the President to the executive branch and have the following characteristics:

- An order having the force of law issued by the President to the Army, Navy, or any other part of the executive branch of the government.

---

[25] Legal definition at *http://legal-dictionary.thefreedictionary.com/Executive+Order*

- Directives executed in those areas where Congress has specifically delegated authority to the President or where Congress has not acted.

Presidential Decision Directives 63, 66, and 67: The late 1990s saw the issuance of several critical Presidential Decision Directives (PDDs), three of which significantly impacted national-level security policy.

PDD 63, Critical Infrastructure Protection Directive, – updated as *Homeland Security Presidential Directive* (HSPD) 7 – was issued on 22 May 1998. It focused on strengthening the national defenses against emerging unconventional threats, such as weapons of mass destruction, terrorism, and attacks on the critical infrastructure (e.g. computer-based attacks). PDD 63 established an entire infrastructure to address these challenges:

- A national coordinator whose scope will include not only critical infrastructure but also foreign terrorism and threats of domestic mass destruction (including biological weapons) because attacks on the US may not come labeled in neat jurisdictional boxes.
- The National Infrastructure Protection Center (NIPC) co-located with the FBI to fuse representatives from FBI, DOD, USSS, Energy, Transportation, the Intelligence Community, and the private sector in an unprecedented attempt at information sharing among agencies in collaboration with the private sector. The NIPC will also provide the principal means of facilitating and coordinating the federal government's response to an incident, mitigating attacks, investigating threats and monitoring reconstitution efforts.
- Information sharing and analysis centers (ISAC) encouraged to be set up by the private sector, in cooperation with the federal government.
- A National Infrastructure Assurance Council (NIAC) drawn from private sector leaders and state/local officials to provide guidance to the policy formulation of a national plan.
- The Critical Infrastructure Assurance Office (CIAO) which will provide support to the national coordinator's work with

government agencies and the private sector in developing a national plan. The office will also help coordinate a national education and awareness program, and legislative and public affairs.

PDD 66, Encryption Policies, issued by the Clinton administration on 16 September 1998, detailed the means by which the administration intended to strengthen its support for electronic commerce by permitting the export of strong encryption when used to protect sensitive financial, health, medical, and business proprietary information in electronic form. The policy provided new opportunities for US companies to sell products containing encryption to an unprecedented 70 per cent of the world's economy.

In 1998, the emerging threat environment, including localized emergencies and military or terrorist attacks, shifted awareness to the need for continuity of operations planning (COOP) that would enable federal agencies to continue their essential functions in the face of an emergency or attack. As a result, *PDD 67, Federal Preparedness Circular*, was issued on 21 October 1998. This PDD outlined the requirement for federal agencies to implement a comprehensive program to ensure the continuity of federal functions under all circumstances.

PDD 67 established the Federal Emergency Management Agency (FEMA) as the executive agent for the federal COOP, as well as the requirement for each federal agency to appoint an emergency coordinator.

Executive Order (EO) 13231, *Critical Infrastructure Protection in the Information Age*: President George W. Bush signed *Executive Order (EO) 13231* in 2001, establishing the President's Critical Infrastructure Protection Board (CIPB) to coordinate cyber-related federal efforts and programs associated with protecting the nation's critical infrastructures. EO 13231 tasked the board with recommending policies and coordinating programs for protecting critical infrastructure protection (CIP)-related information systems.

EO 13231 emphasized the importance of CIP and the information sharing and analysis centers (ISACs), but did not identify any additional requirements for agencies to protect their critical infrastructures or suggest additional activities for the ISACs.

Regulations

Regulation: The word often sends shivers down the spine of business executives and IT professionals.[26]

Congress passes the laws that govern security activities. In order to make the laws work on a day-to-day basis, Congress has authorized certain federal agencies to assist in defining how these laws will be put into effect by creating and enforcing regulations.

And even though they are not laws, regulations can have the force of law since they are created under the authority granted by the law and often include punitive measures for non-compliance. In fact, the hard work of creating the vast and ever-growing volumes of federal regulations, which are the real and enforceable rules behind the Acts, takes place largely unnoticed in the offices of the government agencies and not in the halls of Congress.

Over 50 federal agencies participate in the development of regulations – over 145,000 pages of rules, published to address requirements as varied as the organizations themselves. And all regulations have a cost associated with the development – a so-called "regulatory tax." But the real cost of regulations is the cost of compliance. "Regulatory compliance is a form of asymmetric warfare," claimed Andreas Antonopoulos recently in *Network World*.

It is much faster and easier for Congress to create new laws and agencies to create new regulations than it is for businesses and government offices to meet compliance requirements. For example, the costs of implementing Section 404 of the Sarbanes-Oxley Act, which mandates external auditing of financial reporting in just a few sentences – was assessed in one study to be as high as $1.4 trillion.

---

[26] Jeffery E. Payne, "Regulation and Information Security: Can Y2K Lessons Help Us?" *IEEE Security and Privacy*, vol. 2, no. 2, pp. 58-61, Mar. 2004, doi:10.1109/MSECP.2004.1281248.

To summarize, regulations implement laws. Their definitive characteristics include:

- Promulgated by agencies, such as the Department of Defense, Office of Management and Budget, etc.
- Development often includes industry input.
- Open to public comment before publication is authorized.
- Published in the Federal Register.
- Compliance with requirements can be costly.

Department of Defense Directive 5200.40, *Department of Defense Information Technology Security Certification and Accreditation Process (DITSCAP)*: In 1997, the US DOD jumped on the information systems security policy train with the publication of the DITSCAP, a DOD policy intended to establish a manageable, standard process, set of activities, general task descriptions, and a management structure to certify and accredit DOD information technology (IT) systems. The birth of the DITSCAP can be traced to August 19, 1992, when the Office of Assistant Secretary of Defense directed the Defense Information Systems Agency (DISA) Center for Information Systems Security (CISS) to formulate a standard DOD process for security certification and accreditation.

CISS formed a working group, consisting of service and agency representatives. The working group evaluated ten existing processes, but found none which could be adopted DOD-wide. As a result, it took the working group five years to agree and develop the DOD Information Technology Security Certification and Accreditation Process.

DODD 5200.40 may have been the document that first introduced the idea of maintaining IA throughout the life cycle. In fact, the processes defined in the DITSCAP were specifically designed to ensure that DOD IT systems would meet specified requirements for accreditation and that the system would continue to maintain the implemented security posture throughout its life cycle. The DITSCAP promoted nine characteristics for DOD C&A. It was intended (and advertised) to be:

- Tailorable – applicable to any system at any point along the lifecycle.
- Scalable – can be sized to fit the system and its security requirements.
- Consistent – standard process regardless of the system type.
- Understandable – objective and have clearly defined security objectives.
- Relevant – identifies appropriate security requirements and standards.
- Effective – results in a maintainable accreditation for the information system.
- Evolvable – able to incorporate lessons learned and emerging technologies.
- Repeatable – applicable to similar systems with similar results.
- Responsive – timely systems security changes based on operational needs and priorities.

The DITSCAP also organized the C&A process into four well-defined steps:

- Definition: Key players agree on the intended system mission, security requirements, C&A boundary, schedule, level of effort, and required resources.
- Verification: Verify system's compliance with specific security requirements through testing.
- Validation: Assess implementation of security design through testing.
- Post accreditation: Maintain an acceptable level of residual risk through the system operations and maintenance (O&M).

The primary output from the DITSCAP was called the system security authorization agreement (SSAA), a monumental set of documentation intended to present a comprehensive picture of the security status of an information system. The stated purpose of the SSAA was to serve as a formal agreement between the designated accrediting authority (DAA) and the other participants in the C&A process that would continue to be the basis of the agreement throughout the life cycle of the information system. The body of the SSAA was divided into six major paragraphs, often called sections, numbered one to six, plus (a minimum of) 18 appendices, labeled A through R.

Each of these headings in the SSAA body was mandatory, as was the title of each appendix through to Appendix R. The six major headings were:

- 1.0 Mission description and system identification
- 2.0 Environment description
- 3.0 System architectural description
- 4.0 System security requirements
- 5.0 Organizations and resources
- 6.0 DITSCAP plan.

The 18 appendices, labeled A through R, followed the main body of the SSAA. These included any and all documentation relevant to the C&A process. Organizations could add optional appendices to meet specific needs.

The 18 appendices were:

- Appendix A Acronyms
- Appendix B Definitions
- Appendix C References
- Appendix D System concept of operations
- Appendix E Information system security policy
- Appendix F Security requirements and/or requirements traceability matrix
- Appendix G Certification test and evaluation plan procedures (type only)
- Appendix H Security test and evaluation plan and procedures
- Appendix I Applicable system development artifacts or system documentation
- Appendix J System rules of behavior
- Appendix K Incident response plan
- Appendix L Contingency plans
- Appendix M Personnel controls and technical security

<table>
<tr><td></td><td>controls</td></tr>
<tr><td>• Appendix N</td><td>Memorandums of agreement – system interconnect agreements</td></tr>
<tr><td>• Appendix O</td><td>Security education, training, and awareness plan</td></tr>
<tr><td>• Appendix P</td><td>Test and evaluation report(s)</td></tr>
<tr><td>• Appendix Q</td><td>Residual risk assessment results</td></tr>
<tr><td>• Appendix R</td><td>Certification and accreditation statements.</td></tr>
</table>

As the DITSCAP evolved, so did the amount of documentation – even to the extent of becoming the sole focus of the DITSCAP or a "paperwork drill"[27] – a name still fondly attached to the process by DOD agencies.

But DITSCAP also contributed to C&A by establishing it as an agreement-based approach resting on two primary principles:

- Information systems security is established via agreement between the C&A roles: the designated accrediting authority (DAA), certifying authority (CA), user representative (UR), and the program manager (PM).
- Information systems security is important not only during a system's operational phase, but also during all of the phases contributing to the development of the IS.

These principles could be implemented through three primary operations:

- Establish agreement between all of the role-players (i.e. stakeholders). The key to successful execution of the DITSCAP was agreement between the PM, DAA, CA, and the UR.
- Ensure the output of this agreement was produced as a formal, written agreement (e.g. SSAA), without relying on an informal, verbal agreement to produce effective information systems security.

---

[27] One DOD agency provided an example of a standalone system consisting of a single machine with no network connectivity – and an SSAA of over 300 pages!

- Involve the C&A role participants at each stage in the system life cycle, from design to production, and not just at the end of the development cycle. Make the formal, written agreement a dynamic document, modifying the agreement as required as the IS progresses.

It wasn't until 2000 that DOD issued an implementation guide for the DITSCAP, leaving DOD agencies essentially alone from 1997 to 2000 to design and implement their own, highly individualized processes.

IT personnel decided at some point that DITSCAP was a compliance issue, not a security issue, and so, if they got their 500-page reports done, they were happy and ready to move on. As a result, DITSCAP fundamentally failed to protect DOD systems because the program was implemented as a single snapshot look at security in a world where the potential threats and security requirements are changing every day.[28]

The DITSCAP was superseded by the DOD Information Assurance Certification & Accreditation Process (DIACAP) in 2007. We have kept it as a reference in this book, since many of DOD's information systems still refer to the DITSCAP as their primary source of requirements.

Director of Central Intelligence Directive (DCID) 6/3, *Protecting Sensitive Compartmented Information within Information Systems*: On June 5, 1999, the Director of Central Intelligence (DCI) issued *DCID 6/3*. This directive establishes the security policy and procedures for storing, processing, and communicating classified intelligence information in information systems. An implementation manual corresponding to DCID 6/3 was published on May 24, 2000.

DCID 6/3 provides the overarching security requirements necessary to protect highly classified intelligence information systems. It contains a wide variety of security controls, both technical and non-technical in nature. Examples of the non-technical controls include: labeling procedures, configuration management, and maintenance.

---

[28] Allen Paller, Director of Research for the SANS Institute, speech at the NSA Red Team/Blue Team Symposium, 2008.

In addition, in the DCID 6/3 the DCI designates specific principal accrediting authorities (PAAs) with responsibility for all intelligence systems within their respective purviews.

Certification plays a very important role in the DCID 6/3 process. There are essentially two test and evaluation (T&E) phases. During the first T&E phase a certification test plan and test procedures are developed. The certification test plan outlines the IS certification test. It describes the test sets needed to demonstrate that the IS implements its security requirements. The plan also gives specific guidelines for conducting the tests. Certification test procedures expand the test set descriptions into step-by-step descriptions of the security requirement tests.

Most of the C&A process is conducted during T&E II. Once functional testing is complete, the security test and evaluation is conducted based on the certification test plan and test procedures. Shortfalls and vulnerabilities are identified, and risks are analyzed. The outcome of the risk analysis is used to develop a plan to address shortfalls. The plan includes actions required to fix or work around particular shortfalls.

At the time of writing, the DCID 6/3 – or at least the portions referring to governance and responsibilities – has been rescinded and replaced by Intelligence Community Directive (ICD) 503. The security requirements portion of the DCID 6/3 remains in effect for information systems in the Intelligence Community (IC) and other sensitive DOD activities.

National Security Telecommunications and Information Systems Security Instruction (NSTISSI) No. 1000, *National Information Assurance Certification and Accreditation Process (NIACAP)*: The _NIACAP_ process was issued in April 2000 to create a national standard alternative to the Department of Defense Information Technology Security Certification & Accreditation Process (DITSCAP)[29]. The National Security Telecommunications and Information Systems Security Committee (NSTISSC), that

---

[29] The DITSCAP was rescinded and replaced in November 2007 by DODI 8510.01.

developed and published the NIACAP is part of the National Security Agency (NSA).

It established the minimum security standards for certifying and accrediting national security systems. National security systems are those systems related to intelligence activities, equipment that is an integral part of a weapon system, command and control of military forces, cryptologic activities related to national security, or equipment that is critical to the direct fulfillment of military or intelligence missions. The National Institute of Standards and Technology (NIST) further clarified the definition of national security systems in August 2003 in NIST SP 800-59, *Guideline for Identifying an Information System as a National Security System.*

Though the NIACAP was originally intended for national security systems, any federal agency or even a private enterprise can adopt and use the NIACAP process if their oversight authority allows it. Systems that are classified as national security systems are still required to follow the NIACAP methodology.

The purpose of the NIACAP is to provide a comprehensive and uniform approach to C&A that could be adapted by any agency. The NIACAP also provides guidance to agency departments on measures for securing government information resources and emphasizes management controls and how they are supported by the technical controls. The NIACAP is executed in four phases: definition, verification, validation, and post accreditation.

Department of Defense Directive (DODD) 8500.1, *Information Assurance***:** 2002 was a banner year for information systems security laws and policy. In the same year as FISMA, the DOD signed its first information assurance (IA) regulation, *DODD 8500.1,* into effect on 24 October 2002. This directive became the foundational document for all future DOD IA policy.

The primary purpose of DODD 8500.1 was to establish policy and to assign responsibilities to various DOD agencies in order to promote the objectives of DOD IA. This directive focused on a "defense-in-depth" approach to information systems security integrating personnel, technology and operations. This directive superseded earlier regulations, including DODD 5200.28.

DODD 8500.1 mandated a DOD-wide policy requiring IA requirements to be identified early in the system life cycle and included in the design, acquisition, installation, operation, upgrade, and replacement phases of all DOD information systems.

A DOD spokesperson stated in 2003 that DODD 8500.1:

... was developed largely in response to changing security needs brought about by DOD's growing dependence on interconnected information systems, particularly desktop computer networks, and increased concern about the protection of unclassified but sensitive information.[30]

DODD 8500.1 was written to address all DOD-owned or controlled IS, including:

- IS supporting special environments, such as special access programs;
- platform IT interconnections to external networks, e.g. sensors, weapons systems, medical technologies, utility distribution systems;
- IS under contract to DOD;
- outsourced IT-based information services;
- standalone IS;
- mobile devices, e.g. laptops, handhelds, PDAs, BlackBerries, etc. either wired or wireless.

Four categories of information systems were also defined in DODD 8500.1: Automated information system (AIS) application, enclave, outsourced IT-based process, and platform IT interconnection:

- **Automated information system (AIS) application**

  - Product or deliverable of an acquisition program as defined in DODD 5000.1, *The Defense Acquisition System*. It may be a single software application, multiple applications related to

---

[30] Matt French, "DOD Issues more IA Instructions", *Federal Computer Week*, *http://archives.neohapsis.com/archives/isn/2003-q1/0286.html*

a single mission, or a combination of hardware and software performing a specific support function across a range of missions.

- Performs clearly defined functions for which there are readily identifiable security considerations and needs addressed by the program manager (PM) as part of the acquisition process. These requirements are in part determined by the MAC and CL.
- Has a security design conforming to the DOD component IA architecture and utilizes common information systems security services provided by enclaves.
- May be deployed in an enclave with a higher level MAC or CL, but not in one with a lower level (of course, there are exceptions; but these would require additional security considerations.)
- Deployed to enclaves for operations, which then assume responsibility for operational security.
- Is managed across the life cycle, with the PM responsible for addressing security in new releases.

- **Enclave**
  - Collection of computing environments connected by one or more internal networks under the control of a single authority and security policy, including physical and personnel security.
  - Provides standard IA capabilities, such as boundary defense, incident detection, and encryption key management, and also delivers common applications, such as office automation and electronic mail.
  - Always assumes the highest MAC and CL for interconnection with other enclaves or platform IT. Employs a controlled interface if security domains are crossed and at least one is classified.
  - May be specific to an organization or mission and the computing environments may be organized by physical proximity or by function independent of location.
  - Examples of enclaves include: local area networks (LANs), backbone networks, and data processing centers.

- **Outsourced IT-based process**
  - General term used to refer to outsourced business processes supported by private sector information systems, outsourced information technologies, and outsourced information services.
  - Is not under DOD configuration control and is not dedicated to DOD processing or DOD users.
  - Performs clearly defined functions for which there are readily identifiable security considerations and needs:
    - technical security is the responsibility of the service provider;
    - responsibility for administrative and procedural security is shared between the government and the service provider;
    - security roles and responsibilities are addressed in the service acquisition;
    - information systems security posture is addressed via performance and service level parameters, such as service level agreements (SLA).
  - Can be considered an enclave if established only for DOD purposes, is dedicated to DOD processing, and is under DOD configuration control.

- **Platform IT interconnection**
  - Refers to an external network with access to platform IT.
  - Is always used in conjunction with an enclave.
  - Has readily identifiable security considerations that need to be addressed in both acquisition and operations.
  - Responsible for the security of the information processes inherent to its dedicated function.
  - Interconnecting enclaves are responsible for extending security services, such as identification and authentication to the interconnection and for protecting the platform IT from risks, such as unauthorized access.
  - Can be both hardware and software physically part of, dedicated to, or essential in real time to the mission performance of special purpose systems, such as weapons,

training simulators, diagnostic test and maintenance equipment, calibration equipment, medical technologies, transport buildings, and utility distribution systems , such as water and electric.

The enclave is the primary information system management unit: it provides the majority of the information systems security services and capabilities. The implications of these differing types of information systems on the C&A process will be discussed in greater detail in Chapter 10.

DODD 8500.1 was updated in April 2007 to address changing responsibilities and nomenclature and was renamed DODD 8500.01E.

Department of Defense Instruction (DODI) 8500.2, *Information Assurance Implementation*: <u>*DODI 8500.2*</u>, which was signed into effect on 6 February 2003, is the companion regulation to DODD 8500.1. DODD 8500.1 provides the policy requiring DOD organizations to identify their IA requirements and ensure these are reflected in the design, acquisition, installation, operation, upgrade and replacement of all DOD information systems. DOD 8500.2 provides the detailed instructions on how to execute that policy and how it will be enforced. The timing for issuing these two policies was intentionally close: DOD organizations could not implement the policies in DODD 8500.1 until DODI 8500.2 was issued. DODI 8500.2 was issued to address the significant DOD responsibility for protecting its information assets. In the words of the instruction:

The Department of Defense has a crucial responsibility to protect and defend its information and supporting information technology. DOD information is shared across a Global Information Grid [GIG] that is inherently vulnerable to exploitation and denial of service. Factors that contribute to its vulnerability include: increased reliance on commercial information technology and services; increased complexity and risk propagation through interconnection; the extremely rapid pace of technological change; a distributed and non-standard management structure; and the relatively low cost of entry for adversaries.[31]

---

[31] Department of Defense Instruction 8500.2, *Information Assurance Implementation.*

The most important content of DODI 8500.2 is found in Enclosures 3 and 4. Enclosure 3 provides the overview of DOD's IA program and the expectations of DOD for protecting the GIG. It lays out a multi-tiered management structure and the information standards used to assess, implement, verify, and manage changes to information systems security needs.

The instruction also established the baseline set of DOD IA controls to be applied to all DOD information systems. The DOD IA controls are provided in six attachments in Enclosure 4 of the instruction. Three attachments specify controls necessary to protect the integrity and availability of DOD information through the assignment of a mission assurance category (MAC).

There are three MAC levels: MAC I, MAC II, MAC III – in decreasing levels of stringency, which influences the selection and implementation standards for the IA controls. Each of these levels is described in detail in the table below:

Table 1: Mission assurance categories

	Definition	Integrity	Availability
MA C I	Systems handle information that is determined to be vital to the operational readiness or mission effectiveness of deployed and/or contingency forces in terms of both content and timeliness. Any loss is unacceptable and could result in an immediate/sustained loss of mission capability. Requires the most stringent protective measures.	High	High
MA C II	Systems handle information that is important to the support of deployed and/or contingency forces. The loss of integrity is unacceptable and the loss of availability is difficult to manage; however, it is tolerable for the short term. Loss seriously impacts mission	High	Medium

	effectiveness/operational readiness. Additional safeguards are required beyond best practices.		
MAC III	Systems handle information that is necessary for the conduct of day-to-day business, but does not materially affect the support to deployed and/or contingency forces in the short term. Loss can be tolerated or overcome without significant mission impact; protective measures are commensurate with commercial best practices.	Basic	Basic

The second criterion for determining IA requirements defined in DODD 8500.1 is the confidentiality level (CL), which is based on the sensitivity of the information in the system. Three other attachments address the IA controls necessary to protect classified, sensitive, or public information. Here again there are three levels presented in the directive:

Table 2: Confidentiality level

Confidentiality level	Definition
Classified	Systems processing classified information.
Sensitive	Systems processing sensitive information as defined in DODD 8500.1, to include any unclassified information not cleared for public release.
Public	Systems processing publicly releasable information as defined in DODD 8500.1 (i.e. information that has undergone a security review and been cleared for public release).

Together, these nine elements combine in a two-dimensional Cartesian product[32] to determine a final set of information systems security requirements. As shown in the table below, an IS might determine that it required high availability and basic integrity and had a confidentiality level of sensitive.

Table 3: MAC and CL matrix

		Confidentiality Level		
		Classified	Sensitive	Public
Mission Assurance Category	MAC I			
	MAC II		X	
	MAC III			

Once DODI 8500.2 was published, the DOD 8510.1-M was updated to mandate the use of DOD IA controls as part of the DITSCAP process. This was not, however, fully successful, which led to the development and publication in 2007 of the replacement to the DITSCAP, the DIACAP.

The processes for assigning, implementing, and verifying DOD IA controls as part of the overall DOD C&A process will be addressed extensively in Chapter 11.

Department of Defense Directive (DODD) 8570.1, *Information Assurance Training, Certification, and Workforce Management*: <u>*DODD 8570.1*</u> was published on 15 August 2004 to establish the requirements for an enterprise-wide approach to training, certifying,

---

[32] In the field of mathematics, a Cartesian product (or product set) is a direct product of two sets of content. The Cartesian product is named after René Descartes, whose formulation of analytic geometry gave rise to this concept. A Cartesian product of two finite sets can be represented by a table, such as that depicted by the MAC and CL combination, with one set as the rows and the other as the columns.

and managing the DOD IA workforce. Under this regulation, personnel involved as IA technicians and managers must be trained and certified to a specified DOD baseline.

Much of the DOD directive addresses workforce management issues. DOD agencies are required to identify and document IA personnel and positions in designated databases and ensure that all IA personnel meet the training and certification requirements related to their job function.

The ultimate vision of DODD 8570.1 is a sustainable, professional IA workforce possessing all of the skills needed to effectively prevent, detect, and respond to attacks against DOD information, information systems, and information infrastructures.

The foundation established in DODD 8570 supports the following five strategic IA workforce objectives:

- Certify the workforce: Establish baseline certifications across the enterprise and certify the workforce according to those baselines.
- Manage the workforce: Provide the tools to facilitate both component management of its IA workforce and the insight of the OSD into DOD's overall workforce status and certification posture.
- Sustain the workforce: Enable the DOD workforce to receive continuous learning opportunities to keep their skills current to combat new network threats.
- Extend the discipline: Infuse IA into professional education programs to expand operational leadership's attention to the domain.
- Evaluate the workforce: Establish a means of assessing compliance and measuring program effectiveness.

DODD 8570.1 is supported by a companion implementation manual that was originally published in November 2005. This manual, DOD 8570.01-M, *Information Assurance Workforce Improvement*, was updated in May 2008 and provides detailed guidance for the identification and categorization of positions and certification of personnel conducting information assurance functions within the DOD.

A more detailed account of information systems security training and certification is provided in Chapter 17.

The Common Criteria for Information Technology Security Evaluation: Commonly known just as the "*Common Criteria,*" this security standard took its origin from three existing standards:

- Department of Defense DOD 5200.28-STD, also known as "The Orange Book," part of the original DOD Rainbow Series in the late 1970s and early 1980s.
- The European IT Security (ITSEC) standard, jointly published in the early 1990s by France, Germany, the Netherlands and the UK.
- The May 1993 Canadian Trusted Computer Product Evaluation Criteria (CTCPEC) standard derived from the US DOD standard and used jointly by evaluators from both the US and Canada.

The Common Criteria represented an effort by the governments of Canada, France, Germany, the Netherlands, the UK, and the US to unify these pre-existing standards, with a primary focus on assisting companies selling computer products targeted at the government defense market. This single standard, now recognized as international standard, ISO15408, ensured that companies would be evaluated against only one set of standards regardless of their target market.

A second purpose of the Common Criteria was to provide a level of assurance that the process of specification, implementation and evaluation of a computer security product was conducted in a rigorous and standardized manner.

The Common Criteria methodology has been critically examined. In a column in the August 2007 *Government Computing News,* senior representatives from the security, R&D, and IA communities were interviewed. Their primary objections to the Common Criteria as outlined in the article include:

- Evaluation is a much too costly process (often hundreds of thousands of US dollars) – and the vendor's return on investment (ROI) may not necessarily represent a more secure product.

- The Common Criteria evaluation is primarily focused on reviewed documentation, and not necessarily on the technical correctness of the product itself.
- Level of effort (LOE) and the time required to prepare the required evidence and other evaluation-related documentation is extremely cumbersome and time-consuming, so that by the time the work is completed, the product in evaluation may have become obsolete.

Department of Defense Instruction 8510.01, *DOD Information Assurance Certification & Accreditation Process* (DIACAP): The DIACAP, *DODI 8510.01*, which was signed into effect in November 2007, is DOD's most recent process for the certification of its information systems and for determining whether these systems should or should not be authorized to operate. The DIACAP serves as the DOD policy to support compliance with the information systems security mandates required of all federal agencies under FISMA.

The DIACAP established a modernized DOD information assurance C&A process for authorizing the operation of DOD information systems consistent with the requirements of FISMA, DODD 8500.1, and DODI 8500.2.

DOD considered the development and publication of the DIACAP as an essential response to changes in technology, the way DOD acquires and uses IT, and in order to facilitate compliance with an ever-growing set of federal compliance mandates.

The cost of C&A had continued to grow exponentially without, however, delivering the security return on investment needed by DOD. So, any new C&A process had to be less time consuming, easier to implement, less resource intensive, present clear accountability, implement standardized information systems security, and ensure the ability to report on information systems security status.

Upon its release, DOD emphasized that the DIACAP:

- Satisfies the need for a dynamic C&A process for the global information grid and net-centric applications, neither of which could be met with previous C&A methodologies.
- Focuses on a net-centric approach with emphasis on embedding IA into the information systems development and implementation cycle.
- Enables shared information systems security solutions across system boundaries and eliminates fixed phases to allow for the continuous integration of IA with the system life cycle processes.
- Provides standardized security implementation, security testing, and evaluation processes.
- Replaces DITSCAP and its hard-coded phases with a set of five activities.

The following table compares the DIACAP activities with the DITSCAP phases:

Table 4: DITSCAP vs. DIACAP

DITSCAP	DIACAP
Definition	Initiate & plan
Verification	Implement & validate
Validation	Make C&A decisions
Post-accreditation	Maintain ATO/reviews
	Decommission

DOD developed two supporting tools concurrently with the DIACAP to assist in sharing C&A data across the DOD:

- The DIACAP Knowledge Service (KS), which is a web-based portal containing DIACAP guidelines. The KS allows DOD to maintain and consistently update C&A requirements data, lessons learned, C&A templates, best practice resources, and general certification news. The site is designed to facilitate DOD community-wide collaboration, input, and discussion.

- The Enterprise Mission Assurance Support Service (eMASS) is a standalone or web-based set of computer-based services to facilitate workflow management of the DIACAP. In addition, eMASS can manage the production of certification documentation, verification test data, and other information system-related C&A data throughout the information system life cycle.

The processes for executing a DOD C&A process will be addressed extensively in Chapter 10.

Policy, guidance and standards

Briefly stated, standards are issued in response to a law or regulation. Federal agencies, such as the US Department of Defense (DOD) and others, develop standards and guidance documents designed to provide the basis for planning and designing mechanisms to comply with the requirements stated in law and regulations. These standards can be considered guides for the design and implementation of specific measures. In most cases, standards are well-developed and well-understood and are built on basic principles or on established best practices.

The US National Institute of Standards and Technology (NIST) is the primary developer of information systems security standards and guidance. Standards or guidance documents are defined by certain characteristics:

- Considered to be recommendations.
- Use is voluntary.[33]
- Publicly available.

---

[33] There is an ongoing debate about whether or not the use of certain NIST standards is voluntary. Existing Federal Information Processing Standards (FIPS) – which are considered legal statutes and thus mandatory – often specify the use of the NIST Special Publications as a prerequisite for compliance.

- Often developed by consensus, whether within an agency or across international borders.
- Foundation consists of the results of process, technology and experience.
- Approved and published by a recognized standardization body or responsible agency.

National Institute of Technology (NIST) Special Publication (SP) 800-37, *Guide for the Security Certification and Accreditation of Federal Information Systems*: Although DOD left the information systems security starting blocks first with the development of the DODD 8500.1 and DODI 8500.2, the National Institute of Standards and Technology was not far behind. NIST was given broad responsibilities for the information systems security of federal systems under the Computer Security Act of 1987. Under the Federal Information Security Management Act of 2002, these responsibilities were extended to encompass the following:

- Develop IT standards and guidelines, including minimum requirements, for information systems.
- Develop security standards and guidelines, including minimum requirements, for the security of non-national security systems within the federal government.
- Specifically develop guidelines for: 1) categorizing all federal information and information systems according to a range of risk levels; 2) the types of information systems in each category; 3) minimum security requirements for information and information systems in each category; 4) detecting and handling federal information security incidents; and 5) identification of national security systems within the federal government.
- Consult with other agencies to assure: 1) use of appropriate information security policies and procedures; 2) duplication of effort is avoided; and 3) that standards and guidelines are complementary with those employed to protect national security information and systems.
- Provide assistance to agencies on: 1) complying with NIST-developed standards and guidelines; 2) detecting and handling

security incidents; and 3) security policies, procedures, and practices.

- Submit proposed standards and guidelines, accompanied by recommendation of the extent to which they should be made compulsory and binding, to the Director of the Office of Management and Budget (OMB) for promulgation.
- Conduct security research.
- Develop security performance indicators.
- Evaluate private sector information security policies and practices for potential use in the government;
- Solicit recommendations of the Information Security Advisory Board on proposed standards and guidelines and also submit those to the Director of OMB.
- Report annually to OMB on: 1) compliance with Clinger-Cohen requirements; 2) major deficiencies in federal security; and 3) recommendations for improvement.

In order to enable NIST to perform these responsibilities, in 2002 FISMA agreed to:

- Establish an Office for Information Security Programs at NIST, the director of which would be responsible for administering NIST's information security responsibilities under FISMA.
- Authorize a $20 million level funding for NIST's security program.
- Rename the "Computer System Security and Privacy Advisory Board" as the "Information Security Board," add the Director of OMB (and delete the Secretary of Commerce) as a customer for the Board's advice, and authorize funds for its operation.
- Eliminate the existing process, under limited and specified circumstances, for agencies to waive the use of mandatory and binding security standards.

Under this expanded charter and with the additional budget, NIST has emerged as a pivotal element for issuing federal information systems security guidance.

NIST Special Publication (SP) 800-37[34] was considered an exciting development by the federal community. Its primary purpose is to provide streamlined guidelines for the security certification and accreditation of information systems supporting the executive agencies of the federal government, including their contractors. In doing so, NIST SP 800-37 leveraged the lessons learned from other C&A processes, such as the DITSCAP.

The guidelines in *NIST 800-37* were specifically developed to:

- enable more consistent, comparable, and repeatable evaluations of security controls applied to federal information systems;
- promote a better understanding of enterprise-wide mission risks resulting from the operation of information systems;
- create more complete, reliable, and trustworthy information for authorizing officials – facilitating more informed security accreditation decisions; and
- help achieve more secure information systems within the federal government including the critical infrastructure of the United States.

The guidelines provided in Special Publication 800-37 are applicable to all federal information systems other than those systems designated as national security systems, as defined in 44 USC, Section 3542. The guidelines have been broadly developed from a technical perspective so as to be complementary to similar guidelines issued by agencies and offices operating or exercising control over national security systems. This publication is intended to provide guidelines to federal agencies in lieu of Federal Information Processing Standards (FIPS) Publication 102, *Guidelines for Computer Security Certification and Accreditation*, September 1983, which is being rescinded.

Although NIST SP 800-37 was prepared for use by federal agencies, it has also been adopted for use by non-governmental organizations and commercial entities on a voluntary basis. NIST

---

[34] In August 2008, NIST issued a draft revision of NIST SP 800-37, which is still in public comment as of the drafting of this book.

views security certification and accreditation as "…important activities that support a risk management process and are an integral part of an agency's information security program." The NIST process consists of four distinct, but highly interrelated phases. Each phase contains a series of tasks and sub-tasks for execution by specific roles within the C&A team. The phases are:

- Initiation phase, which consists of:

  - preparation;
  - notification and resource identification; and
  - system security plan analysis, update, and acceptance.

- Security certification phase, with two primary tasks:

  - security control assessment; and
  - security certification documentation.

- Security accreditation phase, which also encompasses two tasks:

  - security accreditation decision; and
  - security accreditation documentation.

- Continuous monitoring phase, with three tasks:

  - configuration management and control;
  - security control monitoring; and
  - status reporting and documentation.

NIST SP 800-37 provides guidelines for the execution of the C&A process, but like DOD, the information systems security controls are listed in a separate publication, NIST SP 800-53.

The processes for executing the NIST C&A process will be addressed extensively in Chapter 11.

National Institute of Standards and Technology (NIST) Special Publication (SP) 800-53, *Recommended Security Controls for Federal Information Systems*: As part of its assigned responsibilities for developing the information systems security standards and guidelines for federal agencies to establish compliance with FISMA requirements, NIST developed and published the first *NIST SP 800-53 – Recommended Security Controls for Federal Information Systems* in 2005.

Since its original publication in 2005, NIST SP 800-53 has undergone several revisions, with the latest being Revision 2 in December 2007.

This NIST publication provides federal agencies with a guide to select the best set of security controls for their information. NIST SP 800-53 presents fundamental concepts concerning the selection and specification of security controls. It organizes security controls, or information system safeguards, into management, operational, and technical countermeasures designed to protect the confidentiality, integrity, and availability (CIA) of an information system and its information.

The structural components of security controls and how the controls are organized into families of controls are described, including the:

- baseline, or minimum, controls and the selection criteria;
- common controls that can be applied in more than one organizational information system;
- additional controls necessary to protect information systems engaged in data exchanges with external information systems;
- controls implementation and how to gain assurance that the controls are effective;
- requirement for a periodic review of the applied security controls;
- maintenance of an effective controls catalog.

The later revisions of the publication also provide tailoring guidance to give federal agencies more flexibility in selecting and implementing their specific security controls in order to cost-effectively meet their unique mission requirements and operational needs.

NIST SP 800-53 was published subsequent to DOD's catalog of controls, DODI 8500.2 – and many consider it to be a considerable improvement on the original.

The processes for identifying and implementing the security controls as part of the NIST C&A process will be addressed extensively in Chapter 11.

National Institute of Standards and Technology (NIST) Special Publication (SP) 800-53A, *Guide for Assessing the Security Controls in Federal Information Systems*: <u>NIST SP 800-53A</u> was published in final form in June 2008 and provides assistance to information system security managers to negotiate the process of implementing and assessing the effectiveness of information security controls derived from NIST SP 800-53. The procedures in the publication define a disciplined and structured process for determining whether information systems security controls in federal information systems have been implemented correctly, are operating as intended, and are producing the desired outcome with respect to meeting organizational security policies.

Although specifically designed to meet the requirements of federal agencies that must satisfy reporting requirements called for in FISMA, NIST SP 800-53A can be useful to IT professionals across the federal government and industry.

The authors of NIST SP 800-53A developed supporting tools and techniques to assist in using the assessment procedures described in SP 800-53A. NIST also worked with representatives from the federal security community to generate a suite of assessment cases based on NIST SP 800-53A procedures. These cases provide additional assessor-related information that can be used for more consistent and cost-effective security control assessments; they can be found at *<u>http://csrc.nist.gov/groups/SMA/fisma/assessment.html</u>*.

The processes for assessing security controls as part of a C&A process will be addressed extensively in Chapter 5 and for the NIST specific processes will be detailed in Chapter 11.

If all of these recently issued C&A processes have caused you some confusion, let's just say – you aren't alone. Deciding which process to use, how to ensure a return on the investment of time and money, and what is required for C&A to be accepted across the US federal agencies has inspired a massive C&A revitalization effort.

Miscellaneous legislation affecting the authorization process

Health Information Portability and Accountability Act (HIPAA)

The privacy portion of the *Health Insurance Portability and Accountability Act* (HIPAA) was enacted on 21 August 1996. This landmark piece of legislation affects almost every entity involved in the health care process – from health care providers to insurance companies to patients. The primary objective of HIPAA was to ensure the portability and continuity of health insurance coverage and to prevent abuse, loss, or unauthorized disclosure of personal information within health insurance and health care delivery.

To achieve that objective, HIPAA requires safeguards that entities involved in health care must meet, but it allows for flexibility in the development of policies and procedures for meeting these standards. The intent was for the implementation of the standards to have sufficient flexibility to adjust to each entity's business, size and resources.

Summary of the rule: HIPAA can be organized into the following major components:

- Security of personal health information:
  - Health care entities must adopt written privacy procedures, which must address access to protected information, how it will be used within the entity, and when the information would or would not be disclosed to others. Each entity must ensure that their business associates also protect the privacy of health information.
  - Health care entities must specifically designate a privacy officer. The officer and the staff must be given sufficient training to ensure they understand the new privacy protection procedures. Furthermore, each entity must appoint an individual responsible for ensuring the procedures are followed.
  - Covered entities must establish a grievance process to provide a means for patients to make inquiries or complaints regarding the privacy of their records.

- Boundaries on the use and release of personal health information:

  - Unless specifically authorized by the individual, health care entities may not use or reveal personal health information for any purpose not related to health care.
  - A health care entity must identify any members who need access to protected health information and assign a level of access which will permit them to carry out their duties. For information disclosures made on a routine and recurring basis, the health care entity must implement policies and procedures to limit the amount of protected health information to that amount reasonably necessary to achieve the purposes of the disclosure.
  - Covered entities must ensure that patient authorization for non-routine disclosures meets the requirements of the Act.

In addition to the Act itself, a specific rule associated with HIPAA and addressing security was also passed. The Security Rule was issued in 2003 and specifically applies to electronic protected health information (EPHI), which is individually identifiable health information (IIHI) in electronic form.

IIHI refers to: 1) a person's past, present, or future physical or mental health or condition; 2) a person's health care; or 3) the past, present, or future payment for health care to an individual. The primary objective of the Security Rule is to protect the confidentiality, integrity, and availability of EPHI during storage, processing or transmission.

The safeguards mandated by the HIPAA Security Rule are divided into three primary areas: technical, administrative, or physical.

Figure 1: HIPAA Security Rule requirements

Administrative	Technical	Physical
– Security management process – Assigned security responsibility – Workforce security – Information access management – Security incident procedures – Contingency plan – Evaluation – Business associate contracts	– Access control – Audit controls – Integrity – Person or entity authentication – Transmission security	– Facility access control – Workstation use – Workstation security – Device and media controls

Health care providers – or covered entities – that do not comply with the HIPAA Security Rule may be subject to penalties. Civil penalties can be up to $100 per violation, and $25,000 per year for each requirement violated. Criminal penalties may range from $50,000 in fines and one year in prison to $250,000 in fines and 10 years in jail.

Additional negatives should an intentional – or unintentional – breach of HIPAA become known are: negative publicity, loss of customers or business partners, and legal liability.

Sarbanes-Oxley

The *Sarbanes-Oxley Act* (SOX) was issued in 2002 in response to the rather large and public failures of corporate governance, such as Enron, WorldCom, and Tyco. SOX was preceded by TV news broadcasts of C-level[35] executives being arrested and walked off in handcuffs.

---

[35] C-level is an adjective used to describe high-ranking executive titles within an organization.

The Sarbanes-Oxley Act was specifically designed to protect individual investors by requiring accuracy, reliability, and accountability of corporate disclosures. It also mandates the implementation of controls to inhibit and deter financial misconduct.

Like HIPAA, there are penalties for failure to comply with Sarbanes-Oxley. Lack of compliance could potentially expose senior management to prison time (up to 20 years), significant penalties (as much as $5 million), or both.

Many consider that Sarbanes-Oxley is one of the most comprehensive laws focusing on and proscribing a range of corporate misbehavior associated with financial responsibility. SOX is very clear on what is not permitted. However, it allows the decision and definition of the implementation to remain in the hands of individual businesses. Many consider this flexibility a plus, since it provides wide latitude in compliance. At the same time, the lack of detail has also led to some confusion about exactly what controls are appropriate and required.

Most of the discussion about Sarbanes-Oxley as it relates to information systems security is focused on two sections: 302 and 404. Section 302: *Corporate Responsibility for Financial Reports* specifies that certifying officers are responsible for establishing and maintaining internal control over financial reporting. It requires:

- A statement that certifying officers are responsible for establishing and maintaining internal control over financial reporting.
- A statement that the certifying officers designed internal controls and providing assurance that financial reporting and financial statements were prepared using generally accepted accounting principles.
- A statement that the report discloses any changes in the company's internal control over financial reporting that have materially affected those internal controls

Section 404 of SOX focuses on the effort required from the financial executives. Section 404 mandates the following:

- Companies must file an annual report, including an internal control report describing management's responsibility for establishing and maintaining an adequate internal controls structure and procedures for financial reporting.
- Execution of an annual assessment of the effectiveness of the internal control structure and procedures for financial reporting.
- A company audit that attests to, and reports on, management's assessment of the effectiveness of the company's internal controls and procedures for financial reporting in accordance with standards established by the Public Company Accounting Oversight Board.

Section 404 also requires companies to establish a security infrastructure to protect financial and personal records and data from destruction, loss, unauthorized alteration, or other misuse. The infrastructure must also ensure there is no possibility for records vital to maintaining the integrity of the business processes to undergo unauthorized changes.

Compliance with this requirement involves determining the necessary controls, conducting a risk assessment, implementing the security controls, creating effective communication and information flows, and monitoring continued compliance. This infrastructure is required to adhere to a structured internal control framework, such as the *Internal Controls – Integrated Framework* of the Committee of Sponsoring Organizations (COSO) of the Treadway Commission. The COSO framework applies to operations, finance, and compliance in the following five areas:

- The control environment
- Risk assessment
- Control activities
- Information and communication
- Monitoring.

Federal Information System Controls Audit Manual (FISCAM)

The *Federal Information System Controls Audit Manual* (FISCAM) provides a methodology for executing information system control audits of federal agencies and other entities in accordance with specific professional standards. It was originally issued in January 1999 and later updated to reflect additional requirements.

FISCAM was developed by the General Accounting Office (GAO) and describes controls that should be considered when assessing the integrity, confidentiality, and availability of information systems and their data.

It is organized to facilitate effective and efficient:

- audit planning;
- evaluation of findings – control hierarchy;
- audit report drafting.

According to FISCAM, both general and application controls must be implemented and tested to ensure the reliability, appropriate confidentiality, and availability of critical automated information.

Figure 2: FISCAM assessment control areas by level

Control areas	Entity wide/ component level	System level			Business process application level
		Network	Operating systems	Infrastructure applications	
Security management					
Access controls					
Configuration management					
Segregation of duties					
Contingency planning					
Business process (incl. interface and data mgmt.)					

Source: Adapted from FISCAM

The manual also provides a methodology for efficiently and effectively evaluating the effectiveness of information security controls from the enterprise to the information system level.

The C&A transformation – The future is here (near)

On 7 June 2006, the Director of National Intelligence (DNI) Chief Information Officer (CIO) and NIST joined with the DOD CIO to sponsor a kick-off event to engage the US security community in a multi-focused effort to revitalize existing C&A processes. The effort sought innovation by mixing teams of specialists and setting them to work on relevant C&A issues. The goal was to develop new policies, processes and ideas for handling C&A that could be used across the federal government.

Retired Major General Dale Meyerrose[36] explained the process as bringing "… competing ideas to war rooms and out of the war rooms, to bring about actionable elements. ODNI[37], DOD and NIST will jointly work on the business of certifying and accrediting."

The intent of the C&A transformation goes far beyond just rewriting existing policies. Of course DCID 6/3, DODI 8500.2, and NIST Special Publication 800 series are all currently part of the C&A process, but this effort is not merely a "rewrite" of these documents. C&A revitalization represents an effort to discover new ways of performing C&A across the board. Government and industry have been working with multiple C&A processes for a long time, often causing confusion and delays. The effort is aimed at understanding what the entire community views as potential solutions and best practices, and then building a fresh approach based on innovative ideas and incorporating only the best solutions and practices.

The full scope of the C&A revitalization and transformation will be addressed extensively in Chapter 15.

---

[36] Former Associate Director of National Intelligence and Chief Information Officer, Director of National Intelligence, and the primary initial motivator behind the C&A transformation initiative.
[37] Office of the Director of National Intelligence.

<table>
<tr><td>Further reading</td></tr>
<tr><td>

Schneier, Bruce. *Beyond Fear: Thinking Sensibly About Security in an Uncertain World,* Copernicus Books, September 2003.

Smedinghoff, Thomas J. *Information Security: The Emerging Standard for Corporate Compliance,* IT Governance Ltd Publishing, October 2008.

Taylor, Laura. *FISMA Certification & Accreditation,* Syngress, November 2006.

</td></tr>
</table>

References

Gill, Kathy. *What is an Executive Order?* Available at: *http://uspolitics.about.com/od/presidenc1/a/executive_order.htm*

Kanellos, Michael. *Gordon Moore on 40 Years of His Processor Law.* Available on: *http://news.cnet.com/Gordon-Moore-on-40-years-of-his-processor-law/2008-1006_3-5657677.html*

Moor, James H. *What is Computer Ethics?* Available at: *http://www.southernct.edu/organizations/rccs/resources/teaching/teaching_mono/moor/moor_definition.html.*

National Institute of Standards and Technology (NIST) Special Publications, *Computer Security Resource Center – Publications*: *http://csrc.nist.gov/publications/PubsSPs.html*

National Institute of Standards and Technology (NIST) Special Publications, *Computer Security Resource Center – Security Drivers*: *http://csrc.nist.gov/drivers/index.html*

Official site for DOD Publications: *http://www.dtic.mil/whs/directives/corres/pub1.html*

Stallings, William. *Official "Internet World" Internet Security Handbook (The Official Internet World).* McGraw-Hill Publishing Co. January 1996.

Ware, William (Ed.). *Security Controls for Computer Systems: Report of the Defense Science Board Task Force on Computer Security.* Rand Report, October 1979.

CHAPTER 3: THE AUTHORIZATION PROCESS FRAMEWORK

High achievement always takes place in the framework of high expectation![38]

Jack Kinder, Management Training Professional

In this chapter:

Common authorization process deficiencies

Authorization process commonalities

The basic authorization framework

Joint or reciprocal authorization

---

[38] Deonaraine, Ramesh, *Power Quotes to Energize Your Life: A Motivational System to Make You More Dynamic* (Paperback), page 11, iUniverse, Inc. (November 17, 2003).

Certification and accreditation (C&A) or the authorization to operate an information system is a process. Despite all of the legislative and regulatory confusion we presented in Chapter 2, *it's really that simple.* You need to understand the supporting laws, regulations, and policies. But after that – if you approach it as a process – you will find that the authorization process can be manageable and produce valid security results.

But before we look at the authorization process, let's discuss some of the most commonly occurring deficiencies found in many of the audits conducted by the General Accounting Office (GAO).

Commonly found authorization process deficiencies

In response to a requirement from the Office of Management and Budget (OMB), the General Accounting Office (GAO) has conducted several evaluations of the authorization processes in federal agencies in recent years. These evaluations revealed a number of weaknesses that were consistent across the federal agencies. It is important to understand what is considered a weakness in order to determine what might be an improvement in your own program.

Risk assessments were not conducted or did not provide an adequate basis for a risk-based decision

Starting with law and ending with agency policies, most federal agencies require a risk assessment for the purpose of identifying system vulnerabilities, threats, and associated impacts.

Identifying and assessing information security risks are essential steps in determining what controls are required. Moreover, by increasing awareness of risks, these assessments can generate support for the policies and controls that are adopted in order to help ensure that these policies and controls operate as intended.

The risk assessment also provides the foundation for determining appropriate and cost-effective protection requirements for the information system. In many cases, the GAO discovered that agencies often relied solely on a security controls checklist and were not able to identify the true risks to their information systems. As a result, the agencies had no means to determine which security controls were really required and whether additional security controls were needed.

Risk assessments, when they did exist, were often found to be outdated and incomplete. For example, federal agencies did not update their risk assessments to reflect significant changes in the network operating environment, such as additional connectivity.

Information system sensitivity levels were inconsistent or incorrect

The information and information system security levels reviewed by the GAO were not always appropriate for the information system. In one case, for example, the security controls were based on an assignment of medium requirements for confidentiality, integrity and availability. The actual plan for the information system, however, indicated that it was a mission essential system with high requirements for confidentiality, integrity, and availability. In other cases, the GAO found that agencies rated their security requirements too high, resulting in unnecessary expenditure for unwarranted levels of protection.

Inadequately assessing information and information system security levels can lead to implementing inadequate or inappropriate security controls that might not address the system's true risk. It also can lead to costly efforts to subsequently implement effective countermeasures.

Inappropriate or insufficient security controls

Linked to the above weakness in correctly determining the information and information security level is the assignment of inappropriate or insufficient security controls. Frequently, agencies were unable to provide adequate information about the security controls that were planned and implemented. In many cases, the description of security controls was merely a repetition from the agency's security policy and not a valid description of the implementation of that security control respective to the information system and its security requirements.

Although the plans should address management, operational, and certain technical controls, other specific technical controls, such as for communication protection, are often not considered. Further, the security controls repeatedly did not reflect the current operating environment because they did not completely address issues such as system interconnectivity. As a result, federal agencies that connect to the network cannot truly ensure that appropriate controls are in place to protect their systems and critical information.

Authorization decisions were based on inadequate and inconsistent testing

Another key element is testing and evaluating system controls to ensure they are appropriate, effective, and comply with policies. An effective program of ongoing tests and evaluations can be very effective in identifying and correcting information security weaknesses.

In many cases, however, certification testing was not rigorous enough to determine where the security control really provided the necessary protection. Testing was often performed by internal agency assets and was inconsistent across the federal government. Test personnel were regularly unprepared and inexperienced, thus putting the results of the testing into question.

Further, inconsistency and lack of standardization in security control testing and the process for making the authorization determination made it almost impossible for the federal government to institute reciprocity between agencies and information systems.

Processes for security controls reviews were inadequate or nonexistent

FISMA requires that agencies test and evaluate the information security controls of their systems. The frequency of these reviews should be based on risk, but should occur no less than annually.

Periodic testing is essential to ensure that the accredited system has maintained its documented configuration baseline and to identify new vulnerabilities that may be inherent in the system and not previously identified.

Although many federal agencies had various initiatives under way to test and evaluate their information systems and the respective security controls, the tests were rarely comprehensive.

If you take a look at the above list of common deficiencies, you will see a common thread: a lack of consistency and standardization in the processes, whether internal to an agency or across the federal government. So, in order for the authorization process to be effective and produce the desired results, we need to focus on the establishment of a common process. Let's start by examining some undeniable commonalities in the authorization process.

Authorization process commonalities

Regardless of whether you are conducting authorization for a federal agency, the Department of Defense, the Intelligence Community, or even a contractor or a commercial business, all of the authorization processes have certain common denominators. A review of all of the legislation and regulations will reveal this very quickly.

First, they are all based on protecting the confidentiality, integrity, and availability of information and information systems. Each of the respective authorization methodologies has unique processes and terminologies for qualitatively categorizing confidentiality, integrity, and availability. And in all authorization methodologies, security requirements of controls are determined by the respective confidentiality, integrity, and availability needs of the information system.

Next, every authorization methodology requires – no, demands – accountability. Accountability for the security of information systems means that:

- actions can be traced back to a person or a process, and
- individuals will be held accountable for their actions.

All of the methodologies require the establishment of certain security roles and the execution of specific authorization related responsibilities. Although the terminology may differ, the essential nature of these roles and responsibilities remain the same.

To varying degrees, the implementation of the required security measures, or controls, is subject to verification and validation. This may differ between methodologies from a "desktop" assessment to comprehensive hands-on testing.

Each methodology has a beginning – initiating the authorization process – and each has an end – decommissioning the information system. Authorization should be a repeatable process, allowing organizations to develop a level of assurance that information system security measures are correctly implemented and maintained throughout the information system life cycle.

In order to introduce you to the authorization process as practiced by varying entities, Chapters 11-13 present an overview of three of the primary methodologies[39]. The goal of this book is to present a generic approach to the authorization process, one that can be used in almost every situation – whether for the federal government, DOD, the IC, or even for commercial organizations. The guidance we will refer to is largely derived from NIST publications – chiefly because the NIST guidance is not only most current, but it is also serving as the primary foundation for efforts to standardize authorization processes across all of the US federal agencies.

---

[39] It makes no sense for us to walk you through all of the different methodologies – especially since the framework for each is essentially the same.

The basic authorization framework

Let's introduce you now to the basic elements of the authorization framework:

- planning, initiation and implementation;
- verification, validation and authorization;
- operation and maintenance; and, at the end of the information system life cycle,
- removal from operation.

These elements may have different names and sub-tasks, but for the most part you will find them in some form in every authorization process.

For the purposes of our discussion in the next chapters, we will break the authorization process down into five essential elements:

- conduct pre-certification
- initiate and implement
- certify and accredit
- operate and maintain
- remove from operation.

The following diagram shows the three primary phases, plus the activities associated with pre-certification and removal from operation.

Figure 3: The primary phases of the authorization process

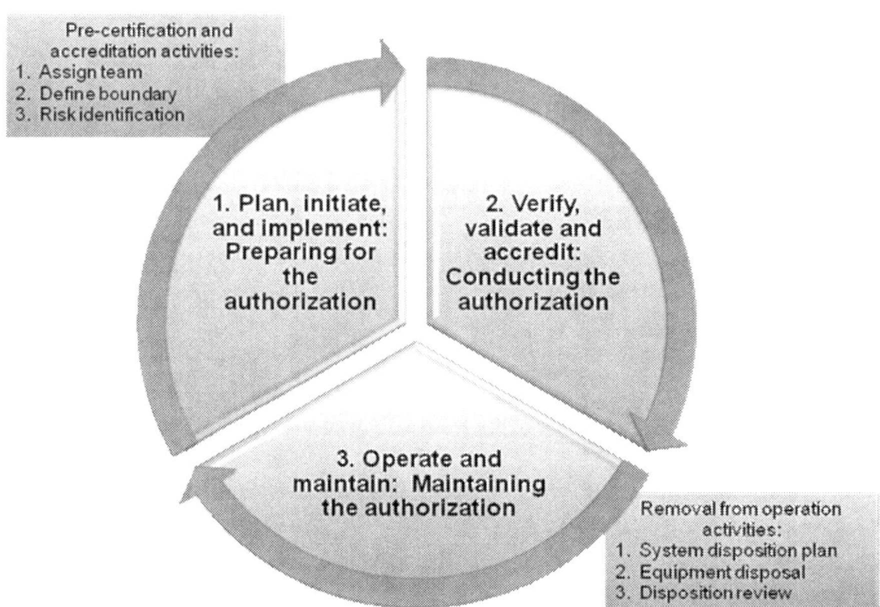

Factors that influence authorization activities

There are several factors that determine which authorization activities must be performed and to which degree. While this book will provide a uniform high-level approach to executing the authorization process, more specific information is necessary to determine how to apply the processes within a given environment, to a particular type of information system, or to a particular stage in the information system life cycle. For example, the authorization activities and requirements associated with a large-scale, interconnected network will be very different from those for a small, local area network (LAN) or a standalone information system.

The **architectural complexity** (e.g. the components and functions) and the **operational complexity** (e.g. the mission and users) of the information system will also affect the approach to authorization. The architectural and operational complexity will be reflected largely in the selection of technical and non-technical safeguards applied to protect the information system.

Another factor affecting the authorization approach is the **level of risk** associated with operating the information system. This includes not only the sensitivity of the information system itself, but also the system criticality and the level and nature of threats and vulnerabilities associated with the system. An office automation system, for example, may be less mission-critical and face fewer threats than a highly sophisticated intelligence analysis system or a financial system in the commercial sector.

Finally, the scope of the authorization activities should also consider the incorporation of previously evaluated or accredited products or systems or security safeguards provided by the environment (e.g. physical security). Every effort should be made to capitalize on authorization work already done by your own or by other organizations.

Joint or reciprocal authorization

Certain environments will require the coordination of two or more authorizing officials in order to ensure that all information systems in the environment have the necessary authorization to operate. These environments can be essentially divided into two types:

- Information systems requiring joint accreditation.
- Information systems consisting of the interconnection of one or more individually accredited systems.

Joint accreditation

Joint accreditation occurs when different operational or mission-related components of an information system are under the jurisdiction of different AOs, requiring them to collectively accredit the information system.

Joint accreditations often require additional planning and coordination to ensure that all of the entities involved in the process share a common understanding of the requirements and their respective responsibilities, the risks involved, and the security needs associated with the operation of the information system. A Memorandum of Agreement (MOA) may be necessary to ensure that roles, responsibilities, and security requirements are clearly defined and documented.

Examples of situations that might require joint accreditations include:

- Information systems that process different types of information, or information that belongs to various organizations within the same system (e.g. command and control and logistics information).
- Information systems used by multiple data owners, but processing the same type of information.
- Information systems supporting multiple organizations with different AOs.
- Information systems connected to a backbone network, where the host system and the backbone accreditor jointly accredit the system as a single entity.

Reciprocal accreditations

When information systems from different organizations and managed by different AOs are interconnected, a process of negotiation must occur to define the conditions for reciprocal acceptance of the existing accreditations and the conditions for interconnection. Each AO must evaluate the situation to determine whether there are any additional risks associated with the interconnection to the other information system(s).

While every effort should be made to minimize additional and unnecessary bureaucracy in this situation, there may be an agreement that the interconnection itself necessitates additional security safeguards and accreditation activities. Again, an MOA may be necessary to document the results of the negotiations that form the agreement between the AOs. In any case, the AOs must be prepared to share their respective accreditation documentation with the other AOs involved in establishing the interconnection.

References

National Institute of Standards and Technology (NIST) Special Publication (SP) 800-37, DRAFT *Guide for the Security Authorization of Federal Information Systems: A Security Life Cycle Approach.* First Public Draft, August 2008. Available at *http://csrc.nist.gov/publications/drafts/800-37-Rev1/SP800-37-rev1-IPD.pdf.*

National Institute of Standards and Technology (NIST) Special Publication (SP) 800-100, *Information Security Handbook: A Guide for Managers,* October 2006. Available at *http://csrc.nist.gov/publications/nistpubs/800-100/SP800-100-Mar07-2007.pdf.*

CHAPTER 4: THE AUTHORIZATION PROCESS – ESTABLISHING A FOUNDATION

Typically in most global organizations, security is viewed at best as a necessary evil and more commonly as a necessary friction. This derives from security's primary focus on attempting to constrain behavior to prevent negative events. Although well-intentioned, the inevitable result is that security practitioners are not viewed as enablers of innovation, but people preventing the business from doing what it needs to do. [40]

Bill Boni, Corporate Vice President, Information
Security and Protection, Motorola

In this chapter:

Designing and implementing an effective security program

Information systems security roles and responsibilities

---

[40] "The Time is Now: Making Information Security Strategic to Business Innovation: Recommendations from Global 1000 Executives," An Industry Initiative Sponsored by RSA, The Security Division of EMC.

Authorization is only one part of an effective security program

Two years ago, the authors were called in by a major international corporation to help them certify and accredit one of their major information systems as a pre-requisite for sales to the US Government. During initial meetings, we discovered that the system development team had included security considerations in their design. We also discovered that this team was working in a security vacuum – there was no corporate level security program that could assist in coordinating all of the efforts essential to effective authorization. As a result, each authorization was an individual, heroic venture – an individual process limited to a single application. The consequence – the company had to "recreate the wheel" for every new accreditation at great expense and cost to the resources of the company.

How much simpler would it have been for this major international corporation if they had a fully integrated security program, including authorization! An effective security program would have institutionalized the processes necessary to support authorization as part of a consistent, standardized enterprise-level effort. Each authorization would build on those that had gone before and could capitalize on coordinated efforts to gather the required information and conduct the activities necessary for a successful authorization.

This chapter will focus on establishing a foundation for an effective security program, focusing on the elements required for successful execution of certification and accreditation at an organizational level.

The first step is to establish that a security program is not only necessary, but that it supports the overall mission of the organization and ensures a return on investment.

Making the business case – what is the ROSI?

Security is viewed today as a significant component of an organization's overall infrastructure. We live in a dynamic environment with a variety of assets that need protection, as well as a large and diverse user population. Information and its associated information technology represent some of the most critical organizational assets. It's not unusual to find that organizations have invested heavily in security technologies, such as firewalls and intrusion detection systems. It is equally common to find that the same organization has not put the same level of investment into establishing and maintaining a security program.

Selling the need for a robust information security program is more important, but may be even more difficult than the complexities of the technical safeguards. Selling an information security program requires an understanding and an ability to address political considerations and business return from the investment in the security program, while the rules are often less clear than those associated with purely technical decisions.

Establishing a security program is serious business, so how should the message be made clear to the senior leaders who make those resource decisions? When it comes to proving the business case for an information security program, it's much more difficult than simply providing a spreadsheet full of return on security investment (ROSI) and risk numbers. The reality is – it's just not that simple.

Let's take a closer look at the essence of ROSI calculations – often defined as the security value received divided by the cost of security over a given time period. So, how does one quantify "value received" when it comes to an information security program? Does a security program save money, make money or does it simply help the organization avoid losing money? If approached from the traditional perspective on ROI, trying to make the business case can feel like an exercise in futility. So, here are a few suggestions on a more productive approach.

Don't sell FUD – tell them what they have to gain

Many leaders simply don't understand the positive impact a secure information infrastructure can have on the business. Some may still believe that information security professionals are simply there to set up new users on the network, manage the firewall, and make sure there are no viruses on the network. In just about every organization, each business process — from customer contact to service delivery — can be directly tied back to the organization's sensitive and fragile computer environment. So, what does the organization have to gain?

- **A good reputation**: An enterprise-level security program can add business value as a competitive differentiator, because there is often a direct link between a company's reputation and its approach to corporate security. The potential benefits to an organization based on having a good reputation include: differentiation in the marketplace, simply keeping the name of the organization off the front page of the *Washington Post*, the ability to attract and retain stakeholders, shareholders and customers, as well as the ability to recruit and retain high quality staff. A good reputation can be the most important asset for an organization. An organization's security reputation will often be of greater concern where security is fundamental to the organization's product or service; in those cases, compromised security will have a much greater reputational impact on some sectors rather than others.

- **Freedom to innovate**: Perception about the role of the security program has an impact on its ability to effectively contribute to the organization. Too often, the security team is viewed as the group that says "no." It's important for the security staff to change the word "no" to the notion of "how." This is the primary step to becoming a trusted partner of the business innovators. The security program can and should be presented as an enabler for innovation by providing a secure infrastructure that frees the other staff to focus on new ideas. And keep in mind, security is NOT about compliance. So, if the security program has fallen into that mindset, switch the focus to looking at the business initiatives and how the security program can support them on a regular, value added basis.

- **Risk management**: Business is all about risks — every organization faces them. The objective of any security program is to help the organization to do new things or to do the old things more securely and efficiently. It's impossible to avoid all risk. As a result, an effective security program is in touch with the organization's tolerance for risk and provides an environment that addresses that level of tolerance.

* **Security consistency**: The security program should focus on creating timely and flexible processes that help to facilitate, not delay, essential projects. And these processes should be consistent, so that the organization learns how these work. Having repeatable processes for security can aid in making the argument for a return on security investment and for security value. Aligning these security "templates" to the organization's business initiatives can actually assist in accelerating the innovation process. Standardized security criteria allow staff to understand how long certain security activities, including authorization, will take and will allow them to include this early in the planning.

So, let's go back to the corporation introduced at the beginning of this section.

An established security program, including the ability to have a consistent, enterprise-level process for authorization would have provided all of

Key features of a successful information security program

- Active board and senior management oversight and direction

- Security charter, policies, standards, and procedures

- Technology and procedural controls to enforce policy

- People in the right numbers, in the right places and with the right skills to efficiently implement the program.

- Measurement systems to gauge the effectiveness of the program

- Process-based security that integrates people, technologies and policies.

the above-listed rewards for their security investment. Information systems security – the pre-requisite for authorization – would have been integrated into the development process. Costs in terms of dollars and time for obtaining authorization would have been significantly reduced. End result – the time to market for their product would decline, quickly giving them a competitive edge over others in their market space.

Designing an effective information security program

Defining the program

Creating an information security program is like putting up a structure. First, the organization has to decide exactly what it wants from its security program – create its blueprint – and build it accordingly. Too often, organizations jump into security – installing firewalls, intrusion detection systems, and configuring information systems without really defining their end goals.

Establishing an information security program and defining the overall information security objectives should be methodical and well-thought out, involving management buy in throughout the process.

The 5000 meter view

In the long term, taking a few steps back at the initiation of a security program will save time and resources by eliminating unnecessary re-work, redundancy, and the need to make dramatic changes mid-stream. This is the foundation of the building, so it's important to take the following steps in launching your information security program:

- Get management support and funding.
- Develop a strategic vision with near-, mid- and long-term goals.
- Align the information security program with the overall business objectives.
- Put a tactical action plan in place.
- Communicate, communicate, communicate – both upward and outward.

Getting and keeping resources

Once the broad objectives have been defined, neither the security program nor the organization can move forward without the necessary resources – monetary and human. Of course, getting the budget for the information security program is only the first step. Those involved in developing and implementing the information security program should always design the means to adjust the budget to meet emerging security needs. Funding and other resources are essentially the materials needed to complete the building.

Security governance – establishing the right roles and responsibilities

Information security responsibility begins at the top of the organization and goes all the way down to the individual user. The members of staff represent the walls and roof of the building – they give the program format and maintain it over time. As you build the governance structure for the information security program, it is also important to ensure that the roles and responsibilities assigned incorporate both the organizational and the security program strategy and mission.

The roles and the related responsibilities discussed here focus on those roles defined as part of an overall security program, but there are also several that are specific to the authorization process. When this is the case, it will be identified in the discussion below. While some of the nomenclature may be different, these same roles and responsibilities could apply to the commercial sector.

So, let's take a look at who is included in the security program governance staff. Nomenclature can be contentious – particularly when positions and staffing are affected. For the purposes of this book, we have decided to use the terminology that has emerged from the DOD and DNI working group on the C&A transformation. So, in many cases you will see position titles joined with "/" – the first title reflects the new terminology

Key roles in a successful information security program

- Senior leadership
- Chief information officer (CIO)
- Senior agency information security officer (SAISO), also referred to as the chief information security officer (CISO)
- Authorizing official (AO), also known as designated accrediting authority (DAA)
- Risk executive (function)
- Information assurance manager (IAM), also known as the information system security manager (ISSM)
- Certifying authority (CA)
- Security control assessor
- Common control provider
- Information owner
- Program manager (PM)
- User representative (UR)
- Users (including contractors)

proposed as part of the C&A transformation efforts and the second reflects the more historical nomenclature.

Most of the roles and responsibilities described here have long been part of the information systems security program staff. However, new positions and tasks are emerging as a result of the efforts of the C&A transformation and ongoing work in NIST. Those unique to the new and emerging information systems security processes are indicated in *gray italics*.

Senior leadership

The senior leadership's responsibility for information security extends beyond the basics of support. They set the tone for the entire program, so it is not enough to utter a few words of blessing for the program. Management must step up to ownership of the security program by becoming a part of the process. The second important role of senior leadership is allocation of the budget for a security program – they decide just how much of the organizational resources can be provided to support the security program.

Senior leadership in the organization bears the final responsibility for information security in both a statutory and a practical sense. In the US federal government, FISMA assigns to senior leadership the responsibility for information security protections commensurate with the risk and the degree of harm that might result from unauthorized access, use, disclosure, disruption, modification, or destruction of an organization's information and information systems. But this level of security responsibility is not unique to the federal agencies. In short, senior leadership in all types of organizations is responsible for:

- oversight of enterprise compliance;
- compliance reporting; and
- actions to enforce accountability.

Chief information officer (CIO)

The Clinger-Cohen Act of 1996 created the role of agency CIO, helping to bring IT to the forefront of agency decision making. Today, the CIO is one of the primary players in information systems security and the authorization process. NIST SP 800-37 states that the CIO is the federal agency officer responsible for the following:

- Appointing the senior agency information security officer.
- Ensuring the development of information security policies, procedures, and control techniques.
- Initial, refresher, and specialized training for personnel with significant responsibilities for information security.

- Advising senior agency officials concerning their security responsibilities.
- In coordination with other senior agency officials, reporting annually to the agency head on the effectiveness of the agency information security program, including progress of remedial actions.[41]

The chief information officer, with the support of the senior agency information security officer (SAISO), works closely with authorizing officials and their designated representatives to ensure that an agency-wide security program is effectively implemented, that the certifications and accreditations required across the agency are accomplished in a timely and cost-effective manner, and that there is centralized reporting of all security-related activities.

The CIO also often executes one additional, critical function. In addition to the above duties, the chief information officer and authorizing officials may be responsible for determining the amount of the organization's budget that should be allocated to information systems security based on organizational priorities.

Senior agency information security officer (SAISO)/chief information security officer (CISO)

The position of CISO or SAISO in federal agencies, a title often used interchangeably with the chief security officer (CSO)[42], is a relatively new position within federal agencies and commercial organizations alike. Senior information assurance officer (SIAO) is the term used specifically within DOD and the IC for this position.

In order to be effective within the organization, this should be a high-level executive position appointed and approved by the senior leadership within the organization. The SAISO carries a heavy burden. He/she must be able to lead and enable the organization in the implementation of security strategy and policies in direct

---

[41] This particular responsibility is limited to US Federal agencies, including DOD, and is not a requirement for the commercial community.
[42] The CSO is usually concerned with business continuity, physical and personnel security.

support of the business. Being an effective business process enabler requires the SAISO to also be an innovative problem solver and a leader who can combine common sense security with efficient and productive business processes.

But just being a leader is not enough. The SAISO must also bring subject matter expertise to the position. Credibility within the information security team, coupled with understanding sufficient to craft an integrated information security strategy, depends on the SAISO's ability to know, value, and effectively articulate the varied security missions. In a few words, the SAISO must successfully fulfill the following (not all security-related) roles:

- **Relationship manager**, who nurtures trust-based connections across the organization.
- **Leader and manager**, who is able to build, motivate and sustain a team of security professionals.
- **Subject matter expert**, who either provides or ensures the availability of technical and procedural expertise.
- **Risk manager**, who identifies, analyzes and communicates the risk posture to the organization and the leadership.
- **Strategist**, who is able to develop and publish a security strategy that aligns correctly with the organization's mission and goals.

In addition to these high level duties, FISMA also assigns specific responsibilities to the CISO/SAISO that support the primary information systems security duty. According to NIST SP 800-100, *Information Security: A Guidebook for Managers*, the SAISO is required to:

- Lead an office with the mission and resources to assist in ensuring agency compliance with information security requirements.
- Periodically assess risk and magnitude of the harm resulting from unauthorized access, use, disclosure, disruption, modification, or destruction of information and information systems that support the operations and assets of the agency.
- Develop and maintain risk-based, cost-effective information security policies, procedures, and control techniques to address

all applicable requirements throughout the life cycle of each agency information system to ensure compliance with applicable requirements.

- Facilitate development of subordinate plans for providing adequate information security for networks, facilities, and systems or groups of information systems.
- Ensure that agency personnel, including contractors, receive appropriate information security awareness training.
- Train and oversee personnel with significant responsibilities for information security with respect to such responsibilities.
- Periodically test and evaluate the effectiveness of information security policies, procedures, and practices.
- Establish and maintain a process for planning, implementing, evaluating, and documenting remedial action to address any deficiencies in the information security policies, procedures, and practices of the agency.
- Develop and implement procedures for detecting, reporting, and responding to security incidents.
- Ensure preparation and maintenance of plans and procedures to provide continuity of operations for information systems that support the operations and assets of the agency.
- Support the agency CIO in annual reporting to the agency head on the effectiveness of the agency information security program, including progress of remedial actions.

Risk executive (individual or function)

The risk executive can be a position or a function. Regardless of whether there is a permanent position with an assigned individual or just an identified organizational function, the risk executive supports an enterprise-wide approach for assessing and addressing risk.

The risk executive provides a holistic view of risk that extends beyond the risk associated solely with the operation and use of individual information systems. The risk executive is an individual or group within an organization that helps to ensure that:

- Security risk-related considerations for individual information systems, to include the accreditation decisions for those systems, are viewed from an organization-wide perspective with regard to the overall strategic goals and objectives of the organization in carrying out its missions and business functions.
- Managing risk from individual information systems is consistent across the organization, reflects organizational risk tolerance, and is considered along with other organizational risks in order to ensure mission or business success.

Authorizing official (AO)/designated accrediting authority (DAA) [43]

The AO, referred to in the DOD and the IC as the DAA, is usually not a member of the security staff, but rather a representative of the senior leadership of the organization. But the role as AO within the authorization process is an important function of that individual. The AO should be a senior management official or executive with the authority to formally assume responsibility for operating an information system at an acceptable level of risk to an agency. Responsibilities of the AO may include oversight of the budget and business operations of the information system within the agency and approval system security requirements, system security plans, and memorandums of agreement (MOA) and/or memorandums of understanding (MOU).

The AO possesses US government authority and, as such, must be a government employee. In other words, accepting risk on behalf of the government is inherently "governmental" and cannot be passed to a contractor – or to a non-US citizen in the case of National Security Systems.

The AO has the following authorization responsibilities:

---

[43] The term "authorizing official (AO)" is used by NIST and is proposed for use across the Federal government. DOD and the IC – at least at the time of publication – plan to continue to use the term "designated accrediting authority (DAA)." The term DAA will be used in those cases specific to DOD or the IC.

- Oversight of the authorization budget and business operations of the system.
- Authority to approve system security requirements, system security plans, and memorandums of understanding (MOU) and/or memorandums of agreement (MOA).
- Make a risk-based decision to grant, conditionally grant, or deny authority to operate a system.
- Appoint, as appropriate, a designated representative to act on the AO's behalf in coordinating and carrying out the necessary activities required during the authorization process.

The AO/DAA may also have a *designated accrediting authority representative or authorizing official designated representative.* Due to the level of organizational responsibility and significant demands on time, an AO/DAA may not always be able to participate directly or on a day-to-day basis in the authorization process. The AO's designated representative can be empowered to act on the AO's behalf in executing the necessary activities required during the authorization process. This includes the authority to make certain decisions with regard to the planning and resourcing of the authorization activities, the acceptance of the system security plan (SSP), and risk determination processes. It can also involve such mundane activities as making routine decisions, attending meetings, and providing coordination of authorization activities.

It is important to note that there is one activity that the AO representative cannot execute. The AO *cannot delegate* the security accreditation decision and the signing of the associated accreditation decision letter (i.e. the acceptability of risk to the agency).

Information systems security manager (ISSM)/information assurance manager (IAM)[44]

The ISSM often serves as the "right-hand man" for the AO and the SAISO. The ISSM provides the focal point for policy guidance on IA matters pertaining to ISs under his/her purview. The ISSM is generally a permanent member of the security staff and, while they often play a role in the authorization process, this may not be their primary function. ISSMs have the following general responsibilities:

- Provide security policy and program guidance to subordinate activities.
- Maintain overall responsibility for the security program within his/her activity by establishing, managing, and assessing the effectiveness of the program.
- Ensure compliance with approved information systems security policies and procedures.
- Ensure that compliance monitoring of ISs under his/her purview occurs, and review the results of such monitoring.
- Ensure that IA inspections, tests, and reviews are coordinated within his/her activity.
- Ensure that all IA management review items are tracked and reported.
- Complete job-specific IA training on an annual basis.

Information system security officer (ISSO)/information assurance officer (IAO)

Simply stated, the information system security officer (ISSO) is the individual responsible to the ISSM for ensuring that the appropriate operational IA posture is maintained for a DOD information system or organization. ISSOs shall access only that data, control information, software, hardware, and firmware for which they are

---

[44] The term "information systems security manager (ISSM)" is used by NIST and is proposed for use across the Federal government. DOD and the IC – at least at the time of publication – plan to continue to use the term "information assurance manager (IAM)."

authorized access and have a need-to-know, and assume only those roles and privileges for which they are authorized.

The next two positions – that of the *certifying authority (CA)* and *security controls assessor* – are both part of the security controls testing process. While there may be some similarities, there are also some primary differences. The role of the CA, which continues to be used by DOD and the IC, has essentially disappeared from the authorization processes as proposed by NIST and the C&A transformation.

In the DOD especially, the CA acts as an advisor to the DAA on making risk-based accreditation decisions. The CA also has the responsibility for ensuring the security control testing teams are properly qualified and trained. Under the C&A transformation, the role and function of the CA is divided between the emerging risk executive function and the security controls assessor.

So, now that we have confused you thoroughly, let's talk about each of these roles separately. Hopefully, the discussion that follows will assist you in understanding the current roles and responsibilities as they apply to each of these positions.

Certifying authority (CA) [45]

The certifying authority (CA) should be an independent entity and not a direct member of the security staff, even though the CA fulfills a critical function in the authorization process. According to the DOD and the IC, the CA has the following responsibilities:

- Performing an independent and comprehensive assessment of information system security controls.
- Issuing a recommendation to the DAA that includes an assessment of risk.
- Recommending the appropriate restrictions and conditions for accreditation.

---

[45] Also known as the certification agent or certifier.

To preserve the impartial nature of the security certification and testing process, the CA should be in a position independent from the persons directly responsible for the development and the day-to-day operation of the information system. The CA should also be independent of those individuals responsible for correcting the security deficiencies identified during the security certification and testing phase.

The DOD and the IC consider that the objectivity of the CA is an important factor in evaluating the credibility of the validation test results and ensuring that the AO receives the most objective information possible in order to make an informed, risk-based, accreditation decision. Within the DOD, the CA is often assisted by an *agent of the certifying authority (ACA)*, who most frequently conducts the actual controls validation testing.

Security controls assessor

The security controls assessor can be an individual, a group, or an organization responsible for conducting independent and objective security controls testing. This role is similar to the validator in DOD and the IC. The primary difference is that the security controls assessor reports to the risk executive while the validator reports to the CA.

Security controls testing, whether in the federal government, DOD or IC, usually takes the form of a comprehensive and independent assessment of the management, operational, and technical security controls in an information system. The security controls assessor, or the validator in the DOD and IC, has the following responsibilities:

- Verify that the controls are implemented correctly, operating as intended, and meeting the security requirements for the system.
- Provide recommendations for corrective actions intended to mitigate or eliminate vulnerabilities in the information system.
- Conduct an independent assessment of the system security plan (SSP) or equivalent documentation to ensure the plan proposes

security controls for the information system that are adequate to meet all applicable security requirements.

- Prepare the validation test report and forward the complete report with an accreditation recommendation. In DOD and the IC, the validator will forward this to the appropriate CA. Under the NIST standard, the security controls assessor will provide the results to the risk executive and AO, and in some instances, directly to the system owner.

Common control provider

The common control provider is responsible for the planning, development, implementation, assessment, authorization, and maintenance of common controls (i.e. security controls inherited by or shared between information systems). Common control providers are responsible for:

- Documenting common controls in a security plan (or equivalent document prescribed by the organization).
- Ensuring that required assessments of common controls are carried out by qualified assessors with an appropriate level of independence defined by the organization.
- Documenting assessment findings in a security assessment report.
- Producing a plan of action and milestones for all controls having weaknesses or deficiencies.

Security plans, security assessment reports, and plans of action and milestones for common controls (or a summary of such information) must be made available to information system owners whose systems might inherit or share those controls after the information is reviewed and approved by the senior official or executive with oversight responsibility for those controls.

Information owner/information steward

The information owner has statutory or operational authority and responsibility for establishing the controls for the secure generation, collection, processing, dissemination, and disposal of information. The alternate term, information steward, emerged to clarify that the information is "owned" only by the people of the United States and that the federal government is only a "steward" on their behalf.

The information owner may not be a permanent member of the security staff or the authorization team, but does have some authorization responsibilities:

- Establishes rules for appropriate use and protection of the subject information (e.g. rules of behavior).
- Communicates the level of assurance required for the information on the system to the appropriate system owner.

Information system owner or program manager (PM)/information system steward

The information system owner or program manager (PM)[46] has overall responsibility for the procurement, development, integration, modification, or operation and maintenance of an information system throughout the system life cycle. As with the information, the people of the United States "own" the information system, and the federal government is only the "steward" – hence the emergence of the new terminology of information system steward.

The information system owner/PM may not be a permanent member of the security staff, or a dedicated member of the authorization team, but does have significant responsibilities in relation to information systems security and authorization:

- Develops and maintains the system security plan (SSP).
- Ensures the participation of IS security personnel early in the IS development life cycle to assist in the identification and selection

---

[46] In order to confuse the reader totally, the term program manager and system manager are also often used interchangeably. However, in most cases, the system manager will be associated with smaller, more mission-specific systems. For example, a PM may be responsible for a major program, such as the Joint Strike Fighter, to include the budget; while the SM will be responsibility solely for the ground system component.

of appropriate security controls, and provides guidance on the authorization process.

- Authors, or ensures the authoring of all required MOAs to address security requirements between: ISs that interface, ISs that are networked and are managed by different DAAs, or ISs networked to non-agency entities.
- Verifies the design of IS security for systems under his/her purview.
- Verifies the implementation of security design in the developed IS by ensuring thorough security testing is performed.
- Initiates protective or corrective measures immediately upon identification of security weaknesses/issues.
- Takes all necessary and appropriate measures to resolve outstanding IS security deficiencies in a timely manner to establish a level of security necessary to achieve authorization to operate.
- Ensures that required security controls are properly implemented and maintained throughout the life cycle of all ISs under his/her purview.
- Ensures that the appropriate functional managers have properly identified and classified the data processed, stored, and/or transmitted by all the ISs under his/her purview.
- Ensures that quality assurance reviews are performed routinely to minimize the risk of errors and preserve IS and data integrity for all ISs under his/her purview.
- Monitors all contractors under his/her purview with access to agency ISs to ensure compliance with this and all other referenced policies and procedures.
- Provides assistance, as needed, to security personnel during the accreditation and re-accreditation processes.
- Assembles the authorization package for submission to the DAA or DAA representative for adjudication.

Information system security engineer (ISSE)

The information system security engineer (ISSE) is a critical component of the IA program staff and should be a permanent member, as opposed to the SME, who may be called in to join the IA program on an as-needed basis. The ISSE focuses on system security engineering as a defined process to capture and refine information system security requirements and ensure that these requirements are effectively integrated into information technology component products and information systems through "purposeful security architecting, design, development, and configuration."[47]

The specific tasks of the ISSE include:

- Coordinating information system security activities with the authorizing official and or the designated representatives, senior agency information security officers, security control implementers and common control providers.
- Recommending and employing system security best practices.
- Ensuring that security is integrated into the information system life cycle.

User representative

Users are found at all levels of an agency – from senior management to office staff. They are often on the front line for identifying mission/operational requirements and for ensuring compliance with the security requirements and security controls described in the system security plan. User representatives speak for the operational interests of the user community and serve as liaisons between users and developers throughout the life cycle of the information system. Although not dedicated to authorization support, user representatives often assist in the execution of the authorization process to ensure mission requirements are satisfied while still meeting the security requirements identified in the system security plan (SSP).

---

[47] From draft NIST SP 800-37, Rev. 1.

Users

Although they are listed close to the end of this section, users are often the most important component of an effective information security program. Information and information system users must know and understand the organization's security policies and be held accountable for meeting their security responsibilities. User understanding and/or recognition of their security responsibilities can be accomplished in various ways.

Initial and refresher security awareness training is one of the most common means used to inform users about security requirements. Many organizations require personnel to sign a user agreement that includes the protection of information assets as a condition of employment, while others are required to sign a user agreement as a condition of allowing their connection to the organization's network.

One highly successful method of ensuring that every user understands that security is a part of his/her job is to include it in the job description and make it part of the annual performance evaluation process.

Subject matter experts (SME)

The Six Sigma dictionary defines a subject matter expert or SME as an "individual who exhibits the highest level of expertise in performing a specialized job, task, or skill within the organization." SMEs are important in the authorization process for those tasks that require a specialized expertise, e.g. implementation of technical controls or development of specific policies, such as disaster recovery and contingency planning.

Generally, SMEs are not a permanent part of the security team or the authorization team, but are called upon to execute a specific task for a specified period of time. In some cases, the SME may be termed an information system security engineer (ISSE).

Contractors

Too often, contractors are seen as "hired hands" to help federal agencies develop, acquire, operate, maintain – and certify and accredit – their information systems. Contractors, like their government or commercial clients, have a responsibility to ensure the security of the information systems and to comply with the security requirements of the information resources they use – whether these are on the premises of the client or within their own information systems.

Contractors provide critical services, but they can also present a risk. "Lack of oversight, combined with contractors' failure to secure their networks, put sensitive government information at risk," said John Grimes, US Department of Defense Chief Information Officer and Assistant Secretary for Networks and Information Integration, during a conference in Orlando, Fla. According to the 2007 annual FISMA report to the Office of Management and Budget (OMB), less than half of the 25 major federal agencies, including the DOD and Veterans Administration (VA), required the information systems used or operated by their contractors to meet the requirements of FISMA, agency policy, or the guidelines established by NIST.

But I'm just a small organization...

Small organizations are not exempt from meeting information system security requirements. In fact, smaller organizations may often need to make their information systems secure with limited staff, many of whom are required to fulfill multiple roles within the agency. A lack of personnel and multiple responsibilities assigned to a single individual make it even more important to understand the various roles involved in securing computers in larger agencies.

Can roles and responsibilities be delegated?

Sometimes it is just not possible for a single individual to execute all of the responsibilities associated with their assigned role. The organization may be too large or too geographically dispersed, or there just may be too much to do. In these cases, senior leadership may decide to delegate certain authorization responsibilities. Appropriately qualified individuals, even contractors, may be appointed in writing to perform the activities associated with almost any authorization role with the exception of certain roles, which are considered inherently government:

- Chief information officer
- Authorizing official
- Certifying authority
- Risk executive
- Senior agency information security officer.

These roles have inherent US Government authority; consequently, the responsibilities associated with these roles must be assigned to government personnel only. Individuals serving in delegated roles may operate with the authority of agency officials within the limits defined for the specific authorization activities. Agency officials, however, always retain ultimate responsibility for the actions taken by those serving in delegated roles.

Systems security training and certification

Most programs do not start out with a ready-made staff, so it is important to determine the required skill sets to meet the overall objectives of the information security program. And don't forget – training is a critical element to preparing the security staff for their responsibilities. Chapter 16 will cover the federal agency requirements for initial and refresher security training and certification in detail.

Developing and publishing plans and policies

Strategies, policies, and procedures are the structure's finishing touches. They are an absolute must for any organization. They provide the virtual glue to hold the security program together.

Imagine how any organization would operate without rules and guidelines? What would life be like?

The first step is to identify the design style for the particular structure represented by your organization and the guiding principles that your organization will follow to secure its information and IT. Our experience working with organizations – both government and commercial – has consistently revealed that just the thought of security policies tends to elevate the level of tension in any given situation. This boils down to a basic human characteristic – people generally do not like rules and they certainly don't want to be restricted in their activities. One reason for the elevated tension level at the thought of policy is that the members of the organization all tend to have different security needs:

- Management is concerned about cost and their return on security investment. They are also worried about the compliance word, thinking that security will be a speed bump to operations.
- Others in the organization worry about still having the ability to accomplish their work without a lot of security restrictions.
- Information system support personnel fear that stringent security measures will impede the capability of the network.

The second step is to firmly entrench guiding principles within the organization through creating strategies and policies within various control domains. These control domains – such as information systems security – represent the highest-level identification of policy. The specific policies within the individual domains specify the desired security course of action. The final step is to implement the authorized courses of action. The results of the implementation step are the operational standards, guidelines, and procedures that govern information systems security for the organization.

Ideally, information security strategies and policies should be the result of a formal policy design process that specifies who develops the initial draft, the policy review process, the approval process, and finally the implementation mechanisms.

NIST describes the basic purpose of security plans and policies as a means to provide an overview of the security requirements of the organization and describe the controls in place or planned for meeting those requirements. The security plans and policies also delineate the responsibilities and expected security-related behavior of the members of the organization. Security policies should emerge as the result of the structured process of planning adequate, cost-effective security protections. And most importantly, the security strategy and policies should reflect input from various organizational leaders and managers, including the information owners, the system owner, and the senior agency information security officer (SAISO).

The following flowchart depicts a decision-based approach to security and strategy policy development.

Figure 4: A decision-based approach to security and strategy policy development

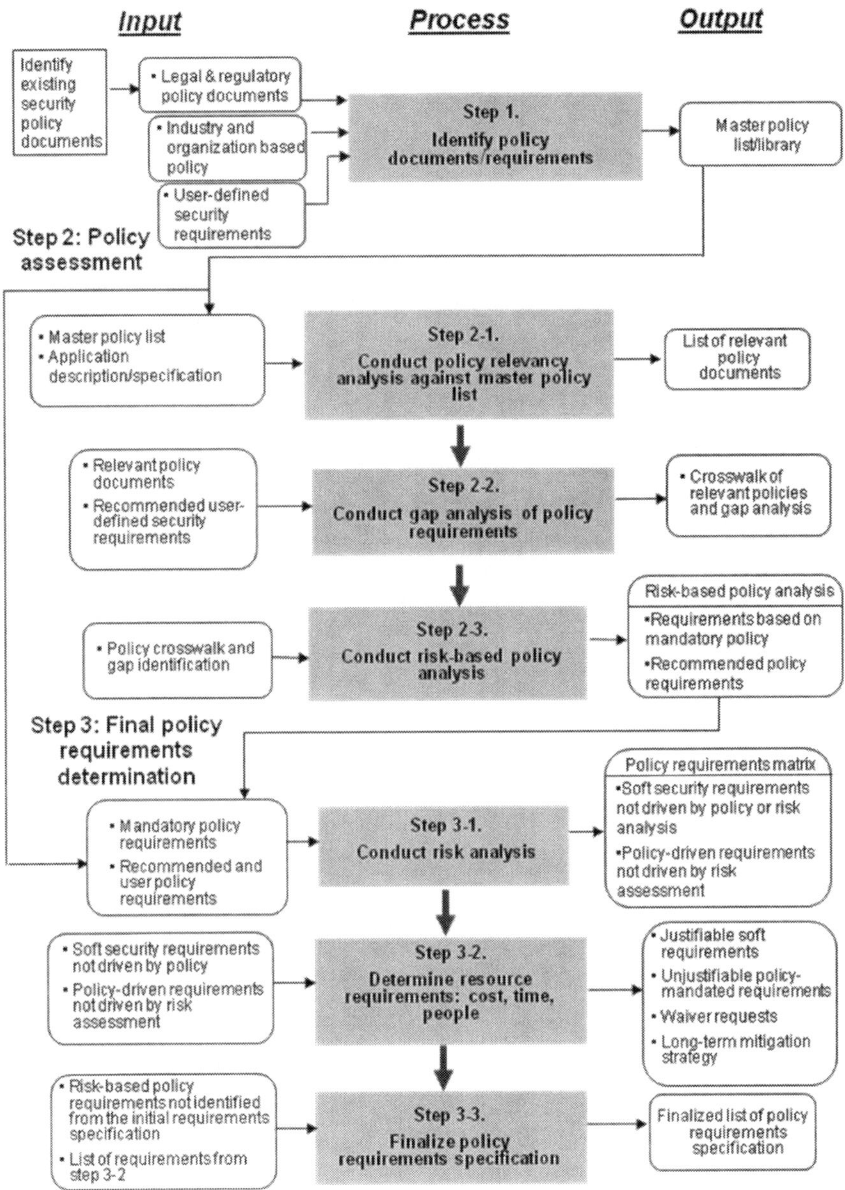

Measuring progress

The final element in an effective security program is the use of the ongoing assessment. Typically, the ongoing assessment will enable the organization to respond more quickly and effectively to change as business models evolve, new technologies are developed, and new legislation is enacted.

But information systems security practitioners are often confronted with the following dilemma in evaluating security progress: If nothing occurs, is it proof that they have done as expected or that simply nothing happened? And if a security event does occur, is this proof that they have done a poor job? So how can their security progress be assessed in a more practical, consistent manner? The answer may be "security metrics".

The right security metrics can help quantify and measure the effectiveness of security operations. The right security metrics can facilitate decision making and improve performance and accountability. The right security metrics can also help management decide where to invest in security and can identify non-productive, costly controls. But what are the right metrics? Metrics must be specific and measurable and must correlate directly to the business risks.

But selecting the right metrics is not the end of the story. Organizations still need to implement a long-term strategy for the collection and analysis of information security effectiveness metrics against established targets in information security effectiveness.

Many of the federal regulations defining security controls also have certain success metrics built into the control description. Where this is not the case, or where these metrics are not sufficient, assistance can be sought in other areas, such as international security standards.

ISO/IEC 27001:2005 (ISO27001) is one of the international standards that can provide guidance in developing, collecting, and analyzing security-related metrics. There are 133 controls in the ISO27001 standard that can be used to assess control effectiveness, but the standard also provides guidance on how to measure the selected controls' effectiveness. In addition to this, ISO27001 requires the measurements to be comparable and repeatable, so they can be used time and time again, and compared on a regular basis to gain a better understanding of trends and progress.

Milestones from the "establishing a foundation" activities

Before proceeding to the next phase, the specific pre-certification and accreditation activities examined in Chapter 5, let's take a final look at what you should achieve in establishing a basic foundation.

- The leadership of the organization understands and supports the business case for information systems security.
- An information systems security program is in place with a governance structure, staff, and budget.
- Information system security policies are developed and published.
- A program for continuous improvement is in place – determining the metrics, collecting and analyzing measurements, and implementing lessons learned into the environment.

By establishing a firm foundation for an overall information systems security program, you will also be setting the stage for a successful authorization program.

<table>
<tr><td>Further reading</td></tr>
<tr><td>

Barman, Scott. *Writing Information Security Policies,* Sams Publishing, November 2001.

Peltier, Thomas; Peltier, Justin; and Blackley, John. *Information Security Fundamentals,* Auerbach, Boca Raton, FL, October 2003.

Tipton, Harold and Krause, Micki. *Information Security Management Handbook, 6th Ed.,* Auerbach, Boca Raton, FL, 2007.

</td></tr>
</table>

References

Government Accounting Office (GAO), *Federal Chief Information Officers: Responsibilities, Reporting Relationships, Tenure and Challenges,* July 2004. Available at *http://www.gao.gov/new.items/d04823.pdf.*

National Institute of Standards and Technology (NIST), Special Publication (SP) 800-18, *Guide for Developing Security Plans for Federal Information Systems, Revision 1,* February 2006. Available at *http://csrc.nist.gov/publications/nistpubs/800-18-Rev1/sp800-18-Rev1-final.pdf.*

National Institute of Standards and Technology (NIST), Special Publication (SP) 800-100, *Information Security Handbook: A Guide for Managers,* October 2006. Available at *http://csrc.nist.gov/publications/nistpubs/800-100/SP800-100-Mar07-2007.pdf.*

RSA, *The Time is Now: Making Information Security Strategic to Business Innovation.* Available at *http://www.rsa.com/innovation/docs/RSA_strategic-security-APR.06.08_wo_mountain_print.pdf*

Westby, Jody R. and Allen, Julia. *Article 2: Defining an Effective Enterprise Security Program (ESP),* Carnegie Mellon University, 2007.

CHAPTER 5: PRE-AUTHORIZATION ACTIVITIES – THE FUNDAMENTALS

Success is neither magical nor mysterious. Success is the natural consequence of consistently applying the basic fundamentals.[48]

Jim Rohn, Motivational Speaker, Philosopher and Entrepreneur

In this chapter:

Establishing the authorization team

Categorizing the information system

Defining the information system boundary

Establishing a risk management process

---

[48] http://thinkexist.com/quotation/success_is_neither_magical_nor_mysterious-success/211597.html

The primary objective of the pre-certification activities is to set the stage for the authorization activities to follow. Certain activities, executed early, will minimize effort later and facilitate the authorization process. These include:

- Establish the authorization team.
- Train the authorization team.
- Define the information system.
- Define the accreditation boundary, which includes identifying the approving authority.
- Conduct the risk assessment.
- Align with the system life cycle.

It is important to note that these activities do not necessarily have to occur in sequence. Some may pre-exist the initiation of an authorization process, such as the authorization team or the overall accreditation boundary. Others may be conducted by external entities, such as the organization risk assessment.

Establish the authorization team

In Chapter 3, we introduced the potential roles that should be part of a successful information systems security program. Here, we reiterate those that are essential to the authorization process.

Basic rule: the composition of the authorization team depends on the size and complexity of the system under examination. Recognizing that organizations have widely varying missions, sizes, and organizational structures, there will be differences in how specific responsibilities are allocated among organizational personnel (e.g. multiple individuals filling a single role or one individual filling multiple roles).[49] However, the basic functions remain the same.

---

[49] Caution should be exercised when one individual fills multiples roles in the security authorization process to ensure that the individual retains an appropriate level of independence and remains free from conflicts of interest.

Accrediting a small or simple information system will certainly not require an entire team. Larger, complex systems or a large network may require a more robust team to implement the controls, conduct the validation testing, gather and analyze the data, and provide the appropriate information to the authorizing official. Where there may be multiple authorizing officials, a more robust team may be necessary to resolve issues that may arise and to provide information needed to form a proper MOA between the authorizing officials.

At the very least, the following roles must be involved in the authorization process:

- Authorizing official (AO)
- Certifying authority (CA)
- Security control assessor
- Information assurance manager (IAM)/information system security manager (ISSM).

These are other roles that may be included in the authorization process as required:

- Program manager (PM) or system owner/steward.
- Data owner/steward.
- Information assurance officer (IAO)/information system security officer (ISSO).
- Information system security engineer (ISSE).
- User representative.
- Subject matter experts (SME) to implement the required security controls or to provide specific area-specialty information.

Unless they are already permanent members of the security staff, authorization team members should be appointed in writing. This can be done with a simple memorandum or with a form. Regardless of the format selected, the appointment orders should state the role to which the team member has been assigned, the responsibilities associated with that role, and the duration of the appointment.

Often, the authorization team consists of a matrix of individuals from various offices within the organization who are temporarily detailed to assist with the authorization activities. While this allows the integration of specialists who may not be available in-house, it is important to recognize that these individuals may not be available full time to work on the authorization process. Also, they may only have limited experience in performing authorization.

In addition to determining the members of the team, it is important to assign one person as the team lead or primary point of contact for authorization activities.

A successful authorization process starts with the assignment of the right leader. The authorization project leader is often the organization's information assurance manager (IAM) or information assurance officer (IAO). For new and significantly modified systems or applications, the authorization project leader often works closely with the system development team.

Seven things to consider in staffing the authorization team

1. Is the team member needed full or only part time?
2. What, if any, are the clearance requirements?
3. Do they have prior C&A process experience?
4. Do they have prior C&A verification and validation (testing) experience?
5. Have they already been trained and certified?
6. How long will they be needed on the authorization team?
7. Can authorization team members be matrixed from other organizations?

In Chapter 4, we introduced the general roles and responsibilities of the members of the organization's security program. Let's now discuss the specific authorization-related roles and how they fit into the authorization of an information system.

Authorization roles by team member

The **AO** plays a central role in the authorization process. He/she is responsible for all accreditation decisions. This starts with approving the determination of the required security measures and safeguards (e.g. IA controls) and ends with the rendering of a risk-based accreditation decision. The AO is the only individual with the authority to assume the risk of operating an information system.

The **CA and the security control assessor** also have crucial roles in the C&A activities. The CA has responsibility for conducting certification activities, such as: assisting in determining system and computing environment security requirements and the associated IA controls; conducting verification and validation testing[50] to determine the level of compliance; assessing and recommending security countermeasures; identifying residual risks; and – most importantly – making an accreditation recommendation to the DAA. The CA and the controls assessor should be independent from the organization responsible for acquiring and operating the information system. This is due to the fact that the CA must review the test results objectively and the security controls assessor must test independently for compliance and make a justified recommendation regarding the information system's level of security and the associated risks of operation.

The **system owner or PM** is ultimately responsible for the system acquisition – from concept, to development, to integration of the information system into its target operational environment. The PM is the best individual to represent the interests of the information system during the authorization process. The PM is also one of the best information resources for the DAA, the CA, and the IAM, since they often have much of the documentation required to ascertain the level of information system security compliance. This includes system description, system design, security architecture, hardware and software inventories, and core services list.

Frequently, it is the **IAM/ISSM** who carries much of the burden of addressing the IA controls implementation and developing the essential evidence of compliance. The IAM/ISSM often prepares the authorization package for the CA and AO to review as part of

---

[50] Also known as Security Testing and Evaluation (ST&E).

the responsibility for establishing, implementing, and maintaining a system level information systems security program. The IAM/ISSM is often supported by an **IAO/ISSO**, who may assist the ISSM in the authorization process.

The **user representative** has a smaller, but no less important role in the authorization process. The user representative functions as the individual and/or organization which represent the user community in the definition of the information system operational and security requirements. Input from the user representative is often critical in establishing the essential balance between utility and security of the information system.

Data owners are responsible for assisting the DAA and the CA in establishing and verifying the necessary level of data protection. The DAA/AO and the CA do not always have the knowledge needed to fully understand the sensitivity of the data processed by the information system – only the data owner can provide this information – which is an essential element of the risk-based authorization decision.

Last, but not least, is the role played by the **SME** during the authorization process. The SME can assist throughout the authorization process in the implementation and testing of the security measures and safeguards, whether technical or procedural. SMEs can be varied, ranging from the system administrator, network architect, and firewall expert to the expert in the development and testing of contingency plans.

SMEs from other security disciplines, such as physical security, can also provide value to the authorization process. These individuals may assist in site surveys, administrative security analysis, and countermeasures analysis. Although funding and training organizations are not directly involved in the authorization process, their support can be critical in the authorization effort by providing the required funding and by supporting the training needs.

If the information system requires a high degree of assurance, the authorization team can work closely with the vendor or the logistical support organization to obtain data on mean time between failure in order to determine if the reliability, maintainability, and availability (RMA) of the system's components meet the criteria for high assurance. Although the authorization team is not directly responsible for information system configuration management, the authorization team must understand the configuration control process in order to determine its strengths and weaknesses. For most information systems, particularly large IS, configuration management responsibilities are usually part of the day-to-day IS life cycle, usually a configuration control board (CCB). This organization can be an important resource for the authorization team.

Training the authorization team should not be an afterthought

In many organizations, the individuals responsible for authorization-related activities and tasks have other job related duties and responsibilities that they perform on a daily basis. For example, the AO is often one of the senior leaders in the organization with responsibility for the overall mission; the SME may be heavily burdened with the operational necessities of maintaining the network. Often, their involvement with the authorization process may only occur sporadically.

At the same time, authorization related duties may be highly complex and technical, influenced by the ever-increasing amount of legislation and compliance requirements, as well as the increasing complexity of the technology itself.

Consequently, early and comprehensive training is essential to ensure that the participating authorization team members have a solid understanding of the regulatory guidance and the prescribed authorization process. Some of the training may be required by regulation, such as the mandatory DAA/AO training and certification requirements. Other may be voluntary, such as the certification of an SME in a particular technology.

Many organizations offer training in specific authorization processes, such as the DIACAP or the processes specified in the NIST guidance. Just a small amount of research into authorization training and certification will result in an abundance of training information – *in fact, a single Google search came up with 138,000 results*. So, before you sign up for training, check out the training provider and the instructors and be sure that they have tangible experience in **successfully** and **cost-effectively** executing authorization activities to completion.

The benefits of ensuring a trained authorization team will be readily apparent as soon as the organization begins to execute its first authorization process. In other words, a small investment up front in proper training and certification can result in larger savings during the authorization process itself.

Categorizing the information system

The simplest definition of an information system is "anything that creates, processes, stores, transmits, displays, and disseminates data." The DOD takes a much broader approach in defining an information system: "A set of information resources organized into an entire infrastructure, organization, personnel, and components composed for the collection, processing, storage, maintenance, use, sharing, transmission, display, and disposition of information."[51]

Take a look at both of these definitions. One concept that should be very clear is that an information system is NOT the hardware inventory. And software alone is also NOT an information system. An information system is a combination of the software and hardware – as well as the workstations, servers, services, and processes that run on them. In fact, the very work "system" implies that there are multiple elements that must be combined to make up the whole of an information system. When considering the definition of an information system in the context of the authorization process, consider too that a system also consists of the business functions defined in terms of mission, processes, and personnel.

---

[51] Source: DODD 8500.1

There are many ways to classify information systems. Some define information systems by the business activities they support.

- Transaction processing systems automate the handling of data about business activities or transactions.
- Management information systems take the information generated by transaction processing systems and convert it into aggregated forms meaningful to managers.
- Decision support systems are designed to help organizational decision makers make decisions by providing an interactive environment that uses data and models.
- Expert systems represent attempts to codify and manipulate knowledge rather than information by mimicking experts in particular knowledge domains.

In the federal government, however, these categorizations are rarely used in the context of the authorization process. More frequently, information systems are defined by the structure and the nature of the system itself. Information systems can range from diverse computing platforms to high-end supercomputers to personal digital assistants (PDAs). Information systems can also be highly specialized systems and devices, such as testing and calibration devices, telecommunications systems, weapons systems, command and control systems, and environmental control systems.

Information systems can also be single standalones, application-based information systems performing single or multiple specific functions, local area networks (LAN), or large and complex systems consisting of multiple LANs. Information systems can be government owned or they can be outsourced information systems owned by contractors, but supporting essential government functions.

Defining the information system – whether by its function, its data, its size, and/or its environment, or a combination of all of these factors – is an essential first step in establishing the scope of the authorization activities. Improperly establishing the information system type can either lead to too much security and the associated costs or too little security and the associated risks.

NIST SP 800-60 specifies a useful methodology for defining information and information systems as a pre-requisite for determining the required IA controls and safeguards and for establishing the accreditation boundary. Let's first take a look at defining the type of information system.

Identifying the type of information system

The type of information processed by the information system is the primary criterion for determining the level of protection necessary for the information system. Determining the actual type of information system is also a factor in determining the scope of the authorization and protection factors.

The federal government, specifically NIST, identifies two primary types of information systems:

General support system (GSS): an interconnected set of information resources under the same direct management control which shares common functionality. A system normally includes hardware, software, information, data, applications, communications, and people. A system can be, for example, a local area network (LAN) including smart terminals that support a branch office, an agency-wide backbone, a communications network, a departmental data processing center including its operating system and utilities, a tactical radio network, or a shared information processing service organization (IPSO)."[52]

---

[52] Definition from OMB Circular A-130, Appendix III.

Major application (MA): an application that requires special attention to security due to the risk and magnitude of the harm resulting from the loss, misuse, or unauthorized access to or modification of the information in the application. It involves the use of information resources to satisfy a specific set of user requirements."[53]

> Some automated information resources may be identified as both a general support system and a major application, as in the case where a database is run from a standalone computer.

Typically, the MA is developed and implemented under the support of a program office/manager and possibly deployed through similar configurations in multiple environments.

> **Major application**
>
> - Developed by a program office
> - Similar configuration deployed to multiple environments
> - May also be known as a "type" or an "AIS application."

If an MA, the authorization team should also identify the GSS upon which it resides. Identifying this link will assist with the identification and implementation of the appropriate security controls for both the MA and the GSS. Additionally, due to the existence of this connection, the security categorization of the GSS might have to be rated, at a minimum, at the same level as the highest-rated MA that resides on that GSS.

The information system categories of major application or general support system address most of the information system types in the federal government's inventory.

The DOD has expanded on these definitions and identified two additional types of information systems. These categorizations are used primarily only in the US DOD, but they are presented here since they offer special consideration of two additional types of information systems: platform IT and outsourced IT.

---

[53] Definition from OMB Circular A-130, Appendix III.

Figure 5: Information system types

Federal information systems	DOD information systems
• Major applications ⟷ • General support systems ⟷	• AIS applications • Enclaves • Platform IT (interconnected) • Outsourced IT

In particular, federal agencies, including DOD, have increased levels of contractor support either on site or on the contractor site. In addition, increased amounts of federal data processing is being managed or executed by externally contracted organizations. The protection of this information is a critical consideration. As a result, the identification and implementation of security controls for outsourced IT takes on increased importance.

While platform IT will likely remain a type of information system unique to the DOD, the concerns of outsourced IT are not unique to the DOD, or even the federal government. It is a concern of almost all organizations – including commercial entities.

So, included here are the definitions of information system types provided by the DOD.

Enclave

The Enclave[54] is the core type of information system. In other publications, the enclave may be referred to as a site. An enclave is essentially a collection of information system environments under the control of a single authority and security policy. The enclave

---

[54] Enclaves are analogous to the general support system identified in OMB A-130.

may provide information systems security capabilities for all of the information systems within it, such as boundary defense, incident detection, and certificate management.

The enclave assumes the highest level of protection required by the information systems supported within the enclave. Generally, an enclave will not change its own security mechanisms when connected with other enclaves, but will generally employ a controlled interface between enclaves. Examples of enclaves include local or wide area networks, backbone networks, and data processing centers.

Automation information system (AIS) application

The AIS application[55] is usually the product of a specific acquisition or development program. It may be a single software application; multiple software applications integrated to provide a single service (e.g. personnel management); or a combination of hardware, firmware, and software designed to support specific functions across a range of missions or organizations. In earlier publications, an AIS application might have been referred to as a type accreditation.

An AIS application performs clearly defined functions for which there are identifiable security requirements that must be addressed during the system life cycle. An AIS application may be deployed within an enclave and often takes advantage of the information system security services provided by the enclave.[56] While the program manager for the AIS application is generally responsible for the integration of security measures within the application, once it is deployed to an enclave for operations, the enclave assumes responsibility for its secure operation.

In order to properly determine the security requirements for the application, program managers for acquisitions of AIS applications

---

[55] AIS applications are analogous to the major application identified in OMB A-130.
[56] In DOD, this is called "inherited controls"; NIST refers to this as "common controls" or "inheritance."

should coordinate early in the acquisition process with the enclaves that will potentially host the applications to address operational security risks the system may impose upon the enclave. This also helps in identifying all system security needs that may be more easily addressed by enclave services than by system enhancement – thus reducing both the cost of development and the resources required for the authorization of the application.

> Do automated information resources not owned by the organization support any required business function?

The AO responsible for the enclave receiving an AIS application is also responsible for accepting the risks of integrating the AIS application into the enclave. The burden for ensuring the AIS application itself is adequately secured is a shared responsibility of both the AIS application system owner or program manager and the AO for the hosting enclave; however, the responsibility for initiation of this negotiation process lies clearly with the system owner or program manager. To the greatest extent possible, systems owners/program managers should capitalize on the common security safeguards that can be provided by the hosting enclave.

Outsourced IT

Increasingly, organizations outsource major elements of their IT support to outside providers. This raises specific security concerns due to the lack of direct control over the information systems. As a result, federal agencies, including DOD, have identified specific authorization requirements for outsourced IT providers.

Outsourced IT may refer to specific business processes supported by private sector information systems, specific information technologies, or specialized information services.

In the case of outsourced IT, the technical security is the responsibility of the service provider; however, procedural and administrative security requirements are often shared between the government client and the service provider. For example, if a payroll system is operated by a contractor, but part of the system is loaded on an agency's computers to perform a business function, the contractor is responsible for ensuring the overall security of the information system, but the agency is responsible for ensuring appropriate security controls are in place for that automated information resource on their computer. In the best of all worlds, the security requirements should be addressed during the contracting phase and defined in the statement of work (SOW) and the service level agreement (SLA).

Platform IT

Platform IT, while not limited to the DOD, is a highly specialized category of information system and will generally not be a consideration for most organizations. Nevertheless, it can be useful to understand the definition. Platform IT refers to specialized mission-related information systems, such as weapons, training simulators, diagnostic test and maintenance equipment, calibration equipment, equipment used in the research and development (R&D) of weapons systems, transport vehicles, medical technologies such as radiology systems, and utility distribution systems such as water and electric.

The PMs for the acquisition of platform IT are ultimately responsible for the platform's overall security requirements. If the platform has an interconnection with the larger network, the system owner/PM is also responsible for identifying the safeguards needed to ensure both the protection of the platform, as well as the interconnecting enclave. The connecting enclaves have responsibility for extending the security services (such as identification and authentication) to ensure a secure interconnection between the platform and the enclave.

Identifying the information

NIST SP 800-60 provides the following methodology for identifying the information processed by an information system:

- Identify the fundamental business areas (management and support) or mission areas (mission-based) supported by the system under review.
- Identify, for each business or mission area, the operations or lines of business that describe the purpose of the system in functional terms.
- Identify the sub-functions necessary to carry out each area of operation or line of business.
- Select basic information types associated with the identified sub-functions.

And, where appropriate:

- Identify any information type processed by the system that is required by statute, executive order, or agency regulation to receive special handling (e.g. with respect to unauthorized disclosure or dissemination). This information may be used to adjust the information type or system impact level.

Once the type of information has been categorized, the organization should review the information processed by the system to determine if there are other information types that need to be categorized for authorization purposes. Knowing the type of information processed by the information system will guide you in knowing what you need to protect, why you need to protect it, and the best safeguards to put in place to protect it. This process will be discussed in greater detail in Chapter 6, since the identification of the information protection requirements is directly linked to the selection of security controls. However, assigning the information to one or more of the above listed categories is generally sufficient to support the identification of the accreditation boundary.

Defining the nature of the information system and identifying the information processed and the associated protection requirements provides the foundation for the next step – defining the accreditation boundary.

Defining the boundary ensures manageable and measurable authorization

Let's say this once more, because it is very important: the goal of defining the accreditation boundary[57] is to ensure that the authorization process is manageable and measurable.

But how difficult is it to define a system boundary and why? Defining the accreditation boundary is one of the most difficult and challenging determinations facing authorizing officials and those responsible for executing the authorization process. **The primary reason – system boundary definition is largely a subjective process.**

But defining the accreditation boundary helps in defining the scope of protection for information systems (i.e. what the organization agrees to protect under its direct control or within the scope of its responsibilities) and identifying the people, processes, and technologies that are part of the systems supporting the organization's missions and business processes. Organizations also need to establish the accreditation boundary before they can determine the security categorization and develop any system security plans.

Organizations have a great deal of flexibility in determining what constitutes an information system and the accreditation boundary associated with that system. The difficulty of defining a system/accreditation boundary is influenced by the complexity of the information system, as well as the environment in which it operates.

So, exactly what does defining an accreditation boundary really mean? It is the "unique assignment of information resources to an information system for the purpose of executing C&A."[58] It is important because it will influence the scope of the accreditation activities – as well as the level of effort and cost.

---

[57] Will be referred to as the "authorization boundary" in upcoming Federal legislation and guidance.
[58] NIST SP 800-60.

Accreditation boundaries which are unnecessarily expansive (i.e. including too many hardware, software, and firmware components or other elements) can make the authorization process unwieldy and complex. Boundaries which are too limited or narrow can actually increase the number of authorization activities that need to be conducted and drive up the total security costs for the organization.

There are some very basic guidelines for establishing the accreditation boundary:

- There is some form of direct management control.
- The information systems have the same function or mission objective and essentially the same operating characteristics and information security needs.
- The information systems reside in the same general operating environment. In the case of geographically distributed information systems, they should have similar operating environments even if they reside in various locations.

You may be one of the fortunate ones – your organization may have already defined your accreditation boundary for you. But if you are not so lucky, what are some of the criteria in determining an accreditation boundary?

First, begin by getting the answers to several important questions about the system itself. These include:

- What is the primary mission of the information system?
- Is it a standalone, a local network, or does it include all of the network domains in a building or a location?
- Is the information system distributed across multiple buildings or even multiple geographic locations?
- Does it process sensitive or classified information?
- Are information systems from multiple data owners and with different accreditation boundaries (AOs or DAAs) interconnected within the same network?

Let's take a detailed look at the primary criteria for making the accreditation boundary determinations. These may be used individually or in a combination of multiple factors.

Authorization boundary criteria

- Network topology or configuration
- Organization
- Mission
- Location
- Data sensitivity or classification

Network topology

The network topology refers to the technical components of the information system, including both the physical and logical features. The physical components consist of the hardware, software and firmware. These include the firewalls, routers, intrusion detection systems, and other boundary protection devices. The logical features of the network topology include IP addresses, network protocols, domains, virtual private networks (VPNs), and trust relationships. Some accreditation boundaries are defined by the topology of the network.

Organization

It is possible to determine the accreditation boundary based on the organization using the information system(s). There are two primary considerations when using organization to determine accreditation boundaries: ownership (who owns it?); and operations (who uses it?). While this seems like a simple determination, it is frequently not quite so easy to define. In many cases, there may be information systems from multiple system owners within a single organization. In this case, the organization may require formal agreements to ensure that the individual information systems comply with the organization's unique requirements.

Mission

The mission of the information system(s) can be a useful criterion for determining the accreditation boundary. Information about the system mission can be acquired from many of the documents generated during the system life cycle, such as the mission need statement (MNS) or statement of need, the mission impact statement (MIS), the operational requirements document (ORD), the system security policy (SSP), and the information system concept of operations (CONOPS). Some of the missions executed by information systems include operational support, administrative office functions, or tactical operations. Part of the mission determination is also identifying how critical the information system is to the overall mission of the organization. Criticality can be based on factors such as:

- loss of life or injury;
- inability to execute the organization's overall mission;
- damage to organizational resources (physical and/or logical);
- damage to the organization's reputation;
- damage to national security.

Location

Some information systems and their accreditation boundaries can be easily defined along geographic boundaries. Information system components can be confined to a single floor, building or region and can be evaluated within these obvious boundaries.

Location may also refer to an operational requirement, such as a remotely deployed element of the organization. For example, mobile or fielded elements of the information system require security safeguards and should be considered part of the accreditation boundary. If the organization is geographically dispersed, each organization will likely have a local area network or enclave that is connected virtually to the larger organizational network. For accreditation purposes, these dispersed organizations may also be considered part of the larger boundary.

Data sensitivity or classification

Data sensitivity or security classification is also a defining factor in determining the accreditation boundary. As a common rule, unclassified (public), proprietary, and classified networks are defined as separate systems. Systems processing information at varying levels of sensitivity or classification may be resident within a single organization and may be included within a single accreditation boundary. In this case, it might be useful to decompose the network into the subsystems with individual accreditations which will contribute to the overall authorization of the enclave.

Boundary considerations: too narrow or too broad

When defining an accreditation boundary, there are still two looming questions: How much is too little? And, how much is too large?

If the accreditation boundary is too narrowly defined, the authorization team may exert great effort and use a lot of resources to achieve a limited objective. The interfaces, both internal and external to the accreditation boundary, may be difficult to define, since the boundary stops short before addressing all of the applicable components "touched" by the information system. There may also be gaps where all relevant devices are not accounted for, leaving the potential for missing significant risks to the information system and the organization.

If the accreditation boundary is too broadly defined, the authorization team may be faced with an overwhelming task. A boundary that is overly expansive will necessitate the evaluation and testing of a multitude of components and information processes. The result: there may not be time for a thorough analysis of the test results. Further, there is increased likelihood of frequent re-accreditation simply because there is an increased chance that something will change due to the massive number of components included in the boundary.

System boundaries may also overlap, causing redundant authorization efforts and an increased possibility for inter-organizational disputes (e.g. "turf battles"). This accreditation boundary error presents the potential for conflicting results stemming from duplicate testing on the same equipment. Conflicting regulatory requirements may also cause problems in determining which one has precedence and where to focus efforts.

Helpful hints

Here are a few ideas that may help in mastering the difficult task of determining the accreditation boundary.

- An information system will have at least one system administrator designated in writing.
- It is often simpler to design in security based on function, so begin with that criterion.
- If your system boundaries extend beyond your location, plan for security for the information systems under your control. Coordinate security on those which you cannot control.
- The accreditor should have some type of configuration control over the information systems within the accreditation boundary.
- Ensure an accurate system definition to avoid disagreements regarding information system boundaries.
- All parties involved in the authorization process must agree on the security requirements prior to the onset of the authorization effort.
- All personnel associated with the authorization effort, especially management, must agree on the accreditation boundary, level of effort, schedule, and security requirements.

Establishing a risk management process

"The first step in the risk management process is to acknowledge the reality of risk. Denial is a common tactic that substitutes deliberate ignorance for thoughtful planning."

Charles Tremper

Security personnel often complain that "leadership just doesn't get it" when they try to discuss risk. An often-cited truism in information systems security is that the only truly secure computer is one isolated in a concrete bunker, without power, and no connection to any network. This may be true – because any exposure opens an information system to potential compromise. An information system like the one described above may indeed be secure, but it certainly doesn't help your organization accomplish its mission. Inevitably, the security of any useful information systems environment will be less than perfect, and that has to be factored into the security planning process.

Any environment involving information systems and information technology includes an element of risk. Even the most rigorously planned information environments contain uncertainties. Unfortunately, in the real world, unexpected events can and often do occur. Planning for and managing these unexpected events is a fundamental element to a secure information environment.

Our experience with organizations has demonstrated that, far more often than not, leaders DO get it. They understand that risk cannot be eliminated, it can only be managed. In fact, leaders are intelligent, sharp individuals who live and breathe risk management as a fundamental element of what they do on a daily basis. Leaders think "risk management", while security people often tend to think "avoidance" – which are subtly, but critically different.

Risk avoidance and risk management are two approaches to dealing with an uncertain environment. Risk avoidance involves implementing all of the necessary countermeasures to eliminate every specter of risk. The question then becomes: when does the expense of eliminating risk overwhelm any potential return on investment.

Risk management is more of a process for selecting and implementing appropriate countermeasures to arrive at an acceptable level of risk at an acceptable cost to the organization. In fact, the risk management model can provide big wins for an enterprise because it directs information systems security spending where it is needed most, often resulting in a stronger security posture. Risk management attempts to answer the question: "What is the best way to invest my constrained, available resources, considering the variety of alternative options, to best accomplish my assigned mission in a potentially hostile threat environment?"

> **Risk management**
>
> - Risk management is the analysis of alternative courses of action.
> - It is the selection and implementation of that course of action, which, in a potentially hostile environment, best supports an organization's operational objectives.

When making decisions that affect our personal lives, we usually have an intuitive understanding of risk concepts without requiring formal definitions or complex analyses.

Here's an example of the risk management decision process based on a highly unlikely event.

We intuitively understand that the destruction caused by a supernova of the sun would be devastating – not only to our way of life, but to our very existence. But, we also intuitively know that this is unlikely to occur in our own lifetime. As we consider both the potential impact and the probability of the event actually happening, we have our own method of determining our personal level of concern for that combined state of impact and probability. What we do about it is dependent upon:

- Our personal fear of the harm that may result.
- Our ability to influence the probability and/or the impact caused by the event.
- Our willingness to invest in influencing either the probability and/or the impact.

We have some choices in this situation:

- Accept the risk and just not worry about it.
- Accept the risk, but continue to worry about it.
- Try to prevent the event from occurring.
- Invest in countermeasures to change the probability and/or the impact.

The choice would most likely be based upon our own individual concern for the risk posed by this event, the costs and benefits of each of the alternatives, and the resources available. The intuitive risk management decision process in this situation might look like this:

Risk management process example

OPERATIONAL OBJECTIVE: Provide a long, safe, and prosperous life for ourselves and our children.

EVENT: A supernova of the sun.

IMPACT: Annihilation of the earth, our way of life, and our existence!

PROBABILITY: Probably won't happen in our lifetime.

LEVEL OF CONCERN: There are probably many other things that have a greater impact than this.

RISK RESULT: This is below the intuitive threshold of concern, so you probably wouldn't invest much, if anything.

ALTERNATIVES:

- Do nothing – accept the risk and not worry about it.

- Worry – accept the risk but continue to worry about it.

- Supernova legislation – establish a policy prohibiting supernovas.

- "Flail at the wind" – invest wildly in various countermeasures to try to change the probability and/or impact.

COST/BENEFIT ANALYSIS:

- Do nothing – no current or future costs; will not waste time or energy on something that probably can't be influenced anyway; does nothing about impact or probability; would be unprepared if the event occurs.

- Worry – no current or future direct expenditure required, but wastes time and energy on something that probably won't occur; does nothing about impact or probability; would be unprepared if the event occurs.

- Supernova legislation – no current direct expenditures. May require future expenditure to enforce the established policy. Enforcement is probably futile with current technology. Since it is unenforceable, any expenditure would be wasteful at this time. When and if the policy is enforceable, establishing the policy may prove to be beneficial. Currently this would waste time, energy and resources on something that probably can't be influenced anyway.

- Flail at the wind – would expend current and long term maintenance resources. Would invest in countermeasures that cannot really do anything about the impact and/or probability. Wastes time, energy and resources on something that probably can't be influenced anyway.

DECISION/SELECTION: Probably alternative 1: Do nothing. By choosing this option, a level of risk is being "accepted," although the possible consequences may be undesirable or meet a standard of "acceptability". But, it is simply the best of the available alternatives at this time.

DECISION RATIONALE: Alternatives 2, 3 and 4 expend resources or energy on an impossible attempt to either reduce the likelihood of a supernova or the consequences if it does occur. There is virtually nothing that can be done to change this event. Since it is futile to develop countermeasures or prohibit the harmful acts, and because the event is so improbable, the decision is to not expend resources on an event that cannot be controlled or prevented.

However, we still might want to be able to choose a more proactive response and invest in a level of research and development to look at future options. These future options may provide the capability to meet a more desired state of affairs.

Risk management is a process and it is cyclical in nature. It must adjust and respond to changes — in the system design and configuration, in the operating environment, and to the organization's mission – since these might result in a change in risk. So, it is necessary to periodically revisit the risks associated with operating within a current and projected environment, and determine if a change in safeguards (e.g. processes, technology, or people) is necessary.

There are six phases of risk management:

- **Definition** – focuses on deriving the security requirements or security policy from the operational need for the information system to provide vital functions and services.
- **Assessment** – focuses on gaining insight into the assets, threats, and vulnerabilities that could or will be incurred based upon system use, design, and the operating environment. This phase includes the vulnerability/attack analysis, threat analysis, and mission impact analysis. These provide guidelines on determining the operational, budgetary, and risk issues that are important to the decision maker.
- **Selection** – focuses on selecting possible courses of action together with the costs and benefits. Options can include "no change," "shut down," or various combinations of technical, procedural, and personnel changes intended to mitigate potential threats and/or vulnerabilities or reduce the impact of a successful attack from a threat source.
- **Decision** – focuses on deciding between the possible courses of action. *This is a critical step in the risk management process.* Up to this point, the whole process is geared toward providing the decision maker(s) with the best possible information about courses of actions available to them. The decision maker must a) have the authority to accept risk on the part of the organization, b) understand the issues and information about the possible courses of action, c) be willing and able to make a decision that reflects the best possible balance between operations and security, and d) have the authority to make sure that the selected course(s) of action will be implemented. The information presented to the decision maker needs to address the decision maker's critical issues, provide objective analysis, and be presented in a format that is useful to the decision maker. The resulting decisions must be documented and then implemented.
- **Implementation** – effective implementation of the selected measures ensures that the risk decisions have the most effect on reducing the potential risk factors.
- **Repeat** – when there are changes to the information system and/or its environment, the risks also change. Changes may initiate a review of the risk assessment process to determine

whether or not the applied safeguards are still providing adequate security to the information system, organization, and mission.

The following diagram portrays a risk management framework. Integrating the risk framework into the overall authorization process will generally involve the functions associated with the **risk executive.**

The scope of this section is to provide introductory information on basic risk assessment and risk management concepts as they apply to information systems. It is not intended to be a comprehensive treatment of the subject. The selection and implementation of the security controls will be discussed in Chapter 6.

The risk assessment process

Just as there is no single approach to forecasting the weather or what's going to happen on the stock market, there is also no single approach to conducting a risk assessment. It is dependent upon a variety of factors such as:

- The availability of the information needed to make a risk decision.
- The quality of the data developed during the assessment.
- The analytical techniques used to develop the results.
- The experience and skills of the individuals conducting the assessment and the analysis.
- The validity of the results of the analysis.
- The risk mitigation strategy.
- The degree of risk tolerance.
- The preferences of the decision maker.

Figure 6: Risk management framework

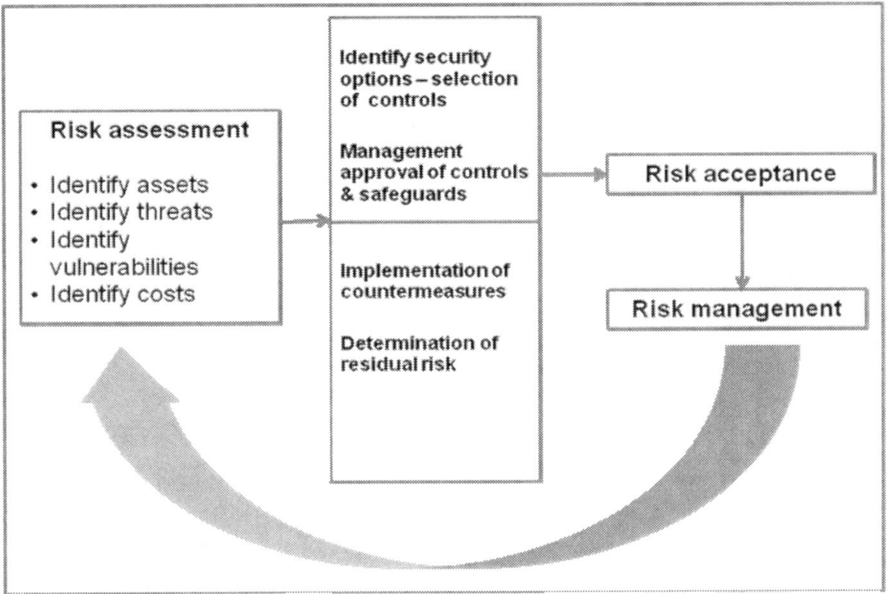

Risk, risk assessment, and risk management are large and complex subjects. So, the authorization team should take advantage of all of the resources at their disposal. Many organizations conduct business impact analyses (BIA) as part of their normal operations, particularly in the corporate world. The BIA has a wealth of information that can contribute to a security-focused risk assessment.

In writing this document, we've tried to balance the need to provide enough information so that risk concepts and the overall framework are clear and useful, while keeping the length manageable. As a result, the discussion that follows can best be described as an introduction and primer for conducting a risk assessment.

This process is not intended to be viewed as an exact mathematical equation to use in quantitative determinations of risk level. It is important to keep in mind that assignment of risk and acceptance of risk will always involve a level of subjective decision making involving the leadership of the organization. But, let's lay a foundation for understanding the language of risk before we proceed.

Ask a hundred information security professionals to define risk and you are likely to get a hundred different responses. Read almost any book on information systems security and you will probably discover that the terms risk, threat, and vulnerability have been used almost interchangeably – and they really aren't the same thing. One of the recurring problems in the information systems security profession has been the lack of a consistent taxonomy.

In informal discussions among security professionals this may not pose a problem, since we can usually understand what is meant within the context of the conversation. But it can become a negative factor when trying to communicate risk concepts to those outside the security profession – particularly to smart leaders who are very familiar with the fundamental concepts of risk management. Misuse of terms and concepts in these situations can potentially damage our credibility as professionals and certainly reduce the effectiveness of our message.

Before we take a closer look at each of these individual elements, let's establish a high level definition of each of the components of the formula **as we use them in this text.**

Assets – the tangible and intangible components of an organization.

Threat – "any circumstance or event with potential to harm an information system through unauthorized access, destruction, disclosure, modification of data, and/or denial of service."

When discussing information systems security, a **vulnerability** is a "weakness in an information system, system security procedures, internal controls, or implementation that could be exploited by a threat." More importantly for our discussion, a true vulnerability is a weakness that – after analysis – is a condition in which the capability of the threat agent to exploit it is greater than the ability to counter the threat agent effectively.

Cost – the total price tag of the impact of a particular threat exercised upon a vulnerable target. Costs can be tangible and intangible. They can be measured in terms of damages to hardware or software, as well as quantifiable IT staff time and resources spent repairing these damages. "Soft" costs can also be incurred; these might include lost transactions during the downtime, lost employee productivity, loss of reputation, damage control, a decrease in user or public confidence, or other lost business opportunities.

Countermeasures, also known as **controls**, can be defined as the processes, tools, technologies, procedures, and configurations that might reduce threats and vulnerabilities, thus mitigating risk until it comes closer to the organization's security acceptance threshold.

And finally, **risk** refers to the probability, frequency, and scale of future loss. Note the use of the term "probability." In the final analysis, risk is not a possibility issue (e.g. either something is possible or not), but a probability issue. In other words, risk lies somewhere on the continuum between the absolute certainty of something happening and the impossibility of its occurrence.

Risk assessments are perishable and should be repeated at discrete time points (e.g. quarterly, once a year, on demand, etc.). After initialization through the results of the risk assessment, risk management becomes an ongoing activity that monitors the implemented safeguards. The role of risk management as part of the ongoing authorization process will be discussed in the subsequent chapters. Here, we are first going to address the risk assessment process.

If you've been in the security field for a while, you probably already know that there are about as many risk assessment methodologies as there are risks themselves. For this book, we have selected a very generic approach. For those interested in exploring other methodologies, we have provided a list of some of the more prevalent of these on the accompanying CD.

The risk assessment process

There are 8 major steps in the risk assessment process we describe. These steps are generic in their approach, so they may be tailored in terms of length and detail depending on the size and nature of the environment under consideration.

Table 5: Steps in the risk assessment process

Step	Output
1. Prepare and plan	Risk assessment plan
2. Identify assets	List of critical assets
3. Perform asset sensitivity analysis	Asset criticality report
4. Conduct a threat analysis	Threat analysis report
5. Conduct a vulnerability analysis	Vulnerability analysis report
6. Execute cost/impact analysis	Cost/impact report
7. Finalize risk assessment	Risk assessment and analysis report
8. Assess residual risk against risk tolerance	Final risk analysis

Let's look at each of these steps in greater detail.

Step 1: Prepare and plan the risk assessment

1.1 Understand the overall process: The risk assessment process is normally initiated based on an identified need. For example, a concern might have been raised because a recent incident occurred or, in the case of this book, the information system is being submitted for authorization. In any event, the responsible individual(s) will initiate a risk assessment for part or all of a specific IT system. The most important aspect of any risk assessment is knowing exactly what it is that needs to be protected, and why.

Normally, the responsible individual will provide the following preliminary information:

- which information system is to be assessed (that is, the boundary of the assessment);
- the reason for the assessment; and
- the urgency or priority of the assessment.

1.2   Determine the scope of the risk assessment: The scope of the risk assessment should be tailored to the needs of the audience. For example, the assessment might require only a high level analysis to support decisions regarding further action made by senior management or it might be a detailed analysis completed for the level of management directly responsible for the information system and its security or operation.

1.3   Identify the required resources: The resources for the risk assessment can include people, time, and funding.   When considering the required resources, identify and record any limitations that might affect the scope of the assessment, along with any assumptions that need to be made because of those limitations.

Examples of limitations that could restrict the scope of an assessment include: departmental policies and standards; available resources; costs; and time limits. Such limitations could greatly affect the focus and the results of the assessment, especially if it is a very complex system.   These limitations need to be properly identified for the decision makers as part of the reporting process.

1.4   Identify the boundary of the assessment: Before starting the assessment, it is critical to identify both physical and logical boundaries by clearly outlining, at a high level, what the assessment will include.

- The physical boundary should include: physical environment; domains; system components and subcomponents; and connections to other internal and external IT systems.
- The logical boundary should include: interfaces with other internal information systems; the information assets that flow between the IT system and other internal systems and through connections to external systems; the methods of transporting these flows; and the end sources (that is, where information originates, as well as its final destination).

1.5   Identify the assessment team: The size of the assessment team depends on the size and complexity of the information system, as well as on the proposed scope and boundary of the assessment. If the magnitude of the risk assessment is such that it requires a larger team, each team member should have a vested interest in the IT system, the business function, the data being processed, or the applications used to process the data.

Assessment team members should know exactly why they are included on the team, and what contributions are expected of them. The more they know before assessment begins, the more likely it is that the assessment will be conducted quickly and successfully.

1.6   Collect the necessary information: Information needed for the risk assessment can include: description of the information system(s), copies of policies and procedures, architecture diagrams and descriptions, organizational charts, and lists of key personnel and others.

The information available for the risk assessment will also depend on when the assessment is being done in terms of the system life cycle. For an information system still in development, available information may be limited; however, more detailed information should be available for an operational information system. It is important to review all of the information collected in order to determine whether there are any aspects of the information system and its environment that may have been overlooked, but should be included in the assessment. As required, the scope of the assessment might have to be revised.

1.7　Develop the risk assessment plan: This sub-task involves developing the assignments for the assessment team; finalizing any materials needed for the assessment, such as questionnaires; identifying any tools required and personnel to be interviewed; and the approximate schedule for completing the assessment.

Step 2:　Identifying assets

2.1　Conduct asset inventory: Too often, organizations view their assets only as the "hard" elements of their information technology. A thorough inventory of assets must include people, all types of property, core business operations, information systems, and information.　The people inventory can include employees, tenants, guests, vendors, visitors, and any others directly or indirectly connected to or involved with the organization and its mission.

Figure 7: Asset categories

Asset categories include, but are not limited to:

People	Property	Core business operations	Information systems and networks
• Agency personnel • Senior leadership • Contractors/ vendors • Visitors • Family • Tenants	• Vehicles • Equipment • Buildings • Power plants • Residences • Intellectual property • Financial data • Classified information • Organization information such as capability • Product design	• Sensitive movement of personnel and material • Business operations • Reputation • Mission-related information	• Communication backbones • Network architecture & operations • Hardware, firmware, software • Web presence • Mobile capabilities (e.g. laptops, BlackBerries)

Property includes both tangible assets, such as the facility and other valuables, and intangible assets, such as intellectual property and critical information. Core business operations consist of the primary mission of the organization, including its reputation. Information systems include all systems, infrastructures, and equipment associated with data, telecommunications, and information processing assets. The primary criterion for selection: does the asset add value to the organization?

2.2   Interview key personnel and asset owners: Asset owners are generally the most knowledgeable about the assets that require protection and which are most sensitive and valuable. To gather asset data in an objective manner, it helps to interview those who know the most about that asset. It is also useful to develop a structured interview process and associated checklists detailing the asset subjects to be covered during interviews with site personnel.

2.3   Conduct site visits: Members of the risk assessment team should also conduct site visits as part of the asset identification process. This provides the opportunity for impromptu interviews, but many also result in the identification of additional assets requiring protection. This may also provide an opportunity to record any existing countermeasures or safeguards.

2.4   Review results and develop asset list: After all of the asset data gathering has been completed, review the results for completeness and develop the final list of assets. A sample list of assets can be found on the CD accompanying this book.

Step 3: Perform asset sensitivity analysis

In order to implement appropriate security safeguards, it is essential to know not only what critical information and assets exist, but also their respective criticality or sensitivity levels. Analyzing asset sensitivity determines the importance of information assets to the business of an organization by identifying and assigning value to those assets. Valuing the assets allows the organization's leaders to determine which areas have the highest priority, and consequently where security efforts should be focused.

3.1 **Analyze the asset sensitivity:** An asset's sensitivity can be rated in terms of confidentiality, integrity and availability and can be measured both qualitatively (in relative terms) as well as quantitatively (in terms of dollar losses).

When assessing sensitivity of an asset, the analysts(s) should also consider other factors, such as the loss of prestige, trust or business opportunity (that is, the impact on intangible assets) that would result as well as the cost of replacement.

- Confidentiality impact is that which would result from the deliberate, unauthorized or inadvertent disclosure of the asset.
- The integrity impact is that which would result from the deliberate, unauthorized or inadvertent modification of the asset.
- An availability impact is that which would result from the deliberate or accidental denial of the asset's use.

(Note that the confidentiality, integrity, and availability impacts can only be determined if the asset owner has defined the required levels of each for the asset in question.)

Finally, the total financial cost to the organization is that which results from the physical or virtual loss or destruction of the asset.

Table 6: Asset sensitivity rating scale

Rating	Sensitivity description
1	Exploitation of the asset could result in little or no loss or injury.
2	Exploitation of the asset could result in minor loss or injury.
3	Exploitation of the asset could result in serious loss or injury; mission or business processes could be negatively affected.
4	Exploitation of the asset could result in very serious loss or injury; mission or business processes could fail.
5	Exploitation of the asset could result in high dollar losses, exceptionally grave loss or injury to the organization and/or individual(s) - including loss of life; mission or business processes will fail.

3.2   Review the asset and asset sensitivity list with the asset owners and create the sensitivity report: After the sensitivity of assets has been initially rated in terms of confidentiality, integrity, availability and replacement value, review these with the asset owners to make sure the list is complete and accurate. The final results should be assembled in an asset sensitivity report. (NOTE: this report can take the form of a matrix, listing the asset and the respective assigned level of criticality/sensitivity.)

Step 4: Conduct a threat analysis

"Currently, approximately 19 million people worldwide have skills to mount a cyberattack."[59]

Frank G. Cilluffo, Director, Task Force on Information Warfare & Information Assurance

Threat identification results in an inventory of realistic threats consisting of the persons, things, events, or ideas that intentionally or unintentionally pose some danger to the information system resources of an organization. The existence of a threat that may have a potential to exploit system vulnerabilities may compromise the confidentiality, integrity, or availability of the system or its data. This threat inventory is then used to focus the process for identifying vulnerabilities.

> **Threat:** potential for a threat source to exercise (accidentally trigger or intentionally exploit) a vulnerability.
>
> **Threat source:** (1) intent and method targeted at the intentional exploitation of a vulnerability or (2) a situation and method that may accidentally trigger a vulnerability.

4.1   Determine sources of threat data: Understanding the threat(s) also involves an understanding of capabilities, intent,

---

[59] How can 19 million people have this capability? Approximately 95% of hacking attacks are executed by "script kiddies" – individuals without extensive computer/programming or security knowledge, but who are able to exploit vulnerabilities with the assistance of tools readily available on the Internet. Most of them know very little about the scripts they use and the potential results.

motives, likelihood, and history. Access to threat-related information is often limited due to security classification issues, so unless the threat has been adequately researched or defined, or information is conclusive, this can be the weakest link in the overall risk assessment process. Information can be obtained essentially from two types of sources: unclassified or "open source" information and classified sources. Depending on the type and depth of the assessment and the access available to the organization, one or both sources may be used.

The primary source of classified threat information is the organization's own internal intelligence resources, if applicable. The second source is information published by various elements of the Intelligence Community. Individuals conducting the risk should determine the type of information needed on a continuous basis, and then register with their supporting intelligence organization for regular updates of the information.

In addition, security surveys, prior internal analyses, and security incident reports may often contain useful information about threats that have resulted in incidents or concerns in the past.

Sources of unclassified threat information are too numerous to list in detail; however, several are worth mentioning. These include media, such as newspapers, websites, magazines, and other publications. The US Government printing office, official Internet sites, individual agencies and departments, think tanks, and other US agencies disseminate information on almost every imaginable threat topic.

Official speeches and open testimony can also be a source of evaluated intelligence that is made available to the public. Directors of agencies, such as the FBI or CIA, provide frequent updates to Congress on threat issues, which are often available to the general public.

Special interest groups and professional associations are also a valuable resource for threat information. These include the Carnegie-Mellon University Software Engineering Institute's Computer Emergency Response Team (CERT) and the respective organizational CERTs, such as the Army CERT. Professional associations, such as the International Systems Security Association (ISSA), may also cover a range of security threat information.

The process outlined will not guarantee that individuals conducting the risk assessment will obtain all the information needed to thoroughly identify and assess the threat(s); however, it does provide a framework for collecting threat information and a process for making judgments about the reality of the threat.

4.2   Identify potential threat agents: We have identified four broad groups of threat agents:

- Intentional human
- Unintentional human
- Nature/natural disasters
- Environmental.

Intentional human threats are defined as malicious, destructive exploits executed against an information system by authorized users or intruders. These can include, but are not limited to:

- **Intrusion or unauthorized access**: Involves the act of gaining access to information system resources for malicious (attack) or non-malicious (curiosity) purposes.
- **Exploitation of known weaknesses/malicious code exploitation**: The deliberate act of bypassing security controls for the purpose of gaining information or privileges. The exploited weaknesses could be at the operating system, application, or access control levels of an information system.
- **Malicious code insertion**: Refers to the intentional release of malicious code against an information system and/or a network in order to affect the system. These include viruses, worms, Trojan horses, logic bombs, and others.
- **Misrepresentation of identity or social engineering**: A technique which capitalizes on interpersonal skills to obtain access to unauthorized information and/or access to information systems.

- **Denial of service or saturation of system resources**: Denial of service (DOS) and distributed denial of service (DDOS) are usually concerted, malicious efforts to prevent an information system, network, or service from functioning. Saturation, a common method for DOS and DDOS, involves a condition in which the information system has reached its maximum traffic handling capacity creating an unstable environment, potentially resulting in lack of availability of a system resource.
- **Tampering**: The unauthorized modification of an information system which alters the proper functioning of the equipment, potentially degrading the security functionality or trust in the information system and/or its information.
- **Eavesdropping:** Deliberate efforts to gain access to information by "listening" using electronic bugs, inductive amplifiers on unprotected cables, packet sniffers, and keystroke monitoring.
- **Espionage:** The covert act of obtaining information through various means. It can be conducted by foreign governments through technical means, such as eavesdropping, or through human means, such as recruiting an agent inside the targeted organization. Espionage can also take advantage of legitimate business agreements, such as licensing and on-site contractors, to gain unauthorized access to information.
- **Terrorism:** The deliberate and potentially violent act undertaken by a group or an individual, whose motives extend beyond the act itself, generally expressing some form of social or political statement. Terrorism can be a physical act or can take advantage of all of the above listed mechanisms to achieve a goal within the realm of cyberspace.
- **Theft, sabotage, vandalism:** Deliberate malicious acts that can result in the damage, destruction, or loss of information system assets.
- **Abuse or fraud by authorized users:** Actions by authorized users to abuse assigned access privileges to gain additional information, privileges, or for personal monetary gain.
- **Procedural violation:** The act of not complying with existing procedures or instructions, which could result in an information system weakness.

Unintentional human threats are those that result from human actions without a clear motive or intent. These can include, but are not limited to:

- **Inadvertent acts or carelessness:** Acts that could cause information system damage, performance degradation, loss, or unauthorized access. These can include:

  - confidentiality breaches, where a user commits an error that allows information access to the wrong individuals or places information in the wrong location;
  - data deletion, where a user accidentally deletes data or changes system data;
  - integrity breaches involving user error that introduces erroneous data into the information system or causes erroneous actions by the information system;
  - system security feature degradation, where a user's inadvertent actions undermines the system security features;
  - programming and development errors which can result in unintentional software performance errors or vulnerabilities.

- **Errors or omissions:** Data entry errors or oversights that can result in information inconsistency or other threats to system resources. These include unintentional data entry mistakes, failure to disable or delete unnecessary or old accounts, or failure to recover common access cards, keys, or other access tools from departed or terminated users.
- **Improper handling of media:** Improper marking, handling, and disposal of sensitive media can result in the unintentional exposure of information to unauthorized individuals.
- **Installation errors:** Errors in the implementation of hardware, firmware, and/or software that could result in information system weaknesses or undermine existing security safeguards. Examples include not implementing built-in software security features, incorrect installation or set up of devices, authorizing users to download and install external and uncontrolled programs, and untested installation of patches.

- **Accidents:** Accidents can result from spills, exposure of the information system to hazardous substances, or physical damage to the information system.

Threats from nature and/or natural disasters are those that are not related to human actions or devices. According to the National Security Institute, more information system loss is associated with natural threats than from more widely publicized threats, such as malicious code or unauthorized network attack. Examples of threats from nature and natural disasters include hurricanes, tornadoes, floods, earthquakes, extreme cold or heat, and lightning.

Environmental threats are those that can be introduced by the conditions in which the information system is operating. These include, but are not limited to:

- **Environmental conditions:** The result of the controlled or uncontrolled environmental conditions in which the information system is operating. Examples include water leaks in server facilities, excess humidity in the network operating center, poor ventilation, or air conditional failures.
- **Power fluctuations/failures**: A power fluctuation is a short-term disruption in the primary power source, such as a power surge, spike, brownout or blackout, resulting in either insufficient or excessive power. A power failure usually involves a much broader effect, such as an overall utility failure or broad scale power disruption.

4.3   Analyze the threat agent: The process of defining threats does not end with a list of all of the potential and relevant threats. Once information is gathered and an inventory of possible threats is developed, the next step is to characterize the threats and assign a level of probability.

- Threat intent is determined most frequently by inference, generally by asking questions such as: Does an adversary have a need for the asset we are trying to protect?
- Could an adversary gain by exploiting or destroying an asset?
- What are the possible motivations, e.g. political agenda, terrorist activity, criminal gain?

Threat characterization and probability determination

- Identify possible threats
- Assess intent and motivation
- Assess capability
- Determine if there is prior history of threat-related incidents.

When assessing a threat capability, there are two general considerations. The first is the capability to obtain, damage, or destroy an asset. The second is the adversary's ability to capitalize on the asset once it has been obtained. Some of the questions to ask include:

- Does the adversary know the asset exists and where it is located?
- What are the adversary's demonstrated modes of operation?

A history of a threat being exercised is another predictor of possible future activity. Reviewing incident data is one method for developing historical data. Here it is useful to address the following questions:

- Can the source of the incident be identified?
- Have there been similar incidents in the past?
- Can they be attributed to the same source?

The following tables demonstrate one way to look at threat agent capability in combination with motivation, intent, and history.

Table 7: Threat agent capability with motivation, intent, and history

Capability	Rating	Motivation, intent, history
Little or no capability to mount an attack.	1	Little or no motivation or demonstrated intent. No history of attack. Not inclined to act.
Moderate capability. Has knowledge, skills to mount attack, but is lacking in some resources. Or, lacking some knowledge but has sufficient resources to mount an attack.	2	Moderate level of motivation or demonstrated intent. Limited history. Would act if prompted, or provoked.
Highly capable. Has knowledge, skills and resources to mount an attack.	3	Highly motivated with demonstrated intent. Prior history of attack. Almost certain to attempt an attack.

Table 8: Threat agent rating combination

Capability rating	Motivation rating		
	1	2	3
1	1	2	3
2	2	3	4
3	3	4	5

Table 9: Overall threat agent rating

Rating	Sensitivity description
1	Little or no capability or motivation, intent and history.
2	Little or no capability; moderate level of motivation, intent and history. Or moderate capability and little or no level of motivation, intent and history.
3	High capability; little or no motivation, intent and history. Or limited capability; high level of motivation, intent and history. Or moderate capability and moderate level of motivation, intent and history.
4	High capability; moderate motivation, intent and history. Or moderate capability; high level of motivation, intent and history.
5	High capability; high motivation, intent and history.

All of these variables and the subtle interactions between them must be considered as part of the likelihood. As a result, defining threat likelihood is often the most difficult aspect of risk to characterize due to the linkages between these various pieces of information. The following table provides three possible definitions of likelihood:

Table 10: Likelihood definitions

Likelihood level	Likelihood definition
High	The threat-source is highly motivated and sufficiently capable, and controls to prevent the vulnerability from being exercised are ineffective.
Medium	The threat-source is motivated and capable, but controls are in place that may impede successful exercise of the vulnerability.
Low	The threat-source lacks motivation or capability, or controls are in place to prevent, or at least significantly impede, the vulnerability from being exercised.

4.4 Summarize the threat analyses in the threat report: The last step is to record the results of the threat analysis in a threat report, indicating those which have the highest likelihood of occurrence.

Vulnerability: A flaw or weakness in system security procedures, design, implementation, or internal controls that could be exercised (accidentally triggered or intentionally exploited) and result in a security breach or a violation of the system's security policy.

Step 5: Conduct a vulnerability analysis

Vulnerability identification is the next step in the risk management process. Due to the very breadth of this subject, the vulnerability discussion presented here cannot be exhaustive. It is intended rather to serve as a guide to spur vigilance and discussion.

Information system weaknesses or vulnerabilities exist everywhere. The mere presence of a vulnerability does not necessarily cause any harm. A vulnerability is merely a condition or set of conditions that might allow an information system and/or its associated activities to be harmed by a threat agent. In other words, a vulnerability for which there is no credible threat does not necessarily require a response by the security processes.

Vulnerabilities can occur whenever systems are not effectively designed, improperly implemented, and/or inadequately protected. The types of vulnerabilities that can be identified may vary depending upon the maturing of that system's development – its phase within the system life cycle:[60]

- If the information system is in the concept phase or very early in the design phase, the identification of vulnerabilities should focus on the design schematics, planned security controls, and the vendor or developer's product analyses and the concept documentation.
- If the information system is at the production and early implementation phases, vulnerability identification should be expanded to include more specific design information, such as the planned security features described in the security design documentation and the results of certification test and evaluation.
- If the information system is already operational, the process of identifying vulnerabilities includes an analysis of the system security features and the security controls and safeguards, technical and procedural, assigned to protect the information system.

5.1 Gather vulnerability information: There are five primary ways to gather vulnerability information:

- Questionnaires/checklists
- On-site interviews
- Document reviews
- Observation
- Testing.

---

[60] Source: NIST Special Publication 800-30, Risk Management Guide for Information Technology Systems.

Questionnaires and checklists: Risk assessment personnel can use questionnaires and checklists to determine the security controls planned for integration into the information system or already implemented. Questionnaires and checklists of this type will generally be provided to technical personnel, developers, system administrators, and non-technical management personnel responsible for designing and supporting the IT system. Questionnaires and checklists are primarily useful for determining if the information system in question addresses known vulnerabilities or has included pre-determined security safeguards.

There are also many credible industry sources that provide information useful in developing the questionnaires, checklists and preparing for the interviews. Many of these can be found on the Internet or in system information descriptions provided by vendors. These will also often include fixes, service packs, patches, or other mitigations for known vulnerabilities.

Industry sources of vulnerability information

- Vulnerability lists, such as the NIST I-CAT database (http://icat.nist.gov)
- Security advisories, such as Fed CIRC
- Vendor advisories
- Commercial computer incident/emergency response teams, such as the Securityfocus.com forum
- Information assurance vulnerability alerts and bulletins (generally available to US DOD)
- System hardware, firmware, and software security analyses.

There are also "pre-made" checklists available for use. Many of these can be found through the Information Assurance Support Environment (IASE) managed by the DOD Information Systems Agency (DISA) located at *http://iase.disa.mil/stigs/stig/index.html*. On this site, there are a number of Security Technical Implementation Guides (STIG) on a number of security configurations, such as application security and development, databases, domain name servers, enclaves, instant messaging, networking, personal computers, remote computing, Unix, voice over IP, web servers, Windows® operating systems, wireless and others.

Interviews: Interviews with information system, network support, and security management personnel can also enable a risk assessment team to collect useful information about the information system, especially how the information system is operated and managed.

Document reviews: Policies, system documentation (e.g. user guides, system design and requirements documents, acquisition documents), and security related documentation (e.g. audit reports, system test results, security plans) are a good source of information about the security controls planned for and implemented in the information system. It is also useful to review the organization's mission and asset criticality assessments for information regarding information system and data criticality and sensitivity.

On-site visits: On-site visits by the assessment team will generally result in observations about the physical, environmental, and operational security of the information system. For information systems still in the concept and design phases, on-site visits provide the assessment team with an opportunity to evaluate the viability of the security safeguards and the target physical environment in which the information system will operate.

Testing: Testing using manual methods and automated scanning tools are another efficient source to gather information system vulnerabilities. For example, an automated vulnerability scanning tool, such as Retina, can identify vulnerabilities and unauthorized services that may be present on an information system. In almost every case, several of the vulnerabilities identified by the automated scanning tool may be false positives, e.g. not real vulnerabilities in the context of the system configuration and/or operational environment. When using these tools, it is important to have a follow on analysis conducted by technical personnel knowledgeable about the information systems configuration, operating requirements, and environment.

Security test and evaluation, also called verification and validation, is another method used to identify information system vulnerabilities. Generally, the purpose of this type of testing is to determine the level of effectiveness of the information systems security controls as they have been applied to the information system and/or its environment. This process will be addressed in greater detail in Chapter 7.

Penetration testing can be used to complement the other methods of information system testing. The objective of penetration testing is to test the security of the information system from the perspective of a threat agent and to identify potential points of failure. *NIST Special Publication 800-42*, *Network Security Testing Overview*, provides a methodology for information systems testing and for the use of automated tools.

5.2 Assign to vulnerability areas: When assessing an information system and its environment for potential vulnerabilities, there are three primary areas to which these can be assigned: management, operational, and technical.

Management area vulnerabilities: Management vulnerabilities are generally evidenced in the lack of proper or comprehensive policies and procedures. While not directly vulnerabilities themselves, these often enable the existence of other vulnerabilities associated with the information system and/or its operational environment. Management area vulnerabilities are divided into:

- administrative policy and procedures;
- physical security policy and procedures;
- personnel security policy and procedures.

Administrative policy refers to the formal, documented procedures for selecting and implementing security measures and safeguards. Vulnerabilities are often found in weak countermeasures and deficiencies in the development and maintenance of procedures, guidance documents, definition of responsibilities, insufficient life cycle management, and lack of security standards.

Physical security vulnerabilities occur when there are weak countermeasures in the physical layout of, or access to, facilities and environments where information systems are located. These weaknesses include inadequate or ineffective physical access controls or intrusion detection (e.g. badge systems, alarms, cameras) and lack of or deficient security controls for the physical site boundary protection (e.g. perimeter fencing, door locks).

Personnel security vulnerabilities are deficiencies in the controls and procedures that ensure that all personnel have the required information access authorization, including clearances, for access to information and information systems. These can be demonstrated in weak safeguards for screening staff, processing background and security checks, hiring and termination processes, and security training.

Operational area vulnerabilities: Operational vulnerabilities are associated with the security procedures in the operational environment in which the information system is being used. Vulnerabilities in the operational area span many practices and procedures, including, but not limited to:

- Security monitoring
- Auditing
- Media protection
- Security documentation
- Account management
- System backup
- Contingency planning
- System maintenance
- Configuration management
- Labeling and data control
- Sanitization and disposal.

Technical area vulnerabilities: Technical vulnerabilities are those weaknesses associated with the hardware, firmware, and software, as well as the information system architecture and technical configuration. Most of the focus on addressing vulnerabilities has been centered on technical vulnerabilities and technical solutions, largely because this is one of the most visible and highly publicized areas. Some of the technical vulnerabilities considerations include, but are not limited to:

- Account management
- Passwords
- System access
- System integrity monitoring and reporting
- Session controls
- External and internal connectivity
- Telecommunications
- Boundary protection, such as firewalls, intrusion detection, proxy servers
- Encryption
- Anti-virus protection
- Audit technology
- Remote access.

A sample list of vulnerabilities is provided on the companion CD.

5.3   Rate likelihood of exploitation: The likelihood of a threat agent exploiting a vulnerability is based on:

- The exposure level of the vulnerability
- The severity level of the vulnerability.

The following tables demonstrate a mechanism for rating vulnerabilities.

Table 11: Vulnerability severity and exposure rating

Severity	Rating	Exposure
Minor: Vulnerability requires significant resources to exploit, with little potential for loss.	1	Minor: Asset is not exposed. Effects of vulnerability tightly contained. Does not increase the probability of additional vulnerabilities being exploited.
Moderate: Vulnerability requires significant resources to exploit, with significant potential for loss. Or, vulnerability requires some resources to exploit, moderate potential for loss.	2	Moderate: Asset has some exposure. Vulnerability can be expected to affect more than one system element or component. Exploitation increases the probability of additional vulnerabilities being exploited.
High: Vulnerability requires few resources to exploit, with significant potential for loss.	3	High: Asset is exposed. Vulnerability affects a majority of system components. Exploitation significantly increases the probability of additional vulnerabilities being exploited.

Table 12: Vulnerability rating combination

Severity rating	Exposure rating		
	1	2	3
1	1	2	3
2	2	3	4
3	3	4	5

Table 13: Overall vulnerability rating

Rating	Description
1	Minor exposure, minor severity.
2	Minor exposure, moderate severity; or moderate exposure, minor severity.
3	Highly exposed, minor severity; or minor exposure, high severity; or moderate exposure, moderate severity.
4	Highly exposed, moderate severity; or, moderate exposure, high severity.
5	Highly exposed, high severity.

5.4 Determine existing countermeasures: In place countermeasures may mitigate the risk to a vulnerability even in the presence of a malevolent and capable threat agent, together with a vulnerability which could potentially be exploited by that threat. All else being equal, more countermeasures can result in less risk, and so countermeasures appear in the denominator to the algorithm presented at the beginning of the section. Countermeasures can reduce the likelihood of a successful attack and so reduce risk.

Information systems security countermeasures can be technical and non-technical in nature. Technical countermeasures are controls that are an integral part of the information system's hardware, software or firmware, including access control mechanisms, identification and authentication mechanisms, encryption and intrusion detection systems. Non-technical controls can be management and operational processes and procedures, such as personnel and physical security procedures. We will discuss the actual selection and implementation of security controls in greater detail in Chapter 6.

The focus of countermeasure analysis is the determination of how effectively the applied control has addressed the risks identified in the risk assessment process. What remains after the controls have been applied and their effectiveness has been evaluated is termed **residual risk.**

The Office of Management and Budget (OMB), Circular No. A-130, defines residual risk as the "risk that remains in operation of an information system after all possible, cost-effective threat mitigation measures have been applied." The level of residual risk presented by system operation is the final output of the risk management process introduced in this section. This residual risk analysis forms the true basis for the determination by the AO to either allow or deny authorization to operate an information system.

Step 6: Execute cost/impact analysis

As part of the risk assessment process, an organization needs to determine the actual costs of theft, modification, or destruction of a critical asset. Often called impact, the cost to an organization can be either tangible or intangible. **Costs or impacts are incurred when a threat agent exploits a vulnerability resulting in some effect on an asset.**

6.1 Assign costs/impact: The costs to an organization of a successful attack depend greatly on the value of the target. If the cost or impact of a security failure is limited, then the allocation of scarce resources to promote security systems and processes should also be limited. For example, the loss of routine office correspondence might occasion little concern. On the other hand, there are some security failures with exceptionally dire consequences.

For example, a failure of the public switched network that carries telephone and computer communications could be devastating and could even inhibit deployment of military forces, emergency response teams or law enforcement officials. In the extreme case of cyberwarfare – attacks on a nation's information infrastructure – the results could be serious enough to affect the outcome of a geopolitical crisis without a single shot being fired. Obviously, as the value of the target rises, the impact of a successful attack goes up as well, and so our sense of risk increases. Consequently, cost is also considered a multiplier in the risk algorithm.

A key point here is that different organizations will have very different cost (impact) concerns. For example, a government agency will have dramatically different areas of consideration than a financial institution. There are also, however, some common considerations related to confidentiality, integrity, and availability of their information and information systems.

Some of the basic cost considerations are:

- How long can we live without access to our information and/or information systems before there is a dramatic impact on mission and operations?
- If we lose the confidentiality of our information or our customer's information, what is the cost to our organization?
- If the integrity of sensitive records is questionable, what is the effect on our organization and our reputation?

The actual determination of cost (impact) will depend heavily on the perspective of the organization. A good starting point for making cost determinations is to begin with those considered high – e.g. having a **dramatic** cost (impact) on the organization. Examples might include:

- Loss of life
- Inability to execute a mission
- Excessive downtime
- Major loss of money.

Typically, a medium cost is one that is considered **significant** by the organization. These might include:

- Loss of customer confidence
- Significant delay in a mission
- Loss of a strategic advantage
- Significant loss of money.

Low cost determinations are reserved for those considerations that might have only a **limited or lesser** cost to the organization. Some examples are:

- Limited loss of money
- Customer complaints
- Limited delay in a mission.

It is not unusual for an organization to feel that any loss, degradation, or delay will present a major cost or impact. So, there is a tendency to rate a large number of possibilities presented by the exploitation of a vulnerability by a threat agent as high. If everything is rated as high, however, this would actually provide little value to the organization. In reality, not all assets (tangible and intangible) deserve the same level of protection.

6.2   Prepare cost/impact report: Once the costs/impacts have been determined, assemble the information in a cost or impact report. This does not have to be a formal or separate report, but can be an association of the level of impact/cost of impact to an asset.

Step 7: Finalize risk assessment and analysis

7.1   Consolidate the asset, threat, vulnerability, and cost/impact information: This is the step where all of the above data is consolidated: the assets and their respective criticalities have been defined; likely/probable threat agents have been determined; the asset vulnerabilities, exposure and existing countermeasures or safeguards have been identified; and the potential costs/impact of a threat agent compromising an asset have been determined.

7.2   Review existing/planned safeguards: An initial review of existing safeguards was conducted when assessing the vulnerabilities. In this step, these safeguards/countermeasures are once again reviewed in light of all of the collected data. In addition, any planned safeguards will be considered.

The following table provides an example listing of threat agents and their interrelationships with the data described in the preceding sections.

Table 14: Assessment interrelationships

Threat agent(s)	Motivation	Capability	Threat	Vulnerability	Asset	Consequence	Safeguard(s)
Hackers	Challenge Status	Knowledge	Unauthorized access	Configuration	Business data Privileges	Disclosure Modification Embarrassment	Technical Administrative Personnel Awareness
Foreign intelligence	Political gain Economic advantage	Skills	Unauthorized access Unauthorized use	Configuration Physical access Employees	Business data	Disclosure	Technical Physical Personnel Awareness
Criminal activity	Financial gain	Skills	Service denial Theft	Configuration Physical access	Business data	Disclosure Modification Destruction	Technical Physical Personnel Awareness
Corporate raiders	Financial gain Economic advantage	Skills Resources	Takeover Hire away	Salaries Working conditions	Employees Knowledge	Loss of talent	Salaries Working conditions
Vandals & terrorists	Revenge	Disgruntled employee Outside personnel Labor problems	Damage Service denial Theft	Configuration Physical access Salaries Working conditions	Employees Facility	Destruction Modification Productivity Service denial Looting	Technical Physical Personnel Awareness
Employees (insiders)	Human error		Damage Service denial Destruction Modification	Configuration Fatigue Training Knowledge	Business data Application programs	Destruction Modification Productivity Service denial Embarrassment	Technical Physical Personnel Awareness
Electrical storm		Varying degrees of severity	Damage Service denial Destruction Safety		Building IT systems	Destruction Modification Productivity	Alternate supply Redundancy Business resumption plan

7.3   Identify residual risk: Determine what, if any, risk remains after consideration of existing and planned safeguards. Also consider possible constraints that might affect the implementation of safeguards/countermeasures, including:

- legal constraints;
- contractual constraints (lease agreements, etc.);
- collective agreements;
- cost;
- potential loss of productivity;
- operational overhead;
- enforceability;
- management style.

7.4   Prepare the risk assessment and analysis report: The risk assessment and analysis report should contain a prioritized record of the assets at risk from the identified threat agents after consideration of all of the data described in paragraph 7.1 and 7.2. This includes a statement of residual risk.

Step 8: Assess residual risk against risk tolerance

The Committee of Sponsoring Organizations of the Treadway Commission (COSO) has defined risk tolerance or "appetite" as "... the amount of risk, on a broad level, an entity is willing to accept in pursuit of value (and its mission)." Risk appetite is influenced by the organization's culture, operational strategies, and infrastructure. It is not a constant; risk appetite is influenced by and must be able to adapt to changes in the environment.

Defining the organization's risk tolerance must be an executive responsibility based on the organization's goals and objectives. Management assesses the alternatives, sets objectives aligned with strategy, develops business processes to accomplish the plan, and manages any inherent risks. Risk tolerance can be defined as the residual risk the organization is willing to accept upon reaching the state of having determined its risk and implemented its set of risk-mitigation and monitoring processes.

The full risk assessment: Yes or No?

It is easy to see from the detailed risk assessment and analysis process described above that this can be a long and costly process. Is it really necessary to conduct the full process in order to determine essential security controls and make an authorization to operate decision?

Some form of risk determination is an essential part of the AO's risk based decision; however, it may not be necessary to exercise the full extent of the process in order to arrive at a reasonable risk determination.

Even though Appendix III of OMB Circular No. A-130 does not require a formal risk assessment such as that described in this section, Appendix III does state that "the need to determine adequate security will require that a risk-based approach be used." This approach should at least consider the major factors in risk management at a high level: the value of the information and the information system, threats, vulnerabilities, and the effectiveness of current or proposed safeguards.

Ultimately, the risk management process is about making decisions. The cost of a successful attack on an organization's information infrastructure and the level of risk that is acceptable in any given situation are by necessity individual policy decisions. The threat is whatever it is and while it may be mitigated, controlled or subdued through the selection of the appropriate countermeasures, it still remains beyond the direct control of the information systems security process.

In order to ensure greater success in managing risk, the process must address weaknesses in the information system's hardware, firmware, software and architecture during the design, development, fabrication and implementation phases of our facilities, equipment, systems and networks.

Risk assessments and the resulting capability to manage risk may seem inherently complex, but even complex issues can be understood when broken down into simple steps. So, let's take this entire section and boil it down into the following simple questions:

- What assets do you want to protect? While this question may seem self-evident, many organizations do not take the time to understand what is really valuable to them.
- What are the threats to these assets and the likelihood that these threats will be exercised? This may never be fully known, but looking at capabilities and history may provide some insight.
- What are vulnerabilities or weaknesses in the system that could be exploited by a willing and capable threat agent? Remember an asset or a vulnerability may not be visible to a threat agent, so it may not warrant the high cost of certain protections.
- What would be the cost of a successful attack? If a vulnerability can be exercised by a threat agent, understanding the cost of protection should be in relationship to the potential cost to the organization as a result of a successful attack.
- What are the potential countermeasures or security safeguards and how well do they mitigate the risk? Residual risk is what remains after looking at the remaining level threat, vulnerabilities, and cost after the application of safeguards.
- How will the above information be analyzed and presented in order to make an appropriate risk management decision? The risk assessment and management process is not a singular activity. Organizations must establish risk monitoring and evaluation activities as part of a continuous process.

This section focused on information system-related security risk. But this is just one component of the large organizational risk that senior leaders tackle as a routine part of their ongoing management responsibilities. Risk can take many forms, e.g. investment risk, budgetary risk, program management risk, legal liability risk, safety risk, inventory risk, and the risk from information systems.

Effective risk managers know that organizations operate in highly complex and interconnected worlds using information systems to accomplish critical missions and to conduct important business. Organizations recognize that well-informed management decisions are necessary in order to balance the benefits gained from the use of these information systems with the risk to the organization posed by the same systems. The risk assessment is the means to provide leaders with the information they need to make these decisions.

Managing risk, either information system-related security risk or other types of risk, will never be an exact science. It can only represent the best collective judgment of those individuals responsible for ensuring the day-to-day operations of organizations.

Align with the system life cycle[61] (SLC)

NIST Special Publication 800-64, Security Considerations in the Information System Development Life Cycle, defines the SLC as "the scope of activities associated with a system, encompassing the system's initiation, development and acquisition, implementation, operation and maintenance, and ultimately its disposal that instigates another system initiation."

Information systems security, including the authorization process, should be considered throughout the SLC, starting with the preliminary system concept. Identifying IA safeguards early in the SLC will ensure that key elements, such as technical security requirements, scheduling, and cost and funding issues associated with executing requirements for IA and authorization, are addressed and maintained.

The security requirements of information resources must be considered as they are planned to operate when fully functional, not necessarily how they currently operate. Security safeguards should be considered for the data that will be processed by the information system and the planned system configuration, even if that information is not yet being processed and the design is not fully solidified. The data requirements and system configuration may change throughout the life cycle of the information system, but it is important to have accurate classifications at each stage of the life cycle, so that appropriate security controls can be identified and

---

[61] Many publications refer to the system development life cycle (SDLC) in this same context. But we feel that the integration of information systems security and information systems life cycle goes far beyond development and extends through the full life of the system until it is removed from service.

applied. As the need for changes to the information classification and the system configuration surface, the system description should be updated to accurately reflect the current state of sensitivity or mission criticality.

As a result, the number and nature of suitable security controls will vary depending on the phase within a SLC and acquisition cycle. The relative maturity of an information system's architecture and design may influence the types of appropriate security controls. The blend of security controls is also dependent upon the mission of the organization and the role of the information system within the organization in supporting that mission. One way to identify the ideal mix of management, operational, and technical security controls is through the risk assessment, analysis management process.

We will provide a more exhaustive description of the relationship between the authorization process and the SLC in Chapter 14.

Milestones from the pre-certification and accreditation activities:

Before proceeding to the next phase, the actual initiation of activities for a specific authorization requirement, let's take a final look at what you should achieve in this preliminary phase.

- The authorization team is established and each member is familiar with their role(s).
- Each member of the authorization team is trained in their respective specialties, as well as in the authorization processes.
- The information and the information system are characterized.
- The accreditation boundary is determined and the AO notified of the pending authorization.
- The enterprise and system level risk assessment is complete and the risk management process is initiated.
- The authorization activities are aligned with the system life cycle and are part of the process of development, deployment, and operations.

Much of the effort you put into this preliminary phase remains in place or "re-usable" for parallel or future authorization efforts. This includes the authorization team, the enterprise risk assessment, and perhaps the accreditation boundary.

<table>
<tr><td>

Further reading

Alberts, Christopher and Dorofee, Audrey. *Managing Information Security Risks: The OCTAVE (SM) Approach*, Addison Wesley Professional, 2002.

Calder, Alan and Watkins, Steve G. *Information Security Risk Management for ISO27001/ISO17799*, IT Governance Publishing, 2007.

OCTAVE (*Operationally Critical Threat, Asset and Vulnerability Evaluation*). Available at *http://www.cert.org/octave/*.

Roper, Carl. *Risk Management for Security Professionals*, Butterworth-Heinemann, 1999.

Schneier, Bruce. *Beyond Fear: Thinking About Security in an Uncertain World*, Springer, 2006.

</td></tr>
</table>

References

Barker, William C. *Guide for Mapping Types of Information and Information Systems to Security Categories*, ITL Bulletin, July 2004.

Department of Defense Instruction 8500.2, *Information Assurance Implementation*, 2003.

National Institute of Standards and Technology (NIST) Special Publication 800-30, *Risk Management Guide for Information Systems.*

National Institute of Standards and Technology (NIST) Special Publication 800-59, *Guideline for Identifying and Information System as a National Security System.*

National Institute of Standards and Technology (NIST) Special Publication 800-60, *Guide for Mapping Types of Information and Information Systems to Security Categories.*

Peltier, Tom. *Information Security Risk Analysis,* Auerbach, 2001.

CHAPTER 6: PLAN, INITIATE AND IMPLEMENT AUTHORIZATION – PREPARING FOR AUTHORIZATION

There are no secrets to success. It is the result of preparation, hard work, and learning from failure[62].

Colin Powell, Former Secretary of State

In this chapter:

Understanding the information and the information system

Registering the information system

Negotiating the authorization approach

Implementing the security controls

---

[62] http://thinkexist.com/quotation/success_is_neither_magical_nor_mysterious-success/211597.html

While many may have a different opinion, we believe that this phase is one of the most important – and challenging – parts of the actual authorization process. That doesn't mean that all the activities done up to this point are unimportant. They are extremely critical, since they provide the overall structure that supports the authorization process.

But here is where the rubber meets the road, at least in terms of actually certifying and accrediting an information system. If the activities in this phase are done correctly, you should breeze through the actual accreditation decision and be able to maintain an information system security environment during system operation. Done inadequately, you may have a significant amount of re-work and considerably more expense.

Process 1 or **plan, initiate, and implement authorization**, begins with acquiring or developing the information necessary to understand the information system and to use that information to prepare for the authorization activities to follow. You should use this information to scope the level of effort (LOE) required to certify and accredit the information system. The LOE can vary with the scale of the information system – from a simple standalone, a large data center running dozens of applications on varied platforms, to a complex, multilevel secure network.

So what, exactly, are the steps you will be following in this phase? Take a look at the following diagram. Each of these steps will be discussed in detail.

Figure 8: C&A process 1

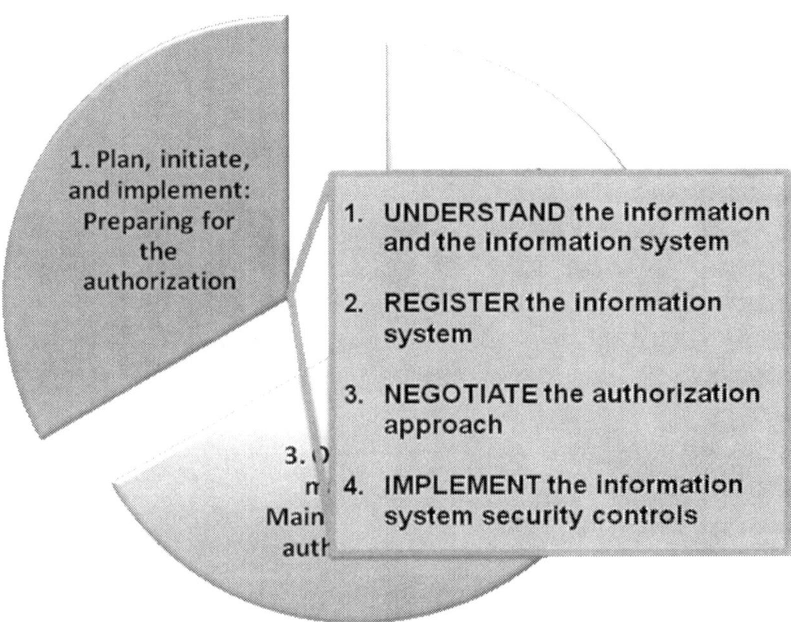

UNDERSTAND the information and the information system

Regardless of where the information system is on the system life cycle continuum, understanding the system and its information is the first and most basic requirement. Based on this understanding, you can determine the certification and accreditation actions, such as:

- Scope and level of effort
- Documentation
- Plan and schedule
- Cost
- System security categorization.

Who is involved?

The primary responsibility for providing the content necessary to understand and characterize the information system and the information is the information system owner, or in the case of developmental systems and certain operational systems, the program manager (PM). The information system owner/PM will recognize that an information system requires an authorization to operate.

Direct supporting roles in Step 1 include the designated accrediting authority/ authorizing official (DAA/AO), the information assurance manager/ information system security manager (IAM/ISSM), the information owner, the certifying authority (CA) and potentially, the senior information assurance officer (SIASO).

Step 1 players

- Primary role: Information system owner and/or program manager
- Supporting roles:
    - DAA/AO
    - IAM/ISSM
    - Information owner
    - CA
    - SIASO

- The DAA/AO should be informed that an information system is entering into the authorization process.
- The IAM/ISSM will be primarily involved in assembling the documentation and starting the process for organizing and planning the authorization effort together with the information system owner/PM.
- The information owner will be able to provide critical information about the sensitivity and criticality of the information to be processed by the information system.
- The CA should be notified early, since he/she can assist in establishing the level of effort and also assist in understanding the information system and its security safeguard requirements.
- The SIASO represents leadership, provides funding and facilitates access to resources.

Other indirect supporting roles include the risk executive, system and/or network administration staff, contracting officials, facilities personnel, and staff in other security disciplines, such as physical and personnel security.

Scope and level of effort

While the authorization process itself remains essentially the same for any information system, the skills needed to perform the authorization, where to focus the implementation and testing, and supporting documentation may vary substantially.

The scope and level of effort required for certification and accreditation of an information system is determined by analyzing the system's mission, information, and availability as follows:

- Criticality to the responsible organization's mission.
- Sensitivity as related to confidentiality, integrity, and availability of system information.

It is a reasonable assumption that the more critical an information system is to the organization and the more sensitive the information, the more secure the information system should be. More security generally means a greater level of effort – for design, development, implementation of security controls, and for the authorization process itself.

Authorization should be integrated into the overall information system development effort as seamlessly as possible. The closer the integration into the SLC, the lower the potential level of effort and associated costs will be for authorization.

Information obtained from documentation

In this case, documentation doesn't refer to the authorization documentation itself. It refers to the data that the authorization team collects as part of understanding the system and preparing for the authorization effort.   The type and detail of the available documentation may vary depending on the stage of the information system life cycle.

Information about the information system is typically documented in the system identification section of the systems security plan (SSP), which we will discuss in more detail later, included in attachments to the SSP[63] or referenced in other standard documents generated as part of the SLC. Preparation of the SSP will be discussed in detail in Chapter 10 and templates are available on the accompanying CD.

Currently, the SSP is used only in federal agencies, the Intelligence Community and for special systems. DOD uses the system identification profile (SIP) and the DIACAP implementation plan (DIP) in lieu of the SSP. These will be described in the chapter on C&A in the US DOD.

Developmental systems

As soon as possible in the life cycle of an information system, the security classification, information sensitivity, security access considerations, and the confidentiality, integrity, and availability requirements of the information system should be determined. This information should be available in documents such as:

- Systems requirements specifications (SRS)
- Mission needs statement (MNS)
- Operational requirements document (ORD)
- System concept of operations (CONOPS)
- Initial capabilities document (ICD)
- Capabilities development document (CDD)
- Capabilities production document (CPD)
- System threat analysis.

---

[63] Since much of the information required in the SSP exists in other documents, it is often sufficient to reference the original document rather duplicate the content in the SSP.

Operational systems

If the information system is already operational, it may already have been accredited – whether under the rescinded DITSCAP or through the earlier federal process under NIST SP 800-37. In this case, there will already be a large amount of documentation that can be reviewed and potentially reused. Other information that can be useful in understanding the operational information system includes:

- Federal and organizational security instructions and policies
- Configuration management documents
- System capabilities
- System architecture and network diagrams
- User manuals
- Risk assessment
- Physical security procedures
- Personnel security procedures
- Operating procedures
- Interconnectivity and data flow
- Level of sensitivity and type of information processed
- Services provided
- Operations supported
- Organizational mission statement.

Plan and schedule

A detailed schedule and plan will assist you in keeping the authorization project on track. It should highlight the big picture and identify executable milestones, tasks and deliverables. If the information system is still in development, it also helps to consider general project information such as estimated costs, key personnel, milestones, specific tasks and deliverables, responsible individuals or offices for each task and deliverable, as well as targeted and actual, completion dates for the overall project.

The overall system development project schedule can also provide insight into changes in costs and resource allocation. This will help to adjust the authorization plan to periods when you may not be able to totally control timelines due to tasks external to the authorization effort, such as developmental testing or debugging.

The authorization schedule itself will work best if it is drafted in as much detail as possible during the very early stages. This notifies key participants about specific activities and may influence the make-up of the authorization team.

The schedule should be reviewed and updated by the authorization team throughout the authorization project. The benefits beyond the obvious ones of monitoring progress and keeping the authorization project on track, is that a completed schedule can also serve as a tool for developing the level of effort and costs for the authorization project.

Cost

Don't forget to consider the costs for authorization early in any information system project. Let's look at a lesson learned from one information system project.

An aerospace company contracted for the development of a complex command and control system. In the concept phase, they developed end-to-end scenarios for performance and target capability.

They then used these end-to-end scenarios as the basis for developing and fielding the information system. Their structured development practices enabled them to deliver the system on-time and within budget. However, their planning included all of the engineering, but NOT the authorization costs.

This became very significant, since the information system could not become operational until authorization was completed. Authorization became an unfunded requirement for the system, including those costs related to security controls implementation and authorization testing. The funding for re-engineering the security portion of the information system and conducting the authorization was taken from management reserves and profit – *to the order of $15 million*. If all of the authorization requirements had been considered from the beginning, the engineers estimated that the cost would have been approximately 1/10th.

The lesson learned here is that the cost for authorization should be calculated into the budget from the system development and design stage.

System security categorization for information

System security categorization for the information processed by the information system is a prerequisite for initiating and executing the authorization process. Security categorization provides the basis for determining the level of security required for the information system based on the need for confidentiality, integrity, and availability. It will also identify additional protections that may be needed (i.e. privacy and critical infrastructure protection (CIP)). Thus, it assists in determining authorization scope, level of effort and schedule.

Traditionally, NIST, DOD, and the Intelligence Community (IC) have had different ways to express the system security categorization. DOD refers to **mission assurance category (MAC)** – a combination of availability and integrity – and **confidentiality level (CL),** which refers to the information sensitivity/classification.

The IC looks at **protection levels (PL),** which are associated with the confidentiality requirements for the information based on classification and levels of personnel clearance and access, and **level of concern (LOC)** for availability and integrity.

NIST focuses on the **level of impact**, which was assigned as high, moderate or low based on an assessment of the needs of the information system for confidentiality, integrity and availability.

One thing should become immediately clear: despite the differences in nomenclature used by each sector, system security requirements are based on the requirements of the information and the information system for confidentiality, integrity, and availability.

To be consistent with the majority of users within the federal government, we will refer to the processes in the *NIST Special*

Publication 800-60, Volume I: Guide to Mapping Types of Information and Information Systems to Security Categories, August 2008. This special publication provides the instructions needed to comply with the Federal Information Processing Standard (FIPS) 199 process for determining system security categorization. FIPS 199 establishes security categories for both information and information systems. The security categories are based on the potential impact to the information and/or an information system and the organization should the system be compromised.

The following table illustrates the NIST SP 800-60, Volume I, process roadmap for determining and assigning the security category and using this to identify the security controls essential to protect the information system and its information. This process assumes that the information system has already been categorized by type, life cycle status, and accreditation boundary (described in Chapter 5) in sufficient detail to initiate the information analysis.

Table 15: Process roadmap

Process	Activities	Roles
Input: information system identification (described in Chapter 5)	Type of information system (e.g. general support system, major application, or even outsourced or platform IT). Life cycle status (e.g. concept, design, development, deployment, operation, or removal from the inventory). Accreditation boundary (e.g. identification of responsible DAA).	CIO, PM, system owner
Subtask 1: identify information type(s)	Determine business and mission area(s). Identify all of the information processed by the information system(s). Document the information types.	Information owner, PM, IAM

Subtask 2: select initial impact level	Determine the security category based on the requirement for confidentiality, integrity, and availability based on FIPS 199 criteria. Document the initial impact level.	Information owner, IAM or IAO
Subtask 3: review initial impact level	Review the initial impact level based on consideration of mission, environment, system use, legal requirements, and interconnection. Adjust as required. Document the adjusted impact level.	CIO, SIASO, PM, information owner
Subtask 4: assign system security category	Determine system security category based on the high water mark for confidentiality, integrity, and availability. Assign the overall information system impact level. Document the system security category.	CIO, SIASO, IAM or IAO, information owner
Output: final security categoriz- ation	Used to determine the necessary security controls required to effectively protect the information and the information system. Use standardized security controls available in the respective security control catalogs.	CIO, IAM or IAO, AO, developers, SMEs

Subtask 1: Identify the information type(s)

The first step in this process is to identify all of the applicable information types transmitted, stored, or processed on the information system. The basis for the identification of information types is Office of Management and Budget's (OMB) Business Reference Model (BRM) described in the October 2007 publication,

Federal Enterprise Architecture (FEA) Consolidated Reference Model Document, Version 2.3.

The BRM reference model is translated into information types in NIST SP 800-60, Volume I, which is used in tandem with NIST SP 800-60, **Volume II:** *Appendices to Guide to Mapping Types of Information and Information Systems to Security Categories*, August 2008.[64] NIST SP 800-60, Volume II, categorizes the specific information types in the federal government and provides a methodology for identifying these information types and assigning provisional security impact levels. While these information types and the associated processes described here focus on the federal government and its information, these same documents can also guide other, non-government organizations in defining their own information types.

NIST SP 800-60, Volume I, organizes federal information into two broad categories: mission-based information types and management and support information types. The information system owner is responsible for identifying to the authorization team the information types stored in, processed by, transmitted by, or generated by an information system.

---

[64] It is important to note that NIST SP 800-60 does not cover information processed by National Security Systems. The guidelines for categorizing this information will be a future issue as part of the authorization transformation.

Mission-based information types are, by definition, specific to individual government agencies or to specific sets of government agencies and focus on services for citizens. The approach to establishing mission-based information types at an agency level begins by determining the agency's primary business and mission areas.

In the case of mission-based information, the responsible individuals, in coordination with management, operational, and security stakeholders, should compile a comprehensive set of lines of business and mission areas conducted by

Mission areas and information types

- D1. Defense & national security
- D2. Homeland security
- D3. Intelligence operations
- D4. Disaster management
- D5. International affairs & commerce
- D6. Natural resources
- D7. Energy
- D8. Environmental management
- D9. Economic development
- D10. Community & social services
- D11. Transportation
- D12. Education
- D13. Workforce management
- D14. Health
- D15. Income security
- D16. Law enforcement
- D16. Litigation & judicial activities
- D18. Federal correctional activities
- D19. General sciences & innovation

Service delivery mechanisms and information types

- D20. Knowledge creation & management
- D21. Regulatory compliance & enforcement
- D22. Public goods creation & management
- D23. Federal financial assistance
- D24. Credit and insurance
- D25. Transfers to state/local governments
- D26. Direct services for citizens

the agency. In addition, the responsible individuals should identify all of the applicable sub-functions necessary to conduct agency business and accomplish the agency's mission.

There are 26 information mission areas sub-divided into 98 supported information types. Details on each of these information types are provided in Volume II, Appendix D, *Examples of Impact Determination for Mission-based Information and Information Systems*.

For example, **mission area 16** is applicable when law enforcement is the agency's primary mission. Sub-functions of the law enforcement mission might include criminal investigation and surveillance, criminal apprehension and incarceration, citizen protection, crime prevention, and property protection. Each of these sub-functions would represent an information type.

A lot of federal government information and associated supporting information systems are not employed directly to provide direct mission-based services, but are primarily intended to support delivery of services or to manage resources.

The **management and support information types** are composed of 13 lines of business subdivided into 72 sub-functions.

The service support functions focus on the

Service delivery functions and information types

- C.2.1. Controls & oversight
- C.2.2. Regulatory development
- C.2.3. Planning & budgeting
- C.2.4. Internal risk management & mitigation
- C.2.5. Revenue collection
- C.2.6. Public affairs
- C.2.7. Legislative relations
- C.2.8. General government

Government resource functions and information types

- C.3.1. Administrative management
- C.3.2. Financial management
- C.3.3. Human resource management
- C.3.4. Supply chain management
- C.3.5. Information & technology management

day-to-day activities that provide the critical policy, programmatic, and managerial activities that are essential to federal government operations. The direct service missions and constituencies that are ultimately supported by the service support functions are significant in determining the security impacts associated with the compromise of information associated with the delivery of services.

The management and support information types also include those back office support activities which enable the federal government to function effectively. There are five government resource management information lines of business and sub-functions associated with each.

Many federal agencies have their own internal support systems. Others may obtain some of their support services from other organizations. As a result, there are some agencies whose mission is to primarily support other federal agencies in the conduct of their direct service missions.

Other information types not identified in the guidelines: It is likely that NIST SP 800-60, Volumes I and II, cannot list *all* of the information types associated with the functions of the federal government. Organizations that identify information that cannot be directly associated with any of these information types are still able to use the guidelines to develop provisional impact levels for their unique information types.

Subtask 2: Select the provisional or initial impact level

Once the information type has been identified, the organization has established the foundation for determining the provisional or initial impact level. The provisional impact level refers to the level assigned to the information based on the confidentiality, integrity, and availability security objectives of an information type derived from NIST SP 800-60, Volume II. This occurs prior to making any organizationally specific adjustments.

In step two, the initial security categorization for the information type is also established and documented. NIST SP 800-60, Volume

II, Appendix C suggests provisional confidentiality, integrity, and availability impact levels for management and support information types, and Volume II, Appendix D provides examples of provisional impact level assignments for mission-based information types.

In those cases where an information type processed by an information system is not categorized by the NIST SP 800-60 guidelines, the organization will have to make its initial impact determination for each information type received by, processed in, stored in, and/or generated by each system for which they are responsible based on the FIPS 199 categorization criteria depicted in the table below. There are three factors that must be considered:

- **Confidentiality:** Confidentiality of information is most frequently associated with its sensitivity or classification level. In most cases, information will be categorized for confidentiality purposes as *public* (open to anyone), *sensitive* (limited exposure of information, such as personal health information), or *classified* (confidential, secret, top secret). *Without exception, the confidentiality level for classified information is considered high.* Use the following questions to guide your determination:

  - Would the loss of confidentiality of the information through an unauthorized or unintentional disclosure result in a limited, serious, or catastrophic effect on the organization?
  - How could an unauthorized or unintentional disclosure resulting in the loss of confidentiality occur?
  - Would an unauthorized or unintentional disclosure violate any laws, regulations, or policies?

- **Integrity:** The loss of information integrity is most frequently associated with unauthorized (or unintentional) modification or destruction. An undetected loss of integrity has the potential for catastrophic results. These could be either direct (e.g. modification of a financial entry, medical alert, or criminal record) or indirect (e.g. facilitation of unauthorized access to sensitive or private information or denial of access to information or information system services). In most cases, the most catastrophic impact would occur on time-critical information, such as the information required in making a rapid battlefield decision.

Some results of an integrity loss could be: reduced public confidence in an organization, the creation of confusion or doubt about the quality of the information, or the intentional or unintentional influence upon a decision making official. Use the following questions to guide your determination:

- Would the unauthorized or unintentional modification or destruction of information result in a limited, serious or catastrophic effect on the organization?
- Would the unauthorized or unintentional modification or destruction of information violate any laws, regulations or policies?

- **Availability:** For many information types and information systems, the availability impact level will depend on how long the information or the information system remains unavailable to authorized users. The undetected loss of availability can be catastrophic for many information types. For example, the permanent or even temporary unavailability of financial or resource management, contingency planning, security management, inventory control, or logistics management information could be serious, or even catastrophic, for almost any agency. Use the following questions to guide your determination:

  - Would intentional or unintentional acts affecting information or information system availability result in a limited, serious, or catastrophic effect on the organization?
  - Would intentional or unintentional acts affecting information or information system availability violate any laws, regulations or policies?

Using the questions above and the FIPS Publication 199 table, an organization can assign an initial impact level for confidentiality, integrity, and availability. For example, information on a public web server may be assigned a low confidentiality impact rating, a moderate integrity impact rating, and a high availability impact rating. Classified research and development information might be assigned a high confidentiality and integrity impact rating, but a low availability impact rating.

Table 16: FIPS Publication 199

FIPS Publication 199	Low	Moderate	High
Confidentiality	The loss of confidentiality could be expected to have a limited adverse effect on organizational operations, organizational assets, or individuals.	The loss of confidentiality could be expected to have a serious adverse effect on organizational operations, organizational assets, or individuals.	The loss of confidentiality could be expected to have a severe or catastrophic adverse effect on organizational operations, organizational assets, or individuals.
Integrity	The loss of integrity could be expected to have a limited adverse effect on organizational operations, organizational assets, or individuals.	The loss of integrity could be expected to have a serious adverse effect on organizational operations, organizational assets, or individuals.	The loss of integrity could be expected to have a severe or catastrophic adverse effect on organizational operations, organizational assets, or individuals.
Availability	The loss of availability could be expected to have a limited adverse effect on organizational operations, organizational assets, or individuals.	The loss of availability could be expected to have a serious adverse effect on organizational operations, organizational assets, or individuals.	The loss of availability could be expected to have a severe or catastrophic adverse effect on organizational operations, organizational assets, or individuals.

This leads us to Step 3, which requires the organization to review and potentially adjust the provisional or initial impact ratings.

Subtask 3: Review the provisional/initial impact levels and adjust

In this step, organizations should review and adjust the initial impact levels for each information type and information system in order to arrive at a finalized statement of impact. This review should consider such items as the agency's mission and its importance to national security or required government functions, system or policy life cycle implications, configuration and security policy related information, special handling requirements, environmental considerations, and any other organizationally-unique specifications.

It is important to consider the impact for an information or information system type throughout its life cycle. For example, contract information may have a moderate or even high confidentiality impact level during the life of the contract, but may have only a low impact level once the contract execution period is completed. Policy-related information may have moderate confidentiality and integrity impact levels during the policy development process, low confidentiality and moderate integrity impact levels during the policy implementation period, and low confidentiality and integrity impact levels once the policy has become obsolete.

Rarely do information systems process a single type of information, nor will all of the information types processed by an information system always have the same security impact levels. The compromise of some information types might cause more damage than the compromise of other information types within the same information system. As a result, system security impact levels must be assessed in the context of system mission and function, as well as on the basis of the aggregate of the component information types.

In addition to the mission-related information processed by the information system, the associated configuration and security policy enforcement information should also be considered in terms of impact level. Configuration and security policy information includes such things as password files, network access rules, hardware and software configuration settings, and documentation affecting access to or the integrity of the information system's data, programs, and/or processes. At a minimum, a low confidentiality and integrity impact level will always apply to this set of information due to the potential for corruption, misuse, or abuse of system information and processes.

As mentioned earlier, classified information will always have a high confidentiality impact. However, there are also other types of information that may have a higher confidentiality impact level based on the organization's mission. These include information types, such as Trade Secrets Act information, information protected by the Privacy Act, Department of Energy Safeguards Information, Internal Revenue Service Official Use Only Information, and Environmental Protection Agency Confidential Business Information.

Another consideration that might affect the impact level of information may be the existence of other, compensating security safeguards. For example, research and development information may be classified, but knowledge of and access to the information could be very strictly limited to only a highly select set of individuals. In this case, the integrity impact – and the associated security requirements – might be reduced to moderate based on the additional access restrictions.

Once all of these additional considerations are applied, the organization may adjust the impact levels for confidentiality, integrity, and availability to either a higher or lower level. Once the final impact levels are determined, the organization will proceed to step four: assigning the overall system security category.

Subtask 4: Assign system security category

The last step in this process is assigning the system security category based on the confidentiality, integrity, and availability impacts determined for the information or the information type aggregate. For federal agencies, the security category is the prerequisite for identifying and assigning the security controls, or the safeguards deemed essential to addressing the requirements of the information and the information system. The individual activities in step four include:

- Review identified security categorizations for the information or the aggregate of information types.
- Determine the system security categorization by identifying the high water mark for confidentiality, integrity and availability based on the aggregate of the information types.
- Adjust the high water mark for each system security objective, as necessary, by applying the factors discussed in the section above.
- Assign the overall information system impact level based on the highest impact level – or high water mark – for the system security objectives.
- Document all security categorization determinations and decisions.

It is a well known fact that information systems consist of information and the software applications that allow that information to be processed, transmitted, and stored. These applications are essential for the information system to conduct its essential business functions and operations. These applications must also be protected and could be subject to security categorization as well. However, in the interest of simplification, federal agencies will provide at least a minimum categorization of low for the information system operations. This is necessary to protect the system-level processing functions and information critical to the operation of the information system itself.

According to FIPS 199, the general formula for determining the security category is:

Security category (**SC**) information type = {(**CONFIDENTIALITY** impact), (**INTEGRITY** impact), (**AVAILABILITY** impact)}, where the acceptable values for impact are **LOW**, **MODERATE**, **HIGH**, OR **NOT APPLICABLE**[65].

Here are a few examples of how the assignment of information security category might work.

---

[65] According to FIPS 199, not applicable can only be assigned to the confidentiality category.

System 1: A public web server

A federal agency provides public information on a publicly accessible e-Government website. Since the information on the web server is public, there is no confidentiality impact associated with its loss or exposure. However, since the information is part of the agency's public information project, a loss of integrity might be considered moderate. Availability is important, but not critical, so any impact to availability might also be considered moderate. Using the formula above, the security category for this information would be expressed as:

SC public information = {(**CONFIDENTIALITY** *not applicable*), (**INTEGRITY** *moderate*), (**AVAILABILITY** *moderate*)} where the high water mark for the overall security categorization = **MODERATE**

System 2: A financial organization

An agency processes highly sensitive financial information. Since this information also involves personal privacy information, a loss of confidentiality and integrity would be considered high. Availability of this information is important, but not necessarily critical, so the impact to availability might be considered moderate. Using the formula for security categorization, the security category for this information would be expressed as:

SC financial and personal information = {(**CONFIDENTIALITY** *high*), (**INTEGRITY** *high*), (**AVAILABILITY** *moderate*)} where the high water mark for the overall security categorization = **HIGH**

Determining the security category of an information system processing multiple types of information is often more difficult and requires additional analysis. For an information system, the overall security category for the information system will be based on the highest values for confidentiality, integrity, and availability that have been determined for *each type* of information resident on the information system. Here is an example:

System 3: A medical management system

An agency is responsible for processing information about medical care provided to a specific group of recipients. This information is personal and confidential and its integrity is essential to providing the correct medical care to its constituency. The agency also uses the information system to process routine administrative information associated with the day-to-day operations of the agency. The agency determines that for the patient information there is a high potential impact from the loss of confidentiality, integrity and availability. It also determines that for the agency's administrative information, the impact of the loss of confidentiality, integrity, and availability are low. Using the formula for security categorization, the security category for this information would be expressed as:

SC patient information = {(<u>CONFIDENTIALITY</u> *high*), (<u>INTEGRITY</u> *high*), (<u>AVAILABILITY</u> *high*)}

SC administrative information = {(<u>CONFIDENTIALITY</u> *low*), (<u>INTEGRITY</u> *low*), (<u>AVAILABILITY</u> *low*)} where the high water mark for the overall security categorization = <u>HIGH</u>

In this case, the resulting security category for the information system using the high water mark would be expressed as:

SC medical management system = {(<u>CONFIDENTIALITY</u> *high*), (<u>INTEGRITY</u> *high*), (<u>AVAILABILITY</u> *high*)} where the high water mark for the overall security categorization = <u>HIGH</u>.

There are other factors that might influence the final assignment of system security category. These include factors such as: information aggregation, system interconnectivity, and extenuating circumstances.[66]

Information aggregation: In some cases, information may not be sensitive in isolation, but an aggregation of the information could reveal sensitive patterns and plans, or facilitate access to sensitive or critical systems. In general, the sensitivity of a given data element is more likely to be greater in a given context than in isolation (e.g. association of an account number with the identity of an individual and/or institution). The availability and sophistication of data aggregation and inference tools are all increasing rapidly, causing a different level of threat environment.

If a review of the information aggregation reveals increased sensitivity or criticality, then the system security impact levels might need to be adjusted to a higher level than necessary for a discrete

---

[66] Extenuating circumstances might include an elevation in the threat environment or in the geographical location.

type of information. This could be explained in a statement that discusses the aggregation and how it affects the security category.

System interconnectivity: Impact of a compromise of the confidentiality, integrity, and availability of some information types may be low in the context of a system's primary function, but may be much more significant when considered in the context of:

- other systems to which the system is connected, or
- other systems which are dependent on that system's information.

Extenuating circumstances: There are times when a security category needs to be elevated based on reasons other than its information or the information system. Examples of extenuating circumstances include:

- Increased visibility of the information system and its information.
- An elevation in the threat environment, for example, an information system in a high threat area.
- An extremely large number of other systems is reliant on its operation.

Additional notes on security category

It is important to note that the use of the high water mark for assigning a security category is unique to the process in NIST SP 800-37. The assignment of security category by this method is scheduled to change in NIST SP 800-37, Revision 1, which is currently in draft, and will be discussed in greater detail in Chapter 17.

In the Department of Defense, there is no equivalent to the process used by the federal agencies in assigning a security category. Although the current DOD process is detailed in Chapter 10, let's have a quick overview here. The process for determining the confidentiality impact is similar – except that in the DOD, information is either public (equivalent to low), sensitive (equivalent to moderate), or classified, which is always high.

The primary difference, however, lies in the assignment of an impact level for availability and integrity. In the DOD, these are currently combined into the *Mission Assurance Category (MAC)* and the impact levels are assigned as below:

- MAC I — information and information systems determined to be vital to the operational readiness or mission effectiveness. Any loss of integrity or availability is unacceptable. MAC I systems require the most stringent protection measures.
- MAC II — information and information systems important to the support of the operational readiness or mission. Loss of integrity is unacceptable; loss of availability would be difficult and tolerated only for a short period of time.
- MAC III — information and information systems handling information necessary for the conduct of day-to-day business. Loss of integrity and availability could be tolerated without significant impacts to mission effectiveness or operational readiness.

The determination of the security category, whether it is NIST's confidentiality, integrity, and availability consideration or DOD's combination of MAC and confidentiality, is the critical prerequisite to identifying the appropriate security safeguards for that information and information system.

The final output: Identification of the security controls baseline

When you consider that 99% of all information system incidents are the result of known vulnerabilities, configuration errors, or operator actions, information system security controls are critically important. Controls have three distinct purposes: threat reduction, vulnerability reduction, and asset value enhancing.

For federal information systems, excluding the Department of Defense, the security controls for information systems are contained in NIST Special Publication 800-53, *Recommended Security Controls for Federal Information Systems. (See the accompanying CD.)* Once the overall impact level of the information system is determined, an initial set of security controls can be selected from the corresponding low, moderate, or high baselines listed in Appendix D or NIST SP 800-53 based on the security category of the information system.

The security controls for DOD information systems are currently listed in Enclosure 3 of DOD Instruction 8500.2, *Information Assurance Implementation.* Aligning these predefined sets of security controls to the information and the information system

> **Sources of security control baselines**
> 1. Required:
>   a. Federal agencies: NIST Special Publication 800-53, *Recommended Security Controls for Federal Information Systems*
>   b. Department of Defense: DOD Instruction 8500.2, *Information Assurance Implementation*
> 2. Supplementary:
>   a. Agency supplementary guidance
>   b. International and national standards
>   c. System-unique requirements

are based on the security categories defined by MAC and confidentiality level.

Whether using the security controls list provided in NIST SP 800.53 for federal agencies or the DOD security controls provided in DODI 8500.2, each provides a baseline or starting point for federal or DOD agencies in addressing the necessary safeguards and countermeasures required for their information systems. The controls for both federal agencies and the DOD are aligned to three control categories: management controls, operational controls, and technical controls.

> **Security control categories**
> - Management
> - Operational
> - Technical

- **Management controls** address those security activities that focus on the management of risk and information system security, such as the establishment and maintenance of an

> **Management controls**
> - Risk assessment
> - Security planning
> - System & services acquisition
> - Security control review
> - Processing authorization

information systems security program. Management vulnerabilities are often rooted in the lack of appropriate or comprehensive policies and procedures. Examples include the security program management, appointment and training of security personnel, and budgeting for security.

- **Operational controls** refer to those security activities that are primarily implemented and executed by people, rather than information systems. Operational controls frequently cross over into management; however, these are often implemented to improve the security of a particular information system or system of systems. They often require technical expertise and rely on the management activities, as well as the technical controls. Operational vulnerabilities are weaknesses in the operational procedures that people execute with respect to an information system. Examples include configuration management, disaster planning, and security training.

> **Operational controls**
> - Personnel security
> - Physical & environmental protection
> - Contingency planning & operations
> - Configuration management
> - Hardware & software management
> - System & information integrity
> - Media protection
> - Incident response
> - Security awareness & training

- **Technical controls** are those that are primarily implemented and executed by the information system through hardware, software, and/or firmware mechanisms. These controls are often dependent upon the proper functioning of the information system for their effectiveness. Also, technical controls must be consistent with the overall security management of the

> **Technical controls**
> - Identification & authentication
> - Logical access control
> - Accountability (including audit)
> - System & communications protection

organization. Technical vulnerabilities are weaknesses in hardware, software, system architecture, and modes of communication. Examples of technical controls include identification and authentication mechanisms, file and system access controls, and anti-virus protection.

Selecting the initial baseline

Both NIST SP 800-53 and DOD 8500.2 provide a mechanism for determining an initial baseline set of controls based on the determined security requirements for the information and the information system. The initial baseline controls are defined as the **minimum** security controls recommended for an information system based on its defined security requirements.

NIST categorizes security controls into the three classes of managerial, operational and technical and then further categorizes the controls within each class into 17 families, or control focus areas. Each security control family contains dozens of specific security controls. Federal agencies select a subset of minimum security controls from the master catalog found in NIST SP 800-53 according to the security categorization for the information system as high, moderate or low.

DOD also categorizes its controls into management, operational and technical classes, but then further categorizes the controls into eight subject areas, each containing multiple individual security controls for a total of 157 controls. The initial security control baseline is determined based on the combination of mission assurance category and confidentiality level.

The initial baseline set of controls serves as the starting point for an organization to identify the protection mechanisms and safeguards essential for their information system. Because the initial baselines are only intended to serve as the minimum basic standard for protection, supplements to the initial

Security control types

* Baseline
* Supplementary
* Complementary

baselines may be necessary in order to achieve the desired level of risk mitigation. The initial baselines can be supplemented or compensated based on organizational assessments of risk and the resulting determination of the need for additional security safeguards.

Supplementing the initial baseline

Organizations should supplement the minimum initial baseline as appropriate, to define, develop, and implement security controls. In addition to the baseline security controls, NIST SP 800-53 provides supplementary enhancements for the minimum baseline controls. In DOD, supplementary guidance or supplementary requirements are specified by the individual DOD entities and not in the basic DOD instruction.

In most cases, the supplemental guidance provides additional detail about the basic controls or specific considerations for implementing the minimum security controls in the context of an organization's operational environment, specific mission requirements, or assessment of risk. In addition, applicable laws, executive orders, directives, policies, regulations, standards, and guidance documents are taken into consideration, when appropriate, for the particular security control.

The control enhancements or supplementation guidance must not contradict or negate the baseline controls. Nor should they degrade interoperability or functionality of the information system.

Control enhancements, or supplementary guidance and requirements, are intended to:

- build in additional, related security functionality to an existing control;
- increase the security strength of an existing control;
- add specific controls to meet unique organizational requirements.

In addition to control enhancements or supplementary guidance, some organizations may find it necessary to identify and implement compensating security controls. A compensating control is a management, operational, or technical control employed by an organization in place of a recommended control defined in NIST SP 800-53 or DODI 8500.2. The compensating control must provide an equivalent or comparable protection for the information system.

A compensating control can only be used under the following conditions:

- The organization has selected a compensating control from another security control catalog or within the same control catalog, and the control represents an upgrade in the stringency requirement.
- The organization provides a complete and convincing justification describing how the compensating control provides an equivalent or comparable protection for the information and the information system.
- The organization assesses and formally accepts the risk associated with employing the compensating control.

Like the baseline control enhancements or supplementary controls, compensating controls must be documented in the system's security plan and approved by the DAA or authorizing official for the information system.

Identifying common or inherited controls

The final action in determining the appropriate set of controls, which will then be implemented by the organization, is the identification of common or inherited controls.[67] Common or inherited controls are the result of a state in which the security control, along with its validation results and compliance status, is shared across two or more information systems for the purpose of authorization.

The use of common or inherited controls reduces the complexity of controls implementation and testing, and eliminates validation test redundancy (and the associated costs). Identifying the specific

---

[67] The term "common controls" is used by NIST while DOD uses the term "inherited controls."

security controls which may be shared is a cooperative effort between the originating and the receiving information systems. It is most effectively accomplished as an organization-wide effort involving the senior leadership of the organization and the security authorization team.

Many of the security controls designed to protect an information system and its information may be excellent candidates for inheritance or as a common control. Examples include contingency planning, incident response, security training and awareness, physical and environmental safeguards, and intrusion detection.

Common or inherited security controls can be applied to:

- all organizational information systems;
- a group of information systems at a specific site;
- common information systems, subsystems, or applications (i.e. common hardware, software and/or firmware) deployed at multiple operational sites.

Common or inherited security controls have the following properties:

- The development, implementation, and validation of the common/inherited security controls may be assigned to responsible organizational officials or organizational elements, who may not be the information system owners whose systems will implement or use the common security controls; and
- The results from the validation of the common/inherited security controls can be applied to support the security certification and accreditation processes of other information systems within the organization where the controls have been applied.

Organizations may also assign a **hybrid** status to a security control in the specific situation where one part of the control is common or inherited, and the other is deemed to be system specific. For example, an organization may view disaster and recovery planning as a master template for all organizational information systems, while individual system owners may tailor the plan as appropriate for system-specific requirements.

While the concept of common/inherited controls is relatively straightforward, the application within an organization takes planning, coordination, and communication. Initially, it may take some time to introduce the concept and to get the benefits. And there is one final consideration: because of the potential dependence on a common/inherited security control by many of an organization's information systems, failure of a common/inherited control could result in an increase in agency-level risk.

Figure 9: Common/inherited controls

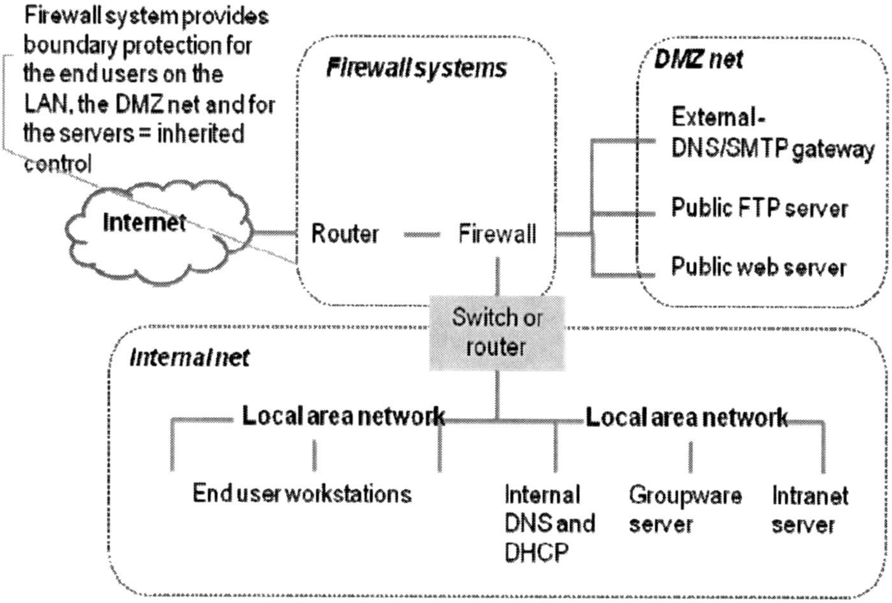

The diagram above depicts a standard network configuration where common/inherited controls might be applied. Here is an enclave hosting three information systems behind a firewall, which is on the boundary of the network. The firewall provides boundary level protection to all of the systems in site two. The overall network would reflect that the boundary defense control(s) are satisfied in part by the shared firewall. All of the systems sharing the firewall, including the network itself, would document this relationship in the system security plan. The status of the boundary defense control for firewall protection, all test results, and supporting materiel would be passed from the network to the sharing systems.

Benefits of common/inherited controls

Partitioning the security controls into common/inherited and system-specific security controls can result in significant savings to the organization in terms of control development and implementation costs. Partitioning can also result in a more consistent application of the security controls across the entire enterprise.

Equally significant savings may be realized in the actual certification and accreditation process. Rather than assessing common/inherited security controls for every individual system, the process can draw upon the results from the most current evaluation of the common/inherited controls at the enterprise level.

Finally, an organization-wide approach to reuse and sharing of validation results can greatly enhance the efficiency of the authorization process.

OUTPUT FROM STEP 1: UNDERSTAND THE INFORMATION SYSTEM

* IDENTIFY THE SYSTEM SECURITY CATEGORY
* DEVELOP THE LIST OF ASSIGNED BASELINE, SUPPLEMENTARY, COMPLEMENTARY, AND COMMON/INHERITED CONTROLS

REGISTER the information system

Registration of the information system is a critical step in ensuring that the information system is recognized in the organization's system inventory. Registration can be as sophisticated as the formal entry in a comprehensive agency-level database or as simple as an entry in a spreadsheet on a laptop.

Depending on your organizational preferences, you may be asked to register the system prior to the security categorization process. And that is how it is done in the NIST SP 800-37. However, most system registrations require an understanding of the information system and some indication of the impact level and protection requirements for that system. So, as a result, we have put system registration after the security categorization process.

Who is involved?

The primary responsibility for information system registration lies with the owner of the information system, often also the program manager (PM). The PM, or system owner, is supported in this process by the information assurance manager (IAM).

Step 2 players

- Primary role: Information system owner and/or program manager
- Supporting roles:
  - IAM/ISSM
  - Information owner
  - SIASO

The registration process

The actual process of registration varies widely according to the organization. But regardless of the process, there is one overwhelming rational for registration. To ensure that information systems are protected and subjected to the certification and accreditation process, the organization must be aware of the existence of its information systems. Otherwise, there is no assurance that the enterprise itself can be adequately protected. Information system registration also provides organizations with an effective management and tracking tool, which provides the essential foundation for security status reporting to meet FISMA and OMB compliance requirements.

Registration begins with the system description and concludes with the preparation of the initial draft of the system security plan (SSP). All of the information collected so far now serves to prepare the preliminary SSP:

- Authorization team

- Risk assessment
- System description, including the system architecture
- Accreditation boundary
- Security category and protection requirements
- Scope and level of effort.

It's all about the money!

But one of the primary reasons for registering an information system is funding. For all information system initiatives, federal agencies are required to report the percentage of resources needed to information assurance (IA) activities for the budget year.

Registration, whether formal or informal, is done in accordance with existing organizational policy. It requires the information generated in Step 1, UNDERSTAND the information system, to inform the governing organization of:

- the existence of the information system;
- the key characteristics of the system; and
- any security implications for the organization as a consequence of system operation.

Each federal agency has its process for information system registration. And at the highest level within DOD, information systems are registered in the *Department of Defense Information Technology Portfolio Repository* (DITPR). At the same time, each DOD service has its own information system database:

- Army Portfolio Management Solution (APMS)
- Air Force Enterprise Information Technology Data Repository (EITDR)
- Department of the Navy Application Database Management System (DADMS).

Some of the registration requirements are mandated under the Federal Information Security Management Act (FISMA) and the requirement to make an annual report of system security status to the Office of Management and Budget (OMB). These include the assignment of a unique OMB identification number for the information system. This number will remain part of the information system security reporting throughout the information system life cycle.

Information that might be included in the system registration includes, but is not limited to:

- Registry number
- Information system name
- Information system acronym
- System description
- Mission criticality
- System life cycle stage
- Program management information
- Designated accrediting authority information
- Security information:

  - Security category
  - Security costs
  - Authorization status
  - Date of accreditation
  - Accreditation expiration date
  - Privacy impact assessment
  - Security controls validation test
  - Annual security controls review
  - Plan of action & milestones
  - Contingency plan
  - Security training
  - Risk assessment
  - Accreditation vehicle (e.g. DOD, NIST, etc.).

OUTPUT FROM STEP 2: REGISTER THE INFORMATION SYSTEM

- SYSTEM ENTERED IN ORGANIZATIONAL INVENTORY

NEGOTIATE the authorization approach

At this point, the information system has been defined, the accreditation boundary established, the security requirements have been identified and the system has been registered in whichever way is mandated by the organization. You've done a lot of work to set your system up for the actual process of executing certification and accreditation.

The next step is a careful negotiation among all key participants – considering all the mission/business requirements of the agency, the technical considerations with respect to information security, and the programmatic costs to the agency.

Step 3 players

- Primary roles: Information system owner and/or program manager and DAA
- Supporting roles:
    - IAM/ISSM
    - Information owner
    - CA
    - User representative
    - Organization management

Participants in the negotiation process include those involved in the information systems development, acquisition, operation, security certification, and accreditation.

The objective of this step is to arrive at an agreement regarding the actions required to adequately address system threats and vulnerabilities, and produce an acceptable level of residual risk. These actions should include incorporating security features into the system design, as well as administrative procedures implemented in the operational environment.

Negotiations will often include the DAA, as well as the CA, PM and user representative. The negotiation process looks at all information system data collected to date and concludes with an agreement regarding the level of effort. The parties to the negotiation have the authority to tailor the authorization process to meet the characteristics of the information system and its operational requirements, security policy, and prudent risk management.

Negotiation is NOT a consideration of which security requirements to implement and which are not applicable. This determination has already been made during Step 1. The real purpose of the negotiation step is to ensure that all participants in the authorization process understand their roles and responsibilities and that the approach and level of effort are properly and clearly defined.

Negotiations associated with system type

In Chapter 5, we discussed types of information systems and some of the accreditation considerations, particularly in connection with determining the accreditation boundary. The type of information system also influences how the authorization process might be approached. This determination is another part of the negotiation. So, to refresh your memory, here are the primary types of information systems:

Major applications (MAs)/AIS applications[68]

The approach to the accreditation of major applications or AIS applications can either streamline or complicate the accreditation process. So, let's look at how you can negotiate to avoid unnecessary complication and facilitate accreditation.

Typically, a major application (MA) or AIS application is developed and deployed under the auspices of a designated program office and has an assigned program manager. In this case, the baseline authorization of the MA should be centralized and managed from a central integration and test facility or at a representative intended operating site. This eliminates the need to conduct the testing of the common system components (e.g. hardware, firmware, and/or software) at multiple sites. At the conclusion of the baseline IA controls implementation, testing, and certification, the test results,

---

[68] In prior documentation, such as the DITSCAP, this might also be referred to as type accreditation.

the CA's recommendation, and the accreditation results can be centrally documented in a baseline system security plan (SSP).

Of course, it is not possible to centrally implement and test the security controls for all possible types of deployments or locations, so the authorization process for an MA or AIS application should focus on a typical operating environment. *The first level of negotiation will focus on identifying this "typical operating environment" and the associated security design, implementation, and testing requirements.* Once completed, this type of accreditation then becomes the official authorization to deploy identical copies of the information system and will be documented in the accompanying SSP.

Site owners must ensure that all of the required documentation – including the C&A documentation – is included with the deployment of an MA or AIS application at their site.

It should not be necessary for each site to repeat the baseline authorization requirements, since the results of the centralized effort will accompany the system to each site where it will be deployed. *In this case, negotiation regarding authorization requirements should concentrate on identifying, implementing, and testing ONLY those security controls associated with the specific system installation and configuration at the target site.*

In every case, the site's information system inventory and associated system security plan (SSP) must be modified to include the documentation on the MA/AIS application. The SSP must identify the specific uses of the system, operational constraints, and operational considerations of including the new MA/AIS application within the existing site or enclave. It will also include the baseline IA requirements/controls necessary to protect the information intended for processing by the MA/AIS application in its target deployments. The receiving organization must ensure that the required documentation, security operating procedures, configuration requirements, and system administrator/user training is included with the system deployment.

General support system (GSS) or enclave

The authorization of a GSS or an enclave can be extremely complicated, particularly if a large number and/or variety of information systems are included within the accreditation boundary. The ***negotiation process will center on the optimal approach to implementation, testing, and accreditation considering the number of information systems, applications, and unique operational characteristics.***

When conducting the authorization of a GSS/enclave, it is very helpful if there is an active configuration control board (CCB) with jurisdiction over and knowledge of the entire GSS/enclave. Their role can be critical in ensuring that all included systems and applications maintain the integrity of the baseline security posture.

A single GSS/enclave SSP can be prepared – but it should include an appendix or a reference to the accreditation documentation for each system or application included in the SSP. Additionally, the GSS/enclave SSP must include the following:

- Site security architecture description.
- List of all information systems and applications.
- Description of how the overall GSS/enclave complies with the identified security requirements.
- Data flow map.
- Information system topology diagram.
- External connections.
- Identification of security controls that are the specific responsibility of the GSS/enclave.

The authorization plan

Information systems security should be as important as system functionality. Therefore, the negotiations should focus on developing an authorization plan that adjusts to the needs of the information system in all phases of its life cycle. The authorization plan should document the tailoring and define the activities negotiated to fit your information system.

In Chapter 5, we discussed how to look at scope, level of effort, and resources. These should be included now in the final authorization plan as it is customized to the requirements of your individual information system. At a minimum, the final negotiated plan should include:

- Accreditation schedule and milestones
- Level of effort
- Authorization team members and their respective roles and responsibilities.

Negotiation ends when the initial SSP is prepared and all responsible organizations and individuals adopt the authorization plan and concur that the required objectives have been reached.

OUTPUT FROM STEP 3: NEGOTIATE THE AUTHORIZATION APPROACH

- RESPONSIBLE ORGANIZATIONS AND INDIVIDUALS AGREE TO THE AUTHORIZATION PLAN
- INITIAL SSP PREPARED

IMPLEMENT the security controls

By this step in the process, you have negotiated an authorization plan specific to your information system and have developed your initial system security plan. If you did your work in defining your information system type and the information properly, you will have also

Step 4 players

- Primary roles: Information system owner and/or program manager, IAM/ISSM, and ISSE
- Supporting roles:
    - Information owner
    - User representative
    - Organization management
    - SMEs
    - Other security managers (e.g. physical, personnel)
    - System/network administrators
    - Etc. as required

identified the security controls needed to properly secure your information system.

Implementation of the security controls is a function of a number of roles, not all of which will be direct members of the IA program or the authorization team. Individuals external to the direct authorization effort, such as the facilities manager, the personnel security manager, network and system administrators and many others are crucial to ensuring that all required security controls and safeguards have been correctly implemented.

While all of these preparatory steps are crucial, the actual implementation of the IA requirements/controls is really where "the rubber meets the road." Both NIST and DOD have provided implementation guidance for the security controls specific to their environments.

For federal information systems, implementation guidance can be derived from the NIST SP 800-53 and the associated testing guide, NIST SP 800-53A. DOD has been a little more direct in providing implementation guidance, which can be found on the DIACAP Knowledge Service website at *https://diacap.iaportal.navy.mil*.[69] Detailed information on implementation guidance for IA requirements/controls is available on the accompanying CD.

Implementation factors

There are several factors to be considered when determining how security controls are best implemented within your environment:

- Technology-related factors
- Infrastructure-related factors
- Public access-related factors

---

[69] Access to this site is restricted to authorized members of the DOD. The entry portal to the site provides information on the criteria for access and the required credentials and permissions.

- Scalability-related factors
- Common security control-related factors
- Risk-related factors.

Each of these will be discussed in more detail in the following sections.

Technology-related implementation factors

Frequently, the type and level of implementation of a security control will be influenced – or even determined – by the existence of or lack of certain types of technologies. Here are some of the considerations:

- **Security controls dependent upon specific technologies** (e.g. wireless, cryptography, VoIP) are only applicable if those technologies are employed or are planned for employment within the information system. If these technologies are not present, the security control cannot be implemented and will be identified as not applicable.
- **Security controls may be specific to the security capability addressed by the control and the associated components of the information system.** For example, audit-related security controls would typically be implemented on those elements of the information system that provide auditing capability (e.g. servers) and not necessarily applied to every user-level workstation. Access controls are not typically applied to devices, such as printers, faxes, or other components of the overall information system that provide only a limited functionality. NOTE: Organizations should, however, carefully assess the individual components of their information system to determine which security controls are applicable to the various components in their security environment. As technology continues to advance, increased functionality present in devices associated with the information system, such as personal digital assistants and cell phones, may require the application of additional security controls in accordance with the organization's identified risk.

Infrastructure-related implementation factors

The infrastructure in which the information system is deployed will influence the level and type of security control that is implemented.

- **Security controls designed for the organizational facilities** (e.g. physical security controls, such as locks and guards; environmental controls for temperature, humidity, fire protection, and power) are considered only in those situations where the facilities provide protection to, support, or are related to the information system. In most cases, implementation of these security controls is NOT the responsibility of the individual(s) responsible for the information system itself. However, responsibility for confirming the implementation is the responsibility of the authorization team.
- **Infrastructure-related security controls are generally not applicable to major applications/AIS applications.**

Public access-related implementation factors

Not all federal or DOD information systems allow public access, but if they do, there are special considerations. These information systems must frequently allow the maximum access, while concurrently provide a level of security essential to the protection of the function of the systems and the information contained within. Security controls for public access information systems must be carefully considered and applied with discretion.

Considerations include:

- **Security baseline controls may not be applicable to information systems where users are accessing the system through a public interface.** For example, both federal and DOD baseline control sets require identification and authentication for access, but these same security controls cannot be applied to publicly accessed systems.
- **Publicly-accessed information systems may require additional levels of implementation of boundary protection security**

controls. Public interfaces are often more exposed to attacks than information systems with a more restricted set of users.

Scalability-related implementation factors

When determining security implementation requirements, **organizations should also consider the size of the organization or the information system being protected – or both.** For example, the IT contingency plan for a large organization with a moderate, or high impact information system could be quite lengthy and complex. In contrast, a contingency plan for a smaller organization or a standalone information system would likely be considerably shorter and contain much less implementation detail.

Common/inherited control-related implementation factors

Security controls can be designated by the organization as common controls or inherited controls. In this case, they may be managed by an organizational entity other than the information system owner. This does not, however, affect the responsibility of the organization with regards to the implementation of the baseline controls. Every control must either be addressed or identified as not applicable. Here are some considerations:

- **Identifying common or inherited controls is a cooperative effort between the organization's "originating" and "receiving" information system(s).** The identification of common controls is most effective when accomplished as an organization-wide activity. By centrally managing the identification, implementation, and assessment of common controls, security costs can often be amortized across multiple information systems.
- **Some controls may be assigned a hybrid status**, i.e. one part of the security control is common, while another part of the security control is determined to be system-specific. For example, the organization may have a master template for a disaster recovery

plan, while individual information system owners may need to tailor the plan, where appropriate, for system-specific issues.

Risk-related implementation factors

With the diverse nature of today's information systems, organizations must consider risk in determining the cost-benefit relationship of implementing security controls. **In some cases, the risk determination may point to the need to identify and employ compensating controls.**[70] In all cases, the organization must assess and formally accept the risk associated with employing a compensating control.

Implementation guidance

By its very nature, implementation guidance for the security controls must be relatively generic – it cannot provide the level of detail needed to address every possible design, configuration, or deployment possibility. More often than not, the implementation guidance itself is not specific and will refer to one or more policy or technical implementation documents.

The examples below indicate the type of implementation guidance one might expect to find.

Operational or management control

Disaster recovery planning falls in the family of operational and/or management controls. The implementation guidance might be written in this way:

A disaster recovery plan will exist that provides for the resumption of business or mission essential functions within 24 hours of activation. Disaster recovery procedures will include business recovery plans,

---

[70] A compensating control can be defined as a management, operational, or technical safeguard employed by an organization in lieu of a control recommended in the basic controls requirements publications.

system contingency plans, facility disaster recovery plans, and proof of plan acceptance and testing.

In most cases, references will be provided for further information. In this case, one might be referred to DOD Directive 3020.26, *Defense Continuity Program*, or to NIST SP 800-34, *Contingency Planning Guide for Information Systems*, which can be found on the accompanying CD.

Technical control

There are a number of technical controls designed to address a variety of operating systems and/or applications. The implementation guidance might look like this:

User interface services will be physically or logically separated from data storage and management services. This is called "Partitioning the Application." Separation may be accomplished through the use of different computers and/or services, operating systems, network addresses, or a combination of these methods as appropriate.

The Defense Information Systems Agency (DISA) has published an extensive library of Security Technical Implementation Guides (STIGs), to include a DISA Web Server STIG. This STIG provides technical level instructions on exactly how to partition an application in order to meet the generic implementation guidance provided by the security control itself.

STIGs and other similar technology implementation guides are updated regularly to reflect changes in information technology. As a result, whenever one of these guides is used, be sure to check the originator to ensure that you are following the most current guidance.

Results of implementation: Evidence or artifacts

Artifacts, or evidence, provide visible proof of the security control implementation. These can be an intentional product of the implementation process, e.g. developed specifically to provide proof of implementation, such as a policy or set of procedures.

Artifacts can also be generated as a by-product of the development, deployment, and operations of the information system(s). Artifacts,[71] or evidence of compliant implementation, can be:

- Information system standard operating policies, such as written data backup procedures, together with the actual backup media.
- Documentation, such as the hardware and software inventories maintained by the configuration management board or by an automated configuration management system.
- Plans, such as the disaster recovery or continuity of operations plan.
- Test results, such as the results of a vulnerability scan from a common scan application, such as Retina or Nessus.
- Technical implementations and the associated operating guides, such as the implementation of an authorized instant messaging capability.

Milestones from the plan, initiate, and implement authorization activities

Before proceeding to the next phase, the verification and accreditation activities within a specific authorization requirement, let's take a final look at what you should have achieved in this phase.

- You have categorized your information and your information system.
- The baseline security controls have been identified based on your security categorization.
- You have determined whether additional, supplementary security controls are required.
- Your information system has been registered with your organization in accordance with its specific requirements.

---

[71] More specific information on artifacts will be provided in the security controls section of the accompanying CD.

- You have negotiated and obtained agreement on the type of system you are accrediting, the scope of the authorization process, and the security requirements of the information system.
- The initial SSP has been created, which documents the negotiated agreement.
- The hard work of implementing the controls has taken place and you have either collected or generated your necessary artifacts and evidence of compliant implementation.

It is now time to move on to the next phase – the validation of your security controls implementation and the process of obtaining the authorization to operate.

<table>
<tr><td>

Further reading

NOTE: There are many excellent books on the various aspects essential to secure security program management, network and system architecture, etc. therefore it is impossible to include them all here.

Ashbaugh, Douglas A. *Security Software Development: Assessing and Managing Security Risks*, Auerbach Publications, October 2008.

Howard, Patrick. *Building and Implementing a Security Certification and Accreditation Program: OFFICIAL ISC2 Guide to the CAPcm CBK*, Auerbach Publications, December 2005.

Tipton, Harold F. and Krause, Micki. *Information Security Management Handbook, Sixth Edition*, CRC Publications, May 2007.

</td></tr>
</table>

References

National Institute of Standards and Technology (NIST) Special Publication 800-37, *Guide for the Security Certification and Accreditation of Federal Information Systems*, May 2004.

National Institute of Standards and Technology (NIST) Special Publication 800-53, *Recommended Security Controls for Federal Information Systems*, December 2007.

National Institute of Standards and Technology (NIST) Special Publication 800-60, Vol. I, *Guide for Mapping Types of Information and Information Systems to Security Categories,* August 2008.

FIPS Publication 199, *Standards for Security Categorization of Federal Information and Information Systems,* February 2004.

FIPS Publication 200, *Minimum Security Requirements for Federal Information and Information Systems,* March 2006.

Department of Defense Instruction (DODI) 8500.2, *Information Assurance Implementation*, 6 February 2003.

CHAPTER 7: VERIFY, VALIDATE & AUTHORIZE – CONDUCTING THE AUTHORIZATION

One must verify or expel his doubts, and convert them into the certainty of Yes or No.[72]

Thomas Carlyle, Scottish Essayist, Satirist, and Historian

In this chapter:

Assessing the security controls

Developing the plan of action and milestones

Authorizing the information system operation

---

[72] http://www.famous-quotes.com/topic.php?tid=171

The previous phase ended with the implementation of a set of security controls as defined in the system security plan. This phase begins with a review of the initial SSP and the independent assessment of the security controls and ends with a risk-based decision to either authorize or deny the operation of an information system.

Figure 10: C&A process 2

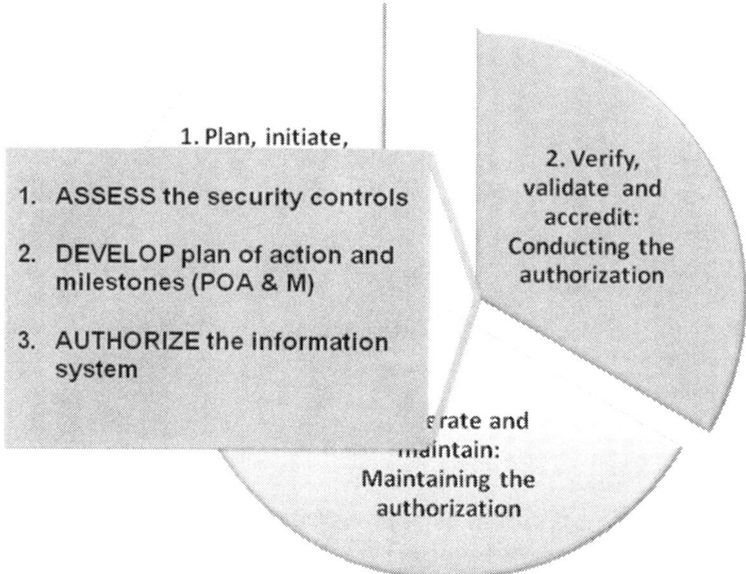

During the implementation activities in the previous phase, evidence and artifacts were collected to support the authorization decision process. These artifacts will be reviewed and tested during this phase to determine if they meet the published compliance standards. In addition, actual testing of the security characteristics of the information system will be conducted.

ASSESS the security controls

In this chapter, you will gain the tools you need to prepare to verify and validate the operational, managerial, and technical controls within your risk or accreditation boundary. You will be introduced to a high level planning process that can be used in any security control testing environment, and

Step 1 players

- Primary role: Security controls assessor, certifying authority
- Supporting roles:
    - Information system owner/steward
    - Information owner/steward
    - IAM/ISSM
    - SME(s)

then provide a methodology for the actual security control testing. Finally, the difference between several commercial and government types of control testing will be illustrated.

As the organization enters this phase, a determination should be made whether the information system is ready to be evaluated and tested.   This decision will be made based on the results of the validation testing, also known simply as security testing.

The verification and validation activities should be tailored to the system life cycle activities to ensure that the tests are relevant and provide the required degree of rigor – but do not test in excess of the system's current life cycle requirements. If a significant period of time has passed since the completion of the activities in the preview phase, or if new individuals are involved in the authorization process, the SSP should be reviewed to determine if the details about the system are still valid.

What is security control testing?

Validation testing, information systems security control testing and information assurance control testing are essentially synonymous for the same action – to certify that the required security controls have been correctly and completely implemented. It includes the examination and analysis of both technical and nontechnical security safeguards of IT resources as they have been applied to the information system.

This process, hereafter referred to security control testing, requires careful planning and a well trained staff to ensure it is executed correctly. It can be arguably one of the most critical steps in the authorization process. Why? There are essentially two reasons:

In fact, certification itself is defined as a "comprehensive assessment of the management, operational and technical security controls in an information system, made in support of security accreditation, to determine the extent to which controls are implemented correctly, operating as intended, and producing the desired outcome with respect to meeting the security requirements for the system."

- On a general level, emphasis is being placed by the government on security control testing. We see this emphasis on the testing and validation of security controls expanding into the private sector, with evidence of the implementation of adequate security controls being demanded by federal and DOD agencies, investors, customers, and eventually and increasingly, the rest of the Internet community. This evolution is analogous to the implementation of mandatory safety inspections of the cars driven on our highways. It is becoming essential that we demonstrate that the mechanisms that are integrated into the information superhighway are built and operated to security standards.
- On a level more specific to the authorization process, security control testing provides the authorizing official (AO) or designated accrediting authority (DAA) with the information needed to make an informed risk-based decision on the authorization for operation or, in some cases, the denial of operation for a system. This includes:

  - evidence about the effectiveness of security controls in organizational information systems;
  - an indication of the quality of the risk management processes employed within the organization; and

- information about the strengths and weaknesses of information systems supporting critical federal missions and applications in a global environment of sophisticated threats. (NIST SP 800-53A)

There are essentially two types of security control testing: self-assessment, which we will discuss in more detail in Chapter 8, and testing by an expert third party. Expert security control testing specifically addresses security control test methods requiring a high level of technical skill and the use of professional tools and methodologies to determine the security profile of the information system. By contrast, self-assessments are more often characterized by a less technical approach to testing the security controls, but usually involve a more direct and complete knowledge of the target information system(s).

Now that you have an idea about what security control testing really is, let's tell you what it is not. Security control testing is not about filling out a checklist or passing an audit or even just getting the information you need to complete the authorization documentation. It is all about developing a credible and significant input to the AO's risk-based decision process.

The primary objectives of security control testing are to:

- discover design, implementation, and operational flaws that might affect the confidentiality, integrity, and availability of the information and information systems;
- determine the adequacy of security mechanisms, assurances, and other properties to enforce the organization's security policy; and
- assess the degree of consistency between the information system security documentation and its implementation.

What should be tested?

Ideally, security control testing should be performed on all hardware and software components to ensure that all baseline security controls are adequately addressed. However, the scope and depth of security control assessments should always be risk-driven.

The security control assessor begins by reviewing the security controls described in the security plan and the purpose of the assessment. A security control assessment could range from a complete testing of all security controls associated with the information system (e.g. during security testing conducted as part of the initial authorization) or a limited assessment of specific security controls in the information system (e.g. during continuous monitoring, post accreditation, or where subsets of the controls in the information system are assessed on an ongoing basis).

When conducting a more limited assessment, the information system owner should coordinate with all of the stakeholders in the security of the information system (e.g. senior agency information security officer, mission/information owners, and/or authorizing official). Together, they should agree which security controls from the security plan should be assessed.

Selection of the security controls may also depend on the continuous monitoring schedule established by the information system owner. All security controls should be reviewed and/or tested at least once during the three-year accreditation cycle. Weaknesses listed on the plan of action and milestones must also be given adequate oversight, and controls with greater volatility should be identified and assessed more frequently.

Who executes security control testing?

The quality of the authorization process is influenced by the quality of the security control testing. Consequently, it is required that the verification and validation of the security controls be performed by an independent, objective – and most importantly – qualified third party. This is particularly important when seeking an initial authorization to operate. Once the authorization has been obtained, self-assessments and internal security control testing may be sufficient.

In this section, we will focus on the more comprehensive, independent, hands-on testing. Self-assessments will be covered in additional detail in Chapter 8, where the focus is placed on maintaining the authorization to operate.

The selection of a qualified security control assessor – whether from an internal team or an independent provider – is a critical decision for organizations seeking authorization to operate an information system. Security control assessment providers should be qualified and able to provide effective and efficient assessments; this will provide sufficiently reliable information to make decisions for authorizing information system operation.

An important note in this time of constrained personnel resources: If the security control assessor also provides other security services to the organization, they may also provide security control assessment services **as long as there is an adequate segregation of responsibilities and accountabilities**. The organization's management should ensure that different individuals are assigned to provide oversight and other security services separate from the security control assessment. They should also ensure that the personnel are not involved in any authorization to operate decision making, and ensure there is no possibility of influencing the outcome of the assessment.

Validation testing in federal agencies

Federal agencies may have internal security control test teams who are responsible for the initial testing associated with the authorization process and for the testing required

by continuous monitoring. They may also contract for independent testing through one of the many government consulting companies specializing in security controls testing.

Validation testing within DOD

While "highly recommended" for federal agencies, independent testing is a DOD mandate. Each of the DOD services has established an independent testing authority, usually reporting to the CA. In the Air Force, the certifying authority is located within the Headquarters, Air Force Communications Agency (AFCA). The Department of the Army certifying authority is centralized in the Office of the CIO/G-6, Senior Information Assurance Officer. Finally, the function of certifying authority for the Department of the Navy is assigned to the Space and Naval Warfare Systems Command (SPAWAR SYSCOM). As required, DOD also augments their security control test team with external contract support.

It is important to note that the testing and validation of security control assessment may differ depending on its status in the authorization process and its life cycle status. Prior to authorization the emphasis is most frequently placed on security control testing by a third-party expert — whether in the federal agencies or in the DOD. After authorization is granted, however, the security control assessments are specifically targeted to ensure continuity of the system security status. Frequently, the security control tests become the responsibility of the system owner, but may also be conducted by third-party experts, internal reviewers or a combination of the two.

Security control test procedures

Security control testing can only meet the above objectives if it is a consistent and standardized process. In order to meet this ideal, both the federal government and the DOD have provided standardized guidance. This guidance is equally applicable for use in conducting the independent test and the self-assessment.

For federal agencies, this guidance can be found in NIST Special Publication 800-53A, *Guide for Assessing the Security Controls in Federal Information Systems*, July 2008. Below is an example of part of a validation test from this guidance document. NOTE: This is not the entire validation test, only a subset which is used here to provide an example of the comprehensiveness of the security control validation test instructions.

Table 17: Sample validation test

Step No.	Assessment procedure	Low	Moderate	High
AC-2	Account management control: The organization manages information system accounts, including establishing, activating, modifying, reviewing, disabling, and removing accounts. The organization reviews information system accounts [Assignment: organization-defined frequency].	X	X	X
AC-2.1	Document: Examine organizational records or documents to determine if the organization establishes, activates, modifies, reviews, disables, and removes information system accounts in accordance with documented account management procedures.	X	X	X
AC-2.7	Interview selected organizational personnel with access control responsibilities and examine organizational records or documents to determine if the organization consistently manages information system accounts on an ongoing basis.	X	X	X

Rather than issuing a written publication, the DOD provides its standardized validation test guidance on the DIACAP Knowledge Service website at *https://diacap.iaportal.navy.mil/*. Here is an example of a DOD validation test. Different from the NIST SP 800-53, DOD provides a description of the steps required to prepare for the test, the execution tests, and the expected results.

Table 18: DOD validation test

Control No.	Control Test No.	Procedure preparation	Procedure script	Expected results
COAS-2	COAS-2-1	1. Obtain system description documentation that identifies and prioritizes system functions by data type, criticality, or other operational criteria. 2. Identify system resources required for duplication of operations, including hardware, software, applications, boundary defense devices, physical and environmental infrastructure, and personnel support. 3. Obtain a copy of the signed service agreement made with the alternate site.	1. Review the primary site's system description documentation to identify mission or business-essential services and functions. 2. Compare the primary site's system description documentation with the service agreement for the alternate site. 3. Verify that the service agreement with the alternate site contains a detailed description of the restoration services to be provided to the primary site in the event of an incident or outage and that all mission or business-essential functions requiring restoration are clearly identified. 4. Report the results.	An alternate site has been identified that has the capability to fully restore mission or business essential functions.

Security control assessment methods

Whether conducting a validation test for federal agencies or the DOD, the methods are essentially the same: examine, interview, and test. Most security controls require a combination of these methods in order to obtain the most comprehensive results.

Let's look at these a little more closely.

Examine — "E"

Specific artifacts are usually the target of examination. The examine method is used to facilitate assessor understanding, achieve clarification, or obtain evidence.

This method may be used to observe a managerial or operational situation or possibly review a technical configuration. Examinations consist of checking, inspecting, reviewing, observing, studying, or analyzing one or more assessment objects to facilitate understanding, achieve clarification, or obtain evidence, the results of which are used to support the determination of security control effectiveness.

Typical actions might include the examination or review of information security policies, plans, and procedures; system design documentation and interface specifications; system backup operations, reviewing and analyzing the results of contingency plan exercises or drills; incident response operations or activities; security configuration settings; or technical manuals and user/administrator guides.

For example, you might examine the rules of behavior to ensure users understand their roles and responsibilities for system access. You would ascertain that all users had signed rules of behavior and that they were stored in the training file.

You might also use the examine method for testing system configurations, particularly where automated means are not applicable or possible. For example, you may examine a system configuration to ensure that the audit log is configured correctly. Then you would examine the actual logs to ensure that all actions that needed to be logged in an application were reflected in the logs.

To reduce the level of effort in examining assessment objects, assessors should, to the maximum extent possible, reuse examination results and evidence from previous assessments. This is useful only in those cases when the results are available, when there have been no substantial security-relevant changes to the information system that could invalidate the results, and when the results are determined to still be credible.

There are three levels of examinations:

- **Generalized:** Brief, high-level reviews, observations, or inspections of security controls using a limited body of evidence or documentation. These are typically conducted using functional-level descriptions of specifications, mechanisms, or activities.
- **Specific:** Detailed analyses of security controls using a substantial body of evidence or documentation. These are typically conducted using functional-level descriptions of specifications, mechanisms, or activities, and where appropriate, high-level design information.
- **Comprehensive:** Detailed and thorough analyses of security controls using an extensive body of evidence or documentation. These types of examinations are usually conducted using functional-level descriptions of specifications, mechanisms, or activities, and where appropriate, high-level design, low-level design, and implementation-related information (e.g. source code).

Interview – "I"

Individuals, or groups of individuals, are usually the target of the interview process. Interviews are usually intended to facilitate understanding, achieve clarification, or lead to the location of evidence, the results of which can be used to support the level of security control implementation and a determination of security control compliance.

Interviews can be conducted with an array of individuals, to include agency heads, chief information officers, senior agency information security officers, authorizing officials, information owners, information system owners, information system security officers, information system security managers, personnel officers, human resource managers, facilities managers, training officers, information system operators, network and system administrators, site managers, physical security officers, and users.

There are essentially three levels of interviews:

- **Generalized:** Broad, high-level discussions with selected organizational personnel on particular topics relating to the security controls being assessed. This type of interview is most often used with a set of general, high-level questions and is intended to obtain a broad, general understanding of the fundamental concepts associated with the security controls.
- **Specific:** Broad, high-level discussions combined with more detailed discussions in specific areas with selected organizational personnel. This type of interview is typically conducted using a set of general, high-level questions together with a set of more detailed questions in specific areas where responses indicate a need for more detailed investigation. Focused interviews are intended to capture the specific understanding of the fundamental concepts associated with the security controls.
- **Comprehensive:** Broad, high-level discussions and more detailed, probing discussions in specific areas with selected organizational personnel on particular topics relating to the security controls being assessed (including the results of other assessment methods). This type of interview is typically

conducted using a set of general, high-level questions together with a set of more detailed, probing questions in specific areas. Comprehensive interviews are used where there is a need for more detailed investigation or where assessment evidence allows and is intended to capture the specific understanding of the fundamental concepts and implementation details associated with the security controls.

Test – "T"

Testing is most often focused on the technical or operational controls. Security control testing occurs under specified conditions and compares actual with expected behavior, the results of which are used to support the determination of security control effectiveness.

Testing is the process of actually exercising one or more assessment objects (i.e. activities or mechanisms) under specified conditions to compare actual with expected behavior. ***Do not confuse a test with an observation***. If you are testing the system to ensure it locks out accounts after three invalid attempts, this requires you to actually try to logon four times (three with the incorrect credential and one with the correct credentials). It does not mean you examine the system configuration documentation and note that the system is set to lockout users after three invalid attempts.

Typical tests include: structural testing of the logical access control and encryption mechanisms; functional testing of the identification/authentication and audit mechanisms; functional testing of the security configuration settings; functional testing of the physical access control devices; penetration testing of the information system and its key components; functional testing of the information system backup operations; and functional testing of the incident response/contingency planning capability.

To reduce the level of effort in testing assessment objects, the assessor should, to the maximum extent possible, reuse test results and evidence from previous security control assessments. This is acceptable when such results are available, there have been no substantive intervening changes to the information system that could invalidate earlier results, and the results are judged to be credible.

There are essentially three depth attributes to testing:

- **Generalized testing:** A test methodology that assumes no knowledge of the internal structure and implementation detail of the assessment object. This type of testing is conducted using a functional specification for mechanisms and a high-level process description for activities. Generalized testing provides a level of understanding of the security control necessary for determining whether the control is implemented and free from obvious errors. Also known as "black box" testing.
- **Focused testing:** Test methodology (also known as "gray box" testing) that assumes some knowledge of the internal structure and implementation detail of the assessment object. This type of testing is conducted using a functional specification and limited system architectural information (e.g. high-level design) for mechanisms and a high-level process description and high-level description of integration into the operational environment for activities. Focused testing provides a level of understanding of the security control necessary for determining whether the control is implemented and free from obvious errors and whether there are increased grounds for confidence that the control is implemented correctly and operating as intended.
- **Detailed testing**: Test methodology (also known as "white box" testing) that assumes explicit and substantial knowledge of the internal structure and implementation detail of the assessment object.
  White box testing is performed based on having knowledge of how the system has been implemented. It includes the analysis of data flow, control flow, information flow, coding practices, and exception and error handling within the system, to test the intended and unintended software behavior. White box testing can validate whether code has been implemented according to the intended design, security functionality has been integrated into the system, and to uncover exploitable vulnerabilities.

White box testing does require access to the source code. Although white box testing can be performed any time in the life cycle after the code is developed, it is a good practice to perform this type of testing during early testing phases.

- Detailed testing provides a level of understanding of the security control necessary for determining whether the control is implemented and free from obvious errors and whether there are further increased grounds for confidence that the control is implemented correctly and operating as intended on an ongoing and consistent basis, and that there is support for continuous improvement in the effectiveness of the control.

Observation – "O"

In addition to the above formal assessment methods, "random" observation can also play a crucial role in the validation process. Observation is often used in two ways:

- The security controls assessor/tester observes the performance of a specific procedure or set of activities.
- The security controls assessor/tester observes an unintended security event during the course of the validation testing that affects one or more of the security controls.

As indicated in each of the assessment methods described above, there is also a set of associated attributes, depth and coverage, which help define the expected level of effort for the assessment. These attributes are hierarchical in nature, providing the means to define the rigor and scope of the assessment for the increased assurance needed for higher impact level information systems.

The depth attribute addresses the rigor of and level of detail in the examination, interview, and testing processes. The values for the depth attribute for examination and interview include generalized, focused, and detailed. The depth values for testing include functional, penetration, and structural testing.

An additional attribute is "coverage." The coverage attribute addresses the scope or breadth of the examination, interview, and testing processes, including the number and type of specifications, mechanisms, and activities to be examined or tested and the number and types of individuals to be interviewed. Values for the coverage attribute include representative, specific, and comprehensive.

The appropriate depth and coverage attribute values for a particular assessment method reflect the values needed to achieve the assessment expectations. This is determined by the characteristics of the information system being assessed (including impact level) and the specific security determinations that need to be made.

Executing the security controls assessment

Successful security control assessments or testing can be broken down into the following steps.

Figure 11: Approach to security control planning

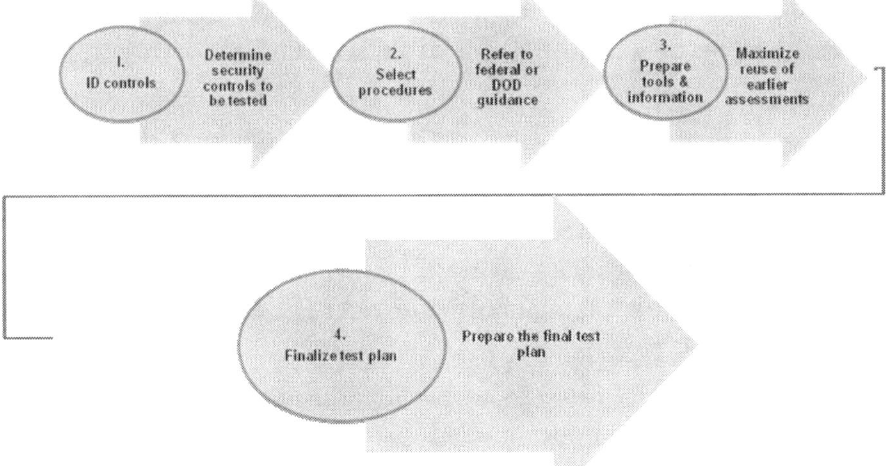

Plan the security controls assessment

The importance of planning as it relates to preparing for an IA control test (sometimes referred to as IA control validation, security test and evaluation (ST&E) and security controls assessment (SCA)) cannot be stressed enough. IA control testing can become a very time consuming, cumbersome, and, all too often, an extremely expensive process for an organization – yet it is too critical to ignore. If the time is taken to plan each IA control test, the cost of testing can be more efficiently managed, it will be more effective, and the results will be more beneficial to the organization.

1. **Determine the security controls to be tested:** Chapter 6 defined the steps for security categorization of your information system and the resulting assignment of the security controls essential to protect your information and information system. You also identified any supplementary or compensatory controls required by specific information system security requirements, such as privacy requirements related to medical information.

This establishes your security controls baseline and the list of all controls that must be verified during the security controls assessment process. But not all of these security controls must be tested!

In order to determine the final set of security controls that must be tested, the security controls tester should identify:

- Common and inherited security controls
- Non-applicable security controls
- Security controls that cannot be tested (e.g. as a result of the life cycle status).

The security controls assessor should note which IA controls (or parts thereof) can be designated as common or inherited. The common or inherited controls may have been previously implemented and tested as part of the organization's enterprise-wide information security program, or there may be a separate plan to assess the inherited controls. Common or inherited security controls can apply to multiple information systems within an organization and the protection measures provided by those controls are inherited by the individual systems under assessment.

The organization must ensure that the impact level associated with the identified common or inherited controls and the level of rigor and intensity of the security control assessments are equivalent to the impact level of the information system(s) inheriting the security controls. In general, the impact level of the common or inherited controls should be the same or higher than the information system being tested.

These are the controls that you do not have to test again, because they are provided as part of the larger system type or environment, for example, if you have several systems in an approved facility (enclave, GSS, SCIF), you will not need to test the access control on the computer room door for each system. Maximizing the use of common controls will reduce costs, make testing more effective, improving the consistency of the testing and results, and reinforcing reciprocity.

Once identified, these security controls can be marked as "compliant" based on the existing test results – without requiring additional testing. If the assessment results are not available for the common or inherited security controls, the assessment cannot be considered complete until the assessment results for the common or inherited controls are either made available or these security controls are included in the test plan.

It is important to coordinate this process with appropriate organizational officials (e.g. chief information officer, senior agency information security officer, authorizing official, information system owner). They may be able to obtain the results of common and inherited security control assessments or (if the inheritable security controls have not been assessed or are due to be reassessed) to make the necessary arrangements to include these controls in the current validation.

Hybrid controls may also be identified. These are security controls that are partially common or inherited controls and partially the responsibility of the information system. CP-2, contingency planning, is an example of a hybrid control. There will generally be a master contingency plan developed by the organization for all organizational information systems. However, individual information system owners may adjust, tailor, or supplement the contingency plan with system-specific aspects of the plan. For each hybrid security control, system-specific assessment procedures must be executed and the results retained along with the results from common control assessments. This way, all aspects of the security control will be assessed.

There may also be security controls that are simply not applicable to the information system being tested. For example, a standalone local area network may not require testing of the security controls for interconnectivity to the Internet. If your system does not have voice over IP (VOIP) – take it off the test list. These security controls can be marked as not applicable or NA. These may not require validation at this time or at all. Again, this should be coordinated with appropriate organizational officials (e.g. chief information officer, senior agency information security officer, authorizing official, information system owner). *NOTE: In the DOD, security controls marked as NA must be indicated as such in the plan of action and milestones (POA&M).*

Next, the IA controls which cannot be tested — based on the system configuration, life cycle status, or type – should be identified as not requiring validation at this time or at all. As with security controls identified as NA, these must be indicated on the POA&M.

Finally, conduct a gap analysis to determine the delta between the security controls, which are common or inherited, non-applicable or not tested, and those which remain valid for the information system. These remaining security controls will form the baseline for the validation test.

2. Select the security test procedures: NIST Special Publication 800-53A for federal information systems and the DIACAP Knowledge Service for the DOD provide comprehensive descriptions of test procedures for each security control in the respective baseline. As a starting point, security control assessors should refer to these provided baseline procedures for each of the security controls remaining after completion of the gap analysis in Step 1 above.

Using these procedures as a starting point, the security control assessors can select the appropriate procedural steps within the procedure. The number and complexity of test procedures may increase based on the impact level determined for the information system. The higher the impact level, the greater the rigor and intensity of the implementation and validation process must be. There is an increased level of assurance required in the effectiveness of the security controls being assessed.

It should be noted during the tailoring process of the initial security control baseline that supplementary security controls may have been added and/or the organization may have decided to employ compensating controls. The assessment procedures and associated procedural steps should be adjusted accordingly to reflect these changes.

Organizations should also be aware that certain changes to the security controls (i.e. adding and/or deleting controls or control enhancements from the security plan) may also affect other controls assigned to the information system. This will, in turn, affect the selection of test procedures and procedural steps required to assess the effectiveness of those controls and control enhancements.

In these situations, security control assessors should use the test framework provided by NIST or found in the DIACAP Knowledge Service to develop tailored test procedures for those supplementary or compensatory security controls. The additional assessment procedures should be integrated into the final security controls test plan.

In addition to the development of new or tailored test procedures, the procedures in the NIST guidance or in the DIACAP Knowledge Service may be extended or adapted to address platform-specific or organization-specific dependencies. If these modifications are made, these must be also noted in the final test.

This situation arises most often in the test procedures associated with the technical security controls (e.g. access control, identification and authentication, etc.). Detailed test scripts may need to be developed for the specific operating system, network component, middleware, or application employed within the information system to adequately validate certain characteristics of a particular security control. These test scripts can be considered extensions of the NIST and/or DOD-provided test procedures.

During the actual testing of an information system, the test procedures may be applied numerous times to a variety of assessment objects within a particular family of security controls. To save time, reduce costs, and maximize the usefulness of the test results, security control assessors should review the selected test procedures and look for opportunities to combine or consolidate procedural steps. For example, the security control assessors may consolidate interviews with key organizational officials to cover a variety of security-related topics.

It is important to realize that the procedures provided by NIST and DOD may not be complete and certainly may not address all of the possible configurations of an information system. Consequently, the security controls assessor should be sufficiently trained and experienced in order to be able to identify those situations where the provided test procedures are not adequate. An assessor should not blindly follow the procedure without taking time to ensure that the procedure is relevant for the information system and configuration being tested.

For example, organizations often integrate new, emerging technologies that have not yet been integrated into the existing test procedures. These may include new types of applications, the addition of cross domain technologies, and the use of emerging wireless capabilities.

Once the final list of security controls to be tested and the test procedures have been identified, selected – and possibly tailored – you should develop a written test plan.

3.   Prepare the security control test tools and gather information: In order to be as time and resource efficient as possible, the security controls assessor should prepare the necessary test tools and gather as much of the required information as possible prior to initiating the actual validation tests.

Testing can be executed manually or by using automated test tools. Manual methods are used most often with people and processes. Automated tools can be very useful in conducting tests of technical security controls.

There is no lack of automated tools and checklists for use in conducting security control tests and evaluations. These tools can facilitate the testing process, but security controls testers should also realize the limitations of these tools. Most security controls assessors will use multiple tools, including commercial and open source tools. Tools generally fall into the following categories:

- Information-gathering tools and techniques
- Scanning tools
- Enumeration tools
- Wireless tools
- Password auditing tools
- Vulnerability scanning tools
- Automated exploit tools.

The main reason for selecting a range of tools and methods is that each tool may only detect some percentage of existing vulnerabilities and, at the same time, potentially generate a number of false positives. Most tools excel in certain types of scenarios, however, a single tool may find less than 50% of known vulnerabilities in a typical information system, at least based on these authors' experience.

Vulnerability assessment products (also known as scanners) are used to support rigorous examinations of information systems in order to determine weaknesses that might allow exploitation by a threat agent. These products generally follow the following steps in executing a vulnerability analysis:

- First, passive, host-based mechanisms inspect system configuration files for unwise settings, system password files for weak passwords, and other system objects for security policy violations.
- Next, these checks are followed, in most cases, by an active, network-based assessment, which reenacts common intrusion scripts, recording system responses to the scripts.

The results of vulnerability assessment tools are only able to present a snapshot of the information system security status at a point in time. Also, these systems cannot reliably detect an attack in progress; they may be able to determine that an attack is possible, and perhaps even identify that an attack has occurred.

Some tools may allow experienced users to augment the baseline product by adding tailored scripts or exploits. This can aid in increasing the number of vulnerabilities found, as well as reducing the false positives. Some may have unrealistic expectations about the capabilities of automated tools. They are not assessment "silver bullets" – so keep in mind that they:

- do not compensate for weak identification and authentication mechanisms;
- cannot conduct investigations of attacks without human intervention;
- will not be able to assess the contents of your organizational security policy;
- are not intended to compensate for weaknesses in network protocols;
- cannot compensate for problems in the quality or integrity of information in the system; and
- are not always current with modern network hardware and features.

As technology progresses and with increased emphasis from customers, such as the federal government, the sophistication of security test tools continues to improve. In the meantime, security control testers should focus on identifying the most critical requirements for the selected commercial tools and especially look for flexibility in extending the product as they prepare for their security control evaluations.

NIST and DOD have collaborated on a suite of tools and checklists to assist in vulnerability management and in the evaluation of the security controls. A list of these tools can be found at the *Security Content Automation Protocol (SCAP)* site, which is part of the National Vulnerability Database (NVD).

Figure 12: SCAP website

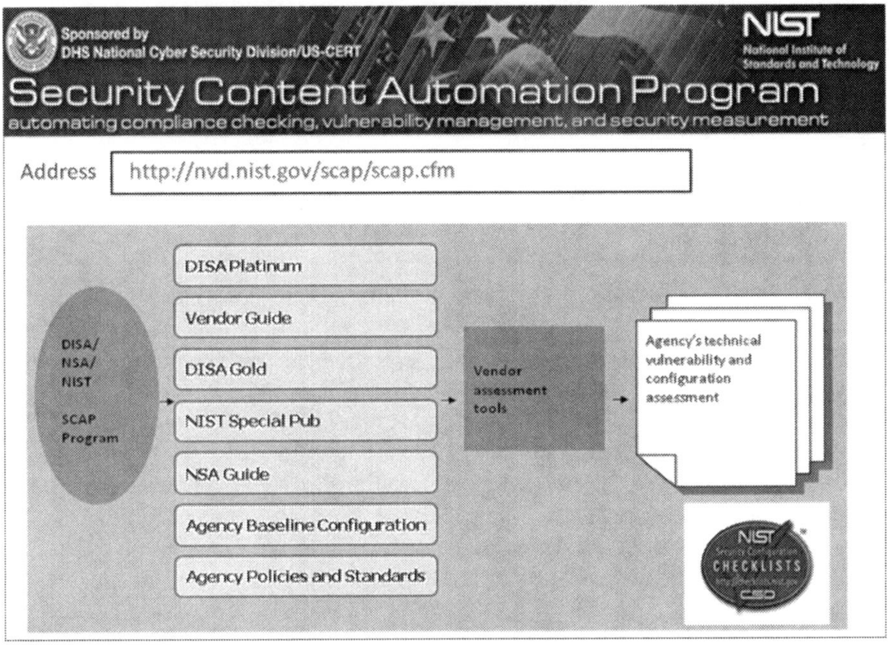

Federal agencies, as well as other organizations, can automate much of their technical security control test activities by using SCAP checklists and associated tools. The SCAP checklists have FISMA compliance mappings embedded within the checklists. SCAP-compatible tools, which are listed on the website, are often designed to automatically generate NIST SP 800-53 compatible security control assessment and compliance evidence. Each security control test or check is mapped to the appropriate high level NIST SP 800-53 security controls and, where appropriate, to the assessment procedures found in NIST SP 800-53A. In addition, the SCAP-compatible tools and checklists also contain mappings to other high level policies (e.g. ISO27000 series, DODI 8500.2) and SCAP tools may also output those compliance mappings.

Table 19: Things to look for in an assessment tool

The ability to keep the assessment tool up-to-date with the latest vulnerabilities easily, efficiently, and economically – environments change constantly and the assessment tool must be able to adjust as well.
A secure interface with critical database software such as Oracle, SQLserver or MS-Access, to further analyze security data and/or tie VA into the back office processes.
Integration with commonly used reporting tools to provide the ability to save, export, print, or email security reports.
Immediate availability of pre-formatted reports that can be customized to fit the needs of the organization.
The capability to intelligently assess security across multiple platforms (UNIX, NT, NetWare, and OpenVMS) and correlate that information into comprehensive report formats.
Requirement for only minimal resources such as network bandwidth – tools that execute on servers through agents typically require less bandwidth as only the report needs to be transmitted over the network.

Develop and/or select test scripts: Most of the controls you will test on a system are not technical. Actually, most of the controls that support an information system fall into the operations and management categories. Luckily, these controls usually have an extensive amount of information about validating these controls and (sometimes) what evidence is required for each control.

If you are testing an information system for a federal agency, you are required to follow NIST guidelines. You will find test procedures in NIST SP 800-53A for most of the operational, managerial, and even technical controls. If you are testing a DOD system under DIACAP, you will be using the DIACAP validation procedures provided on the DIACAP Knowledge Service. If you are testing a National Security System (NSS), then you will use the CNSS 1253A test procedures. For certification purposes, even after you have completed testing of all the baseline controls, you may still be required to perform system component and network assessments depending on the architecture of the information system.

Once you know all the components you are going to test on the system, you should develop/assign a test script (automated tool or manual check) to each component. For example, if you are testing a Windows® 2003 Server with IIS 7.0, and SQL Server 2005, then you will need a test script for each of the named components. If the components connect through the network, you will also want to include a network vulnerability scanner and possibly an application and database scanner.

If you are testing information systems within federal agencies or DOD, you will only be authorized to use certain standards, tools, and scripts for your testing. Be sure to check out the list of authorized tools as you are in the planning process.

You should always include the list of tools you are going to use to test the systems in the test plan, which should be pre-approved by the AO or DAA. Some examples of authorized/provided testing tools include:

- Defense Information System Agency (DISA) Security Test and Implementation Guides (STIG), and NSA System and Network Analysis Center (SCAC) guides: configuration standards for DOD IT, IA and IA-enabled devices/systems.
- A security checklist (sometimes referred to as a lockdown guide, hardening guide, or benchmark configuration) is essentially a document that contains instructions or procedures to verify compliance to a baseline level of security.

- Security readiness review scripts (SRRs) test products for STIG compliance. SRR scripts are available for all operating systems and databases that have STIGs, and web servers using IIS. The SRR scripts are unlicensed tools developed by the Field Security Office (FSO) and the use of these tools on products is completely at the user's own risk.

All DISA STIGS, checklists, and other test resources can be found at: *http://iase.disa.mil/stigs/index.html*

All SRR scripts can be found at: *http://iase.disa.mil/stigs/SRR/index.html*

Gather essential information and artifacts: Next to planning for the security controls testing, identifying, collecting and reviewing artifacts[73] may be the most important step in the authorization process. Before you can properly conduct security control testing, you will need to have a very good understanding of the information system or component you are going to test. Based on the type of test you plan on conducting, it is important to compile all the information you can about the information system.

A good way of knowing what you will need to gather is to co-develop a checklist of the basic documents (or security artifacts) necessary to understand the mission of the organization, the compliance environment (to include the security categorization), and the specifics about the system or component you are going to test. At a minimum, you will need:

- A comprehensive system description. At a minimum the system description should include:

  - full system name and current version;
  - a system identifier (OMB-300 or agency/component registration number);
  - system or security categorization;
  - data types (process, stored, transmitted, and managed);

---

[73] The terms artifact and evidence are often used interchangeably. For the purposes of our text, we will use artifact.

- general description and system purpose;
- system environment.

- System contact information, with at least:

  - system owner/data owner (with related contact information);
  - technical POC;
  - information security POC; and,
  - the system development life cycle (SDLC) or system life cycle (SLC) stage.

- A data flow diagram: A data flow diagram provides an architectural view of the systems, how they interact, and a graphical representation of how data flows from component to component of the system. This will provide a graphical representation of the software and systems functions.
- A network diagram: A network diagram includes all system network devices with all related interconnections. The network diagram should provide information not only about the network (routers, firewalls, etc.), but should include information about communications security, such as VPN and link encryption.
- Software inventory: A listing containing all the software components that support the system, this should include:

  - full software name with current version;
  - patch level if applicable;
  - simple description of how the software is used as it relates to the overall information system.

- Hardware/firmware inventory, including:

  - patch level if applicable;
  - simple description of how the hardware/firmware is used as it relates to the overall information system.

- All documents related to the certification and authorization of the system. These include but are not limited to:

  - previous test results (to include annual assessments and audits);

- system categorization documents (FIPS 199, CNSS 1199, NIST 800-60);
- for DOD: system identification profile, DIACAP implementation plan, security artifacts ;
- the systems security plan (SSP), to include common controls and system specifics;
- risk assessment (RA);
- configuration management plan (CMP), change control board charter, and related meeting notes;
- business impact assessment (BIA), continuity of operations plan (COOP), disaster recovery plan, and/or contingency plan;
- privacy impact assessment (PIA);
- e-authentication risk assessment;
- system standing operating procedures (SOP);
- plan of actions and milestones (POA&M);
- policies, procedures, guidelines, and any other documentation that support the security control compliance related to the system.

- If you are conducting a test for the government in accordance with NIST standards a typical system description includes:

  - the name of the information system;
  - a unique identifier for the information system (OMB-300, or agency/component registration number);
  - the status of the information system with respect to the system development life cycle (phase);
  - the name and location of the organization responsible for the information system;
  - contact information for the information system owner or other individuals knowledgeable about the information system;
  - contact information for the individual(s) responsible for the security of the information system;
  - the purpose, functions, and capabilities of the information system;
  - the types of information processed, stored, and transmitted by the information system;

- the boundary of the information system for operational authorization (or security authorization);
- the functional requirements of the information system;
- the applicable laws, directives, policies, regulations, or standards affecting the security of the information and the information system;
- the individuals who use and support the information system (including their organizational affiliations, access rights, privileges, and citizenship, if applicable);
- the architecture of the information system;
- hardware and firmware devices (including wireless);
- system and applications software (including mobile code);
- hardware, software, and system interfaces (internal and external);
- information flows (i.e. inputs and outputs);
- the network topology;
- network connection rules for communicating with external information systems;
- interconnected information systems and unique identifiers for those systems;
- encryption techniques used for information processing, transmission, and storage;
- public key infrastructures, certificate authorities, and certificate practice statements;
- the physical environment in which the information system operates; and
- web protocols and distributed, collaborative computing environments (processes, and applications) (NIST SP 800-37).

Understand the organization and mission: In order to develop a more comprehensive test plan that will test the system or every system component against the control objectives, and help to provide the AO with risk based information specific to their organization, it is very important to understand as much of the risk associated with the organization as possible. In order to better understand the risks associated with an organization, you must gain a strong understanding of the organization and its related mission.

You must know how the organization works and how the system or facility you are going to test supports the organization and mission. You can gather much about an organization from public websites, news releases, and information provided by the system owners or stakeholders.

If the organization's information security program is fairly mature, critical assets that support the organization and mission will be identified and documented as such. Understanding the organization and mission will also help to provide information on the scope of the test. For instance, if you have been given very limited time or resources to conduct an assessment of the organizational assets – you should choose the assets that are the most critical in the boundary you are testing first.

Understand the compliance environment: Understanding the compliance environment can mean several things. This includes understanding which one of the accreditation methods will be used, such as NIST, NIAP, DIACAP, DCID, or CNSS, etc.

It also requires you to understand any other type of compliance requirements, such as HIPAA, Sarbanes Oxley, FISCAM, PCI, or even agency specific requirements. This will allow you to identify the baseline and tailored controls that will need to be tested if they are not explicitly outlined in the system security plan (SSP).

You should also understand any supplemental and compensating controls that may be required for the system you are going to test. For example, you may plan on testing a DOD system and the military component is the US Army. So you will not only be responsible for testing for the DOD baseline IA controls, but also the US Army IA controls (AR 25-2/380-5). If the system contains personally identifiable information (PII) and medical records, you may also be required to test OMB privacy controls and HIPAA controls. The system security plan should clearly identify the baseline, tailored, supplemental, compensating, or additional requirements, but if it does not you will still be required to include them in the test plan.

Understand the system and related components: In order to test an entire system, you must first decompose the system into its various components and sub-components. Most systems consist of several components and each component must meet the security control baseline and tailored baseline set forward by the organization.

For example, if you had a web-based system, you would most likely have a web server, application server, and a database – each system would also have hardware components, such as servers, telecommunications/network infrastructure and possibly external storage. Next, on each one of the hardware components, you would have an operating system (OS) and possibly several supporting applications.

By identifying every component a system consists of, you can more easily ensure that you are planning to test every control related to the system or facility. For example, you may have to test the identification and authentication (I&A) for the OS, the application, the web server, and the database in order to demonstrate overall compliance of the I&A control for an individual information system.

Decomposing the system into various components and sub-components also allows you to more easily choose the test scripts and tools you will use for the testing.

Finalize the test team: Now that you understand the system, the organization, and have performed all the necessary preliminary de-scoping of controls, it is time to select team members and finalize the test team. Although tests may be limited by time and budget, it is important to put together a team that will provide the most control coverage and understanding of the controls.

This will require a mix of management, compliance, and technical staff. At a minimum you will want to have a team leader that has conducted several similar tests in the past. In addition, just as you tailor specific test scripts for each component of the system testing, you may need to select the personnel that relate to specific test objectives.

NOTE: If you are conducting testing for the DOD, your assessors/testers will be required to meet the educational and certification requirements in DOD 8570-1M. If you are testing for any other organization, ensure you have undertaken due diligence in finding out what specific requirements the organization has for assessors/testers.

It has been our experience that a good testing team needs to have more than just strong technical backgrounds, but also great verbal communication and interpersonal skills. Remember the tester in the federal government is not just supposed to find weaknesses and vulnerabilities, but also provide insight into how the weaknesses and vulnerabilities can be mitigated and remediated.

4. Finalize the test plan: Security controls assessors have flexibility in organizing a security assessment plan that meets the needs of the organization and that provides the best opportunity for obtaining the necessary evidence to determine security control effectiveness. To save time, reduce assessment costs, and maximize the usefulness of assessment results, security control procedures (or parts of procedures) can be combined or consolidated whenever possible or practicable. For example, you can plan to consolidate interviews with key organizational officials dealing with a variety of security-related topics.

Assessors may have other opportunities for significant consolidations and cost savings by organizing groups of related policies and procedures that could be examined as a unified entity in the plan. Obtaining and examining configuration settings from similar hardware and software components within the information system is another example that can provide significant assessment efficiencies.

Also, consider the sequence in which security controls are assessed in the planning process. The results of testing some security controls before others may provide information that facilitates the understanding and assessment of other controls. For example, security controls such as CM-2 (baseline configuration), CM-8 (information system component inventory), PL-2 (system security plan), RA-2 (security categorization), and RA-3 (risk assessment) produce general descriptions of the information system. Assessing these security controls early in the process may provide a basic understanding of the information system that can help in assessing other security controls.

Planning will not only save time, money, and frustration and increase performance, but also help to ensure your staff fully understand and can support the scope and goals of the test. This will allow you to ensure the test provides a full coverage of the information system controls and time is not wasted testing security controls that are either out of scope or non-applicable. As a final note, planning for the security controls testing and actually executing the test plan is not always sequential in nature. So, although the security control testing steps are presented in a sequential manner, it does not mean that several objectives cannot be handled simultaneously.

Based on the planning steps you have conducted thus far, you should have sufficient data to prepare the test plan. The test plan needs to answer the following questions:

- What type of test is being conducted (e.g. independent validation/certification/annual assessment/audit, etc.)?
- What are the key objectives?
- What is the scope of the test (this should correlate directly to the accreditation boundary)?
- What security or IA controls will be covered?
- Who will be conducting the test? What are the team members' roles and responsibilities?
- Where will the test/s be conducted?
- How long will the test be? What are the key dates for testing, interviews, kick-off, and out-brief meetings?
- What is the testing team's understanding of the rules of engagement?
- What test scripts and tools will be used (automated and manual)?
- What assumptions does the test team have?

- Is there any miscellaneous information related to the test, such as terms and conditions of the test, who will receive the test report, how the team will deal with false positives, and customer review period?

Once the security assessment plan is completed, the plan is reviewed and approved in writing by appropriate organizational officials. This helps to ensure that the plan is complete, consistent with the security objectives of the organization and the organization's assessment of risk, and cost-effectively uses the resources set aside for the assessment.

Federal agencies often have their own mandatory format for writing the test plan. We have expanded on the content of the test plan in Chapter 10 and included examples on the CD accompanying this text. One is a written test plan based on the NIST SP 800-53 standards. Another is an example of a security requirements traceability matrix (SRTM).

The SRTM, which can be a subset of the overall requirements traceability matrix (RTM) for the information system, can be used to formally document the specific information system security design requirements and to ensure that these are met. The SRTM document should be formatted so that it can be easily evolved into later serving as the security control test plan.

Execute the security controls test

After completion of the test plan, identification and preparation of the test tools and methods, and development of any additional test scripts, the actual test is scheduled and testing assignments are made.

Figure 13: Approach to security control testing

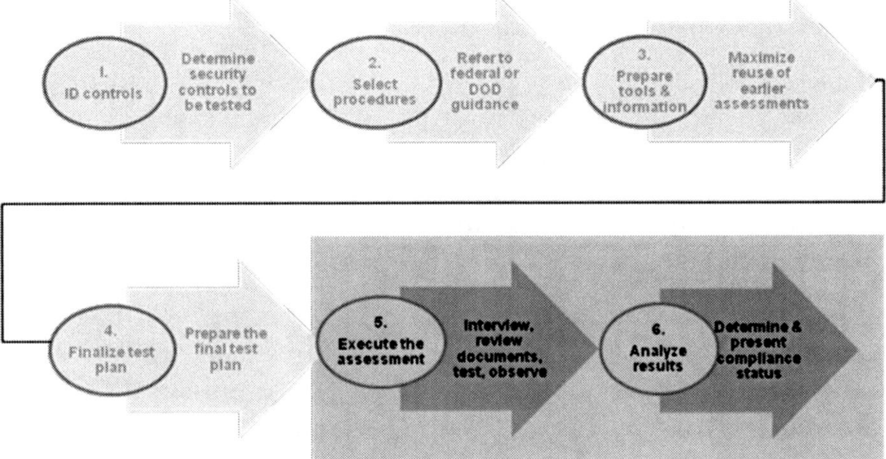

5. Execute the assessment: It is often useful to conduct a dry run of the test on a test bed or virtual information system/network prior to actually putting "hands on" the operational information systems. A dry run verifies that all test objectives, test procedures, and test scripts are appropriate for the system being tested.

The security control assessment team may also include the system owner, ISSO, system and/or network administrators in the dry-run test to assist with refining the test plan. If any of the information contained in the plan is inaccurate or if the proposed tools/methods are not appropriate for the target information system(s), the plan can be corrected prior to formally executing it.

The actual execution phase of the security controls testing can last a couple of days to several weeks – depending upon the size, complexity, and life cycle of the information system. However, the security control assessment team should try to minimize the time on site with the organization as much as possible.

Hold a kick-off meeting: Once arriving at the test location, it is often useful for the security controls assessor to provide the organization's leadership with an overview of the proposed test plan. The control testing kick-off meeting plays an important role in ensuring the system stakeholders of the system being tested have a good understanding of the entire test plan.

This includes understanding what is going to be required of them and their staff; the dates/time of the testing; the components that will be tested, and allows for rules of engagement to be formally vetted and approved. The kick-off meeting is also a good opportunity to obtain answers to any open questions and gather any documentation that you have not received up to this point.

It is always good to go into the kick-off meeting with a project management plan of all of the testing components, dates, who is assigned from the testing team and who is the primary POC from the stakeholders being tested. If you still have a few blanks in your project management plan (PMP), the meeting provides an opportunity to fill those in with the stakeholders in the same room.

Also, ensure you clarify any operational issues regarding the time required for the assessment and the assets being tested. Explain whether your test will obtrusive or non-obtrusive, the tools you will be running, the average time each test takes, and provide the management stakeholders with the contact information of the test management and team leaders should they need to contact anyone during the test.

We always find it works well to include the above information in a presentation where team members can take notes and interact with the system stakeholders. This also helps put "names to faces," which allows for a smoother interview process and configuration-related testing. A sample entrance briefing is included on the CD accompanying this book.

Execute the testing: The security control assessment team and the assigned system personnel will execute the tests in accordance with the test procedures described in the plan. System administrators or other technical personnel should ideally be present during the execution of the actual test. They serve the dual purpose of witnessing the tests and providing subject matter expertise on the target system(s). In fact, multiple technical personnel may be required to execute and/or assist with the test. For example, a team member with training and experience in the UNIX operating system might be needed for specific test procedures or one with Oracle database administration training and experience might be necessary for database testing.

Prior to executing the test plan, the security control assessor and the assessment team should work with system personnel to ensure the following:

- All system components scheduled for testing are available and operational.
- Required organizational personnel are available to participate in the process.

During our careers, we have performed hundreds, possibly thousands of security control tests. One thing has always been consistent across all of our experiences with security control testing: the results obtained from the test often depended on the assessor or tester and not necessarily on the actual requirements. This means that results could vary greatly depending on the individual(s) executing the tests.

Recently, Waylon had a chance to work with many of the brilliant people at NIST and a group of very talented security professionals collaborating in the development of NIST SP 800-53A. Now, instead of a tester spending hours or even days describing a unique step-by-step process on how you should execute your testing, NIST and its team of professionals have already spent thousands of hours refining a process that will allow us to provide a consistent, effective – and hopefully successful – control test.

However, to most effectively use NIST SP 800-53A, you should understand some of the terminology used throughout the publication:

- Assessment objects: identify the specific items being assessed and include specifications, mechanisms, activities, and individuals.

- Specifications: the document-based artifacts (e.g. policies, procedures, plans, system security requirements, functional specifications, and architectural designs) associated with an information system.
- Mechanisms: the specific hardware, software, or firmware safeguards and countermeasures employed within an information system.
- Activities: the specific protection-related pursuits or actions supporting an information system that involve people (e.g. conducting system backup operations, monitoring network traffic, or exercising a contingency plan). Individuals, or groups of individuals, are people applying the specifications, mechanisms, or activities described above.
- Assessment methods: define the nature of the assessor actions and include examine, interview, and test.

As the test is being executed, the security control assessment team should document the initial results for each test executed. Although some preliminary analysis can be conducted, it is important to take the time to carefully review actual against expected results in order to correctly determine the compliance status of the security control.

After the identified system components have been tested and initial results documented, an informal exit brief should be given to the organization's leadership and designated representatives. (There is a sample exit briefing on the CD accompanying this text.) This informal exit brief is intended to provide the organization, especially the system owner and other system personnel, with preliminary findings (e.g. "not met" test objectives) resulting from the test execution.

Some assessment teams may even choose to ensure that functional area results are shared, integrated and incorporated into the subsequent assessment action strategy on a daily basis. The primary means for this information sharing will be a daily "hotwash" meeting. The hotwash is usually held at the end of each work day and attended by all team members and representatives from the assessed organization. The group will review the results obtained during the day and discuss plans and strategies for the following day.

Early disclosure of the findings, particularly any critical findings, gives the organization the opportunity to take immediate corrective action. In fact, many corrective actions can be implemented in real time with the security control tests (and in some cases should be) before the report is finalized. This allows for corrected findings to be documented in the final security control test report.

Analyze, document, and report the results in the security assessment report (SAR)

At the conclusion of the security controls assessment, the assessment team should analyze the results, document the findings, and prepare a security assessment report (SAR).

6. Analyze the results: One of the most difficult tasks associated with performing a security control assessment is analysis of the results. After you compile all of the results from all of the tests (manual and automated), you will often find that some of the actual results do not match up completely with the stated expected result.

Basically, it is highly likely that you will have some false positives. These will need to be evaluated and weeded out of your test results before putting them into the final report.

For example, the assessors may have interviewed the system administrator about the system access policy and – based on the interview – the control appeared to be compliant; however, your automated test scripts found several issues in the configuration of the access policy of the system. This is where your team's experience and raw ability comes into play. An experienced tester will note the discrepancy and be able to evaluate its applicability and validity.

Results of the control assessment may ultimately influence the content of the security plan and the plan of action and milestones (POA&M). As a result, it is important for the information system owner to review the findings of the assessor with the designated organizational officials (e.g. authorizing official, chief information officer, senior agency information security officer, mission/information owners) and determine the appropriate steps required to correct weaknesses and deficiencies identified during the assessment.

Before applying the actual determination of compliant, non-compliant or not applicable to the security control, it may be useful to initially use tags of "satisfied" and "other than satisfied" for the security controls assessment results. This provides visibility for organizational officials of specific weaknesses and deficiencies in the information system and facilitates a disciplined and structured approach to reviewing risk mitigation in accordance with organizational priorities.

For example, the information system owner, in consultation with designated organizational officials, may decide that certain assessment findings marked as "other than satisfied" are of an inconsequential nature and present no significant risk to the organization. Alternatively, the system owner and organizational officials may decide others are significant, requiring immediate remediation actions.

In all cases, the organization reviews each finding of "other than satisfied" and applies its judgment with regard to the severity or seriousness of the finding (i.e. the potential adverse effect on the organization's operations and assets, individuals, other organizations, or the nation), and whether the finding is significant enough to be worthy of further investigation or remedial action.

Senior leadership involvement in the mitigation process may be necessary in order to ensure that the organization's resources are effectively allocated based on organizational priorities. Resources should be provided first to the information systems that support the most critical and sensitive missions for the organization or for correcting the deficiencies that pose the greatest degree of risk.

Ultimately, the assessment findings and any subsequent mitigation actions initiated by the information system owner, in collaboration with designated organizational officials, trigger updates to the risk assessment and the security plan. Therefore, the key documents used by the authorizing official to determine the security status of the information system (i.e. security plan with updated risk assessment, security assessment report, and plan of actions and milestones) are updated to reflect the results of the security control assessment.

The security assessment report (SAR): The SAR includes all of the information from the assessor (in the form of assessment findings) necessary to determine the effectiveness of the controls employed in the information system and the organization's overall security effectiveness determination. The SAR is an important factor in an authorizing official's determination of risk to organizational operations (i.e. mission, functions, image, or reputation), organizational assets, individuals, other organizations, and the nation. This final step is as important – if not more so – than the actual execution of the assessment.

The report should follow guidelines, such as those in NIST Special Publication 800-53A, or utilize a customer-specified report format. It should be written clearly and comprehensively – and remember, the target audience is management. At a minimum, the SAR should include:

- Security control number or IA control number: The security control number refers to the families of security controls as described in the baseline controls being used.
- Finding number: The number in order of the test findings that warranted a recommendation.
- Risk level: Level of risk if the finding is not mitigated. This is usually documented as low, moderate, or high.
- Requirement: The security control from NIST SP 800-53, DODI 8500.2, CNSS 1253, or other.
- Recommendation: The recommended mitigation.

You can find examples of security control test report templates on the CD accompanying this text. The SAR is used to present the following data to the certifying authority and the authorizing official:

- Results of the security controls assessment (i.e. a determination of the extent to which the security controls are implemented correctly, operating as intended, and producing the desired outcome with respect to meeting the security requirements for the system); and
- Recommendations for correcting or mitigating deficiencies in the security controls and reducing or eliminating identified vulnerabilities.

The final report should reflect the fact that you conducted an assessment – not an audit. It should focus on describing the findings and provide recommendations for remediation. It should NOT point out wrong-going or try to point to failures from any specific individual. The report, however, should clearly state the outcomes for the security control tests.

There are four possible outcomes to the test for each individual security control:

- Compliant (C) – the result of the testing demonstrates that the security control fully meets the expected results.
- Non-compliant (NC) – the result of the testing demonstrates that the security control does not meet the expected results.
- Non-applicable (NA) – the security control is not applicable for the information system and/or its current configuration.
- Not tested (NT) – the security control cannot be tested at this time – or at all.

The results of all executed security control tests will be formally documented. These results are also summarized in a written test report that is provided to the requesting organization upon

Protecting the organization's data

- The security control assessment team may obtain information during a security assessment that the customer may not want shared with others.

- The security control assessor has an obligation to protect the confidentiality of all security assessment related records and information, including limiting access within their own organization to the individuals that need to know the information.

test completion.   Further details on the preparation of the test report are provided in Chapter 10 and a template for a report format is on the accompanying CD.

The purpose of a test report is to not only document the security control test results, but also to provide results of analysis of the testing, i.e. what failed and why.   The test report may also make recommendations for further testing or engineering efforts.

DEVELOP the plan of action and milestones (POA&M)

At its most basic, the plan of action and milestones (POA&M), also referred to as a corrective action plan, is a management tool that outlines identified information system security program and information system weaknesses along with the actions necessary to mitigate them. To many, the term POA&M strikes fear and loathing in their hearts.   However, the POA&M is actually a positive resource for planning and monitoring corrective actions.   It defines roles and responsibilities for solving problems; assists in identifying security funding requirements; tracks and prioritizes resources; and informs decision makers.

A POA&M also provides an organization with a capability to highlight progress and demonstrate improvements in the quality of its information security program. It can also serve as a management tool and a point of comparison for an assessment of the organization's overall maturity in comparison to the security status of other federal agencies.

Importance of the POA&M – $$$$

The Office of Management and Budget (OMB) uses the POA&M to assess the state of the federal government's information system security and to assist OMB in providing oversight of the federal government's IT investments. According to OMB direction, agencies are required to link their POA&Ms to the IT budgeting process.

The official word is that OMB penalizes agencies that do not adequately define and implement a plan to mitigate information system security weaknesses. Agency IT programs could be placed at risk and lose critical IT and security funding. In the case of major IT investments, OMB requires the POA&Ms to be cross-referenced through answers to an Exhibit 300 and Exhibit 53.[74]

Table 20: Type of information from Exhibit 300 and Exhibit 53 included on a POA&M

Exhibit 300[75]	Project ID (300)[76]	Project Name	Exhibit 53	Project ID (53)	Security Costs	Auth. Date (Actual or Planned)
Yes	xxx-xx-xx-xx-xx-xxxx-xx-xxx-xxx	CDC Generic	Yes	xxx-xx-xx-xx-xx-xxxx-xx-xxx-xxx	$15k	8/31/08

The security costs column captures the amount required for security based on the following question: "What is the total dollar amount allocated to IT security for this investment?" The response to this question in this section of the Exhibit 300 should align with resources required to remediate the weaknesses reported in the POA&M for that information system.

---

[74] Exhibit 300, or the capital asset plan and business case, is a format used by OMB to make quantitative decisions about budgetary resources consistent with the Federal Administration's program priorities, and qualitative assessments about whether the agency's programming processes are consistent with OMB policy and guidance. Exhibit 300 also supports compliance with the requirements of the 1996 Clinger Cohen Act. Exhibit 53 summarizes federal agency IT spending on all major and non-major IT investments, and is provided to OMB annually as part of the budgeting process.

[75] Exhibit 300 is submitted for every major system or IT investment. See definitions for the criteria for consideration as a major system.

[76] The unique project identifier (UPI), a 23-digit number, must be created for all IT projects. The UPI is based, in part, on the sub-functions found in the business reference model. It will be used on the specific 300 for the investment as well as the Exhibit 53.

How the POA&M fits into the information system security evaluation

Congress uses the agency's own Inspector General's evaluation of its POA&M process in determining the congressional security report card. In fulfilling its oversight role, Congress obtains information about an agency's information system security activities and its FISMA compliance.

Agencies release to Congress, as requested, the following information from their POA&Ms: (1) type of weakness; (2) key milestones; (3) any milestone changes; (4) source of identification of the weakness; and (5) the status of the weakness.

In addition, having a sound POA&M process is essential to achieving a high score on the President's Management Agenda (PMA). The PMA is a strategy for improving the management and performance of the federal government.

Benefits of the POA&M process

Although most agencies view POA&Ms as a necessary evil, there is actually benefit to be achieved from the process of developing and tracking POA&Ms. A good POA&M process has other benefits, such as:

- **Producing valuable trending and analysis:** The POA&M can be used as a historical data source for management on the costs, effort, and time to mitigate system security weaknesses. The type of weaknesses can be tracked, as well as the rate of their recurrence. The POA&M provides the ability to conduct analyses by system, program, or across the entire agency.
- **Supporting IT business cases**: A comprehensive POA&M that contains accurate and reliable financial estimates can provide traceability, as well as the justification for additional security funds.
- **Maintaining institutional knowledge:** A well-executed and maintained POA&M prevents reliance on specific individuals as "the single point of failure" to retain and communicate historical

information relevant to an information system or an entire program.

- **Facilitating effective communication**: The POA&M can serve to facilitate communication and coordination among agency personnel on information system security issues, such as the chief information officer (CIO), information system security officer (ISSO), budget personnel, or program officials.

As a result, the POA&M can provide agencies with tighter control over their IS security program and increase the efficiency of the agency's IS security management.

The POA&M process of weakness remediation

Weakness remediation is a cyclical process with the steps depicted in the following figure. What follows is a brief description of this process. The security controls assessment process was completed in the preceding step.

Note that an assessment is not the only means of identifying system security weaknesses that should eventually wind up on the POA&M. Other means of identifying system security weakness include:

- IG inspections
- Government Accountability Office (GAO) audits
- Self-assessments
- Independent assessments
- Penetration tests.

Figure 14: Weakness remediation cycle

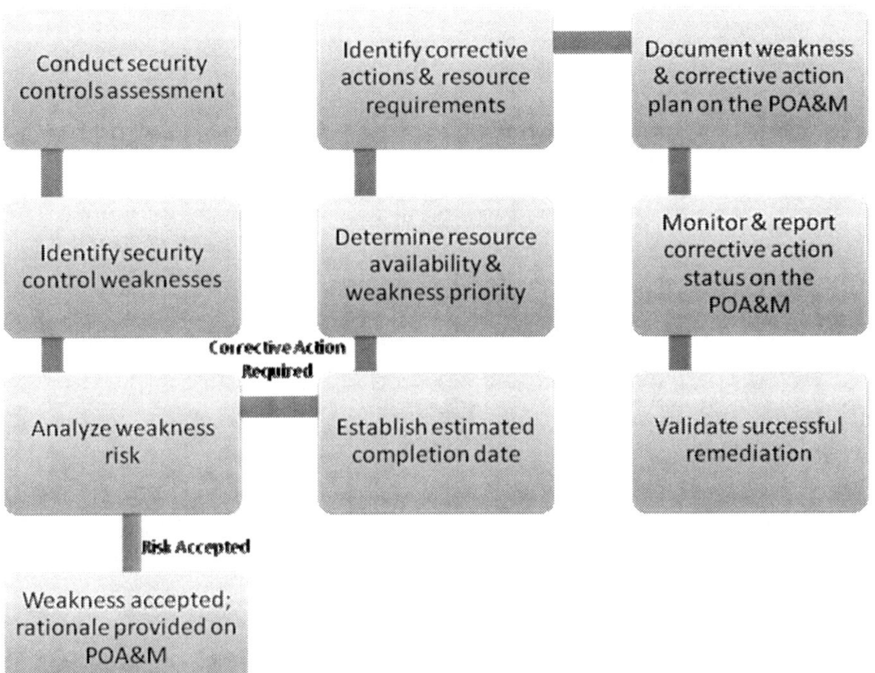

The weaknesses are analyzed to identify if there is a risk as a result of that weakness. In some cases, a specific corrective action may not be necessary when analysis reveals that the weakness can be considered an acceptable risk. In this case, management should sign-off that the risk is acceptable. In this case, the weakness does not have to be included in the POA&M.

Even in this case, a record of the risk acceptance must be documented, particularly since risks can change over time. The agency should record the rationale for accepting the risk. And the weakness should be reviewed periodically for changes in the acceptable risk level.

If analysis of the weakness indicates that action is required to mitigate risk, the agency should identify both the required corrective actions and the required resources. There are often multiple ways to mitigate a weakness, so the various methods should be analyzed for appropriateness in resolving the weakness fully and viewed for long-term implications. At this time, costs for each corrective action plan option must be estimated and analyzed to determine short-term and long-term solution capabilities.

The agency can usually obtain resources for weakness remediation through the following methods:

- Using current resources marked for security management of the system or program.
- Reallocating existing funds or personnel.
- Simply requesting additional funding.

If new or additional funding is needed, it is imperative to take advantage of the capital planning process to request the necessary funds. Integrating IT security costs into the overall capital planning process ensures that security is included in the agency's enterprise architecture, supports business operations, and is funded within each information system over its life cycle.

At its most basic level, weakness prioritization focuses on two essential prioritization criteria: system categorization and weakness risk level. System categorization should have already been determined as part of the system's risk assessment based on the Federal Information Processing Standards (FIPS) Publication 199, *Security Categorization of Federal Information and Information Systems*. According to FIPS 199, system categorization should be classified as high, moderate, or low, according to confidentiality, integrity, and availability criteria.

The second criterion for basic weakness prioritization is the potential impact of the weakness on the organization if it is left unresolved. The identified weakness' potential impact will be listed in the POA&M as high, medium, or low.

The estimated date of completion for the mitigation or removal of each weakness should be based on realistic timelines for resources to be obtained and the associated steps to be completed. Be sure to consider that while it may take 30 days to complete specific weaknesses individually, it may be impossible to address all these weaknesses concurrently, particularly if using the same resources. The completion date should ideally be based on the outcome of prioritization decisions and resource availability.

The POA&M provides the structure and consistency in the presentation of information about system security weakness and the mitigation plan. As a result, you can use the POA&M as a means of documentation, as well as a means to track completion of mitigating actions.

The information in the POA&M should be maintained continuously. Both DOD and the federal government require a quarterly status report to communicate overall progress in identifying and mitigating weaknesses. The table below shows the information required for the quarterly report.

Table 21: Quarterly POA&M report

POA&M updated information	Programs	Systems
Total # of weakness identified at the start of the quarter.		
# of weaknesses for which corrective action was completed on time including testing (by the end of the quarter).		
# of weaknesses for which corrective action is ongoing and is on track for completion as originally scheduled.		
# of weaknesses for which corrective action has been delayed and a brief explanation for the delay.		
# of new weaknesses discovered following the last POA&M update and a brief description of how the security weakness(es) were identified (e.g. IG inspection, audit, self-assessment).		

Finally, FISMA guidance for DOD and federal agencies directs that a **completed** status will only be assigned when a weakness has been fully mitigated and compliance has been validated. Therefore, it is imperative to incorporate follow-on testing of the affected security control(s) into the weakness mitigation process.

A typical POA&M and instructions on its completion are provided in Chapter 10 and a template is available on the accompanying CD. NOTE: Before completing your POA&M, you should check the most current guidance from OMB. This can be found at *http://www.whitehouse.gov/omb*.

Summary

If properly used, the POA&M's benefits can be significant and far-reaching. For federal agencies, the POA&M can provide a comprehensive reference that can be used to support ongoing efforts to address programmatic and system-specific vulnerabilities. The POA&M can be an essential management tool for the oversight and mitigation of security weaknesses.

To function as an effective management tool, the POA&M must be continually and diligently updated. Changes in the operating environment, levels of acceptable risk, and the availability of resources occur on a frequent basis. An effective and successful POA&M process will identify and respond to each one of these changes in a concise and complete fashion.

A mature POA&M program requires that the knowledge and efforts are sustainable over time and independent of any one person or personnel function. As a central repository, the POA&M eliminates the reliance on one resource and secures institutional knowledge. Although the POA&M initially represents a resource and time-intensive effort, if properly maintained, it has the potential to be a valuable tool for management and will improve the overall IT security posture.

AUTHORIZE the operation of the information system

In order to initiate the final step of this phase, the system owner must submit a security authorization package to the authorizing official. The security authorization package documents the results of the security control testing and provides the authorizing official (AO) with the essential information needed to make a credible, risk-based decision on whether to authorize operation of the information system.

The security authorization package

Unless specifically designated otherwise, the system owner is usually responsible for the assembly, compilation, and submission of the security authorization package for the authorizing official. Of course, the system owner cannot do this alone. The system owner receives inputs from the ISSO, certifying agent, security controls assessor, and others during the preparation of the security accreditation package.

The security authorization package

- System security plan (SSP)
- Assessment summary report
- Plan of action & milestones (POA&M)
- Certification statement

Federal laws and regulations mandate that certain documentation must be included in the authorization package. The minimum documentation includes:

The system security plan (SSP)

The SSP is usually prepared by the system owner, provides an overview of the security requirements for the information system and describes the security controls in place or planned for meeting those requirements. System security plans can be developed in accordance with NIST SP 800-18.

The objective is to use the SSP as an evolving, but binding, agreement on the level of security required from initiation of the system development or as changes to a system are made. After authorization, the SSP becomes the baseline security document. The uses of the SSP during the initial authorization phases and during the post authorization phase are shown below.

Figure 15: SSP use during and post authorization

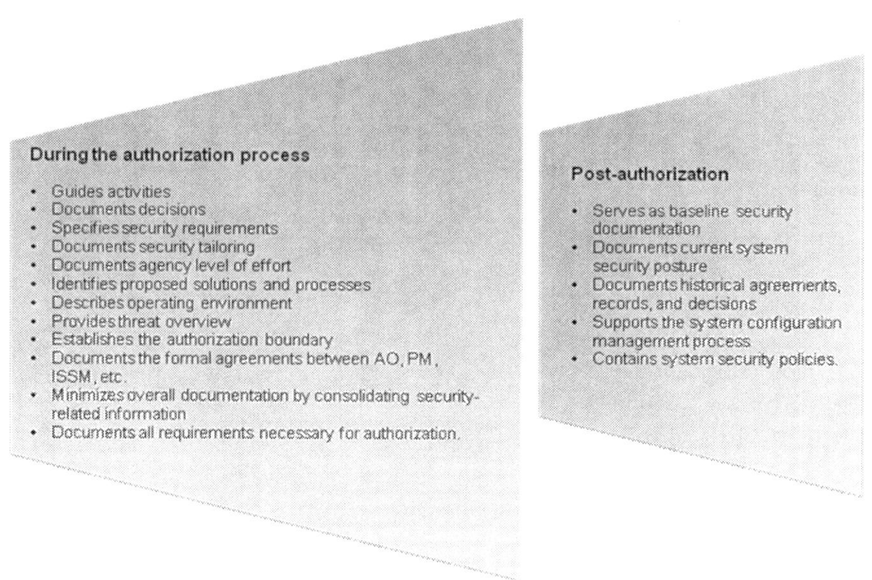

Although the term system security plan is commonly used for the basic security overview documentation, other agencies or environments might use other terminology. DOD currently requires a system identification profile (SIP) and a DIACAP implementation plan (DIP). You may also see a requirement for a system security authorization agreement (SSAA), although the use of this document in DOD became obsolete with the signing of the DODI 8510.01, *DOD Information Assurance C&A Process* (DIACAP). The SSP may also include supporting documentation:

- **A technical architecture document**, which can be prepared as a supplement to the system security plan for information systems to provide more detail on the system description, its environment, and interconnectivity.

- **A hardware and software inventory,** which may also be included as part of the configuration management process.

Assessment summary report

The assessment summary report summarizes the results of the security controls assessment and is usually prepared by the security control assessor. This summary provides an overview of the degree to which the controls have been implemented correctly, are operating as intended, and producing the desired outcome with respect to meeting the specified security requirements. The summary report provides the authorizing official with a synopsis of the findings, which are documented in detail in the security assessment report. The security assessment report should also contain recommended corrective actions for weaknesses or deficiencies identified in the security controls.

A plan of action and milestones (POA&M)

The POA&M identifies tasks that need to be accomplished to mitigate risks to an information system. The POA&M is initiated by the certifying agent for use by the system owner, and it details resources required to accomplish the elements of the plan, any milestones in meeting the tasks, and scheduled completion dates for the milestones.

The certification statement

The certification statement is prepared by the certifying agent to provide information to the designated approving authority to permit an informed decision regarding the secure operation of the system. The statement provides a summary of the results of certification testing; highlights certification activities; records the degree to which security controls are correctly implemented and effective; identifies the level of risk to system assets and to the agency's operations and personnel; states the level of compliance with statutory and regulatory requirements; and documents the certification level of the system.

The security authorization may also contain additional documents or references, including key security-related documents for the information system such as the privacy impact assessment (PIA), incident response plan, configuration management (CM) plan, security configuration checklists, rules of behavior, and any system interconnection agreements. Additional documents that are part of the evidence required in the authorization process, but may not necessarily be provided to the authorizing official as part of the authorization decision process, include:[77]

- The **risk assessment** prepared by the system owner and approved by the authorizing official, which documents risks to the information systems by identifying system assets, evaluating threats to these assets, and vulnerabilities to safeguards protecting system assets. The risk assessment evaluates the effectiveness and applicability of the minimum security baseline control set and recommends adjustments to minimum safeguards according to system-specific risks. The risk assessment will follow a standard methodology approved by NIST (*see* NIST SP 800-30).

- The **contingency plan** documents management policy and procedures that are designed to maintain or restore business operations supported by the system, potentially at an alternate location, in the event of emergencies, system failures, or disaster. However, a contingency plan is not required when the availability of system resources is covered by a contingency plan for another system (i.e. general support system). Contingency plans will be developed in accordance with the standard methodology approved by NIST (*see* NIST SP 800-34).

- The **security test and evaluation (ST&E) plan** and results report, prepared by the certifying agent and approved by the system owner and authorizing official, documents the plan for

---

[77] Samples of these and other documents relevant to the security authorization process are provided on the accompanying CD.

certifying the system and provides the results of the assessment of security controls in the system to determine the extent to which the controls are implemented correctly, operating as intended, and producing the desired outcome. The ST&E plan is generally submitted and approved prior to the beginning of certification testing.

Importance of the certifying authority and the certification statement

The certifying authority[78] (CA) may be an individual, group, or organization responsible for conducting a security certification. This certification is based on a comprehensive assessment by the security controls assessor of the management, operational, and technical security controls in an information system to determine the extent to which the controls are implemented correctly, operating as intended, and producing the desired outcome with respect to meeting the security requirements for the system.

The CA also provides recommended corrective actions to reduce or eliminate vulnerabilities in the information system. Prior to initiating the security assessment activities part of the certification process, the CA may also provide an independent assessment of the system security plan (SSP) to ensure the plan provides a set of security controls for the information system adequate to meet all applicable security requirements.

To preserve the impartial and unbiased nature of the security certification, the CA should be in a position independent from the persons directly responsible for the development and deployment of the information system or the day-to-day operation of the system.

The CA should also be independent of the organization responsible for correcting security deficiencies identified during the security controls testing process. The CA's independence is an important factor in assessing the credibility of the security assessment results

---

[78] Also called certifying authority, certification agent and certifying agent.

and ensuring the authorizing official receives the most objective information possible in order to make an informed, risk-based, accreditation decision. The CA should work closely with the risk executive (function) on assessing the relative risk to the information system posed by the non-compliant security controls.

The certification determination and the associated certification statement to the authorizing official is the certifying authority's validation of the system's compliance with the security controls, the identification and assessment of the risks associated with operating the system, and the balance with the cost to correct or mitigate the security weakness.

The certification determination is based on the actual security control test results. The impact associated with a security control in a non-compliant status, the expected exposure time (i.e. the projected life of the system release or configuration minus the time to correct or mitigate the security control weakness), and the cost to correct or mitigate (e.g. dollars, functionality reductions) are considered.

Certification considers:

- The security posture of the information system itself – the overall reliability and viability of the information system, plus the acceptability of the implementation and performance of the security control mechanisms or safeguards inherent in the system itself.
- How the information system behaves in the larger information environment. In other words, does the information system introduce vulnerabilities into the environment, does the system correctly and securely interact with information environment management and control services, and is its visibility to situational awareness and information system defense services adequate?

The security authorization decision

The security authorization decision is made by the authorizing official and represents a balance of mission or business need, protection of personal privacy, protection of the information being processed, and protection of the information environment, and thus, by extension, protection of other missions or business functions reliant upon the shared information environment.

The authorization package forms the basis for the authorizing official's decision. The CA's recommendation is often heavily weighted in the authorizing official's considerations.

In addition to the CA's recommendation and the package content, the authorizing official should consider many factors when deciding if the risk to agency operations, agency assets, or individuals of operating an information system is acceptable. Balancing security considerations with mission and operational needs is paramount to achieving an acceptable accreditation decision. The authorizing official renders an accreditation decision for the information system after reviewing all of the relevant information and, where appropriate, consulting with key agency officials.

The authorization statement documents the security authorization decision from the authorizing official. The authorization statement usually contains the following information:

- security accreditation decision;
- supporting rationale for the decision;
- summarization of corrective actions required;
- identification of residual risks;
- limitations to operations; and
- terms and conditions for the authorization.

There are two very basic "authorization to operate" decisions: the authorization statement indicates to the information system owner whether the system is either authorized to operate or is not authorized to operate. The supporting rationale provides the information system owner with the justification for the authorizing official's decision. The terms and conditions for the authorization provide a description of any limitations or restrictions placed on the operation of the information system that must be adhered to by the information system owner. The authorization statement is attached to the original package and returned to the information system owner.

Authorization to operate (ATO)

An ATO decision is issued by the authorizing official if, after a review of the authorization package, the risk of operating the information system is determined to be acceptable. An ATO usually means that the information system has no significant restrictions or limitations on its operation. It does not imply that there were no weaknesses determined in the security controls assessment process. In fact, we have not seen an information system that had NO weaknesses.

An ATO does mean that, wherever it is cost effective to do so, the organization should take specific actions to reduce or eliminate identified weaknesses. An ATO generally lasts for three years before re-authorization is required — barring any significant security-related events[79] that might require a re-authorization.

In summary, an ATO (full accreditation) can be granted under the following conditions:

- The certification package is complete.
- No corrective actions are required.
- Residual risks are acceptable to the DAA.

Interim authorization to operate (IATO)

If the authorizing official determines that the weaknesses associated with operating an information system are not acceptable, but there

---

[79] The definition of "significant security-related events" may differ across organizations. It is critical for your organization to define what this means for you. Examples include changes in location, changes in information sensitivity level, changes in the operating system, and/or a major security incident.

is a mission requirement for the information system to be placed into operation or to continue operating, the authorizing official may choose to issue an IATO. An IATO is acceptable only when the identified security weaknesses resulting from the security controls testing are significant, but further analysis indicates they could reasonably be addressed in a timely manner.

An interim authorization allows the information system to operate under specific terms and conditions. It acknowledges that the operation of the information system may pose increased risk to the organization for a specified period of time. The IATO will contain the authorizing official's terms and conditions for operation of the information system.

An IATO accreditation decision is intended to manage system security weaknesses. It is not intended to be a device for signaling an evolutionary approach to information system security. Nor should the IATO be considered a preliminary step to acquiring full authorization to operate. Information systems will continue to change throughout their lifetime, so an organization should not try to wait for an ATO to be granted only for information systems for which no change is planned or foreseen. Such thinking can engender an abuse of the real purpose of the IATO and present an inaccurate portrayal of an information system's security posture.

To summarize, an IATO may be employed in the following situations:

- A new system is in an advanced test phase and may be deployed prior to final design and test of operational capability.
- A survey has concluded that there are no apparent security problems that would allow unauthorized persons to access data in a system, but there has been insufficient time or resources for rigorous hardware and software testing.
- The configuration of an operational system has been altered. Initial security evaluation by appropriate personnel does not reveal any severe problems, but a full evaluation has had scheduling delays.

- A system that will be fielded at multiple sites has been evaluated in a test environment. Full accreditation will occur when it is finalized for deployment.

Denial of authorization to operate (DATO)

The authorizing official always has the option to specifically deny an information system the authorization to operate.[80] A DATO is issued in those cases where the authorizing official considers the risk of operating the information system to be unacceptable. In this case, the information system should not be placed into operation. If it is currently operating, all activity should be halted.

A DATO usually indicates that there are significant security control weaknesses. The authorizing official or designated representative may often set a suspense for the implementation of proactive measures to correct the security weaknesses in the information system and to reapply for authorization to operate.

The DOD allows for an additional authorization category – the interim authority to test.

Interim authority to test (IATT)

The IATT authorization decision is a special case that allows an information system – potentially still in developmental status – to conduct essential tests in an operational information environment or with live data for a specified period of time. An IATT may not be used to avoid ATO or IATO validation activity and certification determination requirements for authorizing a system to operate.

---

[80] The current NIST SP 800-37 and DODI 8510.01 specifically call out the DATO as an authorization option. The proposed revision of NIST SP 800-37 only discusses ATO and IATO, assuming that the absence of either is an indication of an implicit DATO.

Accreditation decision letter

The authorization decision letter transmits the authorizing official's accreditation decision. The AO attaches the certification documentation to the authorization letter and transmits it to the system owner.

Upon receipt of the authorization statement and the associated package, the system owner accepts the terms and conditions of the authorization. The system owner maintains the original authorization statement and package on file. The authorizing official and the IAM/ISSM should also retain copies of the security authorization decision letter. The contents of the security certification and authorization-related documentation (especially information dealing with information system vulnerabilities) will be marked and protected appropriately in accordance with agency policy, and will be retained in accordance with the agency's record retention policy.

Milestones from the verify, validate and authorize activities

Before proceeding on to the next phase, the operate and maintain activities, let's take a final look at what you should have achieved in this phase:

- You determined your security control assessment team.
- The security control test plan was planned and executed.
- The results of the security controls testing were collected and analyzed.
- Security control weaknesses were identified.
- A plan of action and milestones was developed.
- The certifying authority provided a recommendation for authorization.
- The SSP, a summary of the security controls tests, the POA&M, and the CA recommendation were provided as a package to the authorizing official.
- The authorizing official made an authorization decision and provided this decision to the organization.

Further reading
Gregg, Michael and Kim, David. *Inside Network Security Assessment: Guarding Your IT Infrastructure*, Sams Publishing, November 2005. Rogers, Russ et al. *Network Security Evaluation: Using the NSA IEM*, Syngress Publications, July 2005.

References

National Institute of Standards and Technology (NIST) Special Publication 800-18, *Guideline for Developing Security Plans for Federal Information Systems*, February 2006.

National Institute of Standards and Technology (NIST) Special Publication 800-37, *Guide for the Security Certification and Accreditation of Federal Information Systems*, March 2004.

National Institute of Standards and Technology (NIST) Special Publication 800-42, *Guideline on Network Security Testing*, October 2003.

National Institute of Standards and Technology Special Publication 800-53, Revision 2, *Recommended Security Controls for Federal Information Systems*, December 2007.

National Institute of Standards and Technology (NIST) Special Publication 800-53A, *Guide for Assessing the Security Controls in Federal Information Systems*, July 2008.

National Institute of Standards and Technology Special Publication 800-59, *Guideline for Identifying an Information System as a National Security System*, August 2003.

Office of Management and Budget (OMB) Circular A-11, *Preparation, Submission and Execution of the Budget*, (Revised June 26, 2008). Available at *http://www.whitehouse.gov/omb/circulars/a11/current_year/a11_to c.html*.

Office of Management and Budget, Memorandum (M)-02-01, *Guidance for Preparing and Submitting Security Plans of Action and Milestones*, October 17, 2001. Available at *http://www.whitehouse.gov/omb/memoranda/m02-01.html*.

Office of Management and Budget, Circular A-130, Appendix III, *Transmittal Memorandum #4, Management of Federal Information Resources*, November 2000.

Public Law 107-347 [H.R. 2458], *The E-Government Act of 2002 Title III, of this Act is the Federal Information Security Management Act of 2002 (FISMA)*, December 17, 2002.

CHAPTER 8: OPERATE & MAINTAIN – MAINTAINING AUTHORIZATION

The world is not your problem; the problem is your unawareness.[81]

Baghwan Shree Rajneesh, Indian Spiritual Leader

In this chapter:

Monitor the security controls: situational awareness

Conduct the annual review and security reporting

Maintain the authorization

---

[81] http://thinkexist.com/quotes/with/keyword/unawareness/

Wikipedia defines situational awareness as "the perception of environmental elements within a volume of time and space, the comprehension of their meaning, and the projection of their status in the near future. It is also a field of study concerned with perception of the environment critical to decision makers in complex, dynamic areas." More simply, situational awareness is knowing what's happening around you and understanding its importance and relevance to your environment.

Figure 16: C&A process 3

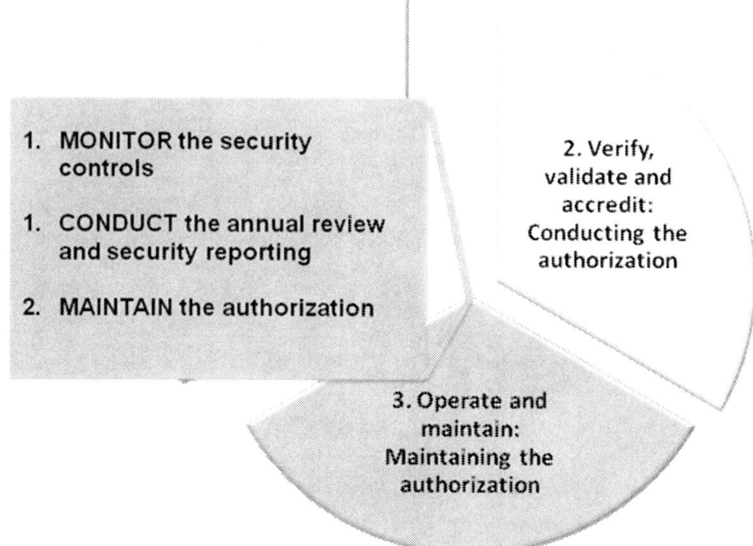

This chapter revolves around the operation of the information system and ensuring that you maintain situational awareness at all times about the status of your system security.

The previous phase ended with the authorization to operate an information system. The post-authorization phase begins with the requirement for continuous monitoring of the security controls and security status reporting – all culminating in the maintenance of the authorization to operate. This phase continues until:

- The information system is removed from service.
- A major change is planned and/or implemented for the information system.
- An updated security control compliance validation is required.

The operate and maintain phase consists of activities required to operate and manage the information system at an acceptable level of risk. Maintaining a secure information system must be an ongoing process. It requires you to continuously weigh the risk of operation against system functionality, the operating environment, and available resources. In order to be effective, you must always maintain what the DOD calls "situational awareness."

MONITOR the security control status: situational awareness

Effective information system security programs must also include an aggressive continuous monitoring program to check the status of the security controls in the information system on an ongoing basis.

Continuous monitoring of the security control status, also called situational awareness, is a proven technique to address the security impacts on information systems resulting from changes to the hardware, software, firmware, or operational environment.

Continued authorization to operate is contingent upon the sustainment of an acceptable security posture, which is accomplished through ensuring continued compliance with assigned security controls. The information system security manager

(ISSM)[82] has the primary responsibility for maintaining situational awareness and initiating actions to improve or restore IA posture.

The primary tasks involved in monitoring support of situational awareness include:

- Continuous change and configuration management.
- Ongoing security control verification.

Change and configuration management

The ISSM and system owner should continuously monitor the information system and its environment for security relevant events and configuration changes to the system or information environment that might negatively impact the security posture. The ISSM and/or the owner of the information system also continuously and periodically assesses the quality of the security controls implementation against performance indicators such as security incidents, feedback from external inspection agencies (e.g. Inspector General, Government Accountability Office), exercises, operational evaluations, etc. Additionally, the ISSM, independently or at the direction of the CA or authorizing official, may schedule a re-validation of any or all IA controls at any time.

What is a security relevant event?

Defining what constitutes a security relevant event often presents a challenge to an organization. Security-relevant events may include:

- Expiration of a security control re-validation period. Certain security controls may have assigned re-validation periods in which the control must be re-validated.
- Security events defined by the security control. The ISSM must also remain particularly cognizant of the security controls related to configuration and vulnerability management, performance

---

[82] Also known as the information assurance manager (IAM).

monitoring, and periodic independent evaluations, e.g. penetration testing.

- Significant changes to an information system. Configuration changes to the system or information environment could impact the security posture of the system. Examples include, but are not limited to:

  - Installation of a new or upgraded operating system, middleware component, or application.
  - Modifications to system ports, protocols, or services.
  - Installation of a new or upgraded hardware platform or firmware component.
  - Modifications to cryptographic modules or services.
  - Changes in laws, directives, policies, or regulations.
  - IAVAs or patch alerts.

Situational awareness is the end result of continuous monitoring. It involves documenting the proposed or actual changes to the information system and subsequently determining the impact of those proposed or actual changes on the security of the system.

Information systems will typically be in a constant state of change as a result of upgrades to hardware, software, or firmware or modifications to the surrounding environment in which the system is deployed. Documenting information system changes and assessing the potential impact those changes may have on the security of the system is an essential aspect of continuous monitoring, situational awareness, and maintaining the security authorization. This critical process is referred to as configuration management (CM) or change management.

Configuration management processes

Having formal configuration management (CM) processes in your organization will ensure that you can manage change in your information systems – SECURELY! In fact, without CM you probably wouldn't even notice when your information system has undergone a security-relevant change.

CM can be defined as the process of establishing and maintaining the technical integrity of an information system throughout its life cycle by systematically identifying, controlling, and accounting for all changes made to that system. A mature CM process is critical to your organization's ability to effectively manage and track system changes.

A configuration management plan (CMP) is essential to this process. Chapter 10 outlines the major elements of a CMP and provides a description of the content that should be included in the plan. In addition, we also provide a high-level introduction to CM and CMPs, including what CM is, what a CMP is, and why and when a CMP should be developed. The section also describes, in depth, the configuration control process (CCP), which is the most important element of the CMP. A template for a CMP can be found on the accompanying CD.

What is a configuration management plan?

A CMP should be a living document that identifies CM roles and responsibilities, resources, and all of the formal processes and procedures needed to ensure that proposed changes to an information system are evaluated and approved prior to implementation. This includes activities, such as system-wide upgrades, replacements, and deployments.

A well-written CMP should include and address CM roles and responsibilities, communications, the system configuration baseline, configuration control processes, and CM resources. A sample configuration management plan is included on the CD.

Why have a configuration management plan?

Many organizations may already be doing some form of CM for their information systems and may question the need for a formal, documented plan. There are two reasons for developing and maintaining a CMP:

- It is the law! OMB A-130, the *Handbook for Information Assurance Security Policy*, and other federal laws and regulations, require you to develop a CM process and document it in a CMP.
- A documented CMP will really help your organization to implement and mature your CM processes.

A well-developed CMP will ensure:

- Changes to the configuration are identified and evaluated to determine the impact to system security before implementation. Ideally, this process will start at the system concept and development and be carried out until the information system is replaced. Since each change is tracked from initial system development through completion, a thorough history of changes is created for that system. For example, an information system running on an older version of the Windows® Operating System (OS) may require an upgrade to a more recent version because of existing vulnerabilities in the older version. Upgrading to the more recent version of the Windows® OS will change the system's configuration. The need for a version upgrade is a configuration change that must be evaluated in terms of impact on the security, system performance, and functionality, as well as that of the overall enterprise.
- Configuration changes are documented, ensuring that version control is maintained. Upgrades and additions are easily implemented as a result of the hardware and software controls in a formal CM process. As part of the CMP, system documentation can easily be checked to verify whether the designed configuration allows the system to achieve its objective. For example, if an information system design needs to be modified to implement a more stringent password policy for users, it could be determined that this change must be included in a planned update. Prior to the new version's implementation, all changes should be documented to ensure that version control is maintained.
- The configuration is verified against the initial baseline ensuring that all changes have been maintained and documented for any

new parties involved in the CM process. Information on the system, including the manufacturer, model type, and software version, is recorded and tracked, ensuring access to the most recent system information.

When should you develop a CMP?

Ideally, you would create your CMP at the beginning of the system life cycle (SLC). This ensures that a CM process has been established to control, track, and maintain all changes that are made to the information system throughout the SLC. Your CMP should be a living document and be reviewed and updated as needed – at least annually.

It is possible to develop a CMP after your information system has already been deployed. In this case, you should maximize the re-use of existing system documentation (i.e. system security plan, system configuration documents, system maintenance records, vendor manuals, system configuration diagrams, and security-related information) in the development of the CMP.

Ongoing security control verification

Organizations should rely on the configuration management process, the most recent assessments, the results of previous security validation tests, and knowledge of the organization's operational requirements – all of which may influence the selection of security controls to be monitored and the frequency of the monitoring process. Top priority for control monitoring should be directed at those security controls that have the greatest potential for change after implementation, have the highest criticality for the system's security, or the controls that have been identified in the organization's plan of action and milestones. Security control volatility is one measure of how frequently a control is likely to change over time after implementation.

For example, security policies and implementing procedures or the physical facility itself are not likely to change from one year to the next and thus might be considered security controls with low volatility. Access control mechanisms, intrusion detection mechanisms, or other technical security controls that are subject to the effects of frequent changes in hardware, software, and/or firmware components may be considered security controls with high volatility.

In most cases, organizations will likely choose to apply greater resources or pay additional attention to security controls deemed to be of higher volatility, and there may be a higher return on investment for assessing controls of this type. Security controls identified in the POA&M may also be a top priority in the continuous monitoring process, since these controls have been deemed to be ineffective to some degree (or in the worst case, non-existent).

In summary, organizations must make informed judgments regarding the application of their limited resources when conducting continuous monitoring activities. There is a responsibility to ensure that security expenditures are consistent with the organization's mission and other requirements.

CONDUCT the annual review and security reporting

The results of continuous monitoring should be reported to the authorizing official and senior agency information security officer regularly or as needed. The continuous monitoring results should also be considered when identifying possible updates to the information system security requirements or the plan of action and milestones. This is important since the authorizing official, senior agency information security officer, information system owner, and security assessor may be using these plans to guide future security assessment activities.

The Federal Information Security Management Act (FISMA) (section 3544(b)(5)) requires each agency to perform "periodic testing and evaluation of the effectiveness of information security policies, procedures, and practices, to be performed with a frequency depending on risk, but no less than annually" for all of their information systems. This review includes the testing of all of the management, operational and technical security controls.

Not less than annually, the program manager/system owner and/or the ISSM will provide a written statement to the authorizing official, based on the review of all of the security controls for continued compliance. Annual security control reviews can consist of one or a combination of: performing security self-assessments, formal security tests and evaluation (ST&E), vulnerability testing, management directed audits, and any continuous monitoring such as intrusion detection.

Consistently, audits of federal agencies highlight deficiencies in this area. Specifically, the annual review of the security controls was often found to be inadequately conducted, and annual self-assessments of security controls were not always completed. In addition, testing itself was sometimes inadequate or conclusions reached did not always reflect the actual status of the control environment. Without adequate security control testing, audits found that management lacked assurance that security controls were operating as intended.

Even when using a self-assessment to review the security controls, you should not rely only on discussions of controls, instead of physically verifying their effectiveness. While this approach may be sufficient for low-risk systems, it certainly does not provide adequate assurance that security controls are correctly implemented and operating as intended on systems with higher risk, such as the financial and SCADA systems.

In some of the organizations we have supported, there were occasionally discrepancies between the certification agent's assessment and the actual security documentation for the systems reviewed. NIST guidance, such as the NIST SP 800-53A, can be used to perform a self-assessment consisting of a table-top exercise, but the results of the assessment should contain explanations as to how the assessment team arrived at its conclusions and which of the system security controls were examined.

We receive a lot of questions about the annual review requirements: how should it be done, are all security controls subject to testing, who should execute the review, and what annual review determinations can be made?

The following activities should be conducted as part of the annual security control testing:

- Direct the system developer/maintainer and the component ISSO/SSO to identify a sub-set of internal controls to test annually. The object is to validate each of the controls at least once every three years using standard testing procedures and techniques.
- Ensure the testing is conducted.
- Submit information regarding any findings in the quarterly POA&M update.

The depth and breadth of an annual system review depends on several factors, such as:

- the potential risk and magnitude of harm to the system or data;
- changes in the information system or its operating environment;
- the relative comprehensiveness of the most recent past review; and,
- the success of the remediation of system security weaknesses identified in the POA&M for that information system.

For example, if a system recently underwent a successful authorization process – including a security controls assessment – then a relatively simple update or maintenance review may be sufficient, provided that the original security assessment results and the POA&M have been adequately documented.

As a result of the annual review and the status of the security controls, the agency can make several possible determinations for action:

- There is no change in the authorization status, no corrective action is required, and the system can remain in operation to the authorization termination date.

- There is no change in the authorization status, the system owner/PM is directed to initiate security improvements, and the system can remain in operation to the authorization termination date.
- The authorization status is downgraded to an interim authority to operate, the system owner/PM is directed to either develop a POA&M or amend an existing POA&M, and the authorization to operate is set to 180 days or less pending weakness remediation.
- The authorization status is downgraded to a denial to operate and the system operation is halted pending weakness remediation.

MAINTAIN the authorization

Current federal and DOD regulations mandate that systems be re-authorized every three years — also called the authorization termination date (ATD) – or when significant changes are made to the system configuration. Program managers and system owners should establish a process to monitor system re-authorization dates.

If the system is not significantly altered, the system owner can begin the process for re-authorization in a timely fashion. With good planning, the process can be complete before the three-year anniversary of the system accreditation has passed.

Potential changes in accreditation status can also be triggered by the annual reviews, as well as the scheduled termination of an authorization, and changes to the system security status may be event-driven. An authorizing official may downgrade or revoke an accreditation decision any time risk conditions or concerns so warrant.

Certain events may also prompt a requirement for re-authorization. In this case, the level of effort required for re-certification and re-authorization can depend on the scope of the change and the degree to which the security control compliance status has been maintained.

The re-authorization process may require the organization to execute many of the same steps needed for the original authorization; however, organizations should seek to maximize re-use of any portions of the security documentation that remains valid.

Below are examples of events that might precipitate a system re-authorization.

- A change in criticality or sensitivity level of the information processed.
- A breach of security or violation of system integrity that reveals a significant flaw in security design, system security management, policy, or procedure.
- A change in the threat environment impacting overall system risk.
- A change in the system security mode of operation.
- A change in the operating system, security software, or hardware that affects the authorized security countermeasure implementation.

Milestones from the operate and maintain activities

Before proceeding to the next phase, the remove the information system from operation activities, let's take a final look at what you should have achieved in this phase:

- You have established a process for continuous monitoring.
- A configuration management process is in place.
- A sub-set of the security controls has been selected for the annual review.
- The annual review is being conducted and the results are documented in the SSP and POA&M as required.
- Quarterly and annual FISMA reports are being prepared as required by law and the agency.
- The authorization to operate is maintained, unless a re-authorization is required.

<table>
<tr><td>Further reading</td></tr>
<tr><td>Lyon, David. *Practical CM: Best Configuration Management Practices for the 21st Century,* Butterworth-Heinemann Publishers, 2000.</td></tr>
</table>

References

ISO10007:2003, *Quality Management Systems — Guidelines for Configuration Management.* International Organization for Standardization, June 2003.

ISO/IEC 27001:2005, *Information technology – Security techniques – Information security management systems – Requirements.* International Organization for Standardization, October 2005.

CHAPTER 9: REMOVE THE INFORMATION SYSTEM FROM OPERATION

A word carries far, very far, deals destruction through time as the bullets go flying through space.[83]

Joseph Conrad, Author

In this chapter:

Required actions to remove an information system from operation

Avoiding self-inflicted security problems

Methods of removing an information system and/or its information

---

[83] *http://www.brainyquote.com/quotes/keywords/destruction.html*

The process of formally removing an information system from operation is a critical, but frequently overlooked, component of the system life cycle. Every information system has a system life cycle and an expiration date. Ideally, removing the system from operation – or decommissioning – should be an important consideration from the inception of the project, during its design and throughout its operation.

A strategy for securely removing the information system from operation should be developed for each of the following circumstances:

- An information system is upgraded and the outdated system is scheduled to be sold, donated, discarded or recycled.
- An information system is fully reconfigured for existing or new users.
- Computer equipment that stores data is returned to a manufacturer or reseller for repair or resale.
- As one method for ensuring that malicious code from a virus attack or hacking attempt is completely removed from the information system.
- A hot spare is put into service and then removed when no longer needed.

Required actions when removing an information system from operation

Several actions are required to effectively and securely remove the information system from operation. First, any inheritance relationships must be identified and assessed for security and operational impact if the system is removed.

Next, it is important to identify any information that needs to be retrieved from the information system and retained. This activity is referred to as information preservation.

Agencies should review the security controls and make sure that all security controls addressing information system decommissioning are implemented. These include security controls for media sanitization, configuration management, and information system control.

In some cases, the storage media associated with the information system will need to be purged, sanitized, degaussed, or even destroyed – depending on the nature and sensitivity of the information contained on the system. There are several regulations that provide useful information on determining the actions required prior to release of the equipment. For example, the DOD 5220.22-M, *National Industry Security Program Operating Manual (NISPOM)*, February 28, 2006 provides specific instructions.

If using configuration management tools, the agency's tracking and management systems should be updated to indicate the specific information system components that are being removed from the inventory. All of the security documentation should be updated to reflect the new status of the information system.

Any external and internal users and application owners hosted on the decommissioned information system should be notified.

The removal from operation or decommissioning plan

Sometimes it helps to develop a formal plan for removing the information system from operation. In some projects, a preliminary plan for removal from operation is developed during the initial system life cycle phases. In others, the plan won't be developed until there is a realization that the information system needs to be removed.

In either case, there are certain actions that should be addressed in the plan:

- Identification of key participants and their respective roles and responsibilities.
- Estimate of the costs/resources associated with the removal of the information system.
- Description of the information system before the removal activities.

- Target description of the information system status after the removal activities.
- Description of the processes and/or tools that will be used during the removal process.
- An estimate of the type and quantity of the information stored on the system and its retention requirements.
- An analysis of any inheritance conditions associated with the information system.
- Relocation and/or destruction information after the removal of the information system.
- Process for notifying any stakeholders.
- Process for retaining the records. NOTE: Once a removal and sanitization process is executed for the DOD, secure execution of the process must be certified and the records retained for six years.

Avoiding self-inflicted security issues through effective system removal

At least once a year or so, there is a report on the front pages of a major newspaper that an organization has allowed data to escape due to ineffective and incomplete removal of the information system from operation. Failure to protect or destroy sensitive and confidential information can potentially have catastrophic consequences to an organization. Financial loss, damage to reputation, civil and criminal liability or even loss of life could result from data that is accessed from information systems that were not thoroughly and securely processed for removal.

This is not just a problem for federal agencies. Any organization with sensitive data can be affected. Simson Garfinkel conducted a study for part of his 2005 dissertation while studying Computer Security at MIT's Computer Science and Artificial Intelligence laboratory. Garfinkel purchased 230 used hard drives from various re-sellers. He reviewed the content and discovered a remarkable amount of sensitive data that could have caused serious harm to the original owners had this information fallen into the wrong hands.

Garfinkel was able to access information, such as corporate trade secrets, financial records, personal medical records and even credit card numbers.

Congress has passed several laws mandating penalties for non-compliance, and restrictions and consequences only promise to become increasingly severe. These include:

Table 22: Penalties for non-compliance

	Gramm Leach Bliley	Sarbanes Oxley	HIPAA	FACTA
	Financial Services Modernization Act	Public Company Accounting Reform & Investor Protection Act	Health Insurance Portability and Accountability Act	Fair & Accurate Credit Transaction Act
Directors & officers - penalty per act	$10K	$1 Million		
Institution - penalty per violation	$100K	$5 Million	$11K	$50 - 250K
Years in prison	5-12	20	1-10	
FDIC insurance	Terminated			
Impact on operations	Cease and desist			
Individual civil fines	$1 Million		$25K	Civil action
Institution civil fines	1% of assets			

So, what are some of the (self-inflicted) possible consequences of an improper or incomplete removal of an information system from operation?

- If the data release results in a security breach which is made public, the resulting firestorm can become a public relations nightmare. The organization's reputation may be severely damaged as the perception may persist that this is an organization that can't be trusted. In the commercial sector, investors may retrieve their investments and look for other opportunities.
- The organization and/or its employees can be held liable for any resulting damages, such as credit card information used for fraudulent charges and civil lawsuits incurred for the release of private records.
- The responsible directors and officers may face embarrassing public trials. Additionally, there can be fines of up to $1 million per violation (note that there can be many potential violations in each information system) and up to 20 years in prison per offense.
- If the security breach and resulting data loss is severe enough, the organization may cease to exist.

Methods of removing an information system and/or its data from operation

There are a number of approved methods of removing an information system and/or its information. For federal agencies and the DOD, there are specific legal and regulatory requirements.

Some of the most common methods include:

- Overwriting: The process of erasing, or "wiping," the contents of an electronic file or disk space, often using specific tools and/or software. Overwriting of data means replacing previously stored data on a storage media device with a predetermined pattern of meaningless information. Depending on the number of overwrites, the data can be effectively rendered unrecoverable. It is virtually impossible to restore data on storage media that has been properly "wiped."

- Physical destruction: The physical destruction of a storage media device is a process whereby the physical storage media is rendered useless and inaccessible. Sometimes older computers are barely worth the effort of carrying to the junkyard or they contain information too sensitive to risk any possibility of its exposure outside of the organization. In these cases, you should understand that junking the computer does not eliminate its data. Recycling may be an enlightened technique for hardware; although it is not always what you need to protect your data. Magnetic storage is remarkably resilient and most physical disposal techniques have little or no effect on the media itself, even if it is not accessible through conventional means. Before final removal of the system, extra care must be exercised to keep that data from reappearing in someone else's files.

- Degaussing. Degaussing is the process of exposing storage media to powerful magnetic fields for the purpose of scrambling the contents of the media into an unrecognizable mess. For relatively low density media, such as CDs, a degaussing tool of adequate power can be a quick and effective way of clearing data. For high-density storage, however, it can be time consuming, less effective, and may have other detrimental effects. Not all degaussing machines are powerful enough to penetrate the cover of a hard drive to get to the storage platters inside. Therefore, the platters must be removed for degaussing, which can also destroy the drive. Machines that are powerful enough to penetrate the shielding are often so powerful that all the controlling circuitry is also destroyed. While destruction of the drive might be one of the acceptable options, you must also consider that there is no simple way to verify that the data has truly been eliminated once the drive itself is no longer useable.

- Transfer. For the purposes of this book, transfer means the physical removal or change of ownership of information technology equipment from one agency to another entity.

- Redeployment. Decommissioning an information system often involves taking a computer initially designated for one task and simply reconfiguring it for another task. It is often cheaper to replace that application server purchased eighteen months ago than to upgrade it and it can often be turned into a great workstation or low-end system somewhere else in the organization. However, such an install does not really remove old information from the storage media. Extra care must be taken to ensure that the sensitive information stored during its previous life doesn't accidentally show up where it doesn't belong.

- Auction or donation. When an information system no longer has a useful purpose within one organization, there are plenty of external entities that may be able to use the computer or its components. Low-cost employee purchase plans are one popular avenue, as well as donating the systems to a charitable organization or school. Some organizations have higher-than-normal performance requirements, and decommissioned systems might still be considered "state of the art" in other organizations. They could also warrant resale or auctioning to recoup some of the investment in newer, cutting edge technology. As with redeployment, special precautions must be taken to ensure that sensitive data on that computer system doesn't show up where it doesn't belong.

Before selecting any process for the secure removal of an information system or its information from operation, be sure to review the current regulations and processes. While there are many guidelines for dealing with the decommissioning of information systems and their media, the recommendations are not always followed or the processes proposed are often no longer effective due to changes in technology.

Data you may not know you have

In addition to the data directly controlled by the system's applications, computers can also store significant quantities of sensitive information that may not be immediately visible to their operators. Many applications and even operating systems store passwords, user information, encryption keys, and other sensitive data in the background and in multiple locations, such as configuration files, registry entries, and temporary files.

Virtual memory systems can write out random contents of application memory to the storage disk in a haphazard manner, so that it may be almost impossible to know exactly what is stored on the system. The challenge in removing an information system is often identifying what information exists, before you can start protecting it from undesired retrieval.

Some examples of tools

Here is a list of tools, some of which have been approved by the DOD, for use in media sanitization.[84]

Tools used for overwriting hard drives using DOD approved packages:

- WipeDrive 3.0 *www.whitecanyon.com*. Windows® platform – DOD approved. Erases files, folders, cookies, or an entire drive.
- CyberScrub *www.cyberscrub.com*. Windows® platform – DOD approved. Erases files, folders, cookies, or an entire drive. Implements Gutmann patterns.
- DataScrubber *www.scsitoolbox.com/products/DataScrubber.asp* Windows®, Unix platforms – DOD approved. Handles SCSI remapping and swap area. Claims to be developed in collaboration with the US Air Force Information Welfare Center.

Tools for degaussing hard drives:

- HD-1 All media degausser. The HD-1 erases virtually all formats of tape, diskettes and hard-disks up to 160 GB. Please note; hard drives are not reusable once degaussed.
- Model 8000 hard drive/media degausser. The Model 8000 Table Top unit is a low noise, compact unit with "industrial strength" flux fields and features a foot-control for hands-free operation.

---

[84] A listing here does not imply an endorsement of the tools.

Tools used for CD/DVD shredding:

- PRIMERA disc shredder – DS360
- Alera Technologies DVD/CD shredder plus XC
- Kobra 240 SS4
- HSM Model 125.2 shredder
- Intimus 502CD CD shredder
- Olympia 1500 CD shredder.

Further reading

Garfinkel, Simson and Spafford, Gene. *Web Security, Privacy and Commerce,* O'Reilly Publishers, January 2002.

Whitman, Michael E. and Mattford, Hebert J. *Principles of Information Security,* Course Technology, December 2007.

References

DOD 5220.22-M, *National Industry Security Program Operating Manual (NISPOM),* February 28, 2006.

National Institute of Standards and Technology (NIST) Special Publication 800-14, *Generally Accepted Principles and Practices for Securing Information Technology Systems*, September 1996.

National Institute of Standards and Technology (NIST) Special Publication 800-88, *Guidelines for Media Sanitization*, September 2006.

NSA/CSS Manual 130-2, *Media Declassification and Destruction Manual*, November 2000.

CHAPTER 10: AUTHORIZATION PACKAGE AND SUPPORTING EVIDENCE

It is wrong always, everywhere and for everyone to believe anything upon insufficient evidence.[85]

W. K. Clifford, British Mathematician and Philosopher

In this chapter:

The package: SSP, POA&M, security control assessment summary, certification statement

Supporting evidence: system inventory, security control assessment plan, security assessment report, configuration management plan, continuity of operations/contingency plan, user guides, incident response plan, privacy impact assessment, interconnection agreements

---

[85] *http://www.brainyquote.com/quotes/quotes/w/williamjam157178.html*

In the previous chapters, we presented a process for approaching information system authorization that will meet the requirements of federal agencies, most of the DOD and the Intelligence Community, and even the commercial sector.

During the discussions, we talked about the "authorization package" and "supporting evidence." Rather than just provide a high-level overview, it is necessary to give you more detailed guidance on format and content for each of the required package elements and for some of the other documents and processes you will have to present as evidence. We don't, however, anticipate that we can provide all of the possible details here – so we have developed a suite of examples and templates that can be found on the accompanying CD.

First, let's take a more detailed look at the authorization package.

The authorization package in detail

System security plan (SSP)

The primary objective of system security planning is the protection of information systems and information. All federal information systems process some degree of sensitive information and need protection as part of good management practice. The protection safeguards for an information system are documented in the system security plan (SSP).

The completion of system security plans is also mandated in the Office of Management and Budget (OMB) Circular A-130, *Management of Federal Information Resources, Appendix III, Security of Federal Automated Information Resources,* and *Title III of the E-Government Act, entitled the Federal Information Security Management Act (FISMA).*

The objective of the SSP is to present a high-level description of the system's security requirements and the security controls in place or planned to meet those requirements. The SSP also defines roles and responsibilities and expected behavior of anyone accessing the system.

You should view the SSP as documentation of your structured process of planning, implementing, and maintaining adequate, cost-effective security protection for a system. It should reflect input from the stakeholders involved with the system, including information owners, the system owner, the information assurance manager (IAM), and the senior agency information security officer (SAISO).

We will present a basic SSP; however, additional information may be included in your agency's version of the plan. You can also modify the structure and format according to your agency's needs, as long as the major sections described in this document are adequately covered and readily identifiable.

Since the SSP establishes and documents the security controls, it should also be the basis for the authorization package, supplemented by the assessment report and the plan of actions and milestones. NIST Special Publication 800-18, *Guide for Developing Security Plans for Federal Information Systems*, provides an excellent resource for developing your plan.

Developing the SSP

In the next paragraphs, we will look at a logical process for developing the SSP, a recommended table of contents, and some useful references for specific sections of the plan.

- **Step 1: Prepare the system identification information**. You should identify the following information about the proposed system:

  - Responsible organization
  - System name or title
  - System code
  - System category:

    - major application: performs clearly defined functions for which there is a readily identifiable security consideration and need;

- general support system: provides general ADP or network support for a variety of users and applications.

- Operational status:

  - operational
  - under development
  - undergoing a major modification.

- General description
- System environment and special considerations

  - system architecture and data flow diagrams
  - system interconnections
  - system dependencies
  - supported programs and applications.

- Information point(s) of contact.

- **Step 2: Identify the information sensitivity**. This activity involves identifying the following:

  - Applicable laws or regulations affecting the system.
  - Description of information sensitivity or the FIPS 199 categorization, indicating which of the following protection requirements apply:

    - confidentiality: system contains information that requires protection from unauthorized disclosure;
    - integrity: system contains information that must be protected from unauthorized, unanticipated, or unintentional modification;
    - availability: system contains information or provides services that must be available on a timely basis to meet mission requirements or to avoid substantial losses.

  - Description of the information handled by the system and the need for protective measures.
  - Estimate of the risk resulting from loss, misuse, or unauthorized access to or modification of information in the system.

- For each of the protection requirements, indicate one of the following risk levels:

  - high (critical concern of the system);
  - medium (an important concern but not necessarily paramount in the organization's priorities);
  - low (requires some minimal level of security but not to the same degree as the previous two categories).

- **Step 3:   Determine the required system security measures** (e.g. security controls).   In this step, you will identify and describe control measures, in place or planned, intended to meet protection requirements of the system. The types of control measures you select should be consistent with the need for protection of the system, as described earlier. Include the following information for this activity:

  - Protection requirements to control the risks.
  - Specific standards used in design, implementation, or operation of protective measures.
  - Security control descriptions indicating whether each is in place, planned, or not applicable.
  - For major applications, also include the following:

    - overall management controls;
    - procedures to assure protection is built into the system;
    - day-to-day procedures and mechanisms to protect systems when operational;
    - security awareness and training;
    - hardware and software controls used to provide automated protection or to facilitate manual protection;
    - complementary controls provided by support systems.

  - For general support systems, include the following:

    - management controls;
    - acquisition, development, and installation controls;
    - day-to-day procedures and mechanisms to protect operational controls;
    - security awareness and training;

- controls to protect the system from unauthorized access or misuse;
- controls over the security of applications.

A sample table of contents (TOC) for your SSP

Here is a simple table of contents that might be considered typical for a federal information system.

System security plan outline

1.0 SYSTEM IDENTIFICATION
    1.1 System name/title
    1.2 Responsible organization
    1.3 Information contacts
    1.4 Assignment of security responsibility
    1.5 Category
    1.6 System operational status
    1.7 General description and purpose
    1.8 System environment and special considerations
    1.9 System interconnection/information sharing
    1.10 Applicable laws, directives and regulations affecting the system

2.0 SENSITIVITY OF INFORMATION PROCESSED
    2.1 Description of data processed
    2.2 Information sensitivity

3.0 MANAGEMENT CONTROLS
    3.1 Risk assessment and management
    3.2 Review of security controls
    3.3 Rules of behavior
    3.4 Planning for security in the life cycle
    3.5 Security control measures

4.0 OPERATIONAL CONTROLS
    4.1 Personnel security
    4.2 Physical and environment protection
    4.3 Production input and output controls
    4.4 Contingency planning
    4.5 Application software and maintenance controls
    4.6 Documentation
    4.7 Security awareness and training

5.0 TECHNICAL CONTROLS
    5.1   User identification and authentication
    5.2   Logical access control
    5.3   Public access controls
    5.4   Audit trail
    5.5   Complementary controls provided by support systems

System security plan approval

Your organization should not only assign responsibility for developing the SSP, but also for ensuring that the plan is approved. As part of the authorization process, the designated authorizing official (AO), independent from the system owner, typically approves the plan – and the earlier in the process, the better.

Once your SSP has been approved, do not put it on a shelf! It is intended to be a living document, so part of your authorization processes and procedures should include one process for the maintenance of the SSP itself. One way to do this is to review your SSP for currency at the same time you prepare your annual security controls compliance report and make any necessary updates at that time.

The POA&M elements and format

Each POA&M has 11 columns containing information about the weakness and associated remediation activities. The following table provides an overview of each column, its title and a general description of the contents.

Table 23: POA&M overview

Column	Heading	Contents (how to fill it in)
1	Weakness identifier	The weakness identifier is an agency assigned identifier that is used to track and correlate the weaknesses throughout the required quarterly and annual submissions.
2	Weakness[86]	Statement presenting the program or system level vulnerability that may pose an unacceptable risk.
3	Point of contact (POC)	The organization, position, and/or individual in the organization responsible for mitigation or correction of the weakness.
4	Resources required	Total amount expressed as $ for the resources required to mitigate or correct the weakness; can include man-hours, equipment, time, etc. The type of funding (e.g. new, ongoing, or re-allocated) should be indicated.
5	Scheduled completion date	An estimated date of completion based on a realistic estimate of the time required to collect resources, procure equipment (if required) etc. in order to implement/test the corrective actions. (NOTE: Cannot be changed.)
6	Milestones/ completion dates	Outline of the high level steps with estimated completion dates that will be executed in mitigating/testing the weakness. (NOTE: Cannot be changed.)
7	Changes to milestones	Used to indicate any changes to the milestones and the associated dates; includes revised milestones and estimated dates of completion. (NOTE: This is the only column where changes to the original POA&M milestones can be made.)
8	Identified in audit or review?	Indicates the type of action (e.g. inspection, audit, self-assessment), the organization, and the date associated with identification of the weakness.

[86] DOD has published standardized weakness statements for each of the DOD IA controls and associated security control validation tests. These statements are available on the DIACAP Knowledge Service and are mandatory for all DOD POA&M submissions.

9	Status	Stage or state of the weakness in terms of the corrective action milestones, etc. (e.g. planned, in progress, completed, delayed).
10	Comments	Used for additional detail or clarifications; required if there is a delay or change to the milestones and/or dates.
11	Risk level	Ranking of the determined level of impact to the information system if the associated weakness would be exploited by a threat agent.

Each of these elements is discussed in more detail in the next sections. For an example of a completed program and system POA&M, see the CD accompanying the book.

Column 1: Weakness identifier

Each weakness on the POA&M should be assigned a unique weakness identifier[87]. The weakness identifier will be used to track the weakness and associated actions in the quarterly and annual submissions. The organization should develop a numbering schema to generate the unique weakness identifier for a system. For example, the identified weakness could use a combination of the name of the associated system, the quarter the weakness is first recorded on the POA&M, the fiscal year the weakness is first recorded on the POA&M, and a sequence number (e.g. SystemName_Quarter_FiscalYear_WeaknessNumber).

When developing a POA&M for a program the weaknesses identifier would substitute the 'program name' for a system name. See the following figure for a sample system weakness identifier.

---

[87] While a required column for each weakness, the weakness identifier is not counted by OMB as one of the 11 columns on the POA&M entry.

Figure 17: Weakness identifier

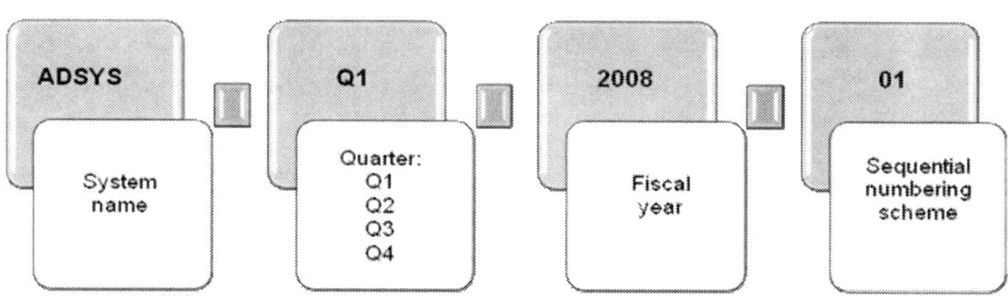

In the sample above, ***ADSYS*** is the information system's name or acronym. This acronym becomes important for sorting POA&Ms by system. ***Q1*** represents the quarter in which the weakness was first identified and entered onto the POA&M. The number ***2008*** indicates the fiscal year in which the weakness was first identified and submitted. The value ***01*** shows the numerical order in which this particular weakness was entered on the POA&M for the ADSYS information system. In this case, this weakness identifier indicates this is the first weakness entered in this submission.

Weaknesses will often be listed on the POA&M by priority. If system X is the highest priority system, its weaknesses should be prioritized first. To prioritize the weaknesses within system X's POA&M, the stakeholders should provide input to ensure the rankings of the security controls represent their interests. This may have to occur through a process of review and consensus.

For example, if the agency's stakeholders ranked privacy protection as the most pressing system security activity, then all weaknesses in system X's POA&M associated with privacy issues would take precedence. Following this prioritization strategy for each system's POA&M, managers can ensure they are using the agency's security budget to most effectively address those weaknesses that are important to the organization.

Column 2: Weakness description

In the world of POA&Ms, the term weakness refers to any program or system-level security vulnerability that poses an unacceptable risk to the information or the information system.

When reporting weaknesses, be careful about the level of detail revealed in the POA&M. Very precise and detailed descriptions are not necessary; provide only the level of data needed to permit oversight and tracking. Also, sensitive information should not be revealed in the description of the weakness or associated milestones.

If sensitive information were to be obtained an unauthorized third party or someone seeking to exploit the information system, the system might be inadvertently exposed to risk. One way to avoid this is to use the type of language commonly found in GAO and IG reports, such as "inadequate password controls," "insufficient or inconsistent data integrity controls," "inadequate firewall configuration reviews," "background investigations not performed prior to system access," and "physical access controls are insufficient."

Another method, and possible preferred method, is to simply reverse the language of the affected security control itself. For example, NIST SP 800-53 control AC-6 refers to least privilege. The stated control requirement is: "The information system enforces the most restrictive set of rights/privileges or accesses needed by users (or processes acting on behalf of users) for the performance of specified tasks." The weakness statement might read: "System does not enforce the most restrictive set of user privileges." If it is necessary to provide more detailed – and most sensitive – data, the POA&M should explicitly note the special sensitivity of the weakness in the comments column.

Here are some useful tips:

- Ensure a weakness statement does not provide system or program specific sensitive information that would compromise the integrity, availability, and confidentiality of the information or the information system.

- Ensure a weakness is described appropriately and not listed as a corrective action. For example:

> *Incorrect* **weakness** *description:* Draft system security documentation.
>
> *Correct* **weakness** *description:* System does not have up-to-date system security plan.

Column 3: Point of contact (POC)

For each weakness listed on the POA&M, a point of contact (POC) must also be identified. The POC is the position/role (e.g. ISSO, system owner) that will be responsible for resolving the weakness. While some organizations may do so, using individual names on the POA&M is less preferable, as personnel may leave and/or responsibilities may change.

Here are some useful tips:

- Ensure that the POC is identified as a designated position/role within the organization.
- Do not identify solely the division or branch name; rather include position/role and if appropriate, the specific office within that division or branch.
- Ensure that a POC is listed for all weaknesses.
- Provide contact information for the POC.

Column 4: Resources required

In order for a weakness to be mitigated or corrected, resources (e.g. equipment procurement, staff, man-hours) must be determined and allocated. It is clear that the type and amount of resources required for corrective actions will vary.

If existing government personnel are able to correct the weakness and no new funding is required, the POA&M should identify the amount of time it will take to complete the corrective action (e.g. 40 man-hours) and that the actions will be carried out by current staff.

The entry for resources required must be based on the total amount of resources needed to fulfill *all* the milestones for each weakness correction. Regardless of the type of resource, the amount will be noted as a dollar figure and identified by type of funding (current, new, or reallocated).

Here are some useful tips:

- Ensure that all weaknesses have resources identified to mitigate the vulnerabilities.
- Ensure that resources are identified as man-hours or monetary values. For example:

> *Incorrect* **resources required** *description:* From existing resources.
>
> *Correct* **resources required** *description:* $75,000 for equipment and man-hours using current resources and staff.

- Identify the required funding as "current resources", "new resources", or "resources reallocated from existing funding" (also suggest indicating whether new staff are required or existing staff will be utilized when listing man hours).

Column 5: Scheduled completion date

The scheduled completion date should be determined based on a realistic estimate of the amount of time it will take to gather the resources needed for the corrective action and to implement and test it. Not all corrective actions or mitigations will be technical in nature – some may involve the development of policy. Note that draft documents do not receive any credit for completion from

OMB and Congress, so it is important to factor required reviews and publication time into the overall timeline to completion.

This column should include the month, day, and year of estimated completion. Once the scheduled completion date has been entered on the POA&M, it cannot be changed. If the time required extends beyond the scheduled completion date, the status of the weakness should be changed to delayed and reasons for the delay will be noted in the comments column.

Here are some useful tips:

- Ensure that all weaknesses have a scheduled completion date. For example:

> *Incorrect **scheduled completion date** description:* 2 years
>
> *Correct **scheduled completion date** description:* 10/31/2004.

- Do not change the initial scheduled completion date if the weakness is mitigated prior to or after the original date.

Column 6: Milestones with completion dates

Column 5 indicated the estimated completion date for all actions required to execute necessary corrections. Column 6 recognizes that the correction of a weakness may have one or more milestones required before corrective action is completed. The key, high level milestones required to complete all corrections should be identified in this column on the POA&M.

Including anticipated completion dates with each milestone will help in tracking progress of the weakness mitigation. Each individual milestone should include its own estimated date of completion. Just like the scheduled completion date, this date should be formatted to list the month, day, and year. Once milestones and completion dates are entered in this column, changes cannot be made. If any of the estimated milestone completion dates change, the new expected date should be recorded in the changes to milestones column and reasons for the change should be noted in the comments column.

The milestones should focus on the major steps needed to mitigate the weakness. Milestones should not simply re-state that the weakness will be completed by repeating the weakness description. For example, appropriate milestones for a weakness such as, "Identification and authentication processes need to be more stringent" might read:

- Milestone 1: Evaluate methods for strengthening identification and authentication;
- Milestone 2: Develop procedures to standardize accepted authentication process; and
- Milestone 3: Implement appropriate authentication process.

Here are some useful tips:

- Ensure that a milestone is described appropriately and listed for all weaknesses.
- The milestone should be detailed as a specific requirement to correct an identified weakness.
- Ensure that all milestones are numbered.
- If there is more than one milestone for a weakness, list and number the milestones in the order they should be executed.
- Ensure that each milestone has an anticipated completion date.

Column 7: Changes to milestones

If a situation exists that prevents a milestone and/or overall corrective action from being completed by the time indicated for the original estimated completion date, the new estimated date of completion will be identified only in the changes to milestones column. No changes can be made to the original estimate in either the scheduled completion date or the milestones with completion date columns.

The date format will include the month, day, and year of estimated completion. The reason for the change in milestone completion should be recorded in the comments column.

Here are some useful tips:

- Ensure that a change to a milestone has been accurately identified in this column.
- Update the date to include the new proposed date.
- Do not change the original date listed in the milestones with completion date column.

Column 8: Identified in audit or review

This column should be used to list the method by which the weakness was identified. The most common sources and methods of identifying POA&M weaknesses include IG inspections, audits, external reviews or self-assessments.

When identifying the source that identified the weakness, ensure that the type of review (e.g. IG inspection, audit, and self-assessment), the organization conducting the review, and the date (month and year) are indicated. In the event that multiple sources cite a specific weakness, list the additional sources and dates in the comments column.

Here are some useful tips:

- Ensure that all weaknesses have corresponding sources identified.
- Ensure the date (month and year), review type, and reviewer is communicated. For example,

IG Inspection, September 2008

NIST-compliant self-assessment, December 2008 (system owner)

Column 9: Status

A status will be assigned to all corrective actions/weaknesses. The status of a corrective action can be designated as planned, completed, ongoing, or delayed.

The completed status should be used only when a weakness has been fully resolved and the corrective action has been tested as compliant. When an action is indicated as completed, also include the date of completion (day, month, year) in this column. This process of updating the POA&M to indicate the current status of a corrective action can demonstrate that the POA&M is truly being used as a management tool and is part of an ongoing process.

Here are some useful tips:

- Ensure that all weaknesses have a status identified.
- Status can be indicated as completed, ongoing, or delayed.
- Status should be accurately reflected based on the scheduled completion date.
- Status refers only to the status of the entire weakness; this area is not used to address the status of individual milestones.

Column 10: Comments

The comments column is the place for any additional detail or clarification about the POA&M weakness. This column may be used to detail additional steps taken to remedy weaknesses or to provide reasons why correction has been delayed.

The comments column should identify other obstacles, such as funding, or challenges to resolving the weakness (e.g. lack of personnel or expertise, or developing a new system to replace insecure legacy system). If the same weakness is found repeatedly in subsequent reviews, list the additional sources and dates of finding in the comments column. This column is useful as a means of accurately conveying to any other external stakeholder what is occurring with a specific weakness.

Here are some useful tips:

- Additional explanations can provide insight into the challenges being faced and likely dependencies that can impact the weakness mitigation.
- If the scheduled completion date has not been met, a weakness that has been listed as delayed can be addressed to provide further clarification or reason for delay.

Column 11: Risk level

The risk level[88] column has been added to the POA&M tool to indicate the potential impact of a weakness on the information system, information, organization, and/or program. The exploitation of weaknesses can result in the loss or degradation of the integrity, availability, and confidentiality of a system.

Some tangible impacts can include loss of confidential or proprietary data, damage to the system, modification of data, loss in revenue, damage to an organization's reputation due to misinformed data to the public, or an increase in the level of effort and manpower required to correct problems caused by an exploited weakness.

A risk level should be assigned to each weakness based on the potential impact and threat likelihood of exploitation of the weakness.[89] Risk level definitions can be designated as high, medium, or low. The risk of the individual weakness should be linked to the overall enterprise risk as determined by the process defined in Chapter 5.

---

[88] While a required column for each weakness, the weakness identifier is not counted by OMB as one of the 11 columns on the POA&M entry.
[89] Draft NIST SP 800-30, Revision A, *Risk Management Guide for Information Technology System*, January 2004.

Risk level determination

Even at the individual weakness level, a risk determination process[90] with the following steps can be adopted:

- Step 1 – Determine the likelihood of the identified system threat exploiting a specific identified vulnerability.
- Step 2 – Determine the impact to a system's operation and information should a threat exploit the specific identified vulnerability.
- Step 3 – Determine the overall risk for the specific identified vulnerability.

For more detailed information on the risk assessment and definition process, refer to Chapter 5.

Establishing a POA&M process

Process can be defined as a series of actions implemented to attain a desired result. The indication of a mature process is consistency, standardization, and repeatability. Establishing a comprehensive POA&M process includes the formalization of a repeatable cycle that effectively corrects weaknesses and facilitates the reporting requirements.

A mature POA&M process should address the following elements.

- formal process development;
- identification of inputs to the POA&M process;
- POA&M documentation development and reporting;
- weakness remediation;
- information verification; and
- post remediation improvement efforts.

We will discuss each of these in greater detail.

---

[90] Process based on Draft NIST SP 800-30, Revision A, *Risk Management Guide for Information Technology Systems*, January 2004.

Formal process development: There are many standards that detail how to identify and implement a formal process. You may already be doing some of these, such as the quality assurance processes from ISO Standard 9000 and 9001 or the security processes from the ISO27000 series. If you have already implemented these process standards, you can capitalize on your existing framework to establish a formal process for managing the POA&M requirements.

In creating a comprehensive, consistent and repeatable process, documenting the policy and procedures related to the POA&M is critical and supports accountability. You should also assign specific roles and responsibilities to personnel, and ensure adequate training is in place to aid personnel in understanding and carrying out their assigned roles and responsibilities. To ensure weaknesses are corrected according to both your organizational standards, as well as external requirements, prioritization criteria should be identified. Finally, you should institute a formal process for identifying the budget requirements and making the necessary budgetary decisions.

Identifying the required inputs to the POA&M process: Identifying what inputs to the POA&M are required and where they will come from is an integral part of the formalization process. The organization should take time to understand all sources of information related to the POA&M process (e.g. internal and external audits or self-assessments).

An organization should formalize the risk executive function to evaluate weaknesses for risk acceptability and ensure discussions take place on a regular basis with management regarding risk-based decisions. Finally, a formal corrective action planning and tracking process should be created for all weaknesses that require remediation.

Preparing POA&M documentation and reporting: POA&M documentation development and reporting is another important component to formalizing the POA&M process. Don't wait until the suspense looms for the required quarterly and annual FISMA reports! You will find the reporting much easier and less resource-intensive if you track the POA&M actions throughout the year.

All of the security control weaknesses that require corrective action should be included in the POA&M documentation. The POA&M documentation should be created according to the standards and recommendations set forth by OMB and your organization. In addition, it is imperative that the mandated reporting guidelines are followed.

The reporting guidelines from OMB change almost every year based on newly emerging threats and technologies. So, be sure to stay informed on the most recent guidelines and requirements being issued. For example, the DOD has a FISMA Integrated Process Team (IPT) that regularly issues the current OMB guidelines, as well as the DOD formats and requirements for reporting.

Remediating the weakness(es): The speed and quality of weakness remediation is one output that can be considered evidence of success in the POA&M process. If an organization's POA&M process is mature, it will quickly highlight successful corrective actions and support mitigation of the organization's weaknesses to reduce risks to an acceptable level.

Verifying the information: A mature POA&M process ensures that activities are built into the organization to verify information. Once weaknesses have been mitigated or corrected, the organization with a mature process should include steps to validate that completed weaknesses meet the security control compliance standards, as well as to ensure the accuracy of the reported information.

Conducting post-remediation improvement: A critical element of any mature process is the establishment of a "lessons learned" activity to collect and analyze program performance metrics. Organizations should be able to apply the knowledge gained from the remediation of weaknesses to future system security improvement efforts. Over time, the information collected from actual POA&Ms, and from the process in general, can be used to advance weakness mitigation effectiveness and to improve information system security in general.

Security assessment report (SAR)

Most of the independent security control assessors you might use will have their own format for the security assessment report (SAR). It is a good idea to review their template before they even begin to test. This will aid in ensuring the test addresses all of your issues and that the final SAR provides all of the information needed to support the authorization decision.

If you are the assessor, it is important that your SAR provides a sufficient level of detail to the federal agency you are supporting. You should have a standardized template for the report that you can show the agency stakeholders early in the assessment process – and you should obtain their approval for the content. A standardized format ensures that all testing results are subject to similar assessment guidelines, and that the initial and final reports include the same types of information.

In any security control assessment, an adequate level of discretion in analyzing and reporting the results should be afforded to the tester. This provides the tester sufficient flexibility to address the test results truly from a "real world" perspective. In order to achieve some degree of standardization, however, the discretion granted to individual testers should be limited and agreed upon in advance in order to prevent inappropriate bias and subjectivity from entering the report.

One key element of the SAR is the assessment of risk level and a proposed remediation effort for each weakness discovered during the testing. This might include the assessor's assessment of the risk level for each weakness, the ease of mitigating or correcting the weakness, and the estimated work effort required to implement reasonable and appropriate controls.

When the final report is delivered to the agency, it should include any and all working papers in hard copy or electronic format, as well as all test results, notes, and screenshots. It also makes good sense to prepare the initial plan of action and milestones (POA&M) along with the final report.

Report structure

The primary purpose of the SAR is to communicate assessment results at the level of the intended audience. In nearly all situations, security test results will be viewed by several different audiences, ranging from senior management to the hands-on technical staff. Senior management is usually not interested in the technical details of any given weakness, but they require the "big picture" in order to make essential risk-based decisions.

The SAR should give high-level audiences the information they need to understand, quickly and proficiently, the potential impact of security vulnerabilities, and what those results mean to the business. This gives them what they need to make informed decisions regarding security priorities, expenditures and staffing.

On the other hand, technical personnel need to have a complete understanding of the details of a given weakness in order to plan and implement appropriate corrective action. For this reason, it is necessary to provide the technical staff with the full details of all weaknesses discovered through security testing.

To accommodate the competing needs of the audience, the report format should provide an initial discussion, followed by technical details at a lower level. The "Executive Summary" section is located at the beginning of the report and presents a high-level overview of the security test results – without the need for non-technical readers to examine the entire report.

Below is a sample table of contents for a security assessment report (SAR):

Security assessment report

1.0 INTRODUCTION

2.0 EXECUTIVE SUMMARY

3.0 DETAILED FINDINGS

    3.1 Methodology for the security control assessment

    3.2 Methodology for security assessment reporting

      3.2.1 Risk level assessment

      3.2.2 Ease-of-fix assessment

      3.2.3 Estimated work effort assessment

   3.3 Procedural business risks (if any were identified)

      3.3.1 Business risk

   3.4 Technical business risks

      3.4.1 Business risk

Submitting the SAR

The SAR package should be prepared by the security controls assessor and delivered in both hard copy and in password protected soft copy. The assessor should always deliver the report only to the requesting agency. Under no circumstances should a copy or any information from the report be provided to any external agencies without the express permission of the requesting agency.

Depending on the security categorization and sensitivity of the information system being assessed, the SAR itself may be extremely sensitive or even classified. Protection of the completed report should also be discussed in advance with the requesting agency to ensure that no information about the agency and its information system(s) is inadvertently compromised.

If you represent a federal agency contracting outside contractor assistance in conducting your security controls assessment, you should include requirements for the protection of your information. These should address the requirements during the conduct of the assessment, but even more important, you should ensure that ALL of your agency information is returned to you upon completion of the assessment.

Certification statement

The certifying authority's (CA) statement completes the authorization package to the authorizing official/DAA. This activity begins after completion of all of the security control assessment tasks and ends with a system authorization recommendation.

If the CA concludes that the information system satisfies the security requirements, the certifier will issue a system certification statement. The CA's statement certifies that the information system is in compliance with the documented security requirements.

The security control assessment may reveal security control weaknesses, but the CA's review may consider that the short-term system operation is within the bounds of acceptable risk. In this case, the CA may recommend an IATO with the understanding that the deficiencies will be corrected in a time period specified by the authorizing official. These weaknesses must be reflected in the POA&M. The authorizing official and the system owner will enter into an agreement detailing the conditions under which the system may be operated and the date when the weaknesses must be corrected.

Supplemental recommendations also might be made in the certification statement to improve the system's security posture. Such recommendations could include input to future system enhancements and change management decisions. Any recommendations will usually be written at a high-level, leaving it to the organization to develop the detailed implementation procedures. Also, any recommendations based on weaknesses should also be reflected in the POA&M.

The CA may also determine that the system does not sufficiently satisfy the security requirements and that the risks of placing the system into operation may put the mission and/or the information in jeopardy. In this case, the CA may recommend that the IS not be accredited until the weaknesses are corrected.

In the case of a recommended IATO or DATO, a new security control assessment is required prior to initiating operation and the CA must be provided the opportunity to review the results and prepare a revised certification statement.

Contents of the certification statement

The certification statement is not intended to be a comprehensive re-hash of the security control assessment results. In addition to a short background statement and a summary of the findings, the CA will provide a statement of compliance and the certification recommendation.

The certification recommendation contained in the overall certification statement might look something like this:

Certification recommendation

Based on my review of documentation contained in the accompanying certification package, I concur with the findings and recommendations of the certifying agent. I certify that <system name> security controls have been tested at the <low or moderate or high> security certification level, which is commensurate with the sensitivity level of the system. As of this date, <system name> meets applicable federal security requirements as it operates in its current environment with the exception of vulnerabilities identified in the attached <system name> POA&M. I recommend that the authorizing official accept the identified residual risks and authorize <system name> to process in its current operational environment under the provision that all risks be mitigated in accordance with the <system name> POA&M. I will ensure that a review of security controls protecting the system is conducted upon any major changes to the current operating environment.

//Signed and dated by the certifying authority//

Supporting evidence for the authorization decision – security control documentation

The documentation required for the authorization package itself may be limited to the four documents described above. But this does not relieve the agency from its responsibility to develop specific security control related procedures and to be able to produce the associated documentation. In the next sections, we will introduce those additional procedures and documents required to provide supporting evidence for the authorization decision.

In addition to providing evidence for the purpose of authorization, some of the processes and documentation are also required by FISMA and are included in the annual report to OMB. These include configuration management, contingency planning and testing, and the privacy impact assessment.

Information system inventory – understand your information systems

The lack of accurate and complete information system inventories remains one of the consistent findings during the evaluations of the annual FISMA reports to OMB. The problems associated with the execution and maintenance of an information system inventory plagues federal agencies and organizations of all sizes and information system density.

Anyone who reads the agency Inspector General reports or the results of the General Accounting Office (GAO) audits will quickly realize that most of the agencies are challenged by the size of this task.

So, why should you inventory your information systems – other than the obvious reason that it is required by FISMA? The first and most obvious reason: *you can't protect what you don't know about.* The next reason: *it is a requirement for your authorization process.*

How to proceed

When executing processes, there are some simple tips for keeping things as smooth and easy as possible:

- Get management support – especially if you are just starting the process. You may need it to ensure cooperation from various elements within your agency.
- Establish roles and responsibilities for executing the inventory and maintaining it. You may want to initially divide these responsibilities in order to "divide and conquer" the inventory.

- Establish a (reasonable) time frame for completion and hold the responsible individuals accountable.
- Have a process. You can either input the inventory information into your data repository as you collect it, or you can use worksheets to collect all of the information, and then enter it into the repository. There are benefits to both methods, so you will have to choose which one works best for your agency. The worksheet method often functions best for large agencies where inventory information may have to be derived from multiple sources and sub-agencies.
- Move as quickly and efficiently as possible through the collection process; don't prolong information gathering.

The overall inventory of information systems

One of the primary challenges is determining exactly what must be included in the inventory and who is responsible for maintaining a current and accurate inventory. First, you will need an inventory of your total information systems in your agency or organization. At a minimum, your overall inventory should include:

- Information system name
- Business function
- Information sensitivity
- Location
- Hardware, software, and firmware list
- External information system dependencies and/or interconnections
- Points of contact
- Recoverability objective
- Contingency plan status.

Next, you should have a complete and current listing of all of the hardware and software associated with each of the information systems in your registry.

Hardware and software inventories

Include as much detail as possible about the hardware associated with your information systems. This will help enormously with your configuration management and in developing/executing your contingency plan. The hardware inventory should also include information about the maintenance plan for each of the hardware components. Here is a sample of what you might want to collect in your hardware inventory:

- Name of the server/system
- Make and model
- Serial number
- Operating system (including patch level)
- Memory (including amount and type)
- Disk controllers
- Disk drives
- Partitions
- Network interface card
- IP address
- Maintenance contracts
- Budget information, such as cost of the hardware components.

You should treat your software inventory as important as your hardware inventory. Knowledge of your software, the versions, and associated information is critical for configuration management and successful recovery processes. It is also useful in making purchasing and upgrade decisions for your agency. This is what you might want to include in your software inventory:

- Application name
- Functional use (e.g. logistics, personnel management)
- Installation path
- Version
- Licensing information
- Maintenance contract
- Hosting server
- Budget information, e.g. cost of the software and licensing fees.

Use of inventory tools

You can manage your inventory information using any form of record management tool – from the back of an envelope to a complex data base. For most organizations, a simple spreadsheet or a database, such as Microsoft® Access, will be sufficient. The real key is to preferably use some form of electronic data repository so the information can be easily and quickly retrieved when needed.

Depending on the size of your agency and the complexity of your inventory, an automated inventory tool might be a wise investment. These tools can be a rich source of information on everything from software usage to user privileges and license management.

There are some important things to consider regardless of which tool you use:

- Keep your inventory current by adding and/or modifying as needed.
- Do not delete your historical records, but maintain them. You may need these at some point.

Most often, the inventory data repository will be maintained by the CCB, as this entity will be the primary user. NOTE: Federal agencies and DOD components may have specific guidance on how to conduct information system inventories, where and how the information will be stored, and how the results of the inventories will be reported. You should always check with your agency prior to establishing and using any information system processes.

The information system inventory and configuration management go hand-in-hand. An accurate and current information system inventory is also essential to effective contingency and recovery planning. Without this, you expose yourself to the possibility of failure when executing either one of these actions.

Security control assessment (SCA) plan[91]

The security control assessment (SCA) plan should be used to identify the tasks and activities needed to ensure that the information system and its security controls are adequately tested and that the system can be securely and successfully implemented.

The assessment provides guidance for the management of test activities, including organization, relationships, and responsibilities.

There are two primary steps involved in writing your security control assessment plan. First, the assessment objectives should be derived from the security controls identified as assigned to the information system. The test objectives should correspond as closely as possible to the technical specifications of the information system. This will focus the test on the specific security features of the hardware, firmware, operating system and software used by the system.

Next, detailed procedures should be written to test each control or requirement. NIST SP 800-53A for federal agencies and the DIACAP Knowledge Service for DOD information systems will provide you with assessment guidance for each security control. These procedures form a standardized foundation for developing and executing the assessment. However, you should still tailor these to your information system and its unique environment.

The extent of the ST&E activities will vary according to the security categorization of the system. Systems that process information at a higher sensitivity or criticality level will need more involved verification activities, such as penetration testing, than systems that process non-sensitive information.

Types of security control assessments

There are two primary types of security control assessments: ***abbreviated*** and ***comprehensive***.

---

[91] Also called the security test and evaluation (ST&E) plan or security control test plan.

The authorizing official will usually determine which type of assessment will be used based on several factors: the system life cycle status, state of authorization, complexity of the system, security categorization, mission of the activity, and the type of information processed.

An **abbreviated security control assessment** is used when there is only a need to determine that the information system is operating within an acceptable level of risk. Depending on the information system and its authorization status, you may be able to use a checklist or self-assessment to meet the requirements of the abbreviated assessment. The results inform the authorizing official if there are security weaknesses in the system and enhance management awareness of known system risks.

One important note: whether executing an abbreviated or comprehensive assessment, the assessment is NOT simply a review of your agency's authorization package documentation. It should always include a review and/or test of each of the security controls assigned to the information system. Beware of any assessment provider that suggests that a documentation review is sufficient for authorization.

This type of assessment has three components:

- a risk analysis review;
- completion of a security control assessment checklist; and
- preparation of the security assessment report.

A **comprehensive security control assessment** is intended for use with systems that process information requiring greater protection. The comprehensive assessment is accompanied by a more detailed risk analysis and requires a more in-depth analysis of the security controls to determine their effectiveness in reducing system vulnerabilities. This level of assessment gives the authorizing official a greater level of assurance that the safeguards implemented truly protect the system from the identified threats by reducing or eliminating weaknesses. There are generally four components in the comprehensive assessment:

- data gathering;
- completion of a formal security control assessment plan;
- execution of the assessment plan; and
- preparation of the security assessment report.

Security control assessment plan contents

In those cases where you are conducting a comprehensive security control assessment, you will have to develop a formal security control assessment plan. Below is an example of the contents of a typical SCA plan:

Security control assessment plan for <system name>

1. Introduction

    1.1 Purpose. Provide a high-level summary of the purpose of this assessment.

    1.2 Background. Standard statement about the supporting background for the assessment (e.g. verify the compliant application of the NIST SP 800-53 security controls).

    1.3 Scope. Define the authorization boundary, high-level system description, and other relevant information that defines the scope of the assessment.

    1.4 Assumptions and constraints. Insert any assumptions regarding the information system and any constraints to the actual assessment (e.g. operational requirements, system life cycle considerations, authorized tools).

    1.5 Assessment team roles and responsibilities. Provide a list of the assessment team members, their assigned roles and a short description of their responsibilities.

    1.6 Organization of the document. Provide an overview of the organization of next sections of the document.

2. Assessment approach. High-level statement regarding the assessment approach (e.g. use of test cases derived from NIST SP 800-53A with tailoring, as required by the information system and its environment).

    2.1 Development of the assessment plan. Provide a short description of the basis for the development of the assessment plan (e.g.

DIACAP Knowledge Service, NIST SP 800-53A, or any other sources used for the plan).

2.1.1 Assessment plan. Describe each of the individual security controls to be assessed, the test case/procedures and tools to be used, pass/fail criteria, type of evidence required, and who is responsible for executing the assessment of this control.

2.1.2 Sample size. Indicate the intended information system sampling size (particularly important for large and/or geographically dispersed systems where you cannot test each and every individual system).

2.1.3 Existing assessment results. If previous assessments have been conducted and are available for review, these will be considered here. Some of the existing results may have continued validity or they may provide a baseline for executing a compliance comparison.

2.2 Assessment execution. Provide a high level description of how the assessment will be executed, points of contact, requirements for the in-brief and out-brief, etc.

2.2.1 Test cases. Provide a general overview of the purpose of the test cases listed in the assessment plan.

2.2.2 Supporting evidence. Describe how supporting evidence will be gathered, stored, analyzed, and protected.

2.2.3 Inherited security controls. If security controls have been inherited, indicate the controls, the source of the inheritance relationship, and how the controls will be addressed during the assessment.

2.2.4 Assessment environment. Provide a short description of the environment in which the assessment will take place (e.g. production environment, dedicated test environment, etc.).

2.3 Documentation of assessment results. Describe how the results of the assessment will be documented and how the report will be provided to the requesting agency. Also, describe how the information about the assessment will be protected, to include, if required, the process for returning all of the test results and evidence to the agency.

3. Assessment schedule. Provide an estimated schedule for each activity involved in the assessment.

Security control assessment plan approval

Once the security assessment plan has been completed, the plan should be reviewed and approved by the appropriate official, usually the authorizing official and/or the system owner, in the agency. This review will ensure that the plan is consistent with the security assessment objectives, their assessment of risk, and is cost-effective with regard to the resources allocated for the assessment. After the security assessment plan is approved, the assessment team can execute the plan in accordance with the agreed-upon milestones and schedule. Once the security control assessment is complete, a comprehensive security control assessment report should be generated.[92]

Security control assessment report (SAR)

In terms of the system authorization process, preparing the security control assessment report (SAR) is certainly as important as actually conducting the assessment. A solid SAR provides detailed descriptions of the results of your assessment, along with prioritized recommendations on what to do about the findings.

You don't have to be an expert writer or even a technical expert to develop effective assessment reports. However, you should be able to differentiate between the urgent weaknesses and the others that may not be as critical and be able to describe the weaknesses and the associated information clearly and logically. Remember that

NOTE: If you are performing a test on a classified information system, the SAR should usually be classified at the level of the system tested. Depending on the weaknesses discovered during the assessment, reports on unclassified or sensitive information systems may require additional protections and/or classification.

you probably won't be submitting the full SAR to the authorizing

---

[92] The SAR is intended to be very detailed and comprehensive; it is not the same document as the assessment summary report provided to the authorizing official in the authorization package.

official. Your target audience is the PM/system owner, IAM, and the security engineers and policy makers responsible for understanding and acting on the findings.

Here are a few tips to consider when preparing the report:

- Include a cover page with the following information: name of the agency, system name, dates the assessment was conducted, date of the report, your name, title and other contact information as needed. It also helps to use page numbers and put the title of the report in the page header on each page. The cover sheet and all internal report pages should include any classification markings and/or protection markings for the report.
- A table of contents is useful as a quick reference and a means to easily navigate the SAR.
- Provide an executive summary with a quick overview of the results, a general statement about the nature of the weaknesses, and any trends you may have noticed during the assessment. NOTE: Streamline your process by writing your executive summary so that it can serve as the assessment summary submitted in the authorization package.

Include a description of any security tools or specific assessment processes used during the assessment, assumptions and miscellaneous notes. You may also want to include a liability disclaimer, for example: "This assessment represents the state of the security controls assigned to <system name> at the time of the assessment and are subject to change."

- In the body of the SAR, prioritize the weaknesses by their impact – high, medium, and low. Provide recommendations for mitigation and, if possible, an estimate of the resources required. This helps the agency program their corrective measures by priority and also assists in the development of the POA&M. If you are assessing a complex information system or network, it helps to categorize your observations by internal systems and external systems and separate the sections with a title page.
- Be as non-technical as possible. It should only take two to three sentences to outline the problem. In addition, we find it useful to

include screenshots of a specific test and the system or information that was exploited. You may also want to include the specific steps that you took to exploit the weakness.

- Always include positive observations, such as good access authorization mechanisms or security awareness training. This provides balance in the report and shows that the agency is responsive to information system security requirements.

We've often heard arguments questioning the need for a detailed report if the results can be shown as a compliance checklist. But consider that a solid security assessment report is a good way to demonstrate to inspectors or auditors that a comprehensive security assessment has been conducted.

SAR template

Many agencies will define their own preferred template for security control assessment reports. So, be sure to gain an understanding of any agency-unique reporting requirements **prior** to beginning the assessment. This will help guide your results collection, analysis, and reporting format.

Below is an example of a table of contents for a generic SAR. A template is provided on the CD accompanying this book.

Security control assessment report for <system name>

Table of contents

Executive summary

1. Introduction

    1.1 Purpose

    1.2 Scope

    1.3 Assumptions and limitations

    1.4 Document overview

2. Assessment configuration

    2.1 System description

    2.2 System components assessed

    2.3 Execution of the assessment

    2.4 Assessment team

3. Assessment results

    3.1 Management controls

    3.2 Technical controls

    3.3 Operational controls

4. Summary

Appendix A: Test procedures, tools, specific processes

Appendix B: Glossary

Configuration management (CM) process and plan

As part of the requirements for obtaining an authorization to operate, each federal agency must develop and implement a configuration management process (CMP). Configuration management is one part of the overall life cycle management plan for the system's security.

Figure 18: The configuration management continuum

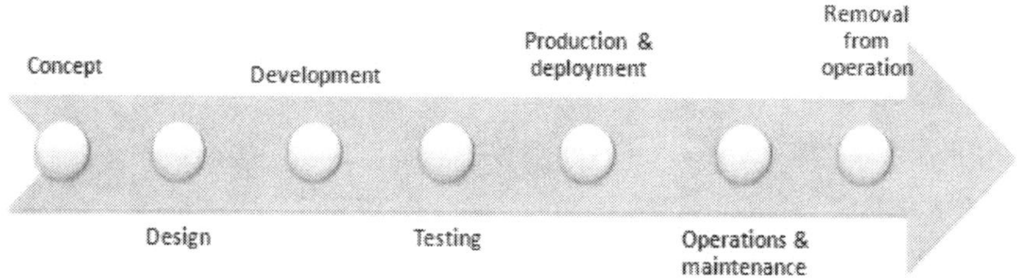

In the above continuum (which mirrors the system life cycle), the information system is placed under configuration control at the point where it is conceived. This is the initial stage at which the concept is captured on paper in the form of specification requirements, white paper, proposal, or other document. The concept leads directly into the design phase, where the security controls are often initially identified and – hopefully – included in the design of the information system prior to development and production.

Next, the information system enters the development stage with hardware being built, software being coded, or a combination of the two. Next, the system is tested to ensure that it operates as originally intended. This includes ensuring operational efficiency, validating that it suits the purpose for which it was intended while operating safely and securely.

Finally the product is produced and deployed, then operated and maintained throughout the life cycle. Versions may be implemented and the product might go through upgrades; however, implementation lasts until the product is removed from active use.

Strong configuration management is a basic requirement for successful security control compliance over the life of the information system. It should manage and document all system and network changes and modifications. A current and comprehensive baseline inventory of all hardware, software (to include mobile code management), and management of ports, protocols, and services is required.

This life cycle configuration management should be defined and documented by the agency. The first step you should take is to formally establish the roles and responsibilities associated with configuration management within your agency.

Typical CM roles and responsibilities

Several members of your agency can and should play a role in the configuration management processes, as indicated in the following table.

Table 24: Typical CM roles and responsibilities

Role	Responsibilities
Chief information officer	The chief information officer (CIO) is responsible for setting forth policies regarding CM and implementing CM at the highest level for the agency.
System owner/ manager	The system owner/manager or other designated individual serves as the authority for all matters of CM for the information system. The system owner/manager is also responsible for developing functional requirements and verifying that the requirements are implemented appropriately. This individual may also play a role in establishing the Configuration Control Review Board (CCRB) and may be involved in the selection of the CCRB members.
CM manager	Depending on the size of the CM effort, a CM manager should be assigned to oversee all aspects of the CMP. The CM manager is responsible for all day-to-day activities necessary to support the CMP and may call on other personnel for assistance. The main responsibilities of the CM manager are to: • Implement the CMP • Provide operational support to the CCRB • Draft the CMP for CCRB approval • Provide the CCRB with information to evaluate changes and screen materials • Arrange CCRB meetings, provide agendas, and prepare meeting minutes • Coordinate implementation of CCRB decisions • Maintain CM library and database • Coordinate CMP with other security documentation, as required.
CM librarian	The CM librarian is appointed by the CM manager and is responsible for storing, retrieving, and distributing CM library materials.

Configuration control review board (CCRB)	The CCRB is the governing body for CM policy and guidance within the organization. A chairperson should be appointed by the CCRB to oversee the activities of the board. The main responsibilities of the CCRB include: • Managing CM operations • Reviewing and approving the CMP • Evaluating, approving, or disapproving change requests • Ensuring proposed changes are limited to those necessary to correct deficiencies • Satisfying changes in operational capability, personnel safety, and logistics support requirements • Effecting substantial life cycle cost savings • Maintaining security requirements • Preventing slippages to approved schedules • Ensuring proposed changes do not adversely affect external systems, subsystems, facilities, software, or services • Establishing system baselines and authorizing changes to applications.
System users	System users are responsible for reporting any weaknesses that are identified in current versions of the hardware, software, and components.
Other roles	Other roles, such as the chief information assurance officer (CISO), information system security officer (ISSO), and system administrator, may also have specific CM responsibilities. Once the extent of these responsibilities is determined, they should be documented within the CMP.

Once the roles and responsibilities are determined, a configuration management board (CMB) and a configuration control board (CCB) should be established.

Configuration management board (CMB) and configuration control board (CCB)

The configuration management board (CMB) should be responsible for conducting an overview of changes being made (including new implementations within the infrastructure). The CMB provides a risk management function to assess any pending implementation in order to provide for approval or rejection of proposed changes prior to implementation. This should limit the failure rate or damage that may be caused by making changes to the configuration of the enterprise.

At a minimum, the members of the CMB should include the designated head of the agency's configuration management processes or an authorized delegate, heads of engineering and information security organizations, representatives from the organizations requiring or representing the effort, and (when invited) vendors responsible for providing and/or integrating the new or upgraded configuration items.

The configuration control board (CCB) is subordinate to the CMB. A CCB may be established to provide special insight into a particular area of an enterprise. The configuration control board should coordinate activities and direct personnel to develop, implement, and follow CM policies as defined by the agency and initiate CM activities as directed by the program manager and/or system owner.

Configuration control boards may be set up only when there is a technical need that is deeper than CMB, or they may be established as a permanent entity in order to address CM issues on a regular basis prior to promoting them for decision to the CMB.

In executing life cycle CM, you should establish and follow a standardized set of processes.

The configuration management process (CMP)

The CMP is the critical element of monitoring the continued status of the information system, as well as the security controls associated with the authorization to operate an information system. One role of the CMP is to provide effective management of changes and a formal, documented, systematic process for requesting, evaluating, tracking, and approving changes to the information system and its approved security baseline.

The diagram below illustrates a simple configuration control process.

Figure 19: A simple configuration control process

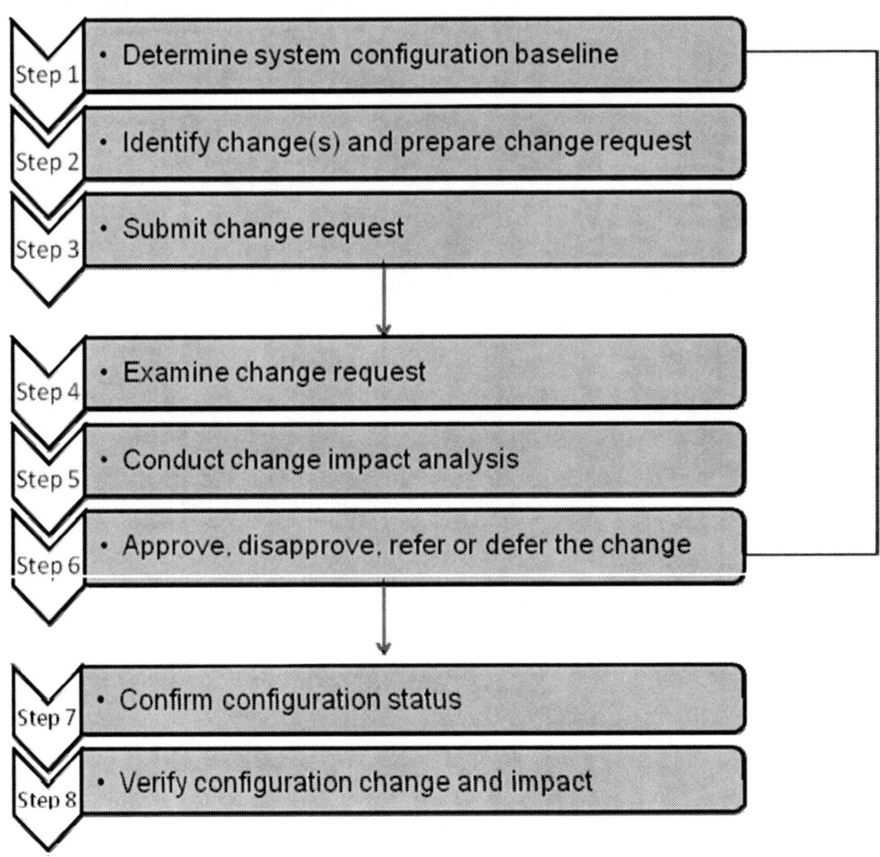

Let's talk about each of the steps in the diagram individually.

Step 1: Determine system configuration baseline. The system configuration baseline is a snapshot of the current design and functionality of the information system and provides details on the hardware, firmware, and software components. The system configuration baseline identifies the servers, workstations, and software applications currently being used and the specific configuration settings for each. If the system is not yet operational, the system configuration baseline should reflect the current status as of that state of the system life cycle. This information may be collected from various system and/or security documentation. The amount of existing documentation may depend on where the system is within the SLC. Specifically, the following items can be included in the system configuration baseline:

- System architecture. A thorough analysis of the system topography should be provided. A diagram may be needed to depict the system hardware and any connectivity devices (hubs, routers, and firewalls). The diagram should also indicate all connections to other systems and/or networks that are either internal or external to the agency.
- System characterization. If a risk assessment report is available for the system, the system characterization may be extracted from the report and used in this section. The system characterization should consist of a description of the information system, providing information such as:
  - purpose and functionality;
  - number of users;
  - system criticality and information sensitivity levels;
  - system confidentiality, integrity, and availability levels; and
  - type of data system.
- Hardware. The hardware used to support the information system should be identified and documented. Additional information, such as vendor support contact information, may also be included as necessary. Listed below is information that should be included for each piece of hardware:
  - manufacturer's name;

- model number;
- serial number;
- configuration settings; and
- hardware specifications, parts, and/or boards.

- Software. The software used to support the information system should be identified and documented. Additional information, such as vendor support contact information, may also be included as necessary. Listed below is information that should be included for each piece of software:

  - title (including acronym or nickname used to reference the software);
  - version number;
  - build number (if appropriate);
  - media (such as 4-mm tape, 8-mm tape, and CD ROM);
  - hardware requirements necessary to run the software (such as available disk space, random access memory, and network connections); and
  - control parameters (password policy, account lockout policy, requirements to change existing passwords, audit policy, user rights assignments, event log policy, restricted groups, system services settings, file permission settings, etc).

- System library. This section should include a list of all system documentation and supporting information, as well as a description of the CM library.

All system documentation, such as the following, used to establish the system configuration baseline should be referenced:

- User manuals
- System reference guides
- System security plan
- Contingency plan
- Risk assessment
- Security test and evaluation (ST&E) plan
- Disaster recovery plan (if applicable).

Supporting information, such as the following, should also be included:

- Glossary of terms
- List of acronyms
- Hardware/firmware/software inventory
- Project procedures and plans
- Development specifications
- System configuration diagrams[93]
- Personnel staffing requirements
- Project standardization documents
- System or subsystem specifications
- Change request form
- Status accounting.

All system documentation and supporting information should include the title, publication date, version number, and revision date of each document, if applicable.

Step 2: Identify changes and prepare the change request (CR) form. At some point, a change to the system may be necessary. To initiate a change, the need for that change should be identified and other relevant information (such as what type of change it is, why the change is necessary, and how the change may be implemented) should be collected.

A change can be categorized as an emergency, major, minor, or optional change. Emergency changes are not always required to undergo the entire CCP; however, they still must be properly documented and authorized. For an emergency change, an emergency CR form should be completed, which provides the justification, timeframe, and the potential impact on security, including a signature from the approving security official (*see the CD for a sample emergency change request form*).

---

[93] System configuration diagrams help to explain various system components. These diagrams explain how other systems are electronically linked to the system as well as their interconnection of user bases. The diagrams include internal and external connections to the system, and are basically a picture of the system's architecture and links to the system. These types of diagrams can be used as an aid when conducting an inventory of system hardware.

For non-emergency changes, a standard CR form should be completed. Information provided on the CR form should include the title and description of the change, impact of the change, justification for the change, and estimated number of staff necessary to implement the change. (*See the CD for a sample change request form.*) The system owner or other designated individual should ensure that all information on the form has been completed before submission.

A security impact assessment form should also be included with the CR form, describing in detail the possible impact that this change could have on system security. (*See the CD for a sample security impact assessment form.*)

Step 3: Submit the change request. The completed CR form should be submitted to the CCRB for approval. Once the CCRB receives the form, a CR tracking number will be assigned to and documented on the CR form. All emergency CR forms should also be submitted to the CCRB for approval within a more critical timeframe and an emergency request number will be assigned to and documented on the emergency CR form. In addition, the CCRB should maintain a CR status log to include all new CRs, including emergency requests, so the change can be tracked (*see the CD for a sample change request status log*).

Not all configuration changes to the information system have to be approved by the CCRB. For example, changes to a Microsoft® Access database field may not have to be approved by the CCRB. However, the system owner or designated individual must review technical and business analyses to determine how the change will impact the system and render a decision based on the information provided. All changes should be tracked in either a CR status log or in an equivalent log that maintains all configuration changes.

Step 4: Examine the change request. In Step 4, the CCRB should carefully evaluate the information provided on the completed CR form to determine whether or not to approve the change. Missing or inadequate information could preclude the CR from being expedited immediately. This section should provide details on how the evaluation is performed and should establish a time frame for decisions to be made regarding regular CRs as well as emergency CRs.

Step 5: Conduct change impact analysis. The CCRB should review both the technical and business effects of implementing the change to the information system. The technical analysis, which is usually conducted first, should determine the following:

- whether the change is technically correct;
- whether the change is technically necessary and feasible within the system constraints;
- how system security will be affected;
- all associated costs for implementing the change; and
- all security components affected (this section will be included in the security impact assessment form; *see the sample on the CD*).

The business analysis should determine the following:

- milestones and if the requested time frames are feasible;
- whether the change affects an existing contractual agreement regarding the system; and
- overall impact agency, associated costs with purchasing the hardware, software, and labor, as well as the impact on personnel schedules.

The CCRB should take into consideration all of the results of the impact analysis review before making a final decision about the change.

Step 6: Approve, disapprove, refer, or defer the change. The CCRB should review the CR and the impact analysis and make a decision based on the information provided. All CRs and corresponding decisions should be entered into the CR log. The CCRB has the option to choose one of the following decisions:

- Approve. Immediate implementation is authorized and may occur at any time after an authorized signature has been documented on the CR.

- Disapprove. Immediate denial of the request regardless of circumstances and information provided.
- Defer. Immediate decision is postponed until further notice. This decision could be due to lack of documentation or results of the technical and business impact analyses.
- Refer. A decision cannot be made by the CCRB alone. In this situation, the CCRB may seek consensus with an independent, objective party to ensure that the decision will not drastically affect system security.

Step 7: Confirm configuration status. This step refers to maintaining records of all changes and ensuring the traceability of each CR from initiation through resolution and disposition. Status accounting accomplishes the following:

- provides historical databases and records;
- provides the status of approved baseline, proposed changes, and implementation of approved status;
- determines the status on all systems in the CM process; and
- tracks changes and action items.

Step 8: Verify configuration change and impact. The final step of the CCP is to verify the configuration and test compliance with the current configuration control requirements. A verification process examines the characteristics of each system and the supporting documents to ensure that the configuration meets the user's needs and reflects the approved system configuration baseline.

An impact analysis can include both the functional and physical configurations. Functional configuration analysis verifies that the system's performance conforms to the stated requirements. Physical configuration analysis ensures the baseline documentation represents a true picture of the software, firmware, and hardware. In addition, as part of the process, the CM documentation can be verified for accuracy. This step ensures:

- changes are properly implemented;
- regulations and standards are followed;

- documentation is accurate (e.g. test results, vendor documentation, system environment, and configuration identification information);
- the system performs its functions; and
- security status is constant.

A robust configuration management process is a major element in the success of the process of verifying the continued compliance status of the security controls.

The configuration management plan (CMP)

The configuration management plan documents the agency's processes for configuration change control during system development, tracking security flaws, authorization of changes, and, for the certification and accreditation process. The CMP may be included in the authorization package, but it is generally sufficient if it is referenced and available for the security control assessment team to review and validate.

What are the basic contents of the CMP?

The following table provides a detailed description of each recommended CMP component and what should be included in each section.

Table 25: Recommended CMP components

CMP section	Description
Cover page	The cover page should include specific information to identify the document, principal owner (PO), title, version number, and date.
Table of contents	The table of contents should provide an outline of the CMP sections, subsections, and appendices with page numbers for each.
Revision or change table	The revision or change table should list date of change/revision, nature of the change/revision, and responsible individual.
Introduction	The introduction should, at a minimum, include the purpose, scope, and structure of the CMP.
Roles and responsibilities	This section should clearly identify CM roles and responsibilities, noting that all CM activities should be performed in accordance with the processes and procedures documented in the CMP.
Communications	The communications section should discuss the methods used to share information regarding CM (e.g. upgrades or application changes, technical notices, and version control). This section should also address items such as who has access to the information and how, when, and what type of information is shared.
Configuration control process (CCP)	This section should identify the CCP that is required to ensure all changes to the information system are properly requested, evaluated, and authorized. The CCP should provide detailed, step-by-step procedures for establishing, processing, tracking, and documenting changes. At a minimum, the following eight (8) basic steps should be included in the CCP: Step 1: Establish system configuration baseline Step 2: Identify change and complete change request

	form
	Step 3: Submit change request form
	Step 4: Evaluate change request form
	Step 5: Review impact analysis
	Step 6: Approve, disapprove, defer, or refer change request
	Step 7: Perform configuration status accounting
	Step 8: Conduct configuration verification and audit.
Configuration management resources	The CM resources section of the CMP should describe facilities and tools used for CM activities. This information serves as guidance for planning the resources required to support the functions throughout the CM process. Because the number of staff, equipment, and space required will vary according to needs, the organization should periodically review the resources involved in CM and verify that the facilities and tools are up-to-date.
Facilities	Facilities consist of dedicated spaces for personnel and equipment. Security controls should be in place to safeguard the materials based on confidentiality and sensitivity requirements. This section should include any physical/environmental security controls that must be in place to protect the information system.
Tools	Using automated tools is an effective way of managing CM activities and maintaining change control. This section should identify any automated software, or support hardware and software that are used in managing the CMP.

A sample table of contents for a configuration management plan follows:

Configuration management plan for <agency name>

1. Introduction

    1.1 Purpose

    1.2 Background

    1.3 Scope

    1.4 References

    1.5 Document overview

2. System overview

3. Configuration management components

    3.1 Organizations and responsibilities

        3.1.1   Information technology services directorate

        3.1.2   Configuration management entities (e.g. CMB, CCB)

    3.2 Configuration identification

        3.2.1   System identification

        3.2.2   System configuration items

    3.3 Configuration change control

        3.3.1   Change control process

        3.3.2   Maintenance of configuration baseline

        3.3.3   Controlling system changes

    3.4 Configuration status tracking

        3.4.1   Status tracking information

        3.4.2   Status tracking process

        3.4.3   Status reporting

    3.5 Configuration reviews

        3.5.1   Configuration review process

        3.5.2   Configuration review reporting

4. Configuration management process

    4.1 Process overview

    4.2 Classification

4.3 Evaluation

4.4 Modeling and testing

4.5 Implementation

5. Other CM information

    5.1 CM implementation plan

    5.2 System inventory

    5.3 CM documentation maintenance

    5.4 CM tools

    5.5 CM training

Appendix A: CM charters

Appendix B: CM forms

Continuity of operations/IT contingency planning

The rapid pace of technological change and the way business is conducted has necessitated that every federal agency's major information systems, those that support the core mission, are able to function in the face of emergencies or disasters. At no time was this more clearly evidenced than during the events surrounding the terrorist attacks of September 11, 2001. From this point on, no one could ignore the fact that our agencies and our information systems are vulnerable to several types of disruptions from a variety of factors, such as:

- Natural – hurricane, tornado, flood, fire
- Human – conflict, sabotage, virus, operator error
- Environmental – equipment failure, outage, electric power failure.

The development and implementation of appropriate plans is critical in ensuring that the federal agency will be able to operate at an acceptable level in the face of a major incident or disaster. Depending on your agency's needs, you might choose to develop a single continuity of operations plan with a series of appendices or you might prepare a suite of plans to properly prepare response, recovery, and continuity activities in the face of disruptions.

In many cases, the plan(s) will be developed based on the results of a business impact analysis (BIA). A BIA is used to evaluate and prioritize the functions needed by the agency to continue to execute its primary mission. A BIA will usually list the essential hardware, software, skills, and personnel functions necessary to ensure the business functions.

Table 26: Continuity plans

Plan element	Description
Continuity of operations plan (COOP)	The COOP focuses on restoring an organization's (usually a headquarters element) essential functions at an alternate site and performing those functions for up to 30 days before returning to normal operations. Since a COOP addresses HQ-level issues, it is often developed and executed independently from the BCP. Presidential Decision Directive (PDD) 67 mandates implementation of a viable COOP capability. Minor disruptions that do not require relocation to an alternate site are typically not addressed; however, the COOP may include the BCP, DRP and BRP as appendices.
Business continuity plan (BCP)	The BCP focuses on sustaining an organization's business functions during and after a disruption. An example of a business function may be a payroll or personnel management process. A BCP may be written for a specific business process or may address all key business processes. Information technology (IT) systems are considered in the BCP in terms of support to the business processes. In some cases, the BCP may not address long-term recovery of processes and return to normal operations, solely covering interim business continuity requirements. A disaster recovery plan, business resumption plan, and occupant emergency plan may be appended to the BCP. Responsibilities and priorities set in the BCP should be coordinated with those in COOP to eliminate possible conflicts.

Business resumption plan (BRP)	The BRP addresses the restoration of business processes after an emergency. Unlike the BCP, it lacks procedures to ensure continuity of critical processes throughout an emergency or disruption. Development of the BRP should be coordinated with DRP and BCP. This plan may be appended to the BCP.
Disaster recovery plan (DRP)	The DRP applies to major, usually catastrophic, events that might deny access to the normal facility for an extended period. Frequently, DRP refers to an IT-focused plan designed to restore operability of the target system, application, or computer facility at an alternate site after an emergency. The DRP scope may overlap that of an IT contingency plan; however, the DRP is narrower in scope and does not address minor disruptions that do not require relocation. Dependent on the agency's needs, several DRPs may be appended to the BCP.
IT contingency plan	A set of advance arrangements and established procedures that provide guidance to enable an organization to recover mission critical IT services at a "local" or alternative site" following a "minor" or "major" disruptive event. Plan duration is for short or long term effects. OMB Circular A-130 requires the development and maintenance of continuity of support plans for general support systems and contingency plans for major applications. This planning guide considers continuity of support planning to be synonymous with IT contingency planning. Because an IT contingency plan should be developed for each major application and general support system, multiple contingency plans may be maintained with the agency or mission area BCP. NOTE: FISMA mandates reporting of the development and annual testing of the IT contingency plan.
Cyber incident response plan (IRP)	This plan establishes procedures to address cyber attacks against agency IT system(s). These procedures are designed to enable security personnel to identify, mitigate, and recover from malicious computer incidents, such as unauthorized access to a system or data, denial of service, or unauthorized changes to system hardware, software, or data (e.g. a

	virus, worm, or Trojan horse). NOTE: FISMA requires an incident response plan as part of the annual report.
Crisis communications plan	This is an often overlooked element of any form of crisis response. Organizations should prepare their internal and external communications procedures prior to a disaster. A crisis communications plan is often developed by the organization responsible for public outreach. The crisis communication plan procedures should be coordinated with all other plans to ensure that only approved statements are released to the public. Plan procedures should be included as an appendix to the BCP. The communications plan typically designates specific individuals as the only authority for answering questions from the public regarding disaster response. It may also include procedures for disseminating status reports to personnel and to the public. Templates for press releases should be included in the plan.
Occupant emergency plan (OEP)	This plan provides the response procedures for occupants of a facility in the event of a situation posing a potential threat to the health and safety of personnel, the environment, or property. Such events would include a fire, hurricane, criminal attack, or a medical emergency. OEPs are developed at the facility level, and are specific to the geographic location and structural design of the building.

Regardless of whether you create a single comprehensive plan or individual plans for each type of crisis response, your plans should have the following common elements:

- Clearly stated objectives.
- Identification of functional roles and responsibilities of internal and external agencies, organizations, departments, and positions.
- Clear lines of authority for the agencies, organizations, departments, and positions involved in the plan.
- Identification of logistics support and resource requirements.
- Definition of the process for managing an event or crisis.
- Description of the process for managing the communication and flow of information, both internally and externally.

You will probably also want to follow a process in developing your plans. The general process of building plans for crisis or contingency response is outlined here:

- Initiate the planning process:

  - Get management support.
  - Identify business requirements.
  - Identify external dependencies.
  - Conduct a business impact assessment.

- Identify recovery strategies:

  - Identify required processes and offsite alternatives.
  - Identify required IT support and offsite alternatives.
  - Identify recovery alternatives (e.g. cold, hot, warm site; outsourcing, etc.).
  - Conduct cost-benefit analysis.
  - Present strategy to management and other stakeholders.

- Develop the plan:

  - Define roles and responsibilities of the response team.
  - Identify required external coordination and associated processes.
  - Develop notification and communication procedures.
  - Define the response procedures.
  - Define the recovery procedures.

- Test the plan:

  - Develop test plans and objectives.
  - Determine test format(s).
  - Execute the test.
  - Evaluate the results.
  - Improve plan based on review of results.

- Maintain the plan:

  - Develop maintenance process.
  - Institute agency awareness program.
  - Develop and implement plan-specific training.

As you can see, this can be a complex process, which should result in a comprehensive plan. There is a great deal of guidance on the preparation of all of these plans, and we suggest you take advantage of them.

The COOP and the IT contingency plan are the two plans that are most relevant for the C&A process. (The incident response plan will be addressed separately.)

A typical COOP will contain the following elements, although you will need to tailor this to the requirements of your agency:

Continuity of operations plan for <agency>

Executive summary

1. Introduction

    1.1 Purpose

    1.2 Applicability

    1.3 Scope

    1.4 References

    1.5 Assumptions and constraints

2. Essential functions

    2.1 Roles and responsibilities

    2.2 Coordination with external entities

3. Critical business functions

4. Concept of operations

    4.1 Planning scenarios

    4.2 COOP execution

    4.3 COOP team

    4.4 Notification and alert

    4.5 Delegation of authority and orders of succession

5. Responsibilities and procedures

    5.1 Responsibilities

    5.2 Procedures

6. Administration and logistics

    6.1 Alternate site

    6.2 Critical records, equipment, and systems

    6.3 Communications

    6.4 Resource management

    6.5 Personnel support

7. COOP maintenance

8. COOP testing

Appendix A: MOUs/MOAs

Appendix B: Personnel contact list

Appendix C: COOP equipment list

Appendix D: Delegations of authority memos

Appendix E: Prioritized list of critical functions

An IT contingency plan will usually have the following elements, although you will also need to tailor this plan to the requirements of your agency:

Information technology contingency plan for <agency>

Executive summary

1. Introduction

    1.1 Purpose

    1.2 Scope

    1.3 References

    1.4 Roles and responsibilities

    1.4 Assumptions and constraints

    1.5 Document overview

2. Concept of operations

    2.1 System description and architecture

    2.2 System interdependencies

    2.3 Notification and activation

2.3.1   Key personnel

2.3.2   Line of succession

2.3.3   Required activities

2.4 Recovery and restoration

2.4.1   Key personnel

2.4.2   Required activities

2.5 Return to normal activities

2.5.1   Key personnel

2.5.2   Required activities

3. After action reviews and reporting

4. Plan maintenance

Appendix A: Personnel contact list

Appendix B: Vendor/supplier contact list

Appendix C: Equipment and specifications

Appendix D: Service level agreements

Appendix E: MOUs/MOAs

Appendix F: Business impact assessment

Appendix G: Related continuity of operations and contingency plans

All of this planning is part of a larger process to ensure the survivability of the agency's critical information and information systems. Survivability implies that the information and the process can be recovered regardless of the disaster or emergency. This can only be assured if the plans are tested on a regular basis, at least annually.

Testing the plan

Testing your plans is critical – and also mandated by FISMA. It may be performed in the following formats:

Tabletop exercise: A tabletop exercise is a prepared simulation that enables the agency to exercise response to a disaster or a crisis situation in an informal, relatively stress-free environment. The name comes from the fact that the participants usually gather around a table to test procedures in the context of an emergency scenario. The focus of this type of exercise is on training and familiarization with roles, procedures, or responsibilities.

Functional exercise: The functional exercise simulates a disaster or crisis in a realistic manner, perhaps only short of moving real people and equipment to an actual site. As the name suggests, its goal is to test or evaluate the capability of one or more required functions in the context of an actual disaster.

Full-scale exercise: A full-scale exercise is as close to the real thing as possible. It can be a lengthy exercise involving several groups and using the facilities, equipment and personnel that might be called upon in a real event. Depending on the size and complexity of the organization, a full-scale exercise may be held at several locations. In some cases, a full-scale exercise may not be feasible since there can be a risk to production systems and the current operational mission.

All testing formats should, after action, be reviewed with the participants and a report. Information collected during an exercise, and discussed during the exercise should be incorporated into a revised version of the plans.

User guides – general and privileged users

Whenever you are dealing with information systems security you will quickly come to the realization that your best assets – and possibly your worst enemy – are your users. So, it is very important that they understand the information systems and that the supporting system security role is established and documented.

The general user's guide (also called the security features user guide – SFUG) and the privileged user's guide (PUG) are both a C&A requirement and a good means to document the role of these important components of your information systems security program.

User's guide

The primary goal of the general user's guide is to describe the operation of the information system, how the security mechanisms in a specific system work, and how the user should interact with both the system and the security components.

User in this context refers to an individual who uses the information system, but has no special privileges that would allow the use to affect the configuration of the system. The user is often assumed to be a person with little or no computer experience, but this is not always the case – certainly not today with the increased exposure to information systems.

In some cases, the user guide requirement can be satisfied in many ways, to include developing it as:

- a summary of the security features and user responsibilities presented as part of the mandatory security training or as a pre-requisite for receiving access to the system;
- a chapter in the agency's security handbook; or as
- a single document.

When developing the user's guide, remember your audience. Its scope should be limited to documenting only those features available to the users and only the user's responsibilities for system security. To accomplish this purpose, you should explain what security means in the context of the system, the security features that are present, how they work, and how to use them properly. As much as possible, the user's guide should be clear, concise, complete, and understandable by the average user.

The typical contents of a general user's guide include:

User's guide for <system>

Executive summary

1. Introduction

    1.1 Purpose

    1.2 Scope

Privileged user's guide

A privileged user has been defined as an individual who has authorized information system capabilities which are significantly greater than those available to the majority of users. Privileged user accounts are usually the most powerful accounts defined within information systems and their supporting applications. These accounts include, but are not limited to, administrator on Wnintel platforms, root on UNIX systems, Cisco enabled, DBA passwords, and the hard-coded passwords found in application scripts throughout an enterprise.

These accounts often provide full access to the information system. If these accounts are not properly managed and secured, it opens up critical applications and the data they contain to deliberate or inadvertent misuse, breaches and potential data theft. Control of these applications could even be transferred to an outside entity not under the agency's control, monitoring or jurisdiction. For this reason, privileged user accounts are under increasing scrutiny. A privileged user's guide or manual is similar to the user's guide, however, it provides details on how the privileged user will implement the security features. It should also describe the protective mechanisms to ensure traceability for the privileged user's interactions with the system.

Like the general user's guide, the privileged user's guide can be part of the overall security handbook, be issued as a part of the information system's operating guidance, or be published as a separate document.

Incident handling and response

Information system-related incidents are an unfortunate fact of life for an agency or company. Incidents can range from completely visible and disruptive (e.g. widespread virus outbreaks) or go entirely unnoticed – and these can often be the most damaging (e.g. loss of confidential growth plans).

There is a lot of information available to help you deal with most types of incidents, but if you haven't prepared in advance, you will struggle to be ready when you need it most. In our experience, incidents are also likely to occur at the least convenient time – when you need your system the most and the right people aren't available.

In addition to just being good commonsense, FISMA also mandates that each federal agency develop, acquire, or coordinate for sufficient capability to detect and respond to information security incidents within their agency. This incident response capability also includes the ability to mitigate the risks of attacks in progress.

In an effort to foster collaboration and communication in responding proactively to incidents, FISMA further specifies that agencies should report all information security related incidents to the US Computer Emergency Response Team (CERT)[94], the central federal information security incident management center. DOD components have their own specific reporting channels through their service or agency CERTs to the Joint Task Force for Global Network Operations (JTF-GNO) (formerly the DOD CERT).

Incident handling versus just incident response

Although your system authorization requires you to have an incident response plan, being ready to deal with incidents is more than just response. It actually starts with a process for incident handling; e.g. detection, response, and recovery.

The real purpose of establishing incident handling procedures is to be able to detect incidents (hopefully before they cause damage to your information system), know what to do when an incident occurs, and what steps to take to recover from the incident. This means anticipating possible incident scenarios before they happen, and making many decisions about how to handle them in advance.

---

[94] *http://www.us-cert.gov/*

Decisions require senior management involvement, so you will need these people on your side early in the development of your incident handling processes. For example, simply knowing who to report to when an incident occurs can be difficult to determine and coordinate. Some incidents may have to be handled as confidential and should be kept at the strictly "need to know" level (e.g. foreign nation involvement). The need to respond quickly to any incident often means after hours support and mixed project/support roles. You may also need to coordinate for external support and this costs money and takes time and effort to select partners.

Figure 20: Incident handling life cycle

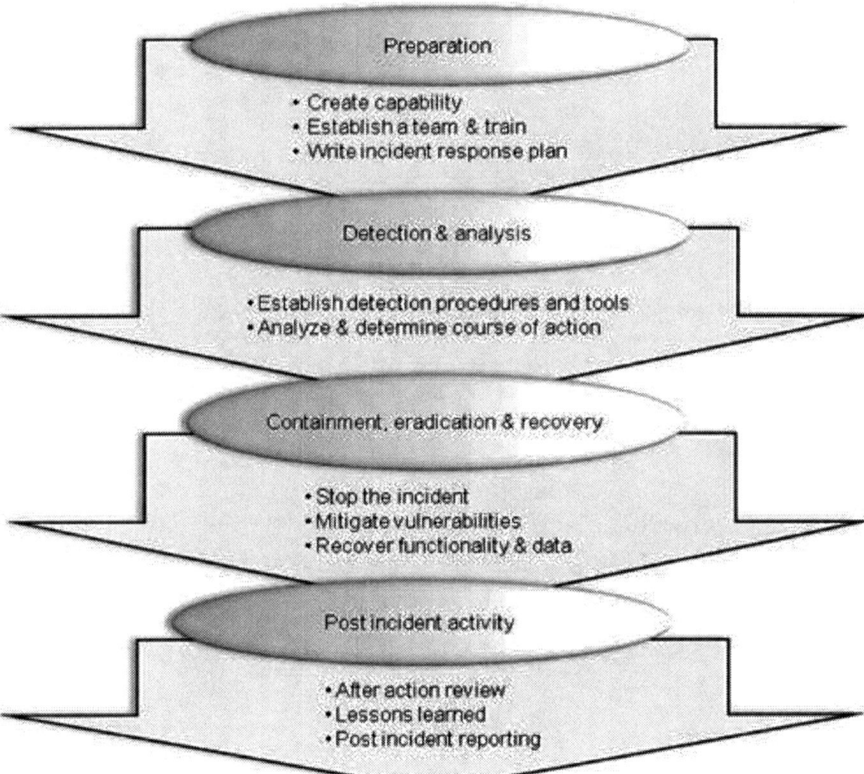

An effective incident handling process is your roadmap for incident identification and response. The figure above illustrates a basic incident handling life cycle adapted from NIST Special Publication 800-61.

As you will note, the initial activity is preparation, which includes the development of an incident response plan (IRP).

Incident response plan (IRP)

The purpose of developing an incident response plan (IRP) is to provide general guidance to your agency's staff – technical and managerial, incident response team member and general users – to:

- enable quick and efficient recovery from security incidents;
- respond in a systematic manner to incidents and carry out all necessary steps to correctly handle an incident; prevent or minimize disruption of critical computing services; and
- minimize loss or theft of sensitive or mission critical agency information.

It also serves as a guide to sharing information with other organizations – internally within your agency and/or externally with other information systems security and law enforcement organizations, as well as a guide for pursuing appropriate legal action. The challenge of incident response is to be able to bring a large number of agency staff with divergent skills together quickly and effectively in a crisis situation. To prepare for this challenge, you need a comprehensive and fully staffed IRP.

Below is an example of the contents of an IRP:

Incident response plan (IRP) for <agency>

Executive summary

1. Introduction

    1.1 Purpose

    1.2 Background

Privacy impact assessment (PIA)

The privacy impact assessment (PIA) provides an analysis of how personally identifiable information (PII) is handled within your federal agency. It evaluates security control compliance with legal, regulatory, and policy requirements; determines risk to the information; and evaluates the controls used to mitigate the privacy-related risks.

The objective of the PIA is to aid federal agencies to identify and address information privacy requirements when planning, developing, implementing, and operating agency information management systems that maintain information on individuals. What follows is the Office of Management and Budget's (OMB) definition of the PIA as stated in the federal requirements for implementing the privacy provisions of the E-Government Act of 2002 (*see OMB memo of M-03-22 dated September 26, 2003*).

A privacy impact assessment (PIA) is an analysis of how information is handled:

1. to ensure handling conforms to applicable legal, regulatory, and policy requirements regarding privacy,

2. to determine the risks and effects of collecting, maintaining, and disseminating information in identifiable form[1] in an electronic information system, and

3. to examine and evaluate protections and alternative processes for handling information to mitigate potential privacy risks.

When is a PIA required?

In accordance with the OMB guidance (M-03-22), the E-Government Act requires federal agencies to conduct a PIA before:

*   Developing or procuring information systems or projects that will collect, maintain or disseminate information in identifiable form[95] regarding members of the public; or

> NOTE: The PIA is only required for those agency information systems that contain personal information about individuals who are in the general public.

*   Initiating, consistent with the Paperwork Reduction Act, a new electronic collection[96] of information in identifiable form for 10 or more persons (excluding agencies, instrumentalities or employees of the federal government);

---

[95] According to the OMB Memo M-03-22, "identifiable form" means information in an IT system or online collection: (i) that directly identifies an individual (e.g. name, address, social security number or other identifying number or code, telephone number, email address, etc.) or (ii) by which an agency intends to identify specific individuals in conjunction with other data elements, i.e. indirect identification. (These data elements may include a combination of gender, race, birth date, geographic indicator, and other descriptors.)

[96] This applies to information collected from interactive forms being placed on DOI websites or terminals which the visitor may fill-out; the information is stored in DOI systems or by a contractor managing systems for the department.

- Whenever a system change creates new privacy risks. Privacy risks may occur when:

  - converting paper-based records to electronic data records;
  - previously anonymous information changes into information in identifiable form;
  - new uses of an existing system significantly change how information in identifiable form is managed in the system;
  - agencies adopt or alter business processes so that government databases holding information in identifiable form are changed;
  - user-authenticating technology (password, digital certificate, biometric) is applied to an information system accessed by members of the public;
  - agencies incorporate into existing information systems information in identifiable form purchased or obtained from commercial or public sources;
  - agencies work on shared functions involving exchanges of information in identifiable form, such as the cross-cutting E-Government initiatives (in such cases the lead agency should prepare the PIA);
  - alteration of a business process results in significant new uses or disclosures of information or incorporation into the system of additional items of information in identifiable form;
  - new information in identifiable form is added to a collection and raises the risks to personal privacy.

When is a PIA submitted?

For information systems that collect and manage information on members of the public (vs. federal employees), **OMB requires that a PIA be submitted with the agency's Exhibit 300s**[97] (*see OMB Circular A-11, sections 31.8, 53.1, and 300.9, available at http://www.whitehouse.gov/omb/circulars/a11/02toc.html*). Exhibit

---

[97] The Exhibit 300 is nothing more than a reporting tool required by OMB to justify agency information technology budget requests and bring standardization to agency budgets.

300, Part I, Questions A. c. and II.B, ask if a PIA or privacy risk assessment was performed. There are also other sections in the Exhibit 300 which address privacy risks and protection measures.

Further, a PIA may be submitted **together with the Paperwork Reduction Act**[98] **submissions** when there is a new electronic collection of information from 10 or more persons (not including agencies, organizations, or employees of the federal government). (*See OMB Memorandum, M-03-22 dated September 26, 2003, Attachment A, II. D for additional information on the E-Government Act and Paperwork Reduction Act interface.*)

Finally, as of 2008, federal agencies' annual FISMA submissions include a privacy section (Section D) which highlights significant accomplishments in implementing requirements of the Privacy Act and E-Government Act. The major components of the FISMA Section D report are:

- inventory of systems that contain federal information in identifiable form which require a privacy impact assessment (PIA) or system of records notice (SORN)[99];
- links to PIAs and SORNs;
- senior agency official for privacy (SAOP) responsibilities;
- information privacy training and awareness;
- PIA and web privacy policies and processes;
- policy compliance;
- agency use of persistent tracking technology; and
- privacy points of contact.

Steps to completing a PIA

The following table identifies some of the primary steps involved with completing a PIA.

---

[98] The Paperwork Reduction Act (PRA) requires that agencies receive Office of Management and Budget (OMB) clearance before requesting most types of information from the public (information collections).

[99] A system of records notice (SORN) in the federal register describes the categories of personally identifiable information collected, maintained and used in an automated system.

Table 27: Primary steps in a PIA

Step	Who does it	What is done
1.	Owner and developer	Obtain a copy of the assessment from your agency's Privacy Act officer or from the department Privacy Act officer or IT portfolio management division, office of the chief information officer (CIO). Request briefings on government and interior privacy, security, records, and Freedom of Information Act requirements.
2.	Owner and developer	Complete questions on the PIA, and consult with other necessary parties (e.g. FOIA officer, data administrator, privacy officer, IT security manager, and information collection clearance officer).
3.	Owner, developer, CIO, privacy officer, IT security officer	All parties should reach an agreement on design requirements and resolve any identified privacy or security risks. Ensure that all appropriate surnames are obtained.
4.	Bureau/owner, IT security manager	Review PIA for information system authorization purposes. Provide completed PIA to the bureau/office IT security manager and bureau/office Privacy Act officer, and provide copy with capital asset planning Exhibit 300.

Contents of the PIA

The contents of the PIA are largely determined by the federally mandated reporting requirements. Most federal agencies have an agency-specific format, so check on your specific agency requirements prior to initiating the PIA.

The following demonstrates the contents of a typical PIA. You will note that the PIA is in the form of a series of questions and answers.

Privacy impact assessment for <system>

Abstract

The abstract should be a minimum of three sentences and a maximum of four, if necessary, and conform to the following format:

- First sentence should be the name of the component and system.
- Second sentence should be a brief description of the system and its function.
- Third sentence should explain why the PIA is being conducted.

Overview

The overview is the most important section of the PIA. A thorough and clear overview gives the reader the appropriate context to understand the responses in the PIA. The overview should contain the following elements:

- The system name and the name of the agency component(s) who own(s) the system.
- The purpose of the program, system, or technology and how it relates to the component's and agency's department's mission.
- A general description of the information in the system.
- A description of a typical transaction conducted on the system.
- Any information sharing conducted by the program or system.
- A general description of the modules and subsystems, where relevant, and their functions.
- A citation to the legal authority to operate the program or system.

Section 1.0 Characterization of the information

The following questions are intended to define the scope of the information requested and/or collected as well as reasons for its collection as part of the program, system, rule, or technology being developed.

1.1 What information is collected, used, disseminated, or maintained in the system?

1.2 What are the sources of the information in the system?

1.3 Why is the information being collected, used, disseminated, or maintained?

1.4 How is the information collected?

1.5 How will the information be checked for accuracy?

1.6 What specific legal authorities, arrangements, and/or agreements defined the collection of information?

1.7 Privacy impact analysis: Given the amount and type of data collected, discuss the privacy risks identified and how they were mitigated.

Section 2.0 Uses of the information

The following questions are intended to delineate clearly the use of information and the accuracy of the data being used.

2.1 Describe all the uses of information.

2.2 What types of tools are used to analyze data and what type of data may be produced?

2.3 If the system uses commercial or publicly available data please explain why and how it is used.

2.4 Privacy impact analysis: Describe any types of controls that may be in place to ensure that information is handled in accordance with the above described uses.

Section 3.0 Retention

The following questions are intended to outline how long information will be retained after the initial collection.

3.1 What information is retained?

3.2 How long is information retained?

3.3 Has the retention schedule been approved by the component records officer and the National Archives and Records Administration (NARA)?

3.4 Privacy impact analysis: Please discuss the risks associated with the length of time data is retained and how those risks are mitigated.

Section 4.0 Internal sharing and disclosure

4.1 With which internal organization(s) is the information shared, what information is shared and for what purpose?

4.2 How is the information transmitted or disclosed?

4.3 Privacy impact analysis: Considering the extent of internal information sharing, discuss the privacy risks associated with the sharing and how they were mitigated.

Section 5.0 External sharing and disclosure

The following questions are intended to define the content, scope, and authority for information sharing external to <agency>, which includes federal, state and local government, and the private sector.

5.1 With which external organization(s) is the information shared, what information is shared, and for what purpose?

5.2 Is the sharing of personally identifiable information outside <agency> compatible with the original collection? If so, is it covered by appropriate routine use in a SORN? If so, please describe. If not, please describe under what legal mechanism the program or system is allowed to share the personally identifiable information outside of <agency>.

5.3 How is the information shared outside <agency> and what security measures safeguard its transmission?

5.4 Privacy impact analysis: Given the external sharing, explain the privacy risks identified and describe how they were mitigated.

Section 6.0 Notice

The following questions are directed at notice to the individual of the scope of information collected, the right to consent to uses of said information, and the right to decline to provide information.

6.1 Was notice provided to the individual prior to collection of information?

6.2 Do individuals have the opportunity and/or right to decline to provide information?

6.3 Do individuals have the right to consent to particular uses of the information? If so, how does the individual exercise the right?

6.4 Privacy impact analysis: Describe how notice is provided to individuals, and how the risks associated with individuals being unaware of the collection are mitigated.

Section 7.0 Access, redress and correction

The following questions are directed at an individual's ability to ensure the accuracy of the information collected about them.

7.1 What are the procedures that allow individuals to gain access to their information?

7.2 What are the procedures for correcting inaccurate or erroneous information?

7.3 How are individuals notified of the procedures for correcting their information?

7.4 If no formal redress is provided, what alternatives are available to the individual?

7.5 Privacy impact analysis: Please discuss the privacy risks associated with the redress available to individuals and how those risks are mitigated.

Section 8.0 Technical access and security

The following questions are intended to describe technical safeguards and security measures.

8.1 What procedures are in place to determine which users may access the system and are they documented?

8.2 Will <agency> contractors have access to the system?

8.3 Describe what privacy training is provided to users either generally or specifically relevant to the program or system?

8.4 Has certification and accreditation been completed for the system or systems supporting the program?

8.5 What auditing measures and technical safeguards are in place to prevent misuse of data?

8.6 Privacy impact analysis: Given the sensitivity and scope of the information collected, as well as any information sharing conducted on the system, what privacy risks were identified and how do the security controls mitigate them?

Section 9.0 Technology

The following questions are directed at critically analyzing the selection process for any technologies utilized by the system, including system hardware, RFID, biometrics and other technology.

9.1 What type of project is the program or system?

9.2 What stage of development is the system in and what project development lifecycle was used?

9.3 Does the project employ technology which may raise privacy concerns? If so please discuss their implementation.

Interconnection agreements

Interconnection agreements describe the management and technical operation between information systems and the required security controls. Depending on the requirements of the agency, the interconnection agreement can be addressed in a memorandum of understanding/agreement (MOU/MOA) and/or interconnection security agreement (ISA).

But what exactly is an interconnection? An interconnection is defined as the direct connection of two or more information systems for the purpose of sharing information and other information resources. It consists of two or more information systems and the mechanism by which they are joined, e.g. the "pipe" through which data is made available, exchanged, or passed.

Why is an interconnection agreement necessary?

Although significant benefits can be realized through system interconnection, it also poses certain risks to all of the interconnected information systems. If the interconnection is not securely designed, a failure could compromise the connected systems and the information they store, process, or transmit. Also, if any one of the interconnected systems is compromised, the interconnection could become a path by which to compromise the other system and its information.

As a result, it is critical that each of the interconnected systems understands as much as possible about the other systems participating in the interconnection. And once the risks are understood, they need a written and signed agreement regarding the management, operation, and use of the interconnection.

Beyond just good commonsense, federal policy also mandates that federal agencies establish interconnection agreements. Specifically, OMB Circular A-130, Appendix III, requires agencies to get written management authorization before connecting their information systems to other systems. The written agreements should define the rules of behavior and controls that must be maintained for the system interconnection. They can either be included in the organization's system security plan or made available as required to the authorizing official, inspectors, or auditors.

MOU, MOA or ISA?

The MOU/A contains the terms and conditions for sharing information and information resources in a secure manner. Specifically, it:

- identifies the purpose for the interconnection;
- names the relevant authorities;
- specifies the responsibilities of both organizations;
- defines the terms of agreement, including cost sharing and the timeline for terminating or reauthorizing the interconnection.

The MOU/A should not include technical details on how the interconnection is established or maintained. That is the purpose of the ISA.

Role of the authorizing official

Once completed, the ISA and the MOU/A must be submitted to the authorizing official of each participating organization, requesting formal approval for the interconnection. Upon receipt, the authorizing official will review the ISA, the MOU/A, and any other relevant documentation or activities. Based on this review, the authorizing official will decide to:

- approve the interconnection;
- grant interim approval; or
- reject the interconnection.

If the authorizing official accepts the ISA and the MOU/A, they should sign and date the documents indicating approval of the interconnection.

Memorandum of understanding/agreement (MOU/A)

The following MOU example is based on the National Institute of Standards and Technology (NIST) Special Publication (SP) 800-47 – *Security Guide for Interconnecting Information Technology Systems.*

Memorandum of understanding/agreement between <agency> and <agency>

1. Supersession

2. Purpose and scope

3. Authority

4. Requirements

5. Architecture/data flow diagram

6. Security responsibilities

7. Communications

8. Responsible parties

9. Cost considerations

10. Timelines/extensions/cancellations

11. Signature of agreement

Appendix A: Architecture/data flow drawing

Appendix B: Interconnection security agreement (if applicable)

Interconnection security agreement (ISA)

Federal agencies, DOD and the Intelligence Community may have different requirements for the ISA depending on the security requirements of the information system(s), so check on the specific requirements before finalizing your ISA. The following example demonstrates the format for a generic ISA:

Interconnection security agreement between <agency> and <agency>

Executive summary

1. Introduction

    1.1 Purpose

    1.2 Scope

    1.3 Assumptions and constraints

    1.4 Roles and responsibilities

    1.5 Organization of the ISA

2. Interconnection statement of requirements

3. Interconnection description

    3.1 <Agency> system

    3.2 Non-<agency> system

    3.3 Architecture and dataflow diagrams

4. Security responsibilities

    4.1 Communications

    4.2 Points of contact

    4.3 Responsibilities

5. Personnel/user security

    5.1 User community

    5.2 Protection of sensitive/classified information

    5.3 Training

    5.4 Personnel changes

6. Policies

    6.1 Rules of behavior

    6.2 Security documentation

7. Interconnection security

    7.1 Management

    7.2 Changes

   7.3 New interconnections

   7.4 System inventory

   7.5 Boundary/firewall management

8. Incident prevention, detection, and response

   8.1 Incident handling

   8.2 Vulnerability scanning and penetration testing

   8.3 Disasters and other contingencies

9. Modifications

10. Compliance

11. Cost considerations

12. Severability

13. Limitation of liability

14. Force majeure

15. Signatories

Further reading

Calder, Alan. *ISO 27001: The Risk Assessment, Control Selection, and Risk Treatment Pla*n. A series of webinars conducted by Alan Calder.

Syed, Akhtar. *Business Continuity Planning Methodology,* Sentryx Publishing, 2003.

US Computer Emergency Response Team website, available at *http://www.us-cert.gov/*.

CERT Coordination Center, Carnegie Mellon University, available at *http://www.cert.org/*.

Forum of Incident Response and Security Teams, available at *http://first.org/*.

References

National Institute of Standards and Technology (NIST) Special Publication 800-14, *Generally Accepted Principles and Practices for Securing Information Technology Systems,* September 1996.

National Institute of Standards and Technology (NIST) Special Publication 800-34, *Contingency Planning Guide for Information Technology*, June 2002.

National Institute of Standards and Technology (NIST) Special Publication 800-37, *Guide for the Security Certification and Accreditation of Federal Information Systems*, May 2004.

National Institute of Standards and Technology (NIST) Special Publication 800-47, *Security Guide for Interconnecting Information Systems*, August 2002.

National Institute of Standards and Technology (NIST) Special Publication 800-53, Revision 2, *Recommended Security Controls for Federal Information Systems*, December 2007.

National Institute of Standards and Technology (NIST) Special Publication 800-53A, *Guide for Assessing the Security Controls in Federal Information Systems* (Final Public Draft), July 2008.

National Institute of Standards and Technology (NIST) Special Publication 800-61, *Computer Security Incident Handling Guide*, January 2004.

National Institute of Standards and Technology (NIST) Special Publication 800-100, *Information Security Handbook: A Guide for Managers*, October 2006.

National Institute of Standards and Technology Interagency Report (NISTIR) 7328, *Security Assessment Provider Requirements and Customer Responsibilities: Building a Security Assessment Credentialing Program*, Initial Public Draft, September 2007.

OMB M-03-22, *OMB Guidance for Implementing the Privacy Provisions of the E-Government Act of 2002*, 30 September 2003.

OMB 08-09, *New FISMA Privacy Reporting Requirements for FY 2008*, 18 January 2008.

CHAPTER 11: C&A IN THE US DEPARTMENT OF DEFENSE

The DIACAP policy is a very critical policy that will set in place a transformative process for having enterprise certification and accreditation…DIACAP is a very important bedrock policy as we move in a net-centric fashion.[100]

Bob Lentz, Director of Information Assurance,
DOD CIO/ASC NII

In this chapter:

Introduction to the DIACAP

DIACAP governance

The DIACAP roadmap

DIACAP support tools

C&A and the DOD components

---

[100] http://www.military-information-technology.com/mit-archives/122-mit-2006-volume-10-issue-7/1099-building-the-ia-offensive-line.html

In the preceding chapters, we provided you with a generic approach to the information system authorization process – one that could be used in federal agencies, the DOD, or even in the commercial sector. In the next few chapters, you will notice similarities between elements of the generic process and the individual processes currently being used in different parts of the federal government. You will also notice the differences. So, let's start with the processes used in the US DOD.

The US Department of Defense (DOD) took the lead in the early 2000s in recognizing the need for a certification and accreditation process that embraced the new and emerging technologies and that considered the ever-increasing levels of interconnectivity. It also had to be a C&A process that aligned more directly with the system (development) life cycle.

The result was the development and publication of the Department of Defense Information Assurance Certification & Accreditation Process (DIACAP), which was signed into effect in November 2007. The DIACAP replaced the earlier methodology, known as the DOD Information Technology Security C&A Process (DITSCAP).

The DITSCAP had long been viewed as onerous and overly resource intensive – particularly when considered in light of the real security benefits emerging from the process. The primary differences between the DITSCAP and DIACAP are:

- The DIACAP is aligned to the system life cycle and supports the way DOD acquires and builds information technology.
- The DIACAP improves compatibility and reciprocity with C&A processes in the federal and intelligence communities.
- The DIACAP represents a focus shift from securing the individual system to supporting security of the enterprise.
- The DIACAP provides both the content and tools to enhance consistency, standardization, and repeatability as well as re-use of C&A products.

The On Cyber Patrol© cartoon and supporting articles are created and made available by the US Army's Office of Information Assurance and Compliance, NETCOM, CIO/G6.

For the purpose of our discussion in this chapter, we will use terminology that is current in the DOD, some of which represents a deviation from that used elsewhere in the book and in federal agencies. So, here is a quick translation of the terms we will use:

- Certification and accreditation (C&A) process instead of authorization process.
- Information assurance (IA) control instead of security control.
- Designated accrediting authority instead of approving official.
- Certifying agent instead of security controls assessor.

Introduction to the DIACAP

The fundamental security requirements for DOD information systems are expressed in the form of graded baseline IA controls (called security controls in federal agencies.) The IA controls for a management framework for the implementation, verification, and monitoring of information systems security are consistent with the federal requirements of OMB A-130.

DODD 8500.1, *Information Assurance*, defines an IA control as an objective IA condition of integrity, availability, or confidentiality achieved through the application of specific safeguards or through the regulation of specific activities. Selected management, personnel, operational, and technical controls are applied to each DOD information system to achieve an appropriate level of integrity, availability, and confidentiality.

The IA controls serve as a common management language for expressing information system security and protection requirements. They also lay a foundation for a shared security dialogue between information owners, program managers, service providers, network and enclave managers, certifying and accrediting authorities, and information system security engineers.

The IA controls and how to use them

DOD's IA controls are found in DODI 8500.2, *Information Assurance Implementation*. They provide the fundamental IA requirements for securing DOD information systems. Unlike the security categorization process described earlier, DOD information systems base their IA controls selection on a determination of mission assurance category (MAC) and confidentiality level (CL).

Table 28: MAC & CL

Requirement	Description	Security focus
Mission assurance category (MAC)	Criticality of the information system to the component; need for availability of the information system to support the mission	Availability and integrity
Confidentiality level (CL)	Criticality of the information's protection to the mission	Confidentiality

There are a total of 157 individual IA controls, from which the baseline set of assigned IA controls is derived. Each IA control describes an objective security condition which can be attained through the implementation of specific technical safeguards or through the use of specified procedures.

The IA controls also provide a common language for expressing IA needs and status. The use of a standard language for information systems security enables a dialogue among DOD information owners, managers, C&A authorities, and others.

Determining mission assurance category

There are three levels of mission assurance category based on the information system's need for availability and integrity.

- Mission assurance category I (MAC I) is assigned to information systems determined to be vital to the operational readiness or mission effectiveness of deployed and/or contingency forces. The consequences of a loss of integrity or availability would be unacceptable and could result in the immediate and sustained loss of mission capability. MAC I information systems are subject to the most stringent protective measures.
- Mission assurance category II (MAC II) is assigned to information systems which are considered important to deployed and/or contingency forces. Consequences of a loss of integrity are unacceptable. Loss of availability would be difficult to manage and could only be tolerated for a short period of time. The consequences could include a delay or degradation in providing important services and could seriously impact mission effectiveness or operational readiness. MAC II information systems require additional safeguards that extend beyond best practices.
Mission assurance category III (MAC III) information systems handle information necessary for the execution of DOD's day-to-day business functions, but do not directly or materially affect deployed and/or contingency forces in the short term. Consequences as a result of a loss of integrity and/or availability are tolerable or could be overcome without significant impact on mission effectiveness or operational readiness. Consequences could include the delay or degradation of services or commodities associated with routing DOD activities. MAC III information systems require protective measures commensurate with commercial best practices.

Table 29: Mission assurance category

MAC	Definition	Integrity requirement	Availability requirement
I	System handles information VITAL to operational readiness or mission effectiveness of the forces. Loss of integrity and availability is UNACCEPTABLE.	HIGH	HIGH
II	System handles information IMPORTANT to the forces. Loss of integrity is UNACCEPTABLE. Loss of availability DIFFICULT, but tolerable for a short time.	HIGH	MEDIUM
III	System handles information NECESSARY for day-to-day activities, but loss would not materially affect the forces in the short term. Loss of integrity and availability are TOLERABLE and without significant impact.	BASIC	BASIC

Determining confidentiality level

In the DOD, the confidentiality level (CL) is primarily used to establish acceptable access criteria for the information system and its information. It is based on the consideration of requirements, such as security clearance, access and need-to-know requirements.

There are three CLs:

- Classified, which is assigned to a DOD information system processing any level of classified information.

- Sensitive, which is assigned to a DOD information system processing information whose loss, unauthorized access to, or misuse of could adversely affect the national interest, federal programs, or individual privacy. This is unclassified information which should not wind up on the front page of *The Washington Post* or any other national newspaper. Examples include financial, logistics, or medical information.
- Public information refers to content which has been reviewed and approved for public release by a cognizant authority and/or the information owner. The primary regulatory guideline for the release of public information is DOD Directive 5230.9, *Clearance of DOD Information for Public Release*, current as of July 1999.

Table 30: Confidentiality level

Definition	Confidentiality level
Information system processing CLASSIFIED information.	CLASSIFIED (HIGH)
Information system processing SENSITIVE information or unclassified information that has not been cleared for public release.	SENSITIVE (MEDIUM)
Information system processing PUBLIC information or unclassified information that has been specifically cleared for public release.	PUBLIC (BASIC)

Selecting the IA control set: Putting MAC and CL together

Assigning the appropriate MAC and CL to information may not be quite as easy as it seems. Well, assigning the CL is usually fairly straightforward. Information is either classified or not; information can either be released to the public or not.

Quantifying requirements for availability and integrity may not be quite as simple. This is usually based on a rather subjective risk assessment based on the information system's operating environment.

Generally, most organizations have at least a general idea of the target operating environment for an information system. A risk-based assessment of this target environment will usually provide the type of information needed to make a valid decision about information and mission integrity and availability requirements. For example, an information system that supports the warfighting environment would usually have higher availability and integrity requirements than one intended for use only as an office administration system.

The following diagram provides a matrix for assigning the MAC and CL. In this particular example, the information system in question processes classified information (=CL CLASSIFIED), has a high integrity and a medium availability requirement (= MAC II). In order to determine the baseline list of IA controls for this information system, you would refer to DODI 8500.2, *Information Assurance*:

- CLASSIFIED information: the IA controls are listed in Enclosure 4, Attachment 4
- MAC II: the IA controls are listed in Enclosure 4, Attachment 2.

Figure 21: Matrix for assigning MAC and CL

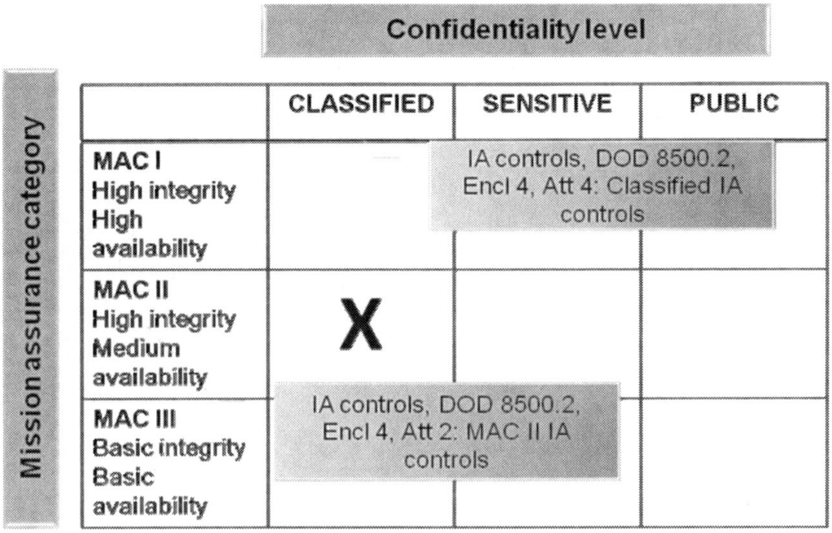

	CLASSIFIED	SENSITIVE	PUBLIC
MAC I High integrity High availability		IA controls, DOD 8500.2, Encl 4, Att 4: Classified IA controls	
MAC II High integrity Medium availability	X		
MAC III Basic integrity Basic availability	IA controls, DOD 8500.2, Encl 4, Att 2: MAC II IA controls		

Confidentiality level

Mission assurance category

Selection of an IA controls baseline for an information system processing classified information and with a high integrity and medium availability requirement.

Source: Adapted from DIACAP Knowledge Service

IA control subject areas

While the NIST SP 800-53 talks about controls in terms of "families," DOD refers to IA control subject areas. The set of IA controls contained in DODI 8500.2 is organized into eight subject areas, which indicate the major subject or focus area of a specific safeguard or countermeasure. The following table shows how the IA controls are organized by subject area.

Table 31: IA control subject areas

Subject area	Abb.	Mgmt	Ops	Tech	Total
1. Security design and configuration	DC	15	8	8	31
2. Identification and authentication	IA	0	1	7	8
3. Enclave and computing environment	EC	1	21	27	49
4. Enclave boundary defense	EB	0	3	5	8
5. Physical and environmental	PE	0	27	0	27
6. Personnel	PR	0	7	0	7
7. Continuity	CO	5	17	2	24
8. Vulnerability and incident management	VI	0	2	0	2
Total		22	86	49	157

As you can see, similar to the security controls specified under NIST, the DOD controls are also categorized as management, operation, or technical controls.

- **Management controls** focus on the management of risk or information system security. These can refer to policies and regulations intended to protect technical environments, information and information system resources, and to guide personnel behaviors. These include security controls addressing areas such as:

  - Risk management: the process of identifying, measuring, and minimizing or reducing security risk to information and information systems. You will note that risk management is a fundamental process within the execution of the C&A process, as well as an individual IA control.

- Annual reviews: under OMB Circular A-130, security controls must be reviewed annually and reports generated.
- Life cycle planning: includes the management process for phasing in of new components and phasing out of old, as well as changes in technology, mission or acquisition process.

- **Operational controls** focus on the day-to-day execution of the activities related to the implementation and maintenance of the security safeguards. Examples of operational controls include:

  - Personnel security: more often than not, the greatest harm or disruption to an information system is a result of the intentional or unintentional actions of individuals. The operational controls focused on personnel are intended to reduce the human potential for damage to the system or the information.
  - Physical security: controls focus on access to and protection of the environment.
  - Contingency planning: describes the mechanisms needed for the recovery of data and/or information systems in the event of a disruption.
  - Security training: a mandatory requirement under the Computer Security Act. Initial, refresher, awareness and job-specific security training are considered essential.
  - Incident response: refers to those procedures needed to ensure an incident response capability.

- **Technical controls** describe safeguards focused on protection of the hardware, software, and firmware, as well as boundary defense for the information system. Examples of technical controls include:

  - Identification and authentication: technical measures that prevent unauthorized personnel and/or processes from accessing an information system.
  - Auditing: the means to maintain a record of system activity by system or application processes and by user activity.

IA control naming convention

Each of the IA controls is uniquely named and catalogued, which allows it to be referenced, measured, and reported against throughout the life cycle of the information system to which it is applied. Each unique name is composed of several elements:

- IA control subject area – indicating which one of the eight groups to which the control is assigned.
- IA control name – a brief phrase with a high level reference to the nature of the individual control.
- IA control number – provides a quick reference to the control as well as an indication of the level of robustness for the IA control. There are three levels of robustness and the higher the number, the more robust the requirements of the control (e.g. a 3 would indicate the highest level of robustness.)

The diagram below provides an example of DOD's IA control naming convention.

Figure 22: IA control naming convention

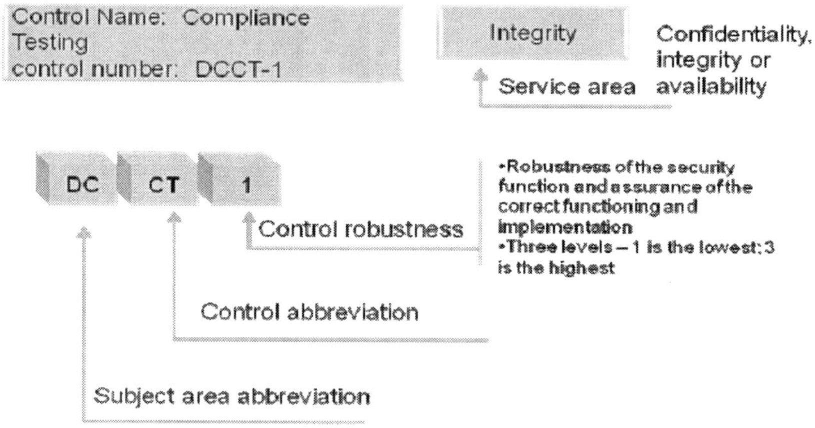

Source: Adapted from DIACAP Knowledge Service

In this particular example, the subject area is security design and configuration, the IA control is compliance testing, and the level of robustness is 1, or the lowest level of the safeguard. There will be more detail about assigning the IA controls in the section on DIACAP stages or activities.

DIACAP governance structure

DOD has established a DIACAP governance structure that is intended to manage and integrate DIACAP relevant activities across all levels of the DOD (e.g. agencies, services, mission areas) and events across the system life cycle (e.g. concept, development, deployment, and operations). There are three primary components of the governance structure:

- An accreditation structure
- A C&A configuration management structure
- C&A process structure.

Figure 23: DIACAP governance structure

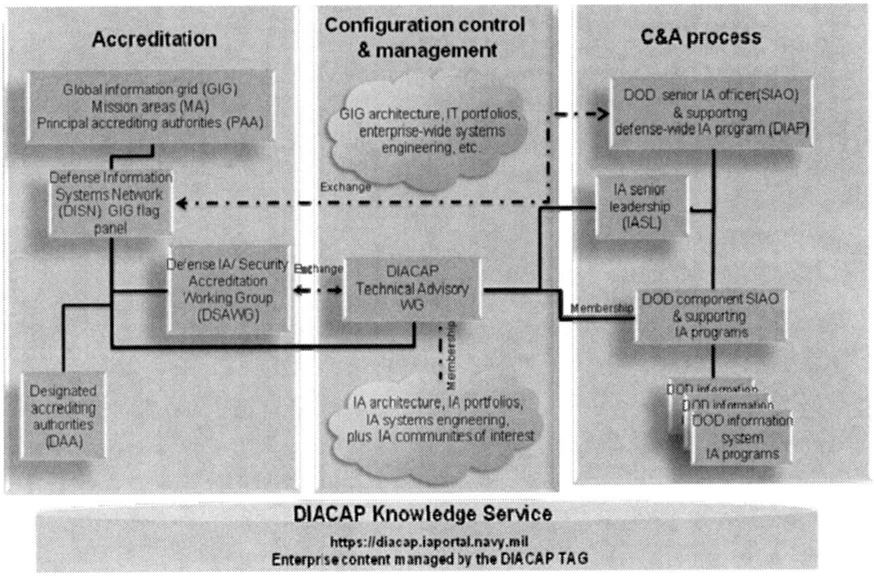

Source: Adapted from DODI 8510.01

The accreditation sub-structure

Principal accrediting authorities (PAA) are appointed for each of the global information grid (GIG) mission areas (MA).[101] The PAAs have the authority to directly appoint a DAA for information systems that directly support their respective mission area and the associated community of interest (COI).

The Defense Information Systems Network (DISN) flag panel acts on behalf and in support of the PAAs. The panel advises the PAAs, has a role in assessing enterprise risk, authorizes information exchanges, and approves proposed changes to the DOD IA control baseline.

The Defense IA Security Working Group (DSAWG), which is under the DISN flag panel, serves as the community forum for reviewing and resolving any C&A decisions and considering the risk to the community of operating an information system. The DSAWG also develops and provides guidance to DOD DAAs on connecting their information systems to the GIG.

Configuration control and management sub-structure

The DIACAP Technical Advisory Group (TAG) provides detailed analysis and authoring support for the enterprise component of the DIACAP Knowledge Service. The TAG interfaces with the DOD components[102], mission areas, IA COIs, and other specialized entities to address issues that are common to all DOD agencies.

The TAG is represented in the DIACAP Knowledge Service. The DIACAP Knowledge Service provides the forum and the structure for the TAG's functions and activities, including: authoring, voting, membership, and configuration control of the IA controls and their content.

---

[101] The GIG MAs are: business mission area, intelligence mission area, warfighting mission area, and enterprise information environment mission area.

[102] A DOD component is defined as a service, agency or combatant command.

C&A process sub-structure

The DOD senior information assurance officer (SIAO)[103] directs and coordinates the DOD IA program. Each of the DOD component SIAOs has authority and responsibility for certification and serves as the certifying authority (CA) for all of the information systems assigned to or governed by the DOD component CIO and supporting IA program.

Each CA may task, organize, staff, and centralize or delegate certifying activities – and you will find that each DOD component approaches this very differently. Regardless of the adopted model, the DOD component's SIAO bears the final responsibility for certification quality, capacity, visibility, and effectiveness.

In addition, each DOD CIO, supported by an appointed SIAO, has overall responsibility for administration of the overall C&A process. This includes:

- the integration of certification with all of the other DIACAP activities;
- participation in the DIACAP configuration management process;
- visibility and sharing of the C&A status of assigned ISs;
- enforcement of training requirements for persons participating in the DIACAP;
- support to DAAs; and
- responsiveness to the DOD CIO.

The information assurance senior leadership (IASL) serves as a community forum for assessing and improving C&A process administration. The IASL, which represents and supports the SIAOs, provides strategic direction and guidance to ensure that IA is integrated across the DOD. It provides for the integrated planning, coordination, and oversight of DOD's IA programs.

This high-level DOD governance structure is supported by a number of other roles and responsibilities at the DOD component

---

[103] The DOD SIAO is located in the Office of the Secretary of Defense / Chief Information Officer.

level. With the exception of the unique role of the PAA, the following roles are very similar to those described in Chapter 5. The following table lists the DOD roles and their respective appointment/delegation authorities.

Table 32: DOD roles

DOD C&A role	Appointed/delegated by
PAA	Mission area owner
DAA	DOD component head; PAA for MA-managed information systems
CIO	DOD component head
SIAO	DOD component CIO (or in organizations where a CIO does not exist, by the DOD component head)[104]
CA	SIAO usually serves as the CA, but may delegate the CA role as required
IAM	Program/system manager
IAO	IAM
User representative	Information owner
DIACAP TAG representative	DOD component SIAO or CIO

A DIACAP roadmap (guide to the stages or activities)

Certification and accreditation of DOD information systems consists of a series of activities or stages and tasks, which may even occur concurrently or at varied frequencies throughout the system

---

[104] The DOD SIAO is appointed by the DOD CIO.

life cycle. To the greatest extent possible, the DIACAP parallels the system life cycle.

Ideally, it should be initiated at system inception (e.g. documented during capabilities identification or at the implementation of a major system modification). But note, failure to initiate the DIACAP process at system inception does not mean that you cannot bring the information system into compliance later in the life cycle. However, the earlier the DIACAP is initiated in the system life cycle, generally the implementation of IA services and safeguards will be less expensive and problematic.

Figure 24: DIACAP stages or activities

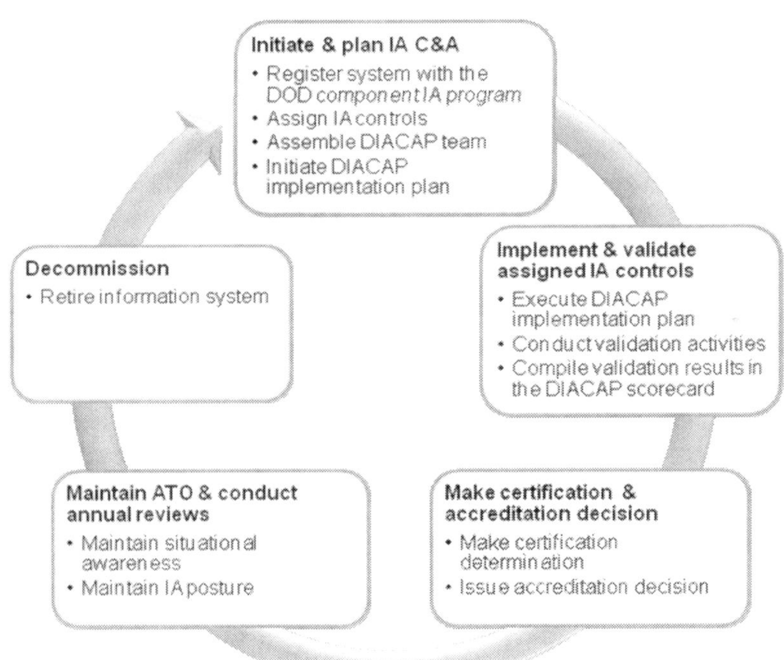

Source: Adapted from the DIACAP Knowledge Service

This diagram depicts the various stages or activities of the DIACAP. We will now discuss each of these in additional detail.

Initiate & plan IA C&A

Initiation and planning for the certification and accreditation process is the first stage or activity in the DIACAP. In involves the following sub-activities:

- Register system with the DOD component IA program.
- Assign IA controls.
- Assemble the DIACAP team.
- Initiate the DIACAP implementation plan.

Let's talk more about each of these individual sub-activities.

Register the information system with the DOD component IA program

In the requirements of the DIACAP, registration of the information system ensures that the system is "visible" to the DOD CIO/SIAO and to the governing component's information assurance leadership. Once an information system is visible, certain management indicators (e.g. C&A status) and FISMA requirements can be more effectively monitored.

The process of registration starts the C&A process between the DOD information system and the responsible elements within the DOD component. These are usually the DOD component's CIO and SIAO. A dialogue regarding requirements and implementation starts with registration and – hopefully – continues until the information system is decommissioned.

There are several events that can start this conversation:

- A new information system development or acquisition has been started and the C&A process is initiated at the same time (the ideal situation!).
- A new information system is being deployed and requires C&A.
- An existing information system is discovered to have no authorization to operate.
- An existing information system has an expiring authorization to operate.

As discussed earlier, there are many ways in which an information system can be registered. The overall DOD registry is called the ***DOD Information Technology Portfolio Repository (DITPR).*** The DITPR was designated as "the Enterprise Shared Space for IT Portfolio Management data for all DOD business IT systems" by the DOD deputy CIO on March 17, 2005. The DITPR is also used as the official unclassified DOD data source for FISMA, e-authentication, portfolio management,[105] privacy impact assessments, and the inventory of all mission critical/mission essential/mission support systems. Even though each of the DOD components has its version of an IT portfolio management system, they must be able to automatically populate information about their systems into the DITPR. Each DOD component also has an agency that controls these databases, for example, the Air Force has the Air Force Communications Agency (AFCA), and the Army has the Installation Management Agency (IMA).

Figure 25: DOD Information Technology Portfolio Repository (DITPR) Connections

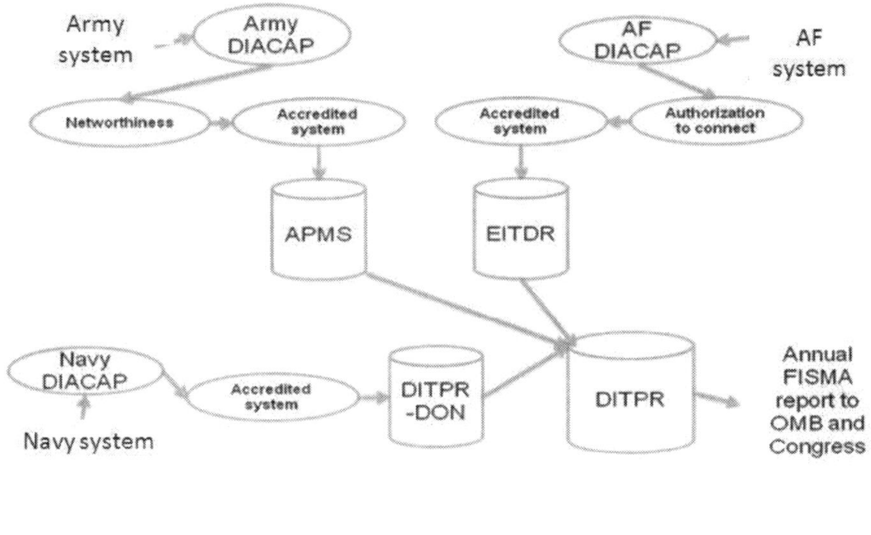

---

[105] Portfolio management is the management of selected groupings of IT investments using strategic planning, architectures, and outcome-based performance measures to achieve a mission capability.

The Air Force's version is the Enterprise Information Technology Data Repository (EITDR). EITDR is used to keep track of new information system acquisitions, new DOD compliance mandates, information technology program management and system engineering documentation. In support of C&A in the Air Force, EITDR also contains a function called security, interoperability, supportability, sustainability and usability (SISSU) for all applicable systems.

The Army Portfolio Management System (APMS) is the Army's IT portfolio management system. APMS is designated as the database of record for Army IT systems. The Army also uses APMS to monitor the C&A and FISMA reporting status of Army information systems.

The Navy uses the DITPR-Department of the Navy (DITPR-DON). DITPR-DON is the single, authoritative source for data regarding DON IT systems, including national security systems. It also has FISMA reporting requirements, and maintains the IT system inventory for compliance with congressional requirements. DITPR-DON is used as a repository for the C&A status of mission critical (MC), mission essential (ME), and mission support (MS) DON IT systems and networks.

The primary means used to initiate the DIACAP process and register the information system is the system identification profile (SIP). This relatively simple document contains the information gathered about the information system during the pre-registration and registration process. The SIP, which is one part of the DIACAP C&A package, is maintained throughout the system's life cycle.

Much of the information contained in the SIP can be found in program documentation, system design documents, requirements specifications, and other documentation normally developed as part of a system acquisition or development.

System identification profile (SIP): The SIP is the first critical component of the DIACAP C&A package. You will use the SIP to provide information needed to clearly identify the information system, the C&A status and the life cycle status.

Several of the information items on the SIP are unique to the DOD C&A process; others are derived from external sources, such as the DITPR or the DOD component equivalent IT portfolio management tools.

So, let's walk through completing the SIP. In order to keep it manageable, we'll break it down into sections. NOTE: A SIP template is available on the CD accompanying the book. We'll look at each entry in detail in the table below, which provides the guidance for entering information into that block.

Table 33: Completing the SIP

ID	Data element descriptor	Example, acceptable values, or comment	Required/ conditional[106]
1	System identification	The system ID is a unique number used by the DOD component to identify the system. It can be derived from the DITPR-assigned number; the unique number assigned by the component-unique IT portfolio management system, or even be a unique numbering system developed by the DOD component for identifying systems that are not officially entered in the IT portfolio management systems.	Required/may be system generated
2	System owner	The system owner is the element or organization within the DOD component that owns, manages, or controls the information system and/or its information.	Required
3	Governing DOD component IA program	The governing DOD component IA program actually refers to the DOD component that owns the information system. This entry	Required

---

[106] Conditional – information will be entered if applicable and available for the information system.

		could be Army, Navy, Defense Logistics Agency, etc. however, it should always be the highest level of the DOD component.	
4	System name	This is the full, descriptive name of the information system, e.g. Defense Personnel Tracking System.	Required
5	Acronym	This is the acronym associated with the information system. For example, the acronym for the system name listed above would be DPTS.	Required
6	System version or release	The system version or release refers to the development/deployed version of the information system, e.g. Ver. 1.1. This is useful in ensuring that the C&A package and its contents refer to the most current version of the IS.	Required
7	System description	In this block, you would provide a high-level description of the information system, its function, and other relevant information. This might include indicating if it is a standalone, or processes classified information, etc. This entry can also require an attachment to the SIP with a system diagram and/or hardware and software listing. This entry should be sufficiently detailed to identify the minimum mandatory system and network security controls required to provide and maintain an adequate security level for the IS.	Required
8	DIACAP activity	The entry here indicates the DIACAP activity in which the information system is currently	Required

		involved. This entry will usually stabilize upon receipt of the authorization to operate and remain the activity "maintain ATO" unless there are significant changes to the IS requiring re-authorization or the system is decommissioned. The possible entries are: • Initiate & plan C&A • Implement & validate assigned IA controls • Make C&A decision • Maintain ATO & conduct reviews • Decommission.	
9	System life cycle phase	DOD system life cycle phases are described in DODD 5000.2, *Operation of the Defense Acquisition System*, December 2008. The authorized entries are: • Concept refinement • Milestone A (MS-A), technology development • MS-B, system development & demonstration • MS-C, production & deployment • Operations & support • Disposal or decommissioning.	Required
10	System acquisition phase	This entry applies to programs of record (POR) and identifies the current acquisition phase of the information system. The possible entries are: • Pre-milestone A (pre-MS A)	Conditional

		(concept refinement)	
		• Post-MS A (technology development)	
		• Post-MS B (system development & demonstration)	
		• Post-MS C (production & deployment)	
		• Post full rate production/deployment decision (FRPD/FRDD)	
11	IA record type	The IA record type refers to the type of DOD IS undergoing C&A. The authorized entries are: • Enclave* • AIS application • Outsourced IT-based process** • Platform IT interconnection *Indicate if the enclave is a standalone or a DMZ. **Indicate if the processes/ services are DOD controlled or if control is shared with an external service provider (e.g. web hosting, external data storage, etc.).	Required
12	Mission criticality	Identify the mission criticality of the IS. Allowed entries include: • Mission critical (MC) • Mission essential (ME) • Mission support (MS) The requirements for mission criticality assignment are described in DODD 5000.2, *Operation of the Defense Acquisition System,*	Required

		December 2008.	
13	Accreditation vehicle	Identify the primary C&A process being used for this IS in terms of the requirements document: DIACAP - DODI 8510.01, NIST SP 800-37, DCID 6/3.	Required
14	Additional accreditation requirements	Based on the function of the IS, there may be additional accreditation requirements. Examples include: privacy (e.g. HIPAA); special access requirements (SAR); cross domain solutions (CDS); ports, protocols, & services (PPS); Non-Classified Internet Protocol Router Network (NIPRNet); Secret Internet Protocol Router Network (SIPRNet); GIG Connection Approval Process (CAP).	Conditional
15	ACAT	This entry refers to the acquisition category. The requirements for ACAT are described in DODD 5000.2, *Operation of the Defense Acquisition System*, December 2008. There are 4 ACATs, each assigned based on a life cycle cost: • ACAT I • ACAT II • ACAT III • ACAT IA	Conditional
16	Governing mission area	Each IS can usually be aligned with a specific mission area (MA) within the global information grid (GIG). The possible entries include: • Business MA (BMA)	Required

		• Defense Intelligence MA (DIMA) • Warfighting MA (WMA) • Enterprise Information Environment MA (EIEMA)	
17	Software category	Every IS has a primary operating system and/or managing application. These are identified here by their procurement type. The possible entries include: • Commercial off the shelf software (COTS) • Government off the shelf software (GOTS)	Required
18	MAC level	This refers to the mission assurance category (MAC) requirements of the IS. Authorized entries are: • MAC I • MAC II • MAC III	Required
19	Confidentiality level	This entry refers to the information sensitivity of the IS. The authorized entries are: • Classified • Sensitive • Public	Required
20	Accreditation status	Identify the current C&A status of the information system. Possible entries include: • Unaccredited • IATO	Required

		<ul><li>IATT</li><li>ATO</li><li>DATO</li></ul>	
21	Certification date	If applicable, enter the date the IS was certified by the certification authority.	Conditional
22	Accreditation document-ation	Often an IS has been previously accredited under a different policy and still has existing accreditation support documentation and evidence of compliance testing results. If this is the case, the entry here would be YES. If not, the entry would be NO.	Conditional
23	Accreditation date	List the date of the current accreditation decision. If there is no current accreditation decision, enter NONE together with the projected accreditation date.	Required
24	Authorization termination date	This is the date that the current accreditation is scheduled to expire (e.g. 180 days for an IATO, 3 years for an ATO).	Conditional
25	DIACAP team roles, member names, contact information	Identify all of the members assigned to the C&A team for this information system. This can also be included as a separate attached list.	Required
26	Privacy impact assessment	A privacy impact assessment (PIA) is required under FISMA for certain IS. Federal requirements for the PIA can be found on the OMB website at *http://www.whitehouse.gov/omb/memoranda/m03-22.html*. The DOD implementation policy is in DOD	Required

		5400.11-R, *DOD Privacy Program.* Answer YES or NO.	
27	Privacy Act system of records notice required	Indicate whether a Privacy Act system of records notice is required in accordance with DOD 5400.11-R, *DOD Privacy Program.* Answer YES or NO. (Although not specifically required in the SIP, referencing the date and location of the PIA in the SIP can be useful.)	Required
28	E-authentication risk assessment required	Indicate whether an e-authentication risk assessment is required in accordance with OMB Memorandum M-04-04, *http://www.whitehouse.gov/omb/memoranda/fy04/m04-04.pdf.* Answer YES or NO.	Required
29	Annual security date of annual security review	List the date of the most recent annual security review for IS with an ATO. Annual assessments are required by FISMA and by DOD for IS with ATOs in effect for one year or longer.	Required
30	System operation	In this entry, identify the primary method of system operation. The possible choices are: • Government (e.g. DOD)-owned, government-operated (GOGO) • Government-owned, contractor-operated (GOCO) • Contractor-owned, contractor-operated (COCO). Includes outsourced IT services. • Contractor-owned, government-	Required

		operated (COGO) • Non-DOD – includes federal, state, and local governments, grantees, industry partners, etc.	
31	Contingency plan required	In accordance with FISMA, each IS must have a contingency plan. Indicate whether a contingency plan addressing disruptions in IS operations is in place. Answer YES or No.	Required
32	Contingency plan tested	In accordance with FISMA, each IS must also test their contingency plan on an annual basis. Answer YES or NO and enter the last date tested.	Required

Assign the information assurance controls

Assigning the appropriate IA controls is arguably one of the most important activities in the DIACAP – as well as in any of the C&A processes. Determining the IA controls is a pre-requisite for execution of the follow-on step in the DIACAP activities, the development of the DIACAP implementation plan. The following diagram will take you through the IA controls assignment process.

Figure 26: IA controls assignment process

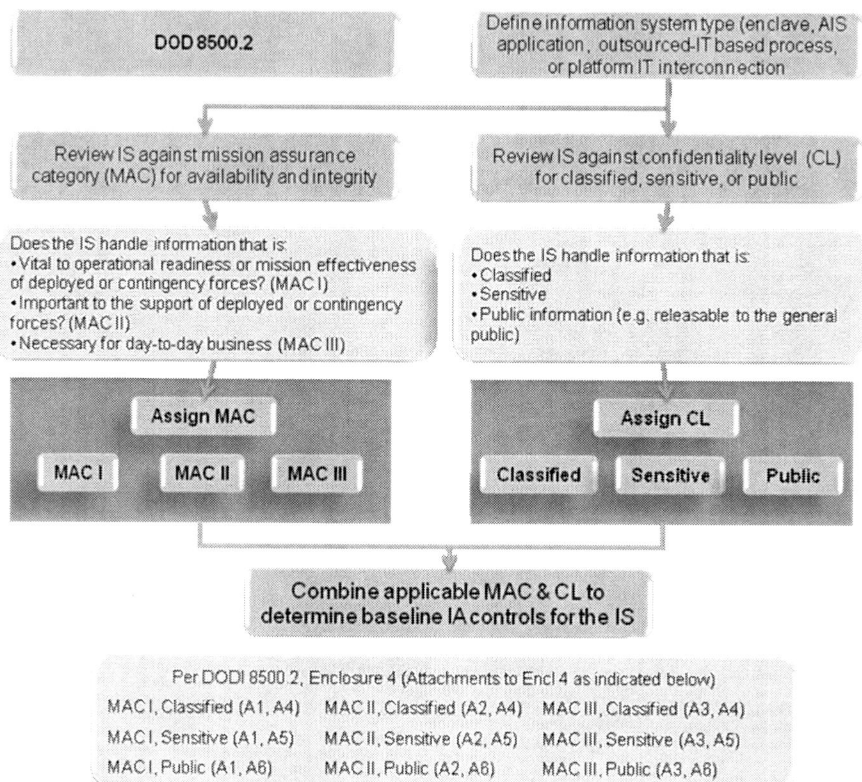

Source: Adapted from the DIACAP Knowledge Service

Here is a condensed overview of the process. Using DODI 8500.2, *Information Assurance Implementation*, as guidance, define the type of information system scheduled to undergo the C&A process. Frequently, the type of information system will influence the MAC and CL, inheritance factors, additional control sets, and ultimately, the selection of controls.

As discussed earlier, DODI 8500.2 defines three DOD mission assurance category levels with associated requirements for availability and integrity. DOD also provides guidelines for determining the confidentiality level.

Once the MAC and CL for the IS have been identified, the initial IA controls baseline can be easily determined. Basically, the initial IA controls baseline is an unrefined, combined list of all of the IA controls associated with the MAC and CL for that IS.

It is important to note that this baseline list of IA controls is not considered final. Further analysis is still required.

- First, you will determine which controls are inherited from other information systems or from the environment.
- Next, determine which IA controls are not applicable to this information system.
- Identify any additional requirements, such as privacy or protections required to interconnect with other information systems.

Only after you have completed this analysis, will you have a final set of IA controls. But wait – you still are not done. Before starting on the implementation of the IA controls, be sure to obtain approval from the DAA and the system owner. Once this process has been completed, you can assemble the DIACAP team and develop the DIACAP implementation plan.

Assigning the DIACAP team

While this is the next "official" step in the DIACAP activities, we believe that your DIACAP team should be largely assembled long before reaching this stage. But if you have not yet determined the structure of your team, this is a good time to finalize this action.

At a minimum, the DIACAP C&A team should consist of:

- Designated accrediting authority (DAA)
- Senior information assurance officer (SIAO)
- Certifying authority (CA)
- Program manager/system manager (PM/SM)

- Information assurance manager (IAM) or information assurance officer (IAO)
- User representative (UR).

Descriptions of these roles and their associated responsibilities can be found in Chapter 5. The members of the DIACAP C&A team should be trained and certified according to the requirements of DODD 8570.01, *Information Assurance Training, Certification, and Workforce Management,* current as of April 2007.

When you are determining the members of the DIACAP C&A team, keep in mind that DOD has established some allowable and unallowable relationships between the team members. The table below shows these relationships:

Table 34: Allowable/unallowable relationships in C&A team

Relationship	Allowed (YES or NO)
PAA may be DAA	YES
DAA reports to the PM, SM or program executive officer (PEO)	NO
DAA and CA are the same individual	YES
CIO may be the DAA	YES
CA reports to the DAA	YES
CA reports to the PM, SM or PEO	NO
PM , SM, or CA report to the DAA	YES
PM, SM, or CA may be the same individual	NO
PM, SM or DAA may be the same individual	NO
PM, SM, or UR may be the same individual	NO

PM or SM reports to the CA	NO
PM or SM reports to the CIO	YES
PM or SM reports to the DAA	YES
UR reports to the CIO	YES
UR reports to the PM or SM	NO
UR reports to the SIAO or CA	YES

Develop the DIACAP implementation plan

The DIACAP implementation plan (DIP) illustrates the strategy for implementation, along with the current implementation/compliance status of the IA controls assigned to the IS. The DIP is the second element in the DIACAP C&A package. At a minimum, the DIP should contain the following information:

- **Assigned IA controls:** This is the final list of all IA controls for that IS. The list can be organized by sub-entities of the DOD IS (e.g. site, subsystem, service, or set of services). NOTE: While only the IA control number is required in this column, it is often useful to include the name of the IA control.

- **Implementation status:** Each listed IA control should also be designated as applicable, not-applicable, or inherited. If the IA control is inherited, specify HOW the inheritance occurs (e.g. enclave firewall, physical security measure, personnel security program, etc.).

- **Responsible entities:** Identify the element or individual responsible for the implementation of the specific IA control. There should be a responsible entity for each control, although one entity may be responsible for more than one IA control.

- **Resources:** This is where you would indicate the personnel, material, or financial resources needed to successfully and completely implement a particular IA control. You should have an entry for each control; however, it is useful to combine IA controls to minimize the resource requirements or to logically organize the implementation of the IA control.

- **Estimated completion date:** You should enter an estimated completion date for each IA control. Again, you may be able to consolidate resources to more effectively implement the IA controls with a combined completion date.
- **Comments:** Use this column to enter any comments relevant to the implementation of an IA control.

The following diagram is an example of a completed DIACAP implementation plan (DIP). Before proceeding to the next stage in the DIACAP, implement and validate IA controls, it is critical to obtain the approval/concurrence of the involved parties in the DIP. This includes the assigned DIACAP team, as well as any external entities or individuals participating in the IA control implementation and/or testing process.

Figure 27: DIACAP implementation plan

DIACAP implementation plan						Mission Assurance Category (MAC)	Confidentiality Level (CL)
Personnel requirements tracking system (PRTS)						**MAC II**	**Sensitive**

C MAC I, Classified   C MAC II, Classified   C MAC III, Classified
C MAC I, Sensitive   C MAC II, Sensitive   C MAC III, Sensitive
C MAC I, Public   C MAC II, Public   C MAC III, Public

Assigned IA control	Implementation status				Responsible entities	Resources	Estimated completion	Comments
	N/A	Inherited	Implemented	Planned				
COAS-2 (Alternate Site Designation)				X	Don Hill	Seek mission area funding to implement this control	31-Jul-09	Requires special funding; resources to be provided by mission area
DCSQ-1 (Software Quality)			X		SW Development Team (Jane Doe)	SW SME required to complete the control	15-May-09	SME was available from 1-15 May to finalize control requirements
PEEL-1 (Emergency Lighting)		X			Facilities (John Doe)			Provided by facilities
EPBW-1 (Public WAN)	X							Information system not connected to the public WAN

Implement and validate assigned IA controls

In the first DIACAP stage or activity, you should have established your C&A team, completed the initial version of the system identification profile (SIP), and assembled the list of required IA controls on the DIACAP implementation plan (DIP). Additionally, all of the required approvals for the SIP and DIP should have been obtained. If yes, then your information system is ready for the IA controls to be implemented and subsequently tested for compliance.

Prior to starting the implementation process, determine which entity(-ies) will be responsible for an IA control, or perhaps even several IA controls. It is best to do this as early in the process as possible to ensure availability of required personnel, materiel support, or funding.

Figure 28: IA control components

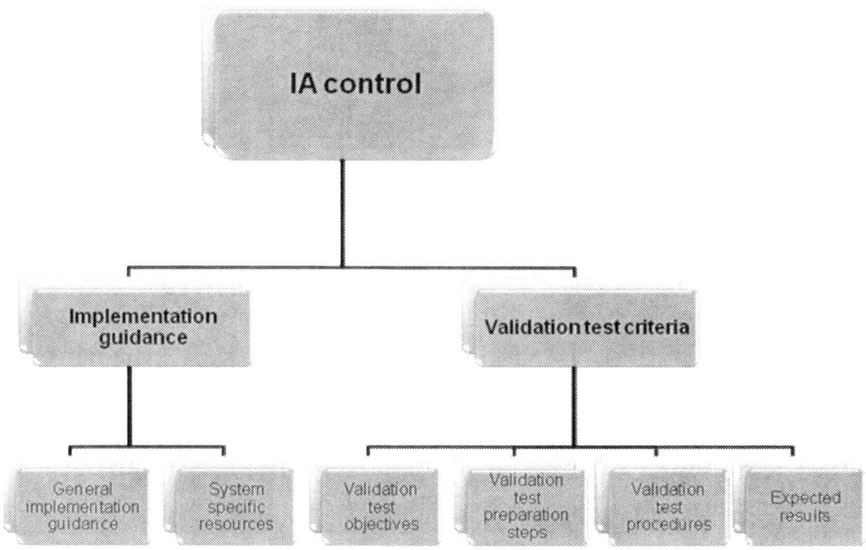

Source: Adapted from the DIACAP Knowledge Service

It is also a good idea to make sure that arrangements have already been initiated for the validation testing. The CA is part of the

DIACAP team and should already have been notified, but now is a good time to confirm their availability for the estimated completion date. This will help you to avoid delays – particularly since most CAs and their staff are extremely busy.

Finding implementation and validation test guidance

The DIACAP Technical Advisory Group (TAG) is responsible for maintaining standardized implementation and testing guidance for each of the IA controls. The anatomy of an IA control and its elements is shown in the diagram below.

Implementation guidance is supported by a high-level set of standards for executing the IA control. The guidance is supplemented with a list of resources, such as other related publications or tools, in the "system-specific resources" area.

The documentation on validation test criteria or procedures includes a statement regarding the objectives of the validation test, a series of steps to prepare for the test, the test procedures themselves, and DOD's expected minimum results. There is a one-to-many relationship between the IA controls and the validation tests, e.g. one IA control may require several discrete tests to ensure that all elements of the IA control are adequately validated for compliance.

Just a note of caution: if you are seeking very specific implementation or validation test guidance – you won't find it here. The standardization information has been developed intentionally at a very high level to ensure that it can be applied to multiple types of information systems and within multiple environments. It is the responsibility of the owning organization to tailor the guidance to fit their particular requirements.

There is an IA controls explorer on the DIACAP Knowledge Service: *https://diacap.iaportal.navy.mil/ks/Site%20Pages/IA%20Controls/I A.4.0.aspx* where the most current guidance for the IA controls can be found. We recommend checking the explorer prior to starting any implementation to make sure that you have the most current information. The DIACAP Knowledge Service maintains a change log, so you can always track any changes to an IA control.

Execute the DIACAP implementation plan

As mentioned above, the DIACAP Knowledge Service is your primary source for information about implementing IA controls. There are also other resources that can assist in the process. These include the Security Technical Implementation Guides (STIG) published by the Defense Information Systems Agency (DISA).

STIGs are essentially configuration guides for DOD information systems and associated IA and IA-related devices. DISA also publishes Security Checklists, which can serve either as an implementation guide or as a checklist to evaluate compliance with a baseline level of security.

The STIGs, Security Checklists and other valuable resources can be found at DISA's Information Assurance Support Environment (IASE) website at *http://iase.disa.mil/stigs/index.html*.

As the IA controls are being implemented, evidence can be developed and retained. In DOD, evidence is referred to as artifacts. Artifacts can be the direct result of IA control implementation, such as the establishment of a password policy. They can also be generated as a part of normal system development, such as configuration management processes. Here are some examples of artifacts:

- System policies, such as the IT contingency plan which includes processes established to meet the requirements of COAS-1, alternate site.
- System documentation, such as the software inventory developed during the configuration management process, which meets the requirements of DCSW-1, software inventory.
- Test results, such as those generated during a vulnerability scan and which meet the requirements of IA control VIVM-1, vulnerability management.

Artifacts provide the tangible evidence of an IA control's implementation. As they are developed, they should be referenced in the DIACAP implementation plan. It is usually not necessary to create a separate document describing the evidence and to attach it to the DIP. But it is useful to reference the artifact, the date of the most current version, and where the artifact can be found in the comment section on the DIP.

Conduct validation activities

Validation testing, or IA controls compliance verification, is the next step in the DIACAP process. It includes all of the tasks related to the execution of the validation tests.

As mentioned above, one or more validation procedures have been developed for each IA control and the most recent procedures are posted on the DIACAP Knowledge Service. These procedures provide guidance on preparing for the validation test, executing the test with test steps, and the expected results. The descriptions may include background material, sample results, and links to automated testing tools.

Although DOD provides the basic guidelines for validation testing, variations in the test procedures may be needed based on system configuration, location, and environment. Some of the testing procedures are largely manual, requiring the direct participation of an individual to initiate the test and collect the results. Other tests may be highly automated and the results will be automatically generated. Regardless of the type of testing, the individuals conducting the test procedures should have security and information system knowledge, such as network security, firewalls, intrusion detection systems, and operating systems.

Using the DOD baseline validation tests – and only modifying as required – ensures that:

- There is standardization of the minimum baseline test plans for all DOD information systems.

- All of the IA controls for an information system are tested to a consistent standard.
- There is a common expectation of test results.
- There is a standard language for expressing the results and sharing them, as required.

While validation testing can be conducted once all of the IA controls have been implemented, we have found that testing each IA control internally as we implement it can save both time and money. First, we see immediately if the implementation has been sufficient – and if not, we can take immediate remediation actions. Also, we may generate artifacts and test results that will be considered sufficient by the responsible certifying authority and/or the CA representative.

This is important to note. In most of the DOD components, IA controls validation testing is conducted by an independent CA on a cost reimbursement basis. If you can reduce the time and scope of the CAs test presence, you can also potentially minimize the time to authorization and the cost of testing.

Prepare the plan of action & milestones (POA&M)

The validation testing will provide a determination if an IA control is compliant or non-compliant. If any of the IA controls is determined to be non-compliant (or not applicable), a system level POA&M must be prepared.

Although FISMA mandates the POA&M as a reporting requirement, it is also:

- an organization's primary tool for tracking the mitigation of any security weaknesses in the information system and in the security program itself;
- a tool to assist an Inspector General (IG) in the evaluation of an organization's overall security performance; and
- assists OMB in its oversight activities.

Once developed, the POA&M is a permanent record. And once a weakness is posted, it can be updated, but not removed, once corrective actions are completed. It is a living document and should be updated as weaknesses are mitigated or as new weaknesses are identified.

The members of the DIACAP Team have certain responsibilities in relationship to the POA&M:

Table 35: POA&M responsibilities

DIACAP team member	POA&M responsibility
DOD component CIO	Monitoring and tracking the overall execution of the component's system level POA&Ms until security weaknesses have been mitigated and the C&A documentation adjusted to reflect the changes.
DAA	Monitoring and tracking the execution of the system-level POA&Ms.
PM/SM	Implementing or overseeing the implementation of the corrective measures identified in the POA&M.
IAM/IAO	Assists the PM/SM in providing the POA&M status to the DAA, SIAO, and CIO.

DOD IT POA&Ms share several characteristics:

- Linked to the organization's budget submission and links security costs with security performance.
- Intended to address all weaknesses associated with an information system, including, but not limited to, those found during validation testing, IG inspections, audits, security tests, and vulnerability assessments.
- Shared as required with the responsible IG.

- Required to follow the mandated format provided by OMB and DOD.
- Submitted to the DOD SIAO when required.

There are three types of DOD POA&Ms:

- System level POA&M, which is a living document designed to be a tool to assist organizations in closing gaps in their security performance. It addresses the IA controls weaknesses from an individual information system.
- Component level POA&M. DOD components are required to prepare and submit a DOD component level POA&M, which compiles the information from system level POA&Ms and systemic weaknesses identified across the DOD component.
- DOD enterprise POA&M. The enterprise POA&M is a roll-up of the component level POA&Ms and includes system weaknesses identified across the enterprise.

Table 36: Types of DOD POA&M

Type of POA&M	Responsible	Submit to	Submission dates
System level	Program managers, information assurance managers	DOD component CIO & SIAO (for all IS with CAT I weaknesses or on the OMB Watch List for security or on request)	1 Dec, 1 Mar, 1 Jun, 1 Sep
DOD component level	DOD component CIO	OSD/NII	1 Dec, 1 Mar, 1 Jun, 1 Sep
DOD enterprise level	OSD/NII	OMB	Included in the October FISMA report – as directed

For the purposes of this book, we will only focus on the system level POA&M. The system level POA&M has a very specific, mandated format. This format is tied to the annual requirements published by OMB and reflects authorized modifications due to specific DOD requirements. The instructions for the DOD POA&M process are developed and issued through the DOD FISMA integrated process team (IPT). The following figure (provided by the DIACAP Knowledge Service as a sample) shows a completed system level POA&M.

Figure 29: System level IT security POA&M example

Date initiated:	October 1, 2005	IS type:	Enclave	OMB project ID:	009-222334-55874
Date last updated:	January 10, 2006				
Component name:	OSD	POC name:	James Avery		
System/project name:	DoD network	POC phone:	703-698-7753	Security costs:	$62,500
DoD IT registration no:	86763	POC E-mail:	james.avery@dod.ctr.mil		

Weakness (1)	CAT (2)	IA control and impact code (3)	POC (4)	Resources required (5)	Scheduled completion date (6)	Milestones with completion dates (7)	Milestone changes (8)	Source identifying weakness (9)	Status (10)	Comments (11)
1 An account management process has not been implemented to ensure that only authorized users can gain access to the DD network and that individual accounts designated as inactive, suspended, or terminated are promptly deactivated.	I	IAAC-1 impact high	IAO	$50,000	5/30/2005	Develop an account management process - 1/15/2005; management review of account management process 3/15/2005; implement/test account management process - 4/15/2005	Implementing and testing the account management process delayed till 10/15/2005 due to inadequate funding	8500.2 IA controls test conducted 5/15/2005	Ongoing	Funding will be available in FY 2006
2 Security plan is out of date, more than one year since last update despite new interconnections.	II	DCSD-1 impact high	IAO	$5,000	11/30/2005	Update plan and obtain independent review - 11/30/2005		8500.2 IA controls test conducted 5/15/2005	Ongoing	
3 Lack of accurate system hardware and software baseline hampers implementation of configuration management processes.	II	DCHW-1/DCSW-1 impact high	IAO	$0	8/31/2005	Establish baseline inventory of the hardware and software and utilize revision control system - 6/15/2005. Implement a software revision control program - 8/31/2005.		Security test and evaluation -4/15/2005	Completed 10/30/2005	
4 Encryption is not certified FIPS 140-2 compliant.	III	DCNR-1 Impact medium	IAO	$5,000	10/21/2005	Upgrade encryption software to FIPS 140-2 certified version 10/21/2005		IG audit 3/21/2005	Ongoing	May slip due to delay in funding

Let's look at each column and the information required.

Table 37: POA&M information requirements

Column	Required information
1	Type of weakness: Use this column to describe the identified security weaknesses. DOD has provided a set of approved weakness statements, one for each IA control, on the DIACAP Knowledge Service. This input cannot be changed.
2	CAT or severity code. This is the code assigned by the CA to a security weakness to indicate the risk level associated with the weakness and the urgency with which the weakness must be corrected. They are expressed as CAT I (greatest risk and urgency), CAT II (moderate risk and urgency), and CAT III (least risk and urgency). In most cases, POA&Ms with CAT I weakness must be protected and possibly classified. Additional detail on the severity codes is provided below.
3	IA control and impact code. This is the number of the IA control associated with the identified weakness and the associated impact code assigned by DOD.
4	Point of contact (POC). Identity of the entity that the DOD component will hold responsible for correcting the weakness.
5	Resources required. Estimated funding and/or manpower required to correct the security weakness. Enter NA for a CAT III weakness that the DAA has accepted.
6	Scheduled completion date. Estimated date for resolving the security weakness. This date cannot be altered. If a security weakness is corrected either before or after the scheduled completion date, the organization should enter the actual date of completion and the status in the status column (10). Enter NA for a CAT III weakness that the DAA has accepted.

7	Milestones with completion dates. Identify the individual requirements essential to resolve a security weakness with estimated completion dates for each requirement. This input cannot be altered. Any changes to the milestones should be noted in column 8, milestone changes. Enter NA for a CAT III weakness that the DAA has accepted.
8	Milestone changes. Include changes to the milestones with completion dates, including the new date and the reason for the change. Enter NA for a CAT III weakness that the DAA has accepted.
9	Source identifying the weakness. The source could be the formal validation test, an IG inspection, audit, or any other means. This input cannot be changed.
10	Status. This must be indicated in the following terms: ongoing, completed, or risk accepted (for a CAT II or CAT III weakness accepted by the DAA). Completed applies only when a weakness has been fully resolved, tested, and validated. Include the date of completion or the date risk accepted for a CAT III weakness, together with the statement "risk accepted by the DAA."
11	Comments. Use this column for any additional information needed to clarify the IA control status. For example, if an IA control is inherited, indicate the originating IS. If NA is used for an IA control, provide the justification here. Issues in the resolution of a weakness (e.g. lack of funding, lack of personnel expertise) can be entered here.

Since the POA&M describes security weaknesses in some detail, the information contained on the document can be quite sensitive. Care should be taken to avoid any sensitive or classified descriptions, but the information provided should be sufficient to permit oversight and tracking. Where it is impossible to avoid sensitive or classified content, the POA&M should note the sensitivity and classified accordingly. In some cases, there may be an unclassified POA&M which provides only high-level data and a reference to the location of the more complete classified or sensitive POA&M.

Compile validation results in the DIACAP scorecard

The results of the validation testing and the review of the associated artifacts should be a matter of record and a permanent part of the C&A package. The detailed results are maintained on file along with the artifacts generated during the validation process, e.g. output from the automated test tools or screen shots depicting certain system configuration aspects.

There are four possible results of the validation testing process:

- Compliant (C) – the control meets all of the requirements of the validation test and is fully compliant with the expected results. This means that each of the sub-validation tests has met all of the requirements of the IA control. If any of the tests related to an IA control in a one-to-many test relationship are not consistent with the requirements, then the entire control is not compliant.
- Non-compliant (NC) – the control has been tested and has failed to meet the expected results, either fully or partially. NOTE: There is no category called partially compliant.
- Not tested (NT) – the IA control was not tested at the time of the validation test due to life cycle status or for other operational or security reasons. A status of NT should be periodically reviewed to determine continued relevance.
- Not applicable (NA) – the IA control was determined not to apply to this information system. A status of NA should be periodically reviewed to determine continued relevance.

The results of the validation testing are recorded on the DIACAP scorecard, one additional part of the DIACAP package. The scorecard is an executive-level summary of the validation test results used to convey the IA controls status of an information system.

An analogy can be made between the scorecard and a university transcript. Once a student has completed a course successfully (or unsuccessfully), the results are retained. If a student transfers to another university or wants to understand the compiled value of his/her studies, the transcript provides a medium by which the student's university participation can be verified. The student does not have to provide copies of all tests taken, papers written, or books read to the other university in order for the transcript to be accepted.

The scorecard provides the medium by which IA controls compliance and weakness information can be shared, either with the authorizing official or with other organizations entertaining a possible connection to the information system.

The scorecard is a relatively simple document to prepare and maintain. The figure below shows a standard DIACAP scorecard. We will talk about each of the required entries in more detail.

Figure 30: DIACAP scorecard

DIACAP Scorecard <Insert System Name Here>	System Owner		IS Type
Designated Accrediting Authority (DAA)	Accreditation Status	Period Covered Accreditation Date ATD	Last Update
Certifying Authority (CA)	Certification Date	Mission Assurance Category	Confidentiality Level (CL)

MAC I, Classified   MAC II, Classified   MAC III, Classified
MAC I, Sensitive   MAC II, Sensitive   MAC III, Sensitive
MAC I, Public   MAC II, Public   MAC III, Public

IA Control Subject Area	IA Control Number	IA Control Name	Inherited?	C/NC/NA	Impact Code	Last Update

Table 38: Instructions for completing the DIACAP scorecard

Scorecard reference	Instructions for completion
System name	This is the name of the information system being certified and authorized for operation.
System owner	The organization/entity within the DOD component that owns, manages, or controls the IS.

IS type	This is the same as the entry on the SIP called IA record type. This will be enclave, AIS application, outsourced IT-based process, or platform IT interconnection. If it is an enclave, indicate whether it is a standalone network or a DMZ.
DAA	The name and signature of the designated accrediting authority. Manual or PKI-certified signatures are both acceptable.
Accreditation status	The authorization decision for the IS: ATO, IATO, IATT, DATO.
Period covered	Date of the authorization (unless the entry is unaccredited) and the authorization termination date (ATD).
Last update	This is the date of the most current change on the scorecard and is primarily driven by the IA controls and their updates.
CA	The certifying authority for the IS.
MAC	The determined mission assurance category for the IS.
CL	The confidentiality level applied to the IS.
IA control subject area	The subject area associated with the specific IA control.
IA control number	The reference number associated with the IA control.
IA control name	The specific name of the IA control.
Inherited	YES or NO indication of the inheritance status of the IA control.
C/NC/NA (NT)	Compliance status of the IA control (compliant, non-compliant, not applicable). Note: DOD does not specify the use of not tested, but this is a viable control status.

Impact code	The impact code is a non-changing evaluation of the impact of a weakness developed and maintained by DOD. It can be found on the DIACAP Knowledge Service.

Make certification determination & accreditation decision

At this point in the DIACAP stages or activities, you have probably completed most of the hard work necessary for obtaining the desired authorization to operate. The following DIACAP package elements have been developed:

- System identification profile (SIP)
- DIACAP implementation plan (DIP)
- DIACAP scorecard
- POA&M.

The next action in the DIACAP is for the certifying authority (CA) to review the validation test results, the associated artifacts, the scorecard, and make a certification determination.

Make certification determination

A certification determination is a pre-requisite to making an accreditation decision, so it is a very important part of the process. It represents the CA's validation that the system is compliant with all of its security requirements, or IA controls.

In making the certification determination, the CA considers a number of factors:

- The IA posture of the information system; the overall reliability and viability of the information system, as well as the acceptability of the implementation and performance of the security safeguards applied or inherent to the information system.
- The behavior of the IS within the larger information environment, including whether or not the IS introduces

vulnerabilities into the environment, interacts securely with the information environment and its services, is visible to situational awareness and network defense services.

An important part of the certification determination is based on an assessment of the risk of operating the information system. This assessment is expressed via impact codes and severity categories.

Impact codes are assigned to the IA controls by DOD and maintained by the DIACAP TAG. They represent DOD's enterprise level assessment of the consequences of a failed IA control to the overall information environment, as well as the urgency of remediation. There are three impact code levels: HIGH, MEDIUM, and LOW. The impact codes are available on the DIACAP Knowledge Service.

Severity category assignments are made by the CA and also indicate the severity of the weakness and the urgency of remediation. There are three severity categories: CAT I, CAT II, and CAT III, as shown in the following table. Once defined by the CA for each weakness, the severity categories are included in the POA&M.

Table 39: Severity category assignments

Category	Criteria
CAT I	Assigned to findings that allow primary security protections to be bypassed, allowing immediate access by unauthorized personnel or the unauthorized assumption of privileges within the IS. An ATO will not be granted if CAT I weaknesses are present in an IS.
CAT II	Assigned to findings that have the potential to allow unauthorized IS access or activity within the IS. CAT II findings that can be or have been successfully mitigated will not preclude the issue of an ATO.
CAT III	Assigned to findings that might impact the security posture of an IS, but must not necessarily be mitigated in order for an ATO to be issued.

The certification determination is actually a recommendation to the DAA. The CA can determine that the information system meets the requirements for an ATO; should be issued an IATO until certain weaknesses can be resolved; has a valid requirement for an IATT and its operation will likely not compromise the enterprise; or the IS has sufficient weakness to justify a DATO.

Even if there is a compelling mission or business need for the rapid introduction of an information system into the DOD information environment, a certification determination is still required.

Once all the information has been received and analyzed, the CA's certification recommendation is provided by the program manager or system owner to the DAA together with the DIACAP package. The certification determination is frequently a primary factor in the DAA's decision.

Issue accreditation decision

The ultimate responsibility for making the final accreditation decision, or authorizing the information system to operate, rests with the DAA. No one else can assume this responsibility.

The final decision to authorize operation of an IS must reflect a balance of the mission or business need for the IS and the risk of operation to the environment. The protections offered by the IS for privacy of information, protection of information, and protection of business functions are included in the consideration.

In those cases where the validation testing is abbreviated in the interests of time and mission, the DAA will not issue an accreditation decision beyond an IATO. If the requirement for the information system is anticipated to extend beyond the immediate need, the validation testing should continue with the goal of obtaining an ATO. The DAA's accreditation decision always applies only to a specific information system. There are four possible accreditation decisions that can be made by a DOD DAA:

ATO – Authorization to operate: An ATO indicates that an IS has met all or most of the criteria necessary to operate securely and the risk is acceptable to the DAA. An ATO may be issued for a period up to 3 years before re-accreditation is required.

Conditions:

- An ATD within 3 years of the authorization date must be specified.
- There are no CAT I weaknesses. (A system can operate with a CAT I weakness *only* when it is critical to a military mission and only the DOD component CIO can make this decision.)
- Any CAT II weakness can be corrected or mitigated within 180 days of the accreditation decision.
- An ATO can be granted with CAT III weaknesses; however, the DAA must indicate that the risk has been accepted.

IATO – Interim authorization to operate: An IATO is a conditional, temporary authorization contingent upon the information system meeting stated conditions or constraints.

Conditions:

- The ATD is within 180 days of the authorization date.
- The request is accompanied by a system-level POA&M.
- CAT II weaknesses must either be corrected within 360 days of the original IATO or the DAA will issue a DATO, unless continued operation is specifically authorized by the DOD component CIO.

IATT – Interim authorization to test: The IATT is unique to DOD and represents the DAA's authorization to operate the IS in a specified environment for a limited time frame in order to conduct an operational test of the IS.

Conditions:

- The IATT is issued only for a special case requiring IS testing in a live environment for a specified time period.

- Applicable IA controls have been tested and validated prior to operation of the IS. The IA controls requiring testing will be approved by the DAA together with the PM/SM.
- The IATT is not being used to bypass the requirements of an ATO or IATO.

DATO – Denial of authorization to operate: A DATO is issued when the DAA determines that the risk of operating the IS may be greater than the mission requirement. A DATO can be issued to prevent an IS from starting operation or to remove an existing system from operational status.

The accreditation decision is indicated on the DIACAP scorecard and the DIACAP implementation plan should also be updated to reflect the current authorization status. Once the accreditation decision has been issued, the IS enters into the DIACAP stage or activity where it will maintain the authorization to operate.

Maintain authorization to operate & conduct reviews

Obtaining the authorization to operate is not the end of the story by any means. In fact, in many cases it is only the beginning of the secure operation of the information system. Initial evaluation of the security controls is a necessity, but is not sufficient to demonstrate due diligence – or meet DOD requirements.

Continued authorization to operate is contingent on the sustainment of an acceptable security posture, which can only be accomplished by ensuring continuous compliance with the security controls.

This is accomplished through continuous monitoring and maintenance of the security controls. Continuous monitoring is one means of obtaining and maintaining situational awareness. The information assurance manager (IAM) usually has the primary responsibility for maintaining situational awareness of an operational information system's security status and for taking actions to maintain or restore its security compliance.

Maintain situational awareness

The term situational awareness is used – at least in the context of C&A – almost exclusively in the DOD. Simply defined it is "an awareness of what is happening around you to understand the impact of information, events, and your own actions." The US military started using the term extensively during the Korean and Vietnam wars. Returning pilots stressed the importance of situational awareness as a decisive factor in the success of their engagements. Survival in any situation, but particularly in war, is typically a matter of observing the opponent's actions and anticipating the next move a fraction of a second before the enemy can observe and anticipate one's own.

Based on the nature of information systems, emerging new technologies and changes in the threat environment, security controls are subject to security volatility. Maintaining situational awareness to address security volatility includes:

- Continuous monitoring of the information system and its environment for security relevant events.
- Assessing configuration changes for impacts to the security of the information system.
- Conducting periodic, at least annual, quality assessments of the security control compliance.

Maintain IA posture

DOD has included security controls that assist the IAM in maintaining situational awareness, such as configuration and vulnerability management, performance monitoring, and periodic independent evaluations (e.g. penetration testing).

Other security performance indicators, such as security incidents, the results of external audits and inspections, exercises, and operational evaluations, can also provide information critical to maintaining the system's security posture. As a result of reviewing the security performance indicators, the IAM may recommend changes or improvements to the implementation of the assigned security controls, additional security controls, or improvements to the design of the information system.

One very important thing to remember: always document any actual or proposed changes to the information system. Information systems are usually in a constant state of migration with upgrades to hardware, software, or firmware or changes to the environment in which the information system operates. If you maintain your documentation, it will be much easier to report the results of your continuous monitoring and your IA status to the stakeholders in the information system and to make sure your system security plan (SSP) and the POA&M are current.

Conduct reviews

FISMA section 3544(b)(5), as well as DODI 8510.01 (DIACAP), require "periodic testing and evaluation of the effectiveness of information security policies, procedures and practices, to be performed with a frequency depending on risk, but no less than annually" as a minimum requirement for maintaining the authorization to operate. You can conduct these reviews in a number of ways:

> Remember to continuously document any changes to the information system or its environment.

- Execute compliance testing for all IA controls.
- Execute periodic, at least annual, testing for volatile IA controls and review the others as part of a self-assessment.
- Execute an annual compliance test for a selected number of IA controls and use a table-top self-assessment for the others.

Regardless of the method you choose for the annual reviews, you must have executed compliance testing for each of the assigned IA controls by the end of the 3-year authorization to operate period.

You should assign greater resources for reviewing security controls with higher volatility, such as vulnerability scans or configurations for firewalls and intrusion detection systems (IDS). Any IA controls identified in the system's POA&M should also receive top priority in the continuous monitoring and review process. Bottom line: you should make informed decisions about how best to apply limited resources to your monitoring and review activities to ensure that expenditures are consistent with your mission requirements, federal mandates, and DOD and component-level policies, directives, and regulations.

For example, if your system was recently accredited and all of the security controls underwent a complete certification test within the past year, then the annual review may consist of a simple update or maintenance review – provided the initial tests and the review are sufficiently documented.

The following factors will influence the depth and breadth of the annual review:

- Potential risk and magnitude of possible harm to the system or its information.
- Comprehensiveness of the most recent past review.
- Adequacy and success of the corrective measures for weaknesses identified in the POA&M.

This review process will ensure that security-relevant events and the appropriate responses are promptly identified. We are often asked what exactly is a security-relevant event? Some examples include:

- Expiration of the revalidation period for an assigned security control. Some of the IA control implementation standards mandate a specific revalidation period or the organization may establish its own revalidation requirements.
- Specific events defined by the IA control. Examples of security controls that may include specific events are configuration and vulnerability management, performance monitoring, and penetration testing.

- A breach of security or violation of system integrity that reveals a significant flaw in security design, information system security management, policy, and/or security procedures.
- Significant changes to the information and/or its environment. Examples include, but are not limited to:
  - Installation of a new or upgraded operating system, for example, moving the information system from Windows® XP to Windows® Vista.
  - Installation or migration of a significant back-end application, for example, changing the database from Microsoft® Sequel to Oracle.
  - Modifications to system ports, protocols, and services, for example, allowing access to a previously denied port to meet a new operational requirement.
  - Modifications to cryptographic modules or services, for example, transitioning to the use of common access cards (CAC) or from the CAC to biometric access.
  - Changes in laws, directives, policies, or regulations, for example, a new threat may drive a change in system configuration requirements.
  - System patch alerts, often issued by DOD in the form of information assurance vulnerability alerts (IAVA).

Not less than annually, the IAM or the PM/SM must provide a written statement to the DAA and the certifying authority (CA) that either confirms the continued effectiveness of the assigned security controls or recommends changes to ensure their continued compliance.

The CA and the DAA will review this statement in light of the mission and the organization's information environment and determine a course of action. Any course of action changing the C&A status will be recorded in the system identification profile (SIP) and reported during the annual FISMA reporting period.

Courses of action can include a decision to downgrade or revoke an accreditation decision if the risk conditions warrant it. The following table shows the possible determinations as a result of the annual review or other events, such as an incident, audit, or inspection.

Table 40: Annual review results

Decision	Description
No change	All of the IA controls remain at a risk-based acceptable level of compliance; there is no change in accreditation status; no corrective action is required, and there is no change in the current authorization termination date (ATD).
Corrective action required	There are continued or new weaknesses in the assigned IA controls; however, a risk-based decision allows the accreditation status to continue with no change; the PM/SM is directed to initiate the required corrective measures; and there is no change in the current ATD.
ATO downgraded to IATO	There are continued or new significant weaknesses in the assigned IA controls; the DAA makes a risk-based decision to downgrade the accreditation status to an IATO; the PM/SM is required to prepare or amend a POA&M; the ATD is set to 180 days or less during which corrective actions must be completed or initiated. In order to upgrade the status, the affected IA controls must undergo compliance testing upon completion of the corrective measures.
DATO	There are continued or new critical weaknesses in the assigned IA controls or there is critical risk to mission and/or environment from the operation of the information system; the accreditation status is downgraded to DATO and operation is halted pending corrective action. In order to re-initiate operation of the information system, the affected IA controls must undergo compliance testing upon completion of the corrective measures.

Initiate re-accreditation

In ordinary circumstances, the DIACAP requires that an information system be recertified and re-accredited upon expiration of the ATO at the three-year mark. ***Important note: if you have been doing your annual reviews and testing of your IA controls throughout the 3-year accreditation period, you may use these results to meet part – if not most – of your re-accreditation requirements.***

In addition to the requirement for re-accreditation at the end of the three-year ATO, the DAA may make a risk-based decision to require re-accreditation based on changes to the information system and/or its operating environment. Here are some of the events that could trigger re-accreditation:

- Change in the criticality or sensitivity level of the information processed by the information system, for example, the system was accredited for sensitive information, but now has a requirement to process classified information. This would result in a change to the MAC and/or confidentiality level of the system.
- A breach of security or a successful violation of the system's integrity reveals a significant flaw in system design, security management practices, or security procedures.
- A change in the system's operational environment that could impact system security, for example, the system is deployed into a war zone or other area of operations with a higher threat environment.
- Significant changes to the operating system, security applications, or hardware that would affect the current security controls, for example, a transition of the information system from a Unix to a Windows® operating system

Decommission the information system

When a DOD information system is removed from operation, there are a number of IA-related activities that must be considered. Here are some of the actions you should consider as you retire an information system containing DOD information.

Retiring the information system

When a DOD information system is retired from operation, a number of DIACAP related actions are required. There are several authorized and appropriate ways to retire your DOD information system. Giving it away, throwing it in the trash, or selling it to your neighbor are not suitable ways to remove your system from operation.

You should consider how you will decommission or retire your information system as you put it into operation. Early planning will allow you to adjust for the potential high costs, slow process times, and the uncertainty involved with each of the authorized decommissioning strategies. Below are some of the actions you will need to take at the time of retirement:

- Any inheritance relationships should be reviewed and assessed for impact.
- The SIP should be updated to reflect the system's decommissioned status.
- Concurrently, the DIACAP scorecard and any POA&M should also be removed from all of the component and DOD tracking systems. Other artifacts and supporting documentation should be disposed of according to its sensitivity or classification, unless these are also relevant to other information systems, in which case they will be retained in association with the other IS.
- Data or objects in IA infrastructures that support the global information grid, such as key management, identity management, vulnerability management, and privilege management, should be reviewed for impact.

The difficulties with retiring your information system are seldom associated with the hardware – in this case, it is all about the information. And this is one area that is often misunderstood – or completely overlooked. ***Prior to disposing of or recycling your***

information system, all DOD data must be completely removed from the system storage.

Data does not just die! This was proven in a 2003 study conducted by two MIT graduate students, Simson Garfinkle and Abhi Shelat. They purchased 158 disk drives from various sources, including eBay, computer stores, salvage companies and swap meets.

> **DATA DOES NOT DIE!** In a 2003 study, 74% of 158 recycled hard drives purchased from eBay and other sources still contained sensitive and personal information.

When they analyzed the hard drives, the students found that 117 (74%) of the purchased drives still contained data that could be recovered and read. 17% of the drives (28) still had fully installed and functional operating systems with easily accessible user data.

The students also proved that formatting the drives is not sufficient for the removal of the data: 36% of the drives (57) had been re-formatted, but contained data that still could be recovered. Of the 158 drives, only 9% – or 12 drives – had been properly sanitized before being purchased by the students.

So, what type of information did they find on the drives? Information retrieved from the disk drives included corporate financial records, personal medical records, credit card numbers, bank account numbers, dates of transactions, and account balances.

The classification level of the information will influence the processes required to ensure that all sensitive and/or classified information, programs, or data files on any storage media associated with the system are completely erased or otherwise made unreadable.

Here are some requirements regarding the disposition of the information and the information system:

- Information preservation — ensure that information is retained, as necessary, to conform to the DOD sensitive information protection requirements or if the information is required for other activities or for historical purposes.

- Media sanitization — ensure that hardware and software are disposed of in accordance with current DOD policy and any applicable DOD component policy or guidance. This procedure also applies to contractor-supplied IT equipment and electronic storage media. Before a computer system is sold, transferred, or otherwise disposed of, all sensitive and/or confidential program or data files on storage media must be completely erased or otherwise made unreadable in accordance with DOD 5220.22-M, *National Industry Security Program Operating Manual (NISPOM)*, February 28, 2006. DOD is also using NIST SP 800-88, *Guidelines for Media Sanitization*, September 2006.
- The information system and any data storage peripherals must be relocated to a designated, continuous physically secure storage area in accordance with DOD 5200.1-R, *Information Security Program*, January 14, 1997 until sanitization is completed.
- Once the sanitization is complete, the success of the process must be certified and the record maintained for a period of six years.

DIACAP support tools

As the DOD was considering the requirements for a new and improved method of executing C&A, it focused on the concept of dynamic policy. DOD defined this as policy that took advantage of the tools in the information environment in order to remain current and relevant to the user.

In order to create this dynamic policy together with the release of the DODI 8510.01, *DOD Information Assurance C&A Process (DIACAP)*, DOD also developed and fielded two supporting tools:

- DIACAP Knowledge Service (KS)
- Enterprise Mission Assurance Support System (eMASS).

Figure 31: Interrelated DIACAP elements

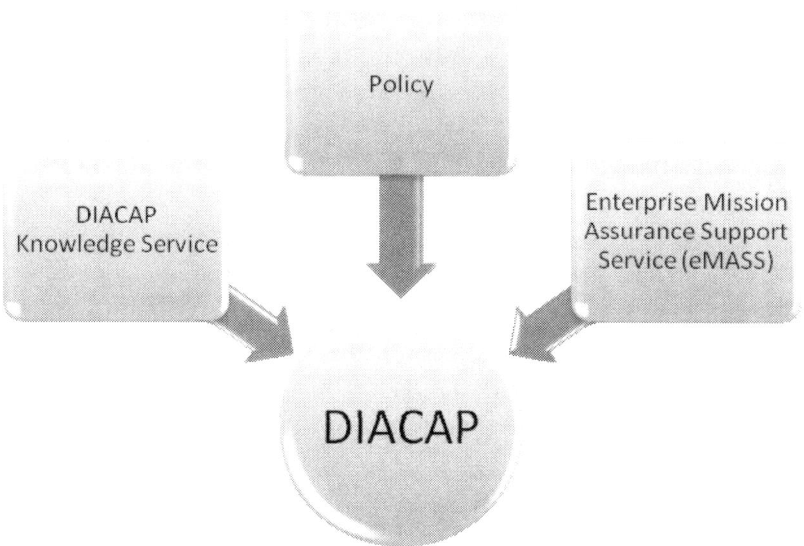

DIACAP Knowledge Service

The DIACAP Knowledge Service is an online repository of information specifically designed to support the execution of the DIACAP. It is available at *https://diacap.iaportal.navy.mil/*.

In order to access the DIACAP Knowledge Service, all users must comply with the following requirements:

- the user must have a valid DOD PKI certificate, such as a common access card (CAC); or
- the user must have a valid ECA PKI certificate[107] AND the user must be sponsored by a DOD employee (this is generally for those users who are not authorized with a DOD CAC).

---

[107] DOD has established the External Certification Authority (ECA) program to support the issuance of DOD-approved certificates to industry partners and other external entities and organizations. The ECA program is designed to provide the mechanism for these entities to securely communicate with the DOD and authenticate to DOD information systems. Additional information about ECA certificates can be obtained from *http://iase.disa.mil/pki/eca/index.html*.

First-time users must go through a series of steps to gain access to the Knowledge Service, including registering an account with the Navy Enterprise Single Sign-On (NESSO) service. Those users holding an ECA certificate must also request and obtain sponsorship from an authorized DOD government employee.

The figure below shows the initial landing page from the DIACAP Knowledge Service and highlights some of the more useful content areas.

Figure 32: DIACAP Knowledge Service

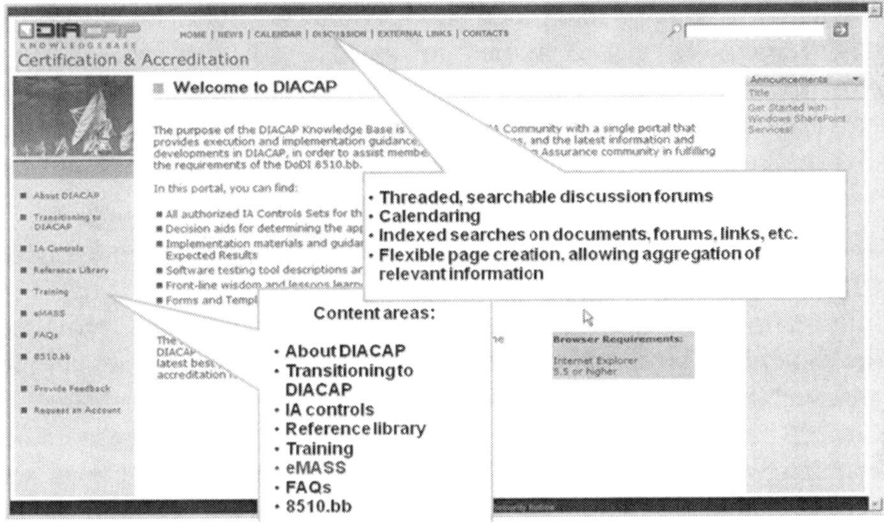

According to the DOD, the DIACAP Knowledge Service is:

- A web-based portal to DIACAP resources.
- A library of tools, diagrams, process maps, documents, and templates, to support the execution of the DIACAP.
- An online repository of the authorized IA control set, including rules for implementation, validation testing, and reporting.
- A collaboration workspace for the DIACAP user community to develop, share, and post lessons learned and best practices.
- A source of IA-related news and links to other information resources.

One important note: The content on the DIACAP Knowledge Service is constantly evolving to keep step with changes in emerging technologies, the DOD threat environment, federal legislative mandates, and DOD policy and regulatory requirements. You should check back regularly to ensure that you are using the most current versions of the IA controls and the supporting guidance.

Enterprise Mission Assurance Support Service (eMASS)

The Enterprise Mission Assurance Support Service (eMASS) is essentially a suite of integrated services that facilitate the workflow management of key activities in the DIACAP process. Using eMASS, a DOD component can automatically initiate the C&A process, manage the requirements for system registration, monitor the implementation and testing of the IA controls, and assign the roles and responsibilities for each of these actions.

The target deployment level for eMASS is the DOD component CIO and the system was designed to be able to exchange information between other web-based services. eMASS provides the capability for information input and exchange through its unique architecture. It is composed of an integrated suite of government-owned, relational-database management systems, based on commercial-off-the-shelf (COTS) components and all functions are accessed through a web interface. The intent of eMASS is to provide a standardized, automated approach for describing and collecting required data for C&A and other core IA functions.

As the required C&A actions are accomplished, they are electronically "moved" along in the workflow and into the "inbox" of the assigned DIACAP team member. Completed actions are digitally signed, allowing for non-repudiation and authentication.

All of the information generated during the C&A process becomes part of the permanent data file for the information system, which enables security to be tracked across the entire system life cycle. eMASS contains a number of standard reports, but also has the ability for the owning organization to develop tailored reports and output.

At the end of the C&A process, eMASS also automatically generates the elements of the C&A package for the information system using the input from the C&A process and then submits the package digitally to the CA and the DAA.

eMASS also correlates the information needed by DOD to meet FISMA reporting requirements and to automatically generate several of the FISMA reports, such as the plan of actions and milestones (POA&M) and self-assessment checklists.

The government-owned component of eMASS software is available free of licensing fees to DOD constituents. Since eMASS does use some COTS, such as the report generation software, there may be some costs for licensing these applications.

However, eMASS currently does not require a large organizational investment in hardware, software licenses, application installation and configuration, or training. Determination of the cost of acquiring and using eMASS will depend on factors such as availability of supporting COTS software/hardware, need for system configuration and database engineering support, and the amount and type of system training required.

The office of DOD Information Systems Agency (DISA) is currently the eMASS sponsor and the final authorizing authority for any eMASS deployment. The DISA office, PEO-IAN, is responsible for reviewing and approving eMASS application deployments and installation. An agreement between DISA and the DOD component installation site is necessary to ensure centralized configuration management needed to maintain the integrity of the system.

C&A and the DOD components

Although the DIACAP was designed to standardize the C&A process and provide consistency and repeatability of results, each of the DOD components has decided to personalize the DIACAP to meet their unique requirements.

In order to discuss each of the DOD component-unique DIACAP implementations, we would need another book. Instead, we will provide the service-specific references here:

- Department of the Army: Army Regulation (AR) 25-2, *Information Assurance*, 24 October 2007.
- Department of the Air Force: Air Force Instruction (AFI) 33-210, *Air Force Certification & Accreditation Program* (AFCAP), 23 December 2008.
- Department of the Navy: Office of the Chief of Naval Operations Instruction (OPNAVINST) 5239.1C, *Navy Information Assurance (IA) Program*, 20 August 2008, and Department of the Navy (DON) *DOD Information Assurance C&A Process (DIACAP) Handbook*, 15 July 2008.

Further reading

Jaquith, Andrew. *Security Metrics: Replacing Fear, Uncertainty and Doubt*, Addison-Wesley Professional Publishing, December 2007.

Taylor, Laura and Shepherd, Matthew. *FISMA Certification and Accreditation Handbook*, Syngress Publishing, 2006.

References

DIACAP Knowledge Service website, available at *https://diacap.iaportal.navy.mil/ks/Site%20Pages/Home/HO.0.0.aspx*.

DOD Directive 8115.01, *Information Technology Portfolio Management*, October 2005.

DOD Directive 8500.01E, *Information Assurance*, current as of April 2007.

DOD Instruction 8500.0, *Information Assurance Implementation*, February 2003.

DOD Instruction 8510.01, *DOD Information Assurance Certification & Accreditation Process* (DIACAP), November 2007.

National Institute of Standards and Technology (NIST) Special Publication 800-88, *Guidelines for Media Sanitization*, September 2006.

CHAPTER 12: AUTHORIZATION IN THE FEDERAL GOVERNMENT

Each federal agency shall develop, document, and implement an agency-wide information security program to provide information security for the information and information systems that support the operations and assets of the agency, including those provided or managed by another agency, contractor, or other source.

Federal Information Security Management Act
(FISMA), 2002

In this chapter:

System security authorization boundaries

Federal security authorization process

So where and how do we start the authorization process in accordance with FISMA? Well, first we need to define the boundary of the information system. We define the boundary through drawing real network boundaries, logical system boundaries, physical boundaries, management, or organizational/ mission based boundaries. These boundaries are also known as authorization or accreditation boundaries.

Draft NIST SP 800-37 Rev.1 states:

Authorization boundaries need to be established before security categorization and the development of security plans. Authorization boundaries that are unnecessarily expansive (i.e. including too many system components) make the authorization process extremely unwieldy and complex. Boundaries that are unnecessarily limited increase the number of security authorizations that must be conducted and thus unnecessarily inflate the total security costs for the organization.

Establishing information system authorization boundaries (also known as accreditation boundaries)

The process of uniquely assigning information resources to an information system defines the security authorization boundary for that system. If you are given the task of setting or defining the security authorization boundary, you should collect a few system artifacts before you start:

- a system description;
- network and dataflow diagrams; and
- the system inventory (all firmware, hardware, and software).

The system description

First you will want to get a system description. At a minimum the system description should include:

- A full system name and current version.

- A system identifier (OMB-300, or agency/component registration number).
- System or security categorization (if completed).
- Data and/or information types (processed, stored, transmitted, reviewed, and managed).
- General description and system purpose.
- System environment. (Where the system will reside both physically and logically. Will it be standalone, dmz, or part of a larger enterprise or organizational system?)
- System contact information (with at least):

  - authorizing official;
  - risk executive function;
  - system owner, data owner, steward (with related contact information);
  - technical POC (sometimes this is referred to as the system subject matter expert);
  - information security POCs (CISO, ISSO, ISSM, and alternates).

- The system development life cycle (SDLC) or system life cycle (SLC) stage that the system is currently in.

Network and dataflow diagrams

Next gather a set of diagrams that describe the agency's networks or systems as a whole – hopefully an enterprise diagram or organizational network diagram. Usually the CIO or CIO's office completes a network diagram of the agency's system assets. Depending on the size, complexity, and locations of the agency's systems this could be one or multiple drawings. It could also include more than network drawings, but system data-flow, and data center physical layout diagrams.

If you are working with an information system with a specific mission function (many times referred to as major application or minor application), it is critical that you obtain or develop a data flow diagram. The data flow diagram provides an architectural view of the systems, how they interact, and the graphical representation of how data flows from component to component of the system. This will provide a graphical representation of the software and systems functions.

These diagrams will allow you to do a few things. First, you will be able to better assess the common controls you will be able to inherit for your system (you may also be given a completed common control SSP). This will help us throughout the process as we decide what controls to implement and monitor. Next, you will be able to more easily establish managerial, physical, and logical boundaries around your system.

The federal C&A process allows for great flexibility in the process of setting security authorization boundaries, so we are not required to physically and logically delineate our systems — although we have found it to be easier to manage the systems and security by doing so.

The system inventory

The next set of information you will need is a system inventory. The system inventory should include a comprehensive list of all firmware, hardware, and software. At a minimum for all firmware, hardware, and software you should include:

- The vendor information (e.g. Microsoft, Cisco, Oracle).
- The specific version or release (e.g. 1.0, 1.1.3.A.02).
- The number of copies (this will help with developing the contingency plans).
- A basic description and/or use.
- Any security relevant information.

It is possible that the system is in the initiation or early stages of development and you have not acquired any firmware, software, or hardware. This is not a problem, but you should still be able to describe the components based on what tasks the components will perform. For example, you may not be able to give the actual technology that will be used to implement a web solution you are developing, such as Microsoft® IIS. However, you should be able to identify that you will be using a web server. You should document this information so that you will be able to more easily identify the technology-specific security requirements later.

Now that we have a base understanding of the system, we can set the authorization boundary. The authorization boundary should be based on the following criteria:

- Be under the same management control. This requires the AO to be responsible for all components of the authorization boundary. For example, a system owner in Treasury should not be making a risk-based decision for the CIO at State Department. However, if a system in Treasury is going to interconnect or share information, the authorizing officials from both agencies should sign an MOU/MOA, or an interconnection security agreement (ISA), based on organizational policy.

- Have the same function or mission objective and essentially the same operating characteristics and information security needs. The same function or mission objective allows you to delineate or group systems based on the information systems' overall processing objective. For example, if you have a mission objective to provide taxpayers with refunds, then you may have several subsystems that allow you to meet that objective. You may have a subsystem that verifies social security numbers and address information with the Social Security Administration (SSA). Or a subsystem that compares the actual returns to information you have collected from banks, creditors, employers, etc. and a subsystem that contacts the Department of Treasury to cut the check or make a direct deposit into the taxpayer's account. You may also decide that each one of the above mentioned subsystems have very specific security needs and do not fall under the same management control in your organization – therefore you will set independent authorization boundaries for each system. The important thing to remember is that you want to keep the authorization boundaries realistic.

- Reside in the same general operating environment (or in the case of a distributed information system, reside in various locations with similar operating environments). This boundary deals specifically with the location where all or most of the important system components reside. For example, you may have a facility in one location that provides many common controls to other information systems that reside on or ride on the facilities' telecommunication backbone. This would be considered a site accreditation based on location. You may also have a large distributed information system that is interconnected to other systems worldwide. In this instance, as long as the facilities (offices, datacenters, etc.) have similar operating environments (perform similar duties with similar security controls in place) then you can consolidate the authorization boundary. This is many times referred to as a type accreditation.

Choose the proper accreditation vehicle

Another initial step in performing any civilian federal C&A is to choose the proper accreditation vehicle. Basically you must ensure your system is not a DOD system or a National Security System (NSS). If the DOD has procured the system (providing funds to develop, procure, or manage the system through the DOD capital planning process) and the system is not a NSS, then read the previous chapter on DIACAP.

With all of the information sharing and intelligence sharing going on, it is very important for you to be able to distinguish whether or not your system is a NSS. By definition, a NSS is any information system (including any telecommunications system) used or operated by an agency or by another organization on behalf of an agency where:

- the function, operation, or use of which: involves intelligence activities; involves cryptologic activities related to national security; involves command and control of military forces; involves equipment that is an integral part of a weapon or weapon system; or is critical to the direct fulfillment of military or intelligence missions (excluding a system that is to be used for routine administrative and business applications, for example payroll, finance, logistics, and personnel management applications); or

- is protected at all times by procedures established by an executive order or an act of Congress to be kept classified in the interest of national defense or foreign policy. [44 USC, Sec. 3542]

Once you are sure you do not have a DOD system or a NSS, let's begin. Federal agencies use the authorization process as defined by NIST SP 800-37 and the risk management framework (RMF), as defined by NIST SP 800-39.

Figure 33: Risk management framework

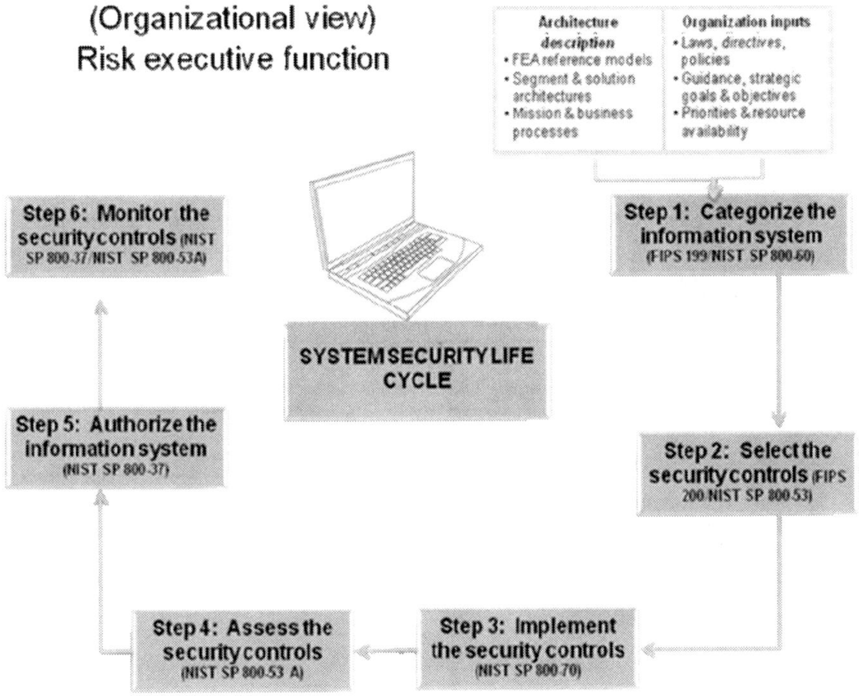

Source: Adapted from the National Institute for Standards and Technology

Security authorization process

C&A, now called the "security authorization process" (SAP), is organized into three steps: preparation, execution, and maintenance. The process is supported by the risk management framework (RFM). The RFM is broken into six steps: categorizing the information system, selecting the security controls, implementing the security controls, assessing the security controls, authorizing the information system, and monitoring the current state. The six primary steps can be further broken down into 13 steps.

The figure below shows the risk management framework (RMF), which supports the life cycle approach to the authorization process.

Figure 34: RMF security/privacy control development

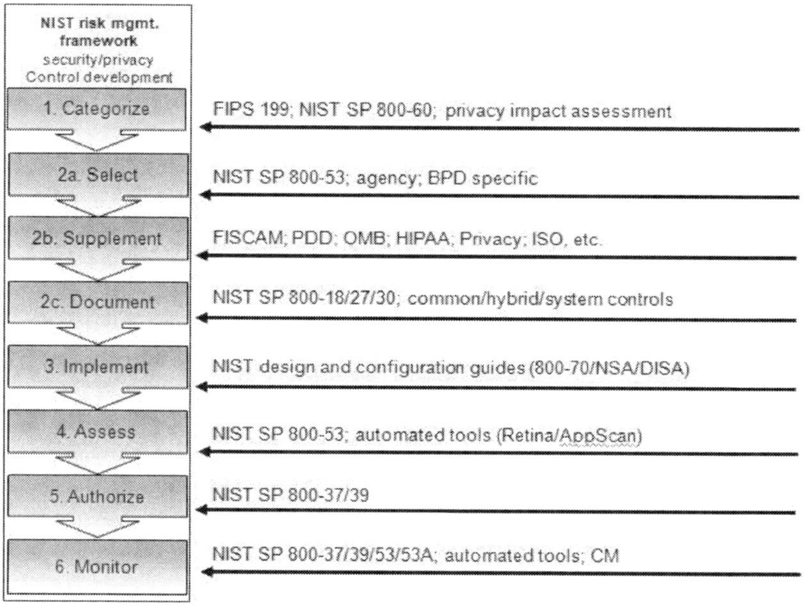

Source: Adapted from the National Institute for Standards and Technology

STEP 1: Categorizing the information system

Once you have established the authorization boundary and ensured you have selected the proper accreditation vehicle, the next step is to categorize the information system. To do this, you will need to know what type of information/data will be stored, processed, transmitted, reviewed, disseminated, and managed by the system.

It is also very important to understand the information system's current or future mission. You will use the information/data types and mission to derive the security categorization using NIST Special Publication 800-60 and FIPS 199 as your guides.

To support the analysis, it is useful to collect the following documents before conducting the security categorization:

- A comprehensive system description that contains information about the system mission on data/information types (see above description of a system description).
- The system's enterprise architecture (EA) and the enterprise architecture security and privacy profile (EA SPP) if it is also available.
- Any documentation relating to the acquisition, development, maintenance, or operation of the system (statement of work, technical description document, data models, data flow diagrams, coding standards, data/information libraries, data schemas, data dictionaries, SOPs, administrator's guide, etc.).

The security categorization is a fairly straightforward process if you have enough information to perform the security categorization analysis. The security categorization analysis is also a very important step that will determine the baseline controls for your information system going forward. To determine the baseline controls, you will use NIST Special Publication 800-60.

NIST Special Publication 800-60 provides the mission-based, management, and support information types used as the foundation for assigning appropriate FIPS 199 impact levels. The FIPS 199 impact levels are based on the security objectives for confidentiality, integrity, and availability. FIPS 199 impact levels will be used to establish the actual security categorization, and correspondingly, the baseline control requirements. NIST Special Publication 800-60 is broken down into two volumes:

- Volume I: *Guide for Mapping Types of Information and Information Systems to Security Categories.*
- Volume II: *Guide for Mapping Types of Information and Information Systems to Security Categories Appendices.*

Volume I outlines the step by step process of categorizing an information system and Volume II provides all of the information types and recommended categorizations. Let's look at the process for properly categorizing an information system.

Before we begin, remember that you will only be performing the categorization on the information/data that is processed, transmitted, stored, disseminated, reviewed, or managed by the system you are analyzing. The rule of thumb is that you will never evaluate any information or data types outside your systems authorization boundary.

- **Step 1**
  - Document the agency's business and mission areas. This will usually be found on the agency's website or in the agency's strategic plan. This will allow us to better understand whether or not our system is mission critical, mission essential, or mission support to the organization.
  - Identify all of the information types that are input, stored, processed, managed, and/or output from each system.
  - Identify mission-based information type categories based on supporting Federal Enterprise Architecture (FEA) lines of business.
  - As applicable, identify management and support information type categories based on supporting FEA lines of business.
  - Specify applicable sub-functions for the identified mission-based and management and support categories [NIST SP 800-60 Volume II, Appendices C and D].
  - As necessary, identify other required information types (these will usually be agency specific). Many times you will find this information in the information system design documentation.

- Document applicable information types for the identified information system along with the basis for the information type selection.

- **Step 2**

  - Select the security impact levels for the identified information types from the recommended provisional impact levels for each identified information type [Volume II, Appendices C and D) or, from FIPS 199 criteria. FIPS 199 is described in detail below:

Federal Information Processing Standard (FIPS) 199 requires organizations to categorize their information systems as low-impact, moderate-impact, or high-impact for the security objectives of confidentiality, integrity, and availability. The potential impact values assigned to the respective security objectives are the highest values (i.e. high water mark) from among the security categories that have been determined for each type of information resident on those information systems.

The generalized format for expressing the security category (SC) of an information system is:

$$SC\ information\ system = \{(confidentiality,\ impact),\ (integrity,\ impact),\ (availability,\ impact)\},$$

where the acceptable values for potential impact are low, moderate, or high.

Since the potential impact values for confidentiality, integrity, and availability may not always be the same for a particular information system, the high water mark concept is used to determine the impact level of the information system for the express purpose of selecting an initial set of security controls from one of the three security control baselines. Thus, a low-impact system is defined as an information system in which all three of the security objectives are low. A moderate-impact system is an information system in which at least one of the security objectives is moderate and no security objective is greater than moderate. And finally, a high-impact system is an information system in which at least one security objective is high.

- **Step 2 (continued)**

  - Determine the security category (SC) for each information type as described using the formula above.
  - Document the provisional impact level of confidentiality, integrity, and availability associated with the system's information type.

- **Step 3**

  - Review the appropriateness of the provisional impact levels based on the organization, environment, mission, use, and data sharing.
  - Adjust the impact levels as necessary based on the following considerations:

    - confidentiality, integrity, and availability factors;
    - situational and operational drivers (timing, lifecycle, etc.);
    - legal or statutory reasons.

  - Document all adjustments to the impact levels and provide the rationale or justification for the adjustments.

- **Step 4**

  - Review identified security categorizations for the aggregate of information types.
  - Determine the system security categorization by identifying the security impact level high water mark for each of the security objectives (confidentiality, integrity, availability):

  SC system X = {(confidentiality, impact), (integrity, impact), (availability, impact)}

  - Adjust the security impact level high water mark for each system security objective, as necessary.
  - Assign the overall information system impact level based on the highest impact level for the system security objectives (confidentiality, integrity, availability).

- Follow the agency's oversight process for reviewing, approving, and documenting all determinations or decisions

Once we have completed the security categorization we can move onto the next steps of registering the information system and selecting the security controls.

Step 2: Registering the information system

Registering the information system is the process of officially identifying and entering the information system in the system inventory. It establishes a relationship between the information system undergoing security authorization and the parent or governing organization that owns, manages, and/or controls the system. It is usually performed by the information system owner.

Registration of the information system requires that you have:

- completed the authorization boundary;
- identified and assigned all key authorization stakeholders (AO, system owner, ISO, and technical POCs);
- completed a comprehensive system description.

Registration, either formal or informal in accordance with organizational policy, uses information in the system identification section of the security plan to inform the parent or governing organization of:

- the existence of the information system;
- the key characteristics of the system; and
- any security implications for the organization due to the ongoing operation of the system.

Information system registration provides organizations with an effective management and tracking tool for security status reporting in accordance with the requirements of FISMA and OMB policy. Registration is also essentially the kickoff of the authorization process. It allows all stakeholders, including the information security engineering team, to start planning on providing information systems security engineering (ISSE) support throughout the information system's development life cycle (SDLC).

Implementation tip: System registration is different in every federal agency (or DOD component). Sometimes it is executed completely outside the security program and performed as part of an information systems acquisition. It can also be tracked through the federal capital planning and investment control process (CPIC).

In most cases, the information system will be assigned a unique identifier during the registration process or it may reuse the OMB-300 number assigned to the system. Often, the registration process requires you to use an organizationally specific workflow tool and requires the system owner to submit the system through the change control board (CCB).

Step 3: Selecting the security controls

After the security categorization process and system registration is completed, the list of appropriate baseline security controls can be specified for each information system. Selection of security controls for an information system is one of the most important tasks in the authorization and security engineering process. The security control selection process, as described in NIST Special Publication 800-53, consists of three activities:

- **Set the baseline:** Use the baseline and supplemental controls as outlined in NIST SP 800-53 and the minimum security requirements defined in FIPS 200. You will use the security categorization (SC) you assigned to your system as the basis for selecting the minimum required controls. The number of baseline controls increases as your SC becomes higher. For a low baseline, you will have fewer controls than you would for a moderate or high baseline. The rigor with which the controls are implemented and tested will also be based on the SC of the system (controls assigned a higher SC will be more comprehensive and tested with more rigor than controls of a lower SC).

- **Tailor the controls as needed:** Tailor the controls with respect to specific mission and business processes, organizational requirements, and environments of operation. Tailoring allows you to decide which baseline controls are applicable to your information system and mission and identify which controls are not. For example, it is probably not a good idea to allow the console on a medical life support system to lock the screen every fifteen minutes – even if this is a requirement in your baseline controls. You may also have instances where the baseline controls are not applicable, simply because your information system does not implement a technology specific control. If your system does not employ Voice over Internet Protocol (VoIP), then you will be able to de-scope the control related to VoIP.

- **Supplement the tailored baseline**: As required, supplement the tailored baseline security controls with additional controls based on an assessment of risk and local conditions including specific and credible threat information, organization-specific security requirements, cost-benefit analyses, and special circumstances. Every system and instance has specific requirements based on risk. For example, you may need to institute specific controls at the Department of Treasury on your systems that perform financial transactions, or you may have to tailor controls to a specific requirement your organization is required to meet. This may sound generic, but every single federal organization has specific mission requirements and, in many cases, specific laws, policies, and standards outside the baseline controls. Some examples would be Health Insurance Portability and Accountability Act (HIPAA) for medical systems and Federal Information System Controls Audit Manual (FISCAM) requirements for financial systems.

The following figure depicts the security control selection process.

Figure 35: Security control selection process

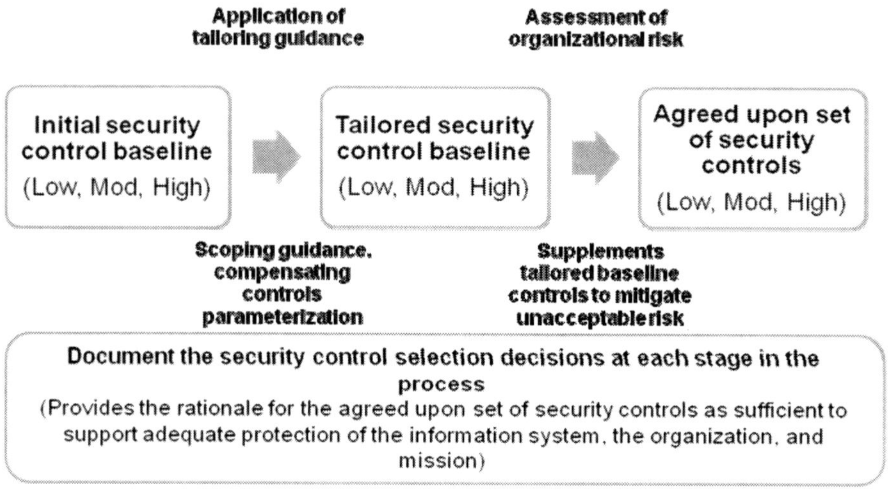

Source: Adapted from the National Institute for Standards and Technology

Security controls are typically characterized as system-specific, common, or hybrid (combination of system-specific and common).

System-specific controls are usually under the direct control of individual information system owners and their associated authorizing officials. They are generally not inherited as common controls, but are the specific technical, operational, and managerial implementations unique to the information system. Frequently, system-specific controls are technical in nature and are implemented at the system level. For example, you may have a common control (e.g. a policy) that requires your system to uniquely identify and authorize each user. In order to meet this requirement, your system uses a pin and biometric device to authenticate the users. The implementation of the common control policy would be the system-specific control.

Organizations may also assign a hybrid status to security controls in situations where one part of the control is deemed to be common, while another part of the control is deemed to be system-specific.

For example, an organization may view the IR-1 (Incident Response policy and procedures) security control as a hybrid control, with the policy portion of the control determined to be common and the procedures portion of the control deemed to be system-specific. In another example, a hybrid control would implement the CP-2 (contingency planning) security control as a master template for a generalized contingency plan for all organizational information systems with individual information system owners tailoring the plan, where appropriate, for system-specific issues.

Many of the security controls needed to protect an information system (e.g. contingency planning controls, incident response controls, security training and awareness controls, personnel security controls, physical and environmental protection controls, and intrusion detection controls) may be excellent candidates for common security control status. By centrally managing the development, implementation, and assessment of the common security controls designated by the organization, security costs can be amortized across multiple information systems. When it comes to common controls the organization is responsible for:

- identifying which security controls are to be considered common controls;
- assigning responsibility for common controls to appropriate organizational entities;
- developing, implementing, and assessing the effectiveness of common controls; and
- ensuring that the appropriate information systems organization-wide can inherit the protection measures provided by the common controls.

The identification of common security controls should be an organization-wide activity and should consider the totality of the organization's mission/business processes and the information systems supporting those processes. For each of the security control baselines defined in Special Publication 800-53 (low, moderate, and high impact), organizations should determine which security controls in each of the baselines are to be designated as common controls. The organization assigns responsibility for the development, implementation, and assessment of the selected common controls to specific organizational entities. The ultimate objective of the organization is to have accountability for every security control supporting the organization-wide protection strategy.

Since common security controls can provide protection for multiple information systems at different FIPS 199 impact levels, it is important for organizations to consider the most appropriate and cost-effective impact level for the common controls to be deployed to best accommodate the information systems using the controls. If the organization chooses to implement common controls at an impact level that falls below the highest impact levels required for individual information systems, then the system owners and authorizing officials for those systems should take appropriate actions to supplement those controls as required for any protection deficits that result at the system level.

If over 70% of your organization's systems are rated moderate or below, it may also be cost effective to develop a separate physical and logical network for your higher categorized assets. For example, if your organization has a primary operations data center and a backup operations data center, it may be more cost effective to build separate rooms with separate logical connections to the rooms for those systems. This will allow your organization to implement more stringent logical, physical, and personnel controls without having to make major investments to protect your less important or lower categorized systems.

It is also important to tailor and supplement the control baseline based on your organization's mission. In many cases, additional security controls or control enhancements will be needed to address specific threats to and vulnerabilities in information systems or to satisfy the requirements of applicable laws, executive orders, directives, policies, standards, or regulations.

Risk assessments at this stage in the security control selection process provide important inputs to determine the sufficiency of the security controls in the tailored baselines – that is, the security controls needed to adequately protect organizational operations and assets, individuals, other organizations, and the nation.

Documenting an organization's protection strategy begins with the enterprise architecture description and the results of the security categorization process for the information and information systems supporting organizational mission/business processes. The security controls allocated to individual information systems and to the supporting infrastructure are documented in the respective security plans as described in NIST Special Publication 800-18.

Security plans provide an overview of the security requirements for the information systems and supporting infrastructure within an organization and describe the security controls in place or planned for meeting those requirements. The plans also describe the rationale for security categorization, tailoring, and supplementation activities, how individual controls are implemented within specific operational environments, and any use restrictions to be enforced on information systems due to high-risk situations.

Security plans provide a description of the risk mitigations that are deemed necessary to reflect the information system trustworthiness which is required to help ensure mission and business success. They are important because the plans document the decisions taken during the security control selection process and the rationale for those decisions. Security plans should be approved by the appropriate authorizing officials within the organization, since they are one of the key documents in security accreditation packages that are instrumental in authorization decisions.

Step 4: Implementing the security controls

Implementing security controls is the point where the information systems security engineering (ISSE) process is aligned with the respective phase of the SDLC. The earlier the information system is in the SDLC, the number of controls you will be able to implement will be limited by the maturity of the system. However, you should be considering the requirements for the later implementation of controls even at this early date.

If you are in the initiation stage of the SLDC, you should be designing many of the controls into your system architecture. You should use your system security plan (SSP) to assign planned controls along with dates based on your proposed operations schedule.

As you get closer to the full operation and authorization of the information system (and or continued maintenance on an existing information system), you will need to implement many more operational and managerial controls, such as patching, personnel training, personal background investigations for users (this may also be a common control). By the time your system is ready for the independent testing all controls will have been "baked into the solution" and you will have adequate documentation to backup the design and implementation.

As you implement the security controls, you should remember a few important things:

- You need to have a clear picture of the system's mission as you design the controls into the information system. You may have selected, tailored, and supplemented controls as needed – but you should not forget the operational deployment scenarios or the end users. Do not lock down a system so well that it does not function, but start implementing and testing the security controls early on in the system life cycle so that the controls are part of the system – not an afterthought that requires you to tradeoff security for functionality.
- Use organizationally approved firmware, hardware, and software that align with the organization's enterprise architecture when possible. This will allow your system to more easily fit, function, and be monitored with the rest of the organization's assets.
- As you are implementing each security control, remember to update your SSP with the most recent information. Keep all system development and vendor related information and documentation as it relates to each security control.
- Cleary define each component in the information system, so you can choose the related lockdown guidance for the specific system components. For example, if you are developing a web-based

application that will have a backend database, you should refer to NIST SP 800-70 and choose the following technology security guides:

- For the application itself, use the Defense Information System Agency (DISA) application – Security Technical Implementation Guidance (STIG).
- For the web server, use the DISA web server STIG (remember, if a technology specific guide does not exist use the generic STIG – in this case, use the web server STIG).
- For the database, use the DISA database STIG (if you were using an Oracle 10.0 database, then you would use the Oracle 10.0 STIG. If you were using a database that did not currently have a technology specific security guide, then use the generic DISA database STIG).
- Use NIST Special Publications when you need to understand a specific technology, such as secure socket layer (SSL), virtual private networks (VPN), intrusion prevention systems, etc.

Once you have completed the implementation of all of the required managerial, operational, and technical controls to the information system, ensure you complete an internal functional quality and security test of the information system and all of the security controls. Document any findings in both your SSP and create a plan of action and milestones (POA&M) for any security controls that are not in place or working as planned.

Step 5: Identify and select the independent security control assessor (assessment team)

The authorizing official (AO) must select a security control assessor that will be independent and impartial in regards to the system development or operation. Often, organizations have a list of approved assessors (internal or external) that are not currently providing system development or operational support to the agencies' systems.

When selecting an assessor you should look for some of the following criteria:

- The assessor(s) or entity that provides the assessor(s) should be independent of the acquisition, development, operation, or management of the system. This ensures the assessor(s) or entity that provides the assessor(s) do not have any organizational conflict of interest.
- The assessor(s) should be trained, qualified, and certified to assess the controls in accordance with the organizational requirements.
- The assessor(s) should undergo at least the same, even preferably more stringent background investigations, as those that are or will be operating the information system.

In small organizations with limited budgets that cannot afford to use a completely independent assessor, the AO should assign separate teams to implement and to carefully review each control together with a government official, such as the ISO. They may also choose to assign one or two individuals to perform independent verification and validation (IV&V) of selected security controls.

Step 6: Develop the security control assessment plan

The security assessor or team should develop a security assessment plan for each engagement. The following items should be considered by assessors in developing plans to assess the security controls in information systems:

- information contacts;
- a system/mission description;
- the purpose of the test (annual assessment, independent authorization test, security impact analysis, etc.);
- scope (authorization boundary);
- objectives;
- the framework being used (800-53A, COBIT, etc.);
- the assessment methods;
- automated tools;

- roles and responsibilities (including testing team); and
- assumptions and constraints.

Some of the actions you should take in developing the security control assessment plan include:

- Determine which security controls/control enhancements are to be included in the assessment based upon the contents of the security plan and the purpose/scope of the assessment. You will need to review the SSP and gain a clear understanding of the system's mission, the various system components, and the authorization boundary.
- Select the appropriate assessment procedures and automated tools to be used during the assessment based on the security controls and control enhancements that are to be included in the assessment.
- Tailor the selected assessment procedures, as needed.
- Develop additional assessment procedures, if necessary, to address security controls and control enhancements that are not contained in NIST Special Publication 800-53, and to address additional assurance needs beyond what is provided in NIST Special Publication 800-53A. Remember that you need to perform complete coverage of all controls for all components.
- Optimize the assessment procedures to reduce duplication of effort and provide cost-effective assessment solutions.
- Finalize the assessment plan and obtain the necessary approvals to execute the plan from the authorization official.

Step 7: Prepare for the test

After the test plan is approved, your next step should be a formal kickoff meeting with the system stakeholders. This is also where you should request any outstanding documentation that you may have not been given at this point. At a minimum you should ask for:

- The completed and updated information system SSP (if it has changed from a version provided earlier)

- The organization's common control SSP, if it exists, to include any testing results to ensure the common controls can be inherited as stated.
- Any documents related to the design, configuration, deployment, security, and or maintenance of the system (these may be appendixes to the SSP).
- Supporting materials such as procedures, reports, logs, and records showing evidence of security control implementation.
- Previous assessment results from tests conducted within the past 365 days that are directly related to the controls stated in the SSP.
- Organizational policies, procedures, guidelines, standards, or written documentation stating organizational security requirements.
- Internet protocol (IP) addresses and any configuration that will be required to perform your automated tests (to include rules of engagement and authorized scanning times).

Step 8: Conduct the security controls assessment test

At this point, you should have a good idea how the actual testing is going to take place based on your test plan, meetings, and any information provided by the system stakeholders. However, here are with some things to remember to do a few days before the actual SCA test:

- Always test your automated tools to ensure they are working correctly and all licenses are up to date. We cannot count the number of times security assessors have shown up to the testing site and they discover the licenses on the assessment software to be tested are either expired or the tool is not adequate or appropriate for the type of system being tested.
- Download the latest patches/updates for your systems and double check to ensure your configurations meet the baseline requirements of the organization to which your systems will connect to perform the automated tests.

- Make sure you have all the authorized tools and media you will need to collect evidence for the test.

What follows is a list of some of the things to remember before you arrive onsite for the SCA test:

- Call your onsite testing POC to make sure everything is a go so that you can make any last minute changes if need be.
- Pre-brief your team and go over any last minute changes to the test plan or schedule.
- Ensure your team has approved identification and clearly understands the sites rules of engagement for testing.
- Ensure you have an updated slide deck for the in-brief and out-brief.

Remember that the controls assessment is used to determine the extent to which the controls are implemented correctly, operating as intended, and producing the desired outcome with respect to meeting the security requirements for the information system. The assessor's job is to help the authorizing official make a truly risk-based authorization decision on the information system being assessed using unbiased, factual reporting.

You are there to help in the authorization process, not hinder the operational mission of the organization. Ensure you provide specific recommendations on how to correct weaknesses or deficiencies in the controls and reduce or eliminate identified vulnerabilities as you proceed through the assessment. Speak with technical POCs and provide suggestions on how they can fix, remediate, and mitigate issues found.

After the test is completed, it is important to provide a high-level report to the stakeholders on any issues, findings, and recommendations from the security control assessment. This should be done in the same or a similar format that you will use for the final assessment report. It is also useful to develop and deliver an executive out-brief in the form of a handout or slideshow. We usually do this prior to sending the final report – there is not as much confusion and it also allows the stakeholders to provide any last minute information that might be needed in the final report.

Some tips for preparing the final assessment report

Here are several useful tips when preparing the final assessment report:

- Remove false positives. You can do this by looking for results and findings that do not match actual evidence. Often, scan results will come back with findings on services or even systems that were not part of the authorization boundary. For example, on many occasions, we have seen scan results that do not properly enumerate systems we know about or list vulnerabilities on printers or devices that were not scanned or are not part of the authorization boundary.
- Perform in-depth analysis on results and prioritize findings based on severity and risk based on organization and mission requirements.
- Research weaknesses found during the assessment and perform analysis to provide possible remediation, mitigation, or acceptance strategies.
- Prepare the final assessment in a format that allows the information system owner the ability to write a clear and concise plan of actions and milestones (POA&M) for each finding.

Step 9: Update the system security plan

Now that the assessment is complete, the security plan should be updated to reflect the actual state of the security controls. Particularly when the plan was developed early in the life cycle, the system owner or whoever completed the SSP may have believed the system met or exceeded certain control requirements. After completion of the test, however, this may no longer be true. As a result, the SSP should contain an accurate list and description of the security controls implemented (including compensating/ supplemental controls) and a list of identified vulnerabilities (i.e. security controls not implemented or not implemented correctly).

Step 10: Develop the POA&M

The POA&M describes the specific measures that are planned to correct any weaknesses or deficiencies in the security controls noted during the security control assessment and to address the remaining known vulnerabilities in the information system.

The actual POA&M document identifies:

- the security control not being met;
- the actual weaknesses or vulnerabilities;
- the tasks needing to be accomplished;
- the resources required to accomplish the elements of the plan (usually quantitative in a dollar amount);
- any milestones in meeting the tasks;
- the scheduled completion dates for the milestones. Thus, the plan of action and milestones is used by the authorizing official to monitor the progress in correcting weaknesses or deficiencies noted during the security control assessment;
- the status of the POA&M:

  - ongoing,
  - completed,
  - non applicable, or
  - not tested; and

- the risk based decision (whether the authorizing official has decided to accept the risk).

It is also possible that the POA&M includes information on the type of POA&M (such as enterprise or system-specific), the level of risk, any ongoing maintenance costs related to the POA&M, who discovered the weakness, and comments related to the POA&M.

Step 11: Security authorization decision

Now that the SSP has been updated to reflect the results of the final security assessment report (SAR) from the SCA test and a current POA&M has been developed, you now have the documents required for a complete authorization package. This package will be sent forward to the AO for an authorization decision.

Figure 36: Security authorization package

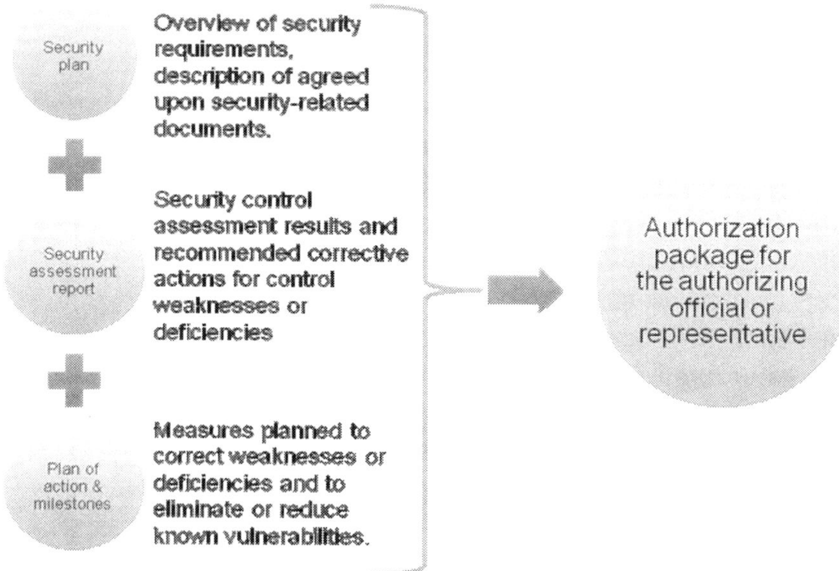

Source: Adapted from the National Institute for Standards and Technology

The AO's risk based authorization decision should be based on the content of the security authorization package as it relates to:

- the system's ability to meet the organizational security and risk objectives;
- the system's operational/mission capability against the system's current residual risk; and
- input provided by system stakeholders, the risk executive or related positions as it relates to the system's risk should it be authorized to operate.

The AO's decision will result in the development of an authorization decision document. The authorization decision document contains the following information:

- authorization decision;
- terms and conditions for the authorization;
- authorization termination date (ATD);
- a formal signature by the AO (digital or non-digital).

The security authorization decision indicates to the information system owner whether the system is:

- authorized to operate (ATO);
- or has been denied authorization to operate (DATO).

The terms and conditions for the authorization provide a description of any specific limitations or restrictions placed on the operation of the information system that must be followed by the system owner.

Step 12: Continuous monitoring and ongoing risk acceptance

Once a system has been authorized for operation, it now needs to be entered into the organization's continuous monitoring program. This allows an organization to maintain the security authorization of an information system over time in a highly dynamic environment of operation with changing threats, vulnerabilities, technologies, and mission/business processes.

Continuous monitoring of security controls should take advantage of automated support tools to facilitate near real-time risk management for information systems. An effective continuous monitoring program includes:

- strict configuration management and control processes;
- security impact analyses on actual or proposed changes to information systems and environments of operation;
- assessment of selected security controls in information systems and controls inherited by those systems (i.e. common controls);
- security status reporting to appropriate organizational officials.

We cannot stress how important the use of strict configuration management and control processes are to the continuous monitoring of your systems. In order for continuous monitoring to work, you need to become situationally aware of your systems and environment. Although automated tools can make this process much easier to manage, nothing replaces a strong and strictly enforced configuration management process. You need to know when and what changes are happening to your environment on an ongoing basis. If you are aware of changes going on in your environment, you can properly perform security impact analysis of these changes.

Your organization should develop a change control board (CCB) if one does not already exist. Both the authorizing official and the security team play an important role in the CCB and should have voting roles. You can also use the CCB to provide the system owner with guidance on updating security authorization packages or when a change is significant enough to require the system to undergo a new authorization process.

Step 13: Decommissioning the information system

This is the last step in the authorization process for information systems in federal agencies. At the end of an information system's life, it is very important to properly decommission the system. Decommissioning an information system allows you to formally remove the system registration from the organization's inventory or registration system.

Some things you should remember when decommissioning your system:

- Ensure to follow organizational media protection requirements. Many times organizations have well established requirements, policies, and system checklists to formally retire a system.
- Do not forget that most systems have records management and data retention requirements – even if the system is going away – the data must usually be retained for an organizationally defined period.
- Ensure the AO formally signs the information system decommissioning paperwork. This will provide the required

information the organizational IG will usually require so that they do not have to report the status of the system.

<table>
<tr><td>Further reading</td></tr>
<tr><td>

National Institute of Standards and Technology (NIST) Special Publication 800-53A, *Guide for Assessing the Security Controls in Federal Information Systems* (Final Public Draft), July 2008.

National Security Systems (NSS) Instruction No. 1253 (ODNI/CIO Draft 4), *Security Control Catalog for National Security Systems*, December 2007.

National Security Systems (NSS) Instruction No. 1253A (ODNI/CIO Draft 2), *Guide for Assessing the Security Controls in National Security Systems*, July 2008.

</td></tr>
</table>

References

Department of Defense (DOD) Directive 8500.1, *Information Assurance*, November 21, 2003.

Director of Central Intelligence Directive 6/3, *Protecting Sensitive Compartmented Information Within Information Systems*, June 1999.

National Institute of Standards and Technology (NIST) Special Publication 800-37, *Guide for the Security Certification and Accreditation of Federal Information Systems*, May 2004.

National Institute of Standards and Technology (NIST) Special Publication 800-53, Revision 2, *Recommended Security Controls for Federal Information Systems*, December 2007.

National Institute of Standards and Technology (NIST) Special Publication 800-53A, *Guide for Assessing the Security Controls in Federal Information Systems* (Final Public Draft), July 2008.

National Institute of Standards and Technology (NIST) Special Publication 800-59, *Guideline for Identifying an Information System as a National Security System*, August 2003.

National Institute of Standards and Technology (NIST) Special Publication 800-60, *Guide for Mapping Types of Information and Information Systems to Security Categories,* June 2004.

National Institute of Standards and Technology (NIST) Special Publication 800-64, Revision 1, *Security Considerations in the Information System Development Life Cycle*, June 2004.

National Institute of Standards and Technology (NIST) Special Publication 800-100, *Information Security Handbook: A Guide for Managers*, October 2006.

National Security Systems (NSS) Instruction No. 1253 (ODNI/CIO Draft 4), *Security Control Catalog for National Security Systems,* December 2007.

National Security Telecommunications and Information Systems Security Instruction No. 1000, *National Information Assurance Certification and Accreditation Process* (NIACAP), April 2000.

Office of Management and Budget, Circular A-130, Appendix III, Transmittal Memorandum #4, *Management of Federal Information Resources*, November 2000.

CHAPTER 13: THE FEDERAL INFORMATION SECURITY MANAGEMENT ACT (FISMA)

That depends on how an agency goes about doing its work. FISMA has put together a framework, but if [an agency] does it just for compliance, then it's purely a paperwork exercise.[108]

Karen Evans, Office of Management and Budget

In this chapter:

The e-Government Act of 2002

FISMA report card

What FISMA is NOT – FISMA misunderstood

FISMA and its achievements

10 questions for FISMA compliance

---

[108] Gauthem Naugesh, "Feds Losing War on Information Security," Government Executive.com, 13 March 2008.

We can truly say that an "A" on the FISMA scorecard does not always mean you are a more secure agency – but it is a start. When we started in C&A in the civilian federal agencies in 2002, it seemed to be an endless labor of developing security documentation for systems that could never meet the requirements. But that did not seem to matter – the systems were accredited anyway.

By "accepting the risk," DAAs or authorizing officials (often agency CIOs) were getting closer to a higher grade in security without doing more than producing more documentation about a system. Coming from the security environment in the Intelligence Community (IC) and DOD, we were very surprised to learn just how most federal agency CIO's looked at security and FISMA (or simply did not). To them, FISMA was only a speed bump and an unnecessary expense to the deployment of their mission systems. To add to the problem, security was often not adequately funded and information security was simply not part of most agencies' cultures.

Working with many federal agency CIOs, we started to understand why information security was considered a pain and not a positive factor in their agencies. The US Federal Government told them to plan and implement security programs, but did not provide funding or training.

Consequently, the agencies had to respond to new requirements (many of which they did not fully understand) with no increase in the funding to do so, but also still had to execute their day-to-day missions. On top of that, information system attacks, although temporarily embarrassing for lower-level officials and sometimes inconvenient to operations, did not get published or reported anywhere else – so with time, they were simply forgotten.

How the world has changed! Many agencies now have mature and funded (some well funded – some less so) information system security programs. Information systems security is becoming a function of the agencies' system life cycle (SLC). Like all things in the government, this took some time.

The e-Government Act of 2002 and FISMA

The E-Government Act was signed in 2002 and we are still changing and maturing security and information assurance to this day. United States Title III of the E-Government Act, known as the Federal Information Security Management Act (FISMA), is where we began to show that we were really serious about information systems security.

The E-Government Act of 2002 (P.L. 107-347) recognized the importance of information security to the economic and national security interests of the United States. Title III of the E-Government Act (FISMA), states that effective information security programs include:

- Periodic assessments of risk, including the likelihood and magnitude of harm that could result from the unauthorized access, use, disclosure, disruption, modification, or destruction of information and information systems that support the operations/assets of the organization.
- Policies and procedures that are based on risk assessments, that cost effectively reduce information security risks to an acceptable level, and address information security throughout the life cycle of information systems.
- Plans for providing adequate information security for networks, facilities, information systems, or groups of information systems, as appropriate.
- Security awareness training to inform personnel (including contractors and other users of information systems that support the operations and assets of the organization) of the information security risks associated with their activities and their responsibilities in complying with organizational policies and procedures designed to reduce these risks.
- Periodic testing and evaluation of the effectiveness of information security policies, procedures, practices, and security controls to be performed with a frequency depending on risk, but no less than annually.

- A process for planning, implementing, evaluating, and documenting remedial actions to address any deficiencies in the information security policies, procedures, and practices of the organization.
- Procedures for detecting, reporting, and responding to security incidents.
- Plans and procedures for continuity of operations for information systems that support the operations and assets of the organization.

FISMA, the Paperwork Reduction Act of 1995, and the Information Technology Management Reform Act of 1996, explicitly emphasize the employment of a risk-based policy for cost-effective security. In support of this legislation, the Office of Management and Budget (OMB) through Circular A-130, Appendix III, *Security of Federal Automated Information Resources*, requires executive agencies within the federal government to:

- plan for security;
- ensure that appropriate officials are assigned security responsibility;
- review the security controls in their information systems; and
- authorize system processing prior to operations and periodically thereafter.

The FISMA report card

OMB has been criticized for creating a paperwork exercise in its implementation of FISMA. One basis for this critique is the use of the FISMA report card to grade federal agencies on certain information systems security elements considered important by OMB.

Many consider that the emphasis on the "good grade" takes away from the real focus on true security and forces agencies to spend their limited IT security budgets on creating this report. The basic criticisms are:

- Security is complex and does not lend itself to an elementary grading scale. The grading committee is often roundly criticized for applying the same standards to all agencies. Their grades are based on a possible 100 points awarded based on a compliance percentage in seven categories. However, the points are the same whether the agency has 100 information systems or 10,000. Also, the grading does not consider whether an agency has an internal policy of addressing mission critical systems first. In other words, a point is a point. And if you lose more than 40 of them, you fail.
- The report card does not really measure security; it measures compliance with the Federal Information Security Management Act itself. FISMA may be an important tool in determining critical elements in an information system security program. But FISMA compliance does not always equate to good security, and poor compliance reporting does not always mean bad security.

The FISMA report requirements

Annually – usually sometime in the summer of the respective reporting year – OMB issues its annual FISMA reporting guidance. This occurs in the form of a memorandum addressed to the heads of executive departments and federal agencies. You should always follow the most recent guidance, as OMB may change the reporting requirements from year to year. For example, 2008 was the first year federal agencies had to report on their privacy practices for the protection of personal information.

The FISMA report card grades on several elements, organized in sections, some of which are directly related to the information system authorization process. In 2008,[109] federal agency CIOs were required to answer the following questions:

---

[109] An example of the 2008 reporting template is included on the CD.

Table 41: FISMA reporting questions

Question	Reporting requirement
1	FISMA systems inventory
2	Certification and accreditation, security control testing, and contingency plan testing
3	Implementation of security controls in NIST SP 800-53
4	Incident detection, monitoring and response capabilities
5	Security awareness training
6	Peer-to-peer file sharing
7	Configuration management
8	Incident reporting
9	New technologies and emerging threats
10	Performance metrics for security policies and procedures

Let's look at each of these reporting requirements from 2008 in more detail.

FISMA systems inventory

To respond to this question, your agency's CIO must report on the number of both federal agency and contractor information systems by component/bureau and FIPS 199 security impact categorization (high, moderate, low). Agency systems include information systems used or operated by the agency; contractor information systems include those used or operated by a contractor to the agency or by another organization on behalf of the agency.

One important note: OMB holds the federal agencies responsible for the security of contractor information systems. As a result, self-reporting by a contractor does not meet the requirements of the law.

Certification and accreditation, security controls testing, and contingency plan testing

For each category of information system listed in the inventory, federal agencies must provide the total number of systems that have a current authorization to operate (ATO), whose security controls have been tested and reviewed within the past reporting year, and which have a contingency plan and have actually tested it.

In addition to the total number of information systems that have met the requirements, the federal agency is required to indicate which percentage of all information systems are represented in that number. For example, if an agency has reported a total number of 100 agency and contractor information systems. Of these, 90 have current certification and accreditation (e.g. authorization to operate). The agency would indicate the total number of 90 systems as meeting the requirement and indicate that this number represents 90% of all the information systems reported. The same would apply for annual testing of security controls and contingency plans.

Implementation of NIST SP 800-53 security controls

In response to this question, the CIO has to provide a YES/NO response. In addition, the federal agency must describe its process for annual security controls testing and continuous monitoring.

NOTE: DOD does not use the NIST SP 800-53 security controls baseline, so the FISMA report for DOD would indicate compliance with the DODI 8500.2 IA control baseline as an alternative.

Incident detection, monitoring, and response

Federal agencies are required to implement a process for incident detection, monitoring and response. This requirement can be met with either an internal capability, or for smaller agencies, by an agreement with another federal incident response team.

In addition to the YES/NO response to the primary question, the agency must also indicate which tools are used to conduct incident detection, monitoring, and response. The number of information systems protected by the incident detection, monitoring, and response capabilities must also be provided.

Security awareness training

Each federal agency is responsible for implementing a security awareness training program that meets the requirements of NIST SP 800-50, *Building an Information Technology Security Awareness and Training Program*, and NIST SP 800-16, *Information Technology Security Training Requirements: A Role- and Performance-Based Model*. The 2008 FISMA report required the agency to provide the total number of employees trained in accordance with the established program – both government and contractor. The total cost for providing this training is also part of the report.

NOTE: DOD has issued DOD 8570.1-M, *Information Assurance Workforce Improvement Program*, which prescribes the DOD standard for information assurance training. As an alternative to reporting compliance in accordance with the NIST special publications, DOD reports the status of compliance with the standards in the DOD 8570.1-M.

Peer-to-peer file sharing

Here, the agency is required to answer YES or NO to the question of whether the use of collaborative technologies and peer-to-peer file sharing are addressed in the annual security awareness training, ethics training, or in some other agency-wide training program.

Configuration management

In addition to the simple YES/NO response to the question of whether the agency has implemented configuration management processes, this question requires the agency to also provide an estimate of the percentage of systems that employ a common configuration baseline.

The federal government has also developed a federal desktop core configuration (FDCC) standard, and agencies are required to indicate the percentage of information systems that are compliant with the FDCC.

Incident reporting

Here the federal agency responds YES or NO to several questions about its use of documented policies and procedures to report incidents internally, to the US CERT, or to law enforcement.

NOTE: The DOD has established its own robust computer network defense service provider (CNDSP) with a mandated set of policies and procedures.

New technologies and emerging threats

There is no way to stem the emergence and use of new technologies and capabilities. Since this is a recognized fact, federal agencies must be able to implement processes and procedures for reviewing these new technologies for their security implications and for ensuring the secure integration of new capabilities into the existing information infrastructure.

This question requires each federal agency to indicate YES or NO regarding whether it has addressed the emergence of new technologies and threats. If they respond YES, they are further required to provide a brief synopsis of the procedures they have established.

Security performance metrics

Finally, in 2008, federal agencies were required to provide three metrics for evaluating the performance of their policies and procedures. The metrics had to be different from those in the

FISMA reporting requirements, but could be derived from NIST SP 800-55, *Performance Measurement Guide for Information Security.*

2008 was also the first year that OMB required agencies to formally report on how they meet the privacy requirements for the protection of personally identifiable information (PII). According to the January 2008 memorandum from OMB announcing this additional reporting requirement, federal agencies were required to report on the following:

- By agency, the number of each type of privacy review conducted during the last fiscal year.
- Information about the advice – formal written policies, procedures, guidance, or interpretations of privacy requirements issued by the agency – provided by the senior agency official for privacy during the last fiscal year.
- The number of written complaints for each type of privacy issue allegation received by the senior agency official for privacy during the last fiscal year to include: (1) process and procedural issues (consent, collection, and appropriate notice); (2) redress issues (non-Privacy Act inquiries seeking resolution of difficulties or concerns about privacy matters); or (3) operational issues (inquiries regarding Privacy Act matters not including Privacy Act requests for access and/or corrections).
- For each type of privacy violation issue received by the senior agency official for privacy during the last fiscal year, the number of complaints the agency referred to another agency with jurisdiction.

FISMA misunderstood – What FISMA is NOT

Every year, OMB announces the annual FISMA grades for federal agencies with a great deal of hoopla and pronouncements of dire security results. In response, the grim state of affairs at the federal agencies is portrayed by the media, which often interprets these grades as the single benchmark for measuring information systems security in federal agencies. But let's take a closer look at this and about how FISMA and its intentions are often misunderstood by both the federal agencies and the reporting media:

First, FISMA really does not provide a means to accurately measure the security posture of all of the federal agencies. In fact, if you just look at the final grades issued by OMB, most of the US's largest and perhaps most critical agencies appear to be doing an awful job of security for their information systems. For example, the DOD, the Department of Veterans Affairs (VA) all received very low grades on the 8th FISMA Report Card on Information Security issued by OMB in May 2008, as indicated in the figure below.

Figure 37: FISMA report card

Federal computer security report card		May 2008			
Government-wide grade 2007: C (2006: C-)					
	2007	2006		2007	2006
DEPARTMENT OF JUSTICE	A+	A-	NATIONAL AERONAUTICS AND SPACE ADMINISTRATION	C	D-
AGENCY FOR INTERNATIONAL DEVELOPMENT	A+	A+	DEPARTMENT OF STATE	C+	F
ENVIRONMENT PROTECTION AGENCY	A+	A-	DEPARTMENT OF EDUCATION	C-	F
NATIONAL SCIENCE FOUNDATION	A+*	A+	DEPARTMENT OF COMMERCE	D+	F
SOCIAL SECURITY ADMINISTRATION	A+*	A	DEPARTMENT OF TRANSPORTATION	D	B
HOUSING AND URBAN DEVELOPMENT	A	A+	DEPARTMENT OF LABOR	D	B-
OFFICE OF PERSONNEL MANAGEMENT	A-	A+	DEPARTMENT OF DEFENSE	D-	F
GENERAL SERVICES ADMINISTRATION	B+	A	DEPARTMENT OF THE INTERIOR	F	F
DEPARTMENT OF ENERGY	B+	C-	DEPARTMENT OF TREASURY	F	F
DEPARTMENT OF HOMELAND SECURITY	B+	D	NUCLEAR REGULATORY COMMISSION	F	F
DEPARTMENT OF HEALTH AND HUMAN SERVICES	B	B	DEPARTMENT OF VETERANS AFFAIRS	F	N/A
SMALL BUSINESS ADMINISTRATION	B	B+	DEPARTMENT OF AGRICULTURE	F	F

* Based on Financial Statement reporting and audit results showing "no significant deficiencies" we have confidence these grades accurately reflect agencies' ability to secure data. All other agencies showed "material weakness" or "significant deficiency," which made it more difficult to use FISMA criteria alone to evaluate an agency's information security posture.

Source: Adapted from the National Institute for Standards and Technology

However, the truth regarding the security of these agencies is quite complex – and perhaps not as dire as originally thought. For example, the DOD plays a major role in the design and development of many of the policies and processes used worldwide by the DOD, the private sector, and even other countries to secure information, networks, and information systems. So, what is the reason the DOD has consistently scored so poorly on eight straight

FISMA audits? Well, it is really because the FISMA reports don't actually measure security – they really measure how well an organization can demonstrate its compliance with the annual FISMA reporting requirements.

Next, the FISMA reporting process does not align well with measuring systems security progress over time. If you look only at the scores over the past eight years, you would think that the US government hasn't made much progress in its pursuit of better information security. Taking eight years to raise the overall grade from an F to a C isn't exactly an indicator of rapid progress! However, as we noted earlier, OMB may change the reporting criteria and/or the scoring methodology every year.

Also, the FISMA grade is a composite of both the agency's self-reporting and the results of an IG audit. The office of the IG assigned to each agency also reviews the agency data and provides an analysis of the FISMA results. However, the skill and personnel resources of the agency IG offices can vary widely.

For example, a large agency may have in excess of 100,000 systems, but may have an IG staff of less than 10. This means that the IG might only be able to test a percentage of the agency's systems. On the other hand, a federal agency with a larger IG staff might be able to actually investigate more than 90% of the agency's systems – perhaps with a more incriminating result. Additionally, the FISMA requirements are not always specific, perhaps leading the IGs to interpret them differently.

Finally, the scores from the IG's FISMA audit might even be impacted by the CISO's working relationship with the agency's IG and the ability to agree on the reporting requirements.

FISMA and its achievements

Despite much of the wailing about FISMA and its burdensome reporting requirements, FISMA has resulted in several tangible information system security benefits. First, it has had a good degree of success in motivating government executives to pay attention to information systems security – if only because it has been linked to their budgets!

There has been an increase in security awareness by both the members of Congress and the members of the individual federal agencies. Prior to FISMA, information systems security was often a neglected requirement – well, certainly not always a top priority.

Lessons learned from the failures in the FISMA reporting progress have led to the recognition that it must and can be made better. Optimal security would really require federal agencies to monitor their information systems, conduct penetration testing and forensic analysis, and mitigate vulnerabilities in a timely manner. FISMA further reinforces the need for federal agencies to develop and implement robust security plans and policies.

In a statement before the House Oversight and Government Reform Committee in February 2008, Tim Bennett, President of the Cybersecurity Industry Alliance made the following recommendations as a result of FISMA lessons learned:

- Provide CIOs and chief information security officers (CISOs) with authority over information systems security. This would include both the power to ensure and to enforce.
- Give the CIOs and CISOs the staff and funding to accomplish the mission of information systems security.
- Hold management accountable for meeting information systems security requirements.
- Develop a comprehensive approach to information systems security, to include assessment, continuous monitoring, and speedy remediation.
- Mandate more effective and accurate inventories of the information systems supporting federal agencies, to include both government and contractor.
- Implement useful performance metrics for information systems security.
- Support efforts to institutionalize a culture of security in federal agencies.

- Increase information systems security funding at the federal level.
- Seek better efficiencies in the federal procurement process.
- Improve the protection of privacy information and require accountability for measures to protect personally identifiable information.

10 critical questions for FISMA compliance

If your agency can respond YES to the following list of 10 most critical questions, you have a reasonable indication of a viable information system security program – and a good likelihood of passing your FISMA grade. So, here they are:

1. Do you have a complete and current inventory of your information systems? Can you produce the required evidence?
2. Have you established an ongoing configuration management process? Do you have the associated documentation?
3. Do you have a consistent, executive level process for assessing, analyzing, and managing risk?
4. Have you developed IT contingency plans and have you tested these at least annually? Can you produce the evidence?
5. Do your information systems have current authorizations to operate? Do you have the associated documentation?
6. Are your security controls reviewed and/or tested at least annually? Do you have evidence of compliance?
7. Have you prepared a POA&M for any security control weaknesses and is your POA&M updated as required, or at least quarterly?
8. Does your agency maintain and document a formal security education training and awareness program?
9. Have you conducted a privacy impact assessment and do you have the associated documentation?
10. Do you have an incident response plan? Do you have an internal agency computer incident response capability or have you coordinated with another agency to provide that support?

The 30,000 foot view of FISMA compliance

Compliance with the requirements of FISMA may appear to be impossible initially, but if you take a look at the FISMA mandates from the 30,000 foot view, it may be somewhat simplified. The figure below provides the birds-eye perspective of FISMA compliance.

Figure 38: A FISMA compliance model

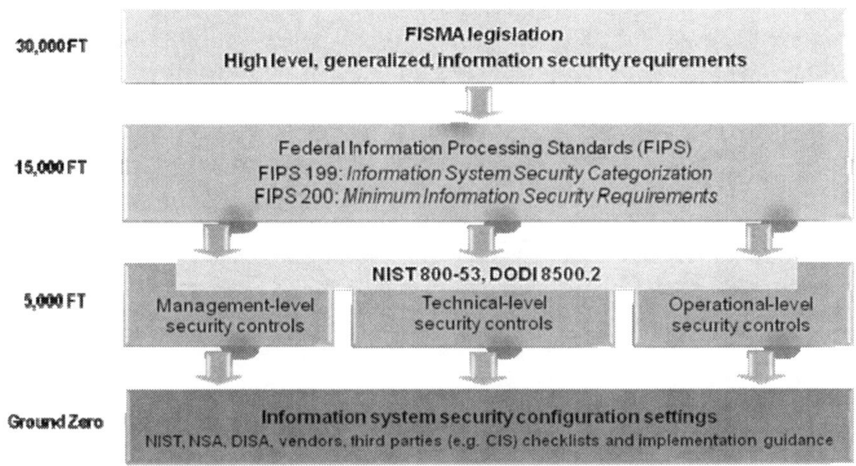

Source: Adapted from the National Institute for Standards and Technology

Automated C&A tools can help!

Despite the simplicity of this model, there is still a lot of underlying complexity. Automated tools can help – a lot! So, here is a list of some of those C&A and FISMA compliance tools, all of which can assist in facilitating the process of automation. *NOTE: This list is not intended to be all inclusive, nor does it represent any form of endorsement for these tools.*

- DIACAP toolset: a free automated tool, information available at *http://www.i-assure.com/products/diacap/diacap_scorecard.htm*.

- Enterprise Mission Assurance Support Service (eMASS): developed under the auspices of the US DOD; information available at *http://www.disa.mil/peo-ian/*.
- SecureInfo Risk Management System (RMS): information available at *http://www.secureinfo.com/solutions/certification-accreditation/rms.aspx*.
- Trusted Agent FISMA (TAF): developed under the auspices of the US Department of Justice; information available at *http://www.trustedintegration.com/ti/TAFISMA.html*.
- Xacta IA Manager: information available at *http://www.telos.com/solutions/information%20assurance/*.

Further reading

Taylor, Laura and Shepherd, Matthew. *FISMA Certification & Accreditation Handbook*, Syngress Publishing, November 2006.

References

Federal Information Security Management Act 2002, Title III, the full text: *http://csrc.nist.gov/drivers/documents/FISMA-final.pdf*.

National Institute of Standards and Technology (NIST) Special Publication 800-37, *Guide for the Security Certification and Accreditation of Federal Information Systems*, May 2004.

Office of Management and Budget Memorandum, FY 2008 *Reporting Instructions for the Federal Information Security Management Act and Agency Privacy Management*, 14 July 2008.

Prepared Testimony of Tim Bennett, President, Cybersecurity Industry Alliance to the House Oversight and Reform Committee, 14 February 2008. Available at: *http://informationpolicy.oversight.house.gov/documents/200802141 32119.pdf*.

CHAPTER 14: AUTHORIZATION AND THE SYSTEM LIFE CYCLE (SLC)

A common mistake that people make when trying to design something completely foolproof is to underestimate the ingenuity of complete fools.[110]

Douglas Adams, author of *The Hitchhiker's Guide to the Galaxy*

In this chapter:

Phases of the system life cycle

The phases and associated documentation

---

[110] http://thinkexist.com/quotation/a_common_mistake_that_people_make_when_trying_to/10630.html

When do you really have to start paying attention to security requirements for your information system? The answer is – from the very earliest stages of planning for the system to its final disposal. By considering security early in the information system life cycle (SLC)[111], you might avoid higher costs later on and even have a more secure information system.

Federal agencies spend millions of dollars each year on the acquisition, design, development, implementation, and maintenance of information systems essential to their mission and day-to-day operations. The need for safe, secure, and reliable information systems is heightened by the increased need for these systems to provide services and develop products, administer daily activities, and perform short- and long-term management functions. There are also additional mandates to ensure privacy and security when developing and operating information systems, to establish uniform privacy practices, and to develop acceptable implementation strategies for these practices.

Sound system life cycle management practices include planning and evaluation in each phase of the information system life cycle. The level of planning and evaluation should be commensurate with system cost, the stability and maturity of the technology under consideration, how well defined the user requirements are, the level of the program's stability, user requirements, and security considerations.

The SLC is applicable to all information technology (IT) environments (e.g. mainframe, client, and server) and applies to contractually and in-house developed applications. The participants in the life cycle process, the necessary reviews and approvals, and the security requirements will vary from project to project.

There are several views of the system life cycle and the relationship to the authorization process. The following figure depicts the NIST view of the system life cycle as described in National Institute of

---

[111] Also called the system development life cycle (SDLC). Since the relationship between systems and authorization extends beyond development, we will use the term system life cycle (SLC).

Standards and Technology (NIST) Special Publication 800-64, *Security Considerations in the Information System Development Life Cycle.*

Figure 39: NIST's view of the system life cycle

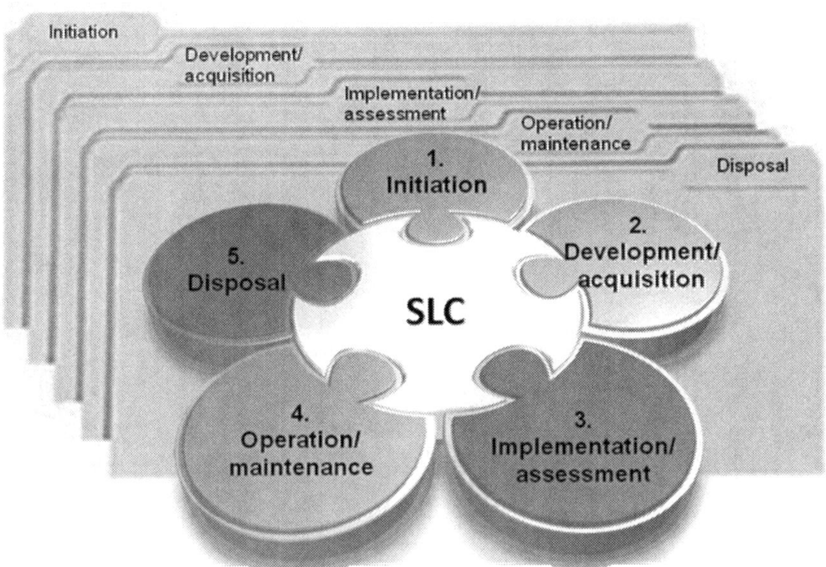

Source: Adapted from the National Institute for Standards and Technology

NIST SP 800-64 describes five stages and the security actions associated with each phase:

- Initiation
- Development/acquisition
- Implementation/assessment
- Operation/maintenance
- Disposal.

NIST's guidance is extremely useful; however, we will expand upon these five stages in the SLC to give you a better idea of how to integrate security and associated authorization requirements. By providing greater detail to NIST's five-stage process we present a logical order of events for conducting system development and integrating authorization that is controlled, measured, documented, and ultimately improved.

Figure 40: The 10-phase SLC and the authorization process

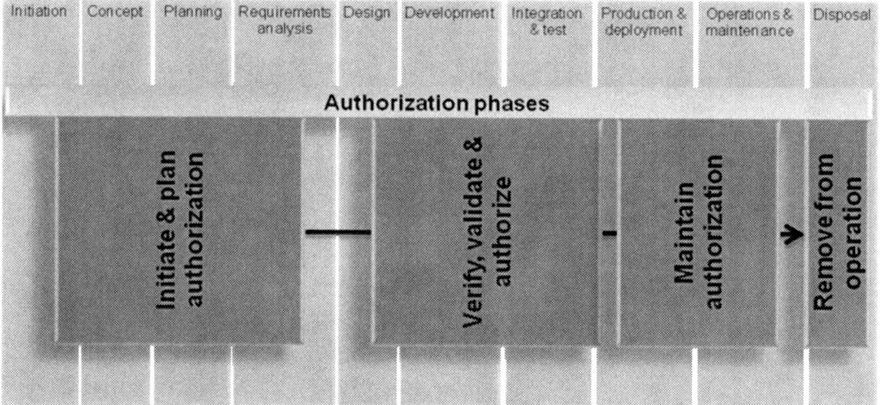

Source: Adapted from the National Institute for Standards and Technology

Phases of the system life cycle (SLC)

The SLC we present involves ten phases, during which defined SLC-related work products are created and/or modified. The last phase occurs when the information system is removed from operation and the tasks performed by the system are either eliminated or transferred to other systems.

The tasks and work products for each phase are described in the following sections. Not every project requires you to execute it sequentially; however, the phases are interdependent. Depending upon the size and complexity of the information systems project, phases may be combined or overlapped.

Here is an introduction to the individual phases and the associated system security/authorization considerations.

Initiation phase

The initiation of an information system starts when an agency identifies a business need or opportunity. As soon as it is initiated, a project/program manager should be appointed to manage the system development. The agency's business need is documented in a concept proposal. After the concept proposal is approved, the system concept development phase begins.

During this initial phase, security is not necessarily paramount. Nevertheless, it is not too early to start looking at some security considerations. These include:

- Probable sensitivity of the information to be processed.
- Threats to the information system and information based on probable deployment environments.
- Possible interdependencies of the information system.
- Legal or regulatory requirements/restrictions.

System concept development phase

Once a business need is approved, possible approaches for the system development are reviewed for feasibility and appropriateness as the system concept is refined. The system's boundary document identifies the scope of the system and requires senior official approval and funding before beginning the planning phase.

As the system concept itself is refined, the security requirements should also acquire additional detail. Here you would start to think about the security features that need to be included in the design.

Planning phase

The concept evolves to planning as it is further developed to describe how the business will operate once the approved system is implemented, and to assess how the system will impact employee and customer privacy. Project resources, activities, schedules, tools, and reviews are defined to ensure the products and/or services provide the required capability on-time and within budget.

At this time, formal security certification and authorization activities can begin with the further identification of system security requirements and the completion of a high level risk assessment.

Requirements analysis phase

Functional user requirements are formally defined and requirements in terms of data, system performance, security, and maintainability are established. All requirements are refined to a level of detail sufficient for the system's design to proceed. All requirements need to be measurable and testable and relate to the business need or opportunity identified in the initiation phase.

Design phase

The physical characteristics of the system are designed during this phase. The operating environment is established, major subsystems and their inputs and outputs are identified, and resources are allocated. Everything requiring user input or approval must be documented and reviewed. The physical characteristics of the system are specified and a detailed design is prepared. Subsystems identified during design are used to create a detailed structure of the system.

The design phase should include the process for integrating the security requirements into the system development. The program manager should involve the information assurance manager in all of the design discussions. The IAM will ensure that the architecture and engineering documents and all design proposals include security considerations. Some of the security and authorization related considerations at this phase include:

- Required technical and operational controls (the management controls can be considered, but these are often solidified later).
- Security specifications (e.g. encryption, access authorization).

- Process for conducting the security control assessments.
- Personnel security requirements.
- Risk analysis and risk management process.
- Security documentation requirements.

Development/acquisition phase

The detailed specifications produced during the design phase are translated through development into hardware, communications, and executable software. Software shall be unit tested, integrated, and retested in a systematic manner. Hardware is assembled and tested.

Only reliable and/or authorized sources should be used for the acquisition of information systems and software. Additionally, at this time specialized security hardware, firmware, and software should be procured and integrated into the development. Be sure to acquire only DOD and/or NIST authorized security-related system components.

During this phase, the identified security safeguards (e.g. security controls) should be integrated into the system development process. NOTE: There may be several security controls that cannot be applied until after deployment.

Integration and test phase

The various components of the system are integrated and systematically tested. The user tests the system to ensure that the functional requirements, as defined in the functional requirements document, are satisfied by the developed or modified system. Prior to installing and operating the system in a production environment, the system must undergo certification and authorization activities.

During the development process, programs will generally conduct a series of tests to verify that the information system is operating as intended. Security related tests can also be built into this process, which will also assist in mitigating the costs of security testing.

Production and deployment phase

The system or system modifications are installed and made operational in a production environment. The phase is initiated after the system has been tested and accepted by the user. This phase continues until the system is operating in production in accordance with the defined user requirements.

At the end of the system's development, a security controls assessment should be conducted and the formal authorization process should be nearing conclusion. Deployment of the system should not begin until it has received an authorization to operate.

Operations and maintenance phase

The system operation is ongoing. The system is monitored for continued performance in accordance with user requirements, and necessary system modifications are incorporated. The operational system is periodically assessed through in-process reviews to determine how the system can be made more efficient and effective. Operations continue as long as the system can be effectively adapted to respond to an organization's needs. When modifications or changes are identified as necessary, the system may re-enter the planning phase.

Security requirements do not end when the system is fielded and operational. In fact, this is where the requirement for continuous monitoring of the security status occurs. Certain security tools, such as vulnerability scanners, can be essential during this phase.

Disposal phase

The disposal activities ensure the orderly removal of the system from operation and preserve the vital information about the system so that some or all of the information may be reactivated in the future if necessary. Particular emphasis is given to proper preservation and protection of the information processed by the system, so that the information can be effectively migrated to another system or archived in accordance with applicable records management regulations and policies, for potential future access.

As discussed in earlier chapters, the requirement to ensure security doesn't stop during the process of removing an information system from operation. In fact, you will want to dispose of the information system properly in order to avoid the possibility that information systems will be released with sensitive government data.

NOTE: Project/program documentation can often be used to assist in preparing the authorization documents.

Life cycle phases and documentation

Some documentation remains unchanged throughout the system's life cycle while other documentation will continue to evolve throughout the life cycle. Recommended documents and their project phase are shown in System Life Cycle and Documentation Table on the CD-ROM. Documents directly related to the authorization process are highlighted.

Why link authorization to the SLC?

There are several requirements that link the system security authorization process to the system life cycle. These include:

- FISMA: Requires a life cycle approach to continuous security management; evidenced in the mandate to conduct annual reviews.
- OMB 130-A, Appendix III: Focuses security across the life cycle and gives NIST the authority to develop and publish guidance.
- FIPS 200: Mandatory security standard that specifies minimum security requirements for information systems and requires a risk-based process for selection of security controls to meet the minimum system security requirements.
- NIST 800-53 Security Control SA-3: A security control directly related to the requirement to link security and the system life cycle. It states: "The organization manages the information

system using a system development life cycle methodology that includes security considerations."

- DODI 8510.01, DIACAP: States that the program manager/ system owner is required to "Plan and budget for IA controls implementation, validation, and sustainment throughout the system life cycle, including timely and effective configuration and vulnerability management."

Further reading

International Council on Systems Engineering (INCOSE). *Systems Engineering Handbook – A Guide for System Life Cycle Processes and Activities, Version 3* (INCOSE-TP-2003-002-03), Seattle, WA: INCOSE, June 2006.

Lippner, S. et al. *The Trustworthy Computing Security Development Lifecycle*, Microsoft, March 2005, available at *http://msdn.microsoft.com/en-us/library/ms995349.aspx#sdl2_topic1_2*.

References

Department of Homeland Security: Cyber Security Division. *Build Security In* website, available at *https://buildsecurityin.us-cert.gov/daisy/bsi/home.html*.

ISO/IEC 15288: 2002(E), *Systems Engineering – system life cycle processes*. Geneva, Switzerland: International Organization for Standardization, 1 November 2002.

National Institute of Standards and Technology (NIST) Special Publication (SP) 800-64, *Security Considerations in the Information System Development Life Cycle*, October 2008.

US Department of Defense Instruction 5000.2, *Operation of the Defense Acquisition System*, 8 December 2008.

CHAPTER 15: INFORMATION SYSTEMS SECURITY TRAINING AND CERTIFICATION

We need both education and training to reach maximum potential in the shortest amount of time.[112]

Dave Ladd, Blog on The Security Development
Life Cycle (2007)

In this chapter:

Leverage your most important asset

The drivers

Security education, training, and awareness (SETA) – and certification

---

[112] *http://blogs.msdn.com/sdl/archive/2007/05/02/security-education-v-security-training.aspx*

Leverage your most important asset

Organizations frequently focus on mitigating risk by investing in and implementing new technologies. But they often fail to leverage their most critical asset – people. Your personnel are both your greatest security resource and your greatest potential source of security vulnerability.

They have access to your agency's most vital information. They may either have the knowledge to circumvent the systems that have been put in place to protect the organization's information, or a lack of knowledge about what is needed to protect this information.

People can be the last line of defense in a network. But if they don't have the tools or the knowledge to protect the information and the information systems, they are about as effective as a firewall still in its original packaging.

Information system-related incidents attract an ever increasing share of the headlines. One can read about the loss of unencrypted personal information on stolen laptops, stolen credit card numbers, business disruptions due to computer outages, and failing information technology infrastructures.

The drivers

Proper training and education can turn employees from risks themselves into key players in mitigating system risks. According to a report issued by Gartner, implementing an effective security awareness, education and training program can eliminate time spent reacting to security incidents and lead to productivity savings of 25 percent.[113]

But, in addition to the good commonsense reason to train and educate your staff, there are also legal and policy-based mandates.

---

[113] Gartner: *Information Security Awareness Training Is Essential to Protect IT Assets.* Witty, Roberta J. et al. 11 January 2005.

Policy foundation

OMB Circular A-130, Appendix III, looks at training and education as a required element in a system security plan. The Circular states:

Ensure that all individuals are appropriately trained in how to fulfill their security responsibilities before allowing them access to the system. Such training shall ensure that employees are versed in the rules of the system . . . and apprise them about available technical assistance and technical security products and techniques. Behavior consistent with the rules of the system and periodic refresher training shall be required for continued access to the system.

The Federal Information Security Management Act (FISMA) tasks the head of each federal agency with ensuring that there are "trained personnel sufficient to assist the agency in complying with (these requirements) and related policies, procedures, standards, and guidelines." FISMA also requires that the head of each agency "delegate to the agency Chief Information Officer (CIO) (or a comparable official), the authority to ensure compliance with the requirements imposed on the agency, including…training and oversee personnel with significant responsibilities for information security…(.)" FISMA also requires that an "agency wide information security program" must include "security awareness training to inform personnel, including contractors and other users of information systems that support the operations and assets of the agency, of:

- information security risks associated with their activities; and
- their responsibilities in complying with agency policies and procedures designed to reduce these risks(.)"

Security education, training, and awareness (SETA) – and certification

Security education, training, and awareness (SETA) are tools to modify any employee behaviors that might endanger the security of the agency's information and information systems. This is the cornerstone of an effective information systems security program.

So, why does an effective security education program require all of these elements? An effective program cannot consist only of an annual refresher briefing or as training that only takes place in a classroom.

Each of these elements has a specific role to play in the security learning process. The table below illustrates the unique characteristics of education, training, and awareness as proposed by Dorothea de Zafra, Director of Curriculum Development, National Institutes of Health, in her "Comparative Instructional Levels." By looking at this table, you can easily see that any effective security program must integrate all three approaches to security learning.

Table 42: Approaches to security learning

	Education	Training	Awareness
Attribute	Why?	How?	What?
Level	Insight	Knowledge	Information
Goal	Understanding	Skill	Acknowledgement
Method	Theoretical instruction	Practical instruction	Multiple media (posters, briefings, etc.)
Time-frame	Long-term	Mid-term	Short-term

Security education and training go a long way towards providing a foundation for security learning, but it may not provide everything required to be effective – particularly for those individuals in positions that can have a more direct security impact. These include members of the security staff, as well as the system administrators who are responsible for the security configuration of the agency's information systems.

Specific, targeted certification is one means of ensuring that users and security staff alike have a level of security knowledge sufficient for the performance of their functions. FISMA stipulates that any individual who performs an IA function be certified in order to retain his or her job. So, security certifications are about the hottest thing out right now.

In addition, government agencies are required to report annually to the Office of Management and Budget (OMB) and Congress about their compliance with the law, and they could lose funding if they don't meet compliance thresholds. The US Department of Defense has implemented the most comprehensive program for defining security training and certification requirements for military, government employees, and contractors working in security and security-related positions.

DOD Directive 8570.1, *Information Assurance Training, Certification and Workforce Management*, was issued in August 2004. In December 2005, the accompanying implementation guidance, DOD 8570.01-M, was published. This manual details the requirements for training, certification, and implementation of the directive. DOD Directive 8570.1 requires all DOD components to identify personnel with direct or indirect responsibility for any aspect of information assurance (IA). DOD agencies must ensure that each worker obtains the appropriate certifications required for that position as established by DOD policy.

Why certification?

The real value of certifications is that they can provide an external validation of a baseline standard of knowledge. Like a degree in a specific subject, a security certification can set a level for exchange based on a common set of experiences with others in the security field.

DOD has specified certain certifications that meet the standards of ISO/IEC 17024, *General Requirements for Bodies Operating Certification of Persons*. ISO/IEC 17024 is the internationally recognized standard which identifies the requirements that certification bodies must meet for the development and maintenance of certification schemes for individuals.

Certifications can be vendor-neutral or vendor-specific. Examples of vendor-neutral certifications accepted by both DOD and federal agencies include:

- CISA (Certified Information Systems Auditor)
- CFE (Certified Fraud Examiner)
- CPP (Certified Protection Professional)
- CISSP (Certified Information Systems Security Professional)
- SANS GIAC (Global Information Assurance Cert).

Of these, the CISSP is probably the most well-known.[114]

Some of the more well-known vendor-specific certifications are:

- Cisco Security Specialist
- Checkpoint Certified Security Program
- RSA Certified Professional Program
- Symantec Certified Security Professional
- IBM SecureWay Specialist.

Managers and technical staff

DOD identifies a specific set of training requirements for security managers and for technical staff. The following figure shows authorized certifications for staff involved in either managing security or in the technical implementation and maintenance of safeguards.

---

[114] More information is available at *http://www.isc2.org/*.

Figure 41: IA workforce certifications

Table AP3.1 IA Workforce Certifications		
Technical I	**Technical II**	**Technical III**
A+	GSEC	CISSP
Network+	Security+	SCNA
TICSA	SCNP	GISA
SSCP	SSCP	GSE
Management I	**Management II**	**Management III**
GSLC	CISSP	CISSP
Security+	GSLC	GSLC
GISO	CISM	CISM
TISCP		

Source: DOD 8570.01-M

Understanding the requirements and whether you are technical or management and at what level can be confusing, so here are some guidelines:

There are two basic questions to help identify IA technical positions:

- (1) Does the position require privileged access to a DOD information system environment?
- (2) Does the position include any of the functional requirements listed in Chapter 3 of the DOD 8570 Manual for that level of the information system architecture?

If the answer to both 1 and 2 is yes the position is an IA technical position. If the answer is no to both then it is not an IA technical position. If the answer is no to either 1 or 2 it is not an IA technical position. If the answer is yes to 1 and no to 2 it is not an IA technical position, but if the answer is no to 1 and yes to 2 it may be an IA manager or other IA position.

Two basic questions can also help identify IA management positions:

- (1) Does the position have responsibility for managing information system security for a DOD information system environment?
- (2) Does the position include any of the functions listed in Chapter 4 of the DOD 8570 Manual for that level of the information system architecture?

If the answer to both 1 and 2 is yes then the position is an IAM position. If the answer is no to both 1 and 2, it is not an IAM position. If the answer is yes to 1 and no to 2 it is not an IAM position. But, if the answer is no to 1 and yes to 2 it may be an IA position but not an IAM position as currently defined in the Manual.

<table>
<tr><td>Further reading</td></tr>
<tr><td>

Blokdijk, Gerard. *CISSP: 100 Success Secrets*, Emereo Pty Ltd Publishing, December 2007.

Howard, Patrick D. *Building and Implementing a Security Certification and Accreditation Program*, Auerbach Publications, December 2005.

Roper, Carl; Grau, Joseph; and Fischer, Lynn F. *Security Awareness, Education, and Training: SEAT from Theory to Practice*, Butterworth-Heinemann Publishing, September 2005.

</td></tr>
</table>

References

Department of Defense Directive 8570.1, *Information Assurance Training, Certification, and Workforce Management*, 15 August 2004.

International Standards Organization/International Electronics Commission (ISO/IEC) 17024, *General Requirements for Bodies Operating Certification of Persons*, April 2003.

National Institute of Standards and Technology (NIST) Special Publication (SP) 800-16, *Information Technology Security Training Requirements — A Role- and Performance-Based Model*, April 1998.

National Institute of Standards and Technology (NIST) Special Publication (SP) 800-50, *Building an Information Technology Security Awareness and Training Program, October 2003.*

National Institute of Standards and Technology (NIST) Security Awareness & Training website available at *http://csrc.nist.gov/groups/SMA/ate/index.html*.

CHAPTER 16: THE FUTURE – REVITALIZING AND TRANSFORMING C&A

We need to establish a community environment, across security domains, equipped with standard enterprise services and universal data access.[115]

Dale Meyerrose, former Chief Information Officer, Director of National Intelligence Office

Certainly the most change will result from the actions we take to reduce redundant activity, unnecessary documentation and shorten the overall process.[116]

John Grimes, Chief Information Officer, Department of Defense

In this chapter:

Why transform?

Goals of the transformation

The transformation process

Proposed approach to C&A

Status of the transformation

Transition

What is the value-added by the transformation?

---

[115] *http://www.prnewswire.com/cgi-bin/stories.pl?ACCT=104&STORY=/www/story/03-27-2007/0004554328&EDATE*

[116] *http://www.prnewswire.com/cgi-bin/stories.pl?ACCT=104&STORY=/www/story/03-27-2007/0004554328&EDATE*

There is a revolutionary top-to-bottom transformation of certification and accreditation (C&A)[117] in progress that is really about changing the way the entire national community manages security risk. One of the primary goals of the C&A transformation has been to break down unnecessary barriers between its members and to improve information sharing and reciprocity among the information systems security, information technology provider, and information technology user communities. The partnership encompasses the Department of Defense (DOD), the Director of National Intelligence (DNI), the Committee on National Security Systems (CNSS), the National Institute of Science and Technology (NIST), the Office of Management and Budget (OMB), and industry.

Why transform?

C&A first originated at a time when there were only a few, large standalone mainframes with custom code and security risks which were simpler to quantify. But now, in this environment of globally interconnected information systems, the legacy, system-centric practice of C&A obstructs information sharing and can impede the timely delivery of mission-critical information.

According to Sharon Ehlers, Planning Division of the CIO, Director of National Intelligence, the national community needed to find "an innovative and efficient way to perform Certification and Accreditation (C&A) activities across the National Security Community."

Goals of the transformation

In January 2007, the DOD and DNI CIOs published seven specific goals of the transformation. Many of these highlight the DOD-IC partnership. But, federal agencies, such as the National Institute of

---

[117] We use the term "C&A" here, since the official name of this effort is the "C&A transformation."

Standards and Technology, have been primary contributors to the outcomes of the transformation.

The seven goals are listed here, together with information on how each goal is being achieved:

- Define a common set of trust (impact) levels and adopt and apply them across the Intelligence Community (IC) and DOD. Organizations will no longer use different levels with different names based on different criteria.

  Execution: The process for assigning trust and impact levels is being defined in the pending CNSS Instruction (CNSSI) 1199. This document is being written with an understanding of the authorities, complexities, classification needs, and special risks inherent in the national security community.

- Adopt reciprocity as the norm, enabling organizations to accept approvals by others without retesting or reviewing.

  Execution: Commonly recognized types of national security information and systems are being described in the new CNSSI 1260. These will be supported by generic reciprocity profiles and tailored sets of security controls for information sharing among specific types of national security information or systems. This will assist the national security community in reaching agreement on security objectives. The use of common security control, compliance criteria, and assessment methods will provide transparency of security implementation across the national information systems.

- Define, document, and adopt common security controls, using NIST Special Publication (SP) 800-53 as a baseline.

  Execution: The pending CNSSI 1253 is a comprehensive information system security controls catalog that used NIST Special Publication 800-53 as its basis. The document normalizes and consolidates security controls extracted from DODI 8500.2, DCID 6/3, the Unified Cross Domain Management Office (UCDMO), and CNSS policies. New controls have been developed to reflect emerging security considerations, such as outsourcing, supply chain risk, and service-oriented architecture. The CNSSI 1253A, which is based on NIST SP 800-53A, is a companion document that defines common assessment objectives (i.e. expected results) and methods for the common controls.

- Adopt a common lexicon, using CNSS Instruction 4009 as a baseline, thereby providing DOD and IC with a common language and common understanding.

Execution: The pending revision of the current CNSSI 4009 will serve as a shared dictionary of security-related terminology across the national security community.

- Institute a senior risk executive function, which bases decisions on an "enterprise" view of risk considering all factors, including mission, IT, budget, and security.

Execution: The complex, many-to-many relationships among the missions, business functions, and supporting information systems of the national security community require a holistic, enterprise-wide view to managing risks. DOD is meeting this goal through DIACAP governance structure established in DODI 8510.01. Other federal agencies are establishing governance structures to define system security authorization (C&A) roles and responsibilities and collaboration mechanisms at every organizational level, from heads of agencies and their chief information officers down to the individual system program managers, security staff, developers, and operators. A comprehensive governance structure with an executive level risk function is necessary to understand the relationship between aggregated information security risks and organizational or enterprise mission and business risks. Individuals with responsibilities for system security implementation and operations will obtain the support they need to better understand how the information security issues associated with their specific information systems can affect organizational or enterprise security concerns. Over time, the national security community will continue to improve this structure and strengthen its interfaces across federal agencies.

- Incorporate information assurance (IA) into enterprise architectures and deliver IA as common enterprise services across the IC and DOD.

  Execution: The national security community is addressing this goal by means of an integrated architecture concept and a suite of system security capabilities and services being made accessible to the national security community and supporting industry.

- Enable a common process that incorporates security within the "life cycle" processes and eliminates security-specific processes. The common process will be adaptable to various development environments.

  Execution: As part of the next generation, NIST Special Publication 800-37, the DOD, NIST and the DNI are collaborating to establish C&A processes that will span the national security enterprise, to include systems and services that can span departments and agencies, coalitions, industry, and international strategic partners.[118]

The transformation process

The C&A transformation was officially kicked off during a meeting jointly hosted by Dale Meyerrose, the CIO, Director of National Intelligence; John Grimes, the CIO of the Department of Defense; and Dr Ron Ross, National Institute of Standards and Technology.

The fact that these three agencies were standing together to establish a new C&A process made it immediately clear to over 600 attendees that this effort was something new and clearly intended to bring massive change to existing C&A processes. Anyone who had

---

[118] As we are writing this book, NIST has issued NIST SP 800-37 Rev 1 for public comment. It is anticipated that it will be issued by March 2009.

ever been involved in developing national level policy also recognized that this transformation process would proceed in a very non-traditional way.

The participants in the C&A transformation process used highly collaborative technologies, such as Internet collaboration forums for sharing information. Input from government, industry and academia was assembled by volunteer "Tiger Teams" and evaluated by a multi-group and multi-national "War Room" panel. Over 1000 individuals participated in the process.

The processes targeted a unified federal approach to C&A by integrating organizations and capabilities across the national security community:

- Committee on National Security Systems (CNSS). CNSS is the organization tasked to update and publish a series of publications reflecting the C&A transformation results.
- National Institute of Standards and Technology (NIST). NIST Special Publications 800-37, 800-53, and 800-53A provided the baseline. NIST – as represented by Dr Ron Ross – provided both advice and "sanity checks" to ensure the efforts remained aligned and coordinated.
- Office of Management and Budget (OMB) Information Systems, Security Line of Business (ISS LOB). The transformation effort was linked to OMB to ensure that best practices were shared across federal agencies and that the efforts were in sync with the FISMA oversight requirements.
- Program Manager Information Sharing Environment (PM-ISE). PM-ISE helped to define C&A requirements that would facilitate information sharing.
- Unified Cross Domain Management Office (UCDMO). UCDMO provided input to the security controls focused on the challenges of sharing information across multiple domains.

In addition to these participants in the process and their insights, the C&A transformation process also sought input from the financial sector to obtain a better understanding of the rapid integration of technology and risk management processes.

Approach to developing the revised C&A policy

The transformation team determined that the best results would be obtained by leveraging existing C&A policies and directives. A multifaceted approach was taken:

- Leverage existing NIST Special Publications as written, e.g. NIST SP 800-37, NIST SP 800-53, and NIST SP 800-53A in order to:

  - bring the Intelligence Community closer to FISMA requirements;
  - facilitate compliance with Inspector General (IG) audits, which are based on NIST standards;
  - align with rest of federal government to support reciprocity.

- Where necessary, CNSS instructions and supplements to Federal Information Processing Standards (FIPS) and NIST Special Publications are being developed

  - Reflect and normalize "differences" between national security systems in terms of their processes for:

    - system categorization;
    - security controls catalog;
    - risk management/assessment.

Figure 42: C&A transformation policy structure

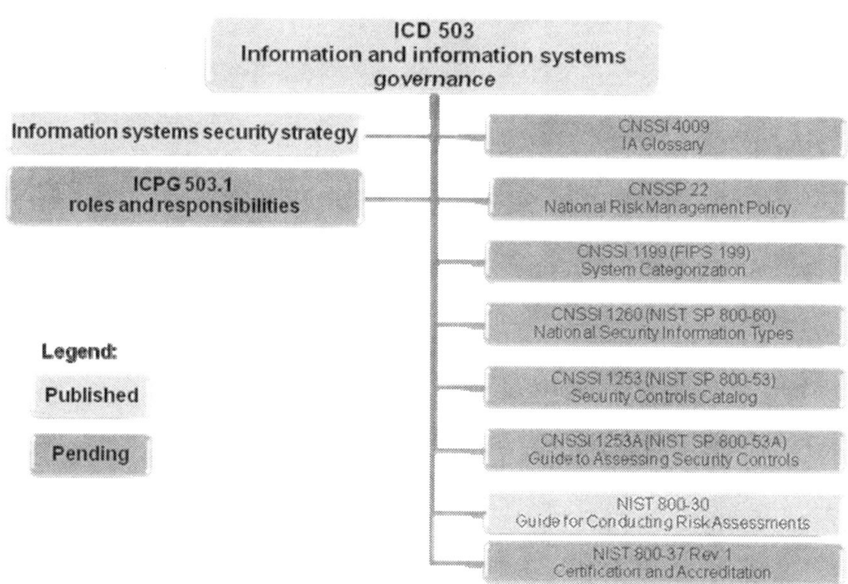

Source: Adapted from ODNI

Proposed approach to C&A

The C&A approach proposed by the transformation effort encompasses a consistent set of policies and processes together with supporting tools. The primary elements are:

- Committee on National Security Systems (CNSS) issuances, which will supplement the NIST risk management framework (RMF) and provide guidance to the national security community.
- Single, four step C&A processes that can be easily integrated into the federal, DOD, and IC acquisition models.
- Automated tools and templates to streamline reporting.
- Continuous monitoring to provide real-time view and eliminate the need for the standard three-year re-accreditation.

- Realistic requirements to meet agency mission needs including the ability (and responsibility) to "tailor" security controls to agency and system requirements.
- Enterprise risk approach which includes more than just technical security requirements.

The elements of the enterprise risk perspective

The enterprise risk perspective is based heavily on NIST's risk management framework (RMF). The key activities of addressing risk – the key words are in bold – from an enterprise view are:

- **Categorize** the information and systems (impact/criticality/ sensitivity).
- **Select and tailor** the security controls.
- Supplement the security controls based on risk assessment.
- **Document** the security controls as required essential information (iterative process).
- **Implement** the security controls in the information system.
- **Assess** the security controls for effectiveness.
- Decide the enterprise/agency-level risk and risk acceptability and **authorize** information system operation.
- **Monitor** security controls on a continuous basis.

Combining the processes with the system life cycle views

The authorization processes issued in NIST SP 800-27 and the C&A processes published by DOD in DODI 8510.01, as well as those from the Intelligence Community all stress the need to link security and the C&A process to the system life cycle. NIST clearly calls out the role of the information system security engineer (ISSE) as a critical element in ensuring that systems security engineering is a part of the process.

Information system acquisition and development follows a number of different models that vary from agency to agency. The figure below shows several of the most common models and their relationship to the C&A process proposed by the transformation team.

The basis for reciprocity

One of the primary objectives of the C&A transformation has been to improve system security reciprocity across the federal government, contractors, and industry. While this may sound simple, it is a daunting task. Over the many years of approaching C&A as an agency-unique process, each of the agencies has developed an approach that mimics their culture and risk tolerance. It is hard for them to let go.

Figure 43: Mapping C&A through acquisition, system (development) life cycle, and the risk management framework

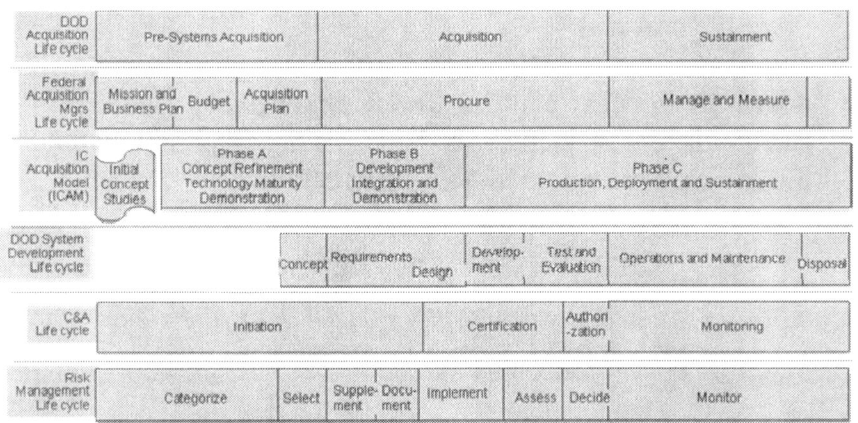

Source: Adapted from ODNI

The transformation process has approached this thorny problem by including all of the stakeholders in the process and by seeking to achieve concurrence on the proposed content. The foundation for achieving reciprocity is represented in the following concepts:

- Utilizing a common set of baseline requirements and standards (CNSS 1253 and CNSS 1253A).
- Adopting a common lexicon (CNSS 4009).
- Leveraging previously certified technologies for re-use.
- Centralizing certification results and accreditation approvals.
- Providing a knowledge repository of approved and validated components (the Information Security Automation Program and the Security Content Automation Protocol available at *http://nvd.nist.gov/scap.cfm*).
- Contributing to trust relationships by establishing one approach based on input from the stakeholders.

Status of the C&A transformation and transition

Although the C&A transformation remains under the joint sponsorship of the DOD and DNI CIOs, significant progress could not have been achieved without the integration and support of key partners, including CNSS, and NIST, particularly the computer security division under Dr Ron Ross.

The engagement and sponsorship of CNSS has facilitated the development of the central policies and guidelines. Close coordination with NIST allows for a synchronization of concepts, standards, and guidelines across all federal agencies. Some of the policy documents have already been issued (e.g. Intelligence Community Directive (ICD) 503). Others are currently undergoing a formal community review; while others are still in the drafting stage. The following table provides a status of the policies as of June 2009:

Table 43: C&A transformation document status as of April 2009

NIST documents in progress	Topic	Status
SP 800-37	Guide for the Security Authorization of Information Systems	Delayed approximately one month in restarting. Final publication target 30 Sep 09.
SP 800-53 (Rev 3)	Security Controls	Highest NIST priority: Final publication target 31 Jul 09.
SP 800-30	Risk Management Guide	Will focus on risk assessment concepts within RMF.
SP 800-39	Managing Risk from Information Systems: An Organizational Perspective	Will "operationalize" risk assessments and focus on tools.

CNSS documents in progress	Topic	Status
CNSSI 1253	Information and Systems Categorization and Security Control Selection (Formerly Security Controls Catalog)	Will be a "delta" document: Will point to SP 800-53 and also include key parts of (former) 1199 plus NSS controls selection guidance.

CNSSI 1253A	Guide for Assessing the Security Controls in National Security Systems	V1 complete: V2 Draft projected completion TBD
CNSSI 1199	Security Categorization	Cancelled (CNSSI 1253 will have equivalent content)
CNSSP 22	National Risk Management Policy	Approved
CNSSI 1230	Risk Assessment Methodology	Postponed
CNSSI 4009	Information Assurance Glossary	WG meeting weekly to adjudicate comments: 40% complete

Intelligence community documents in progress	Status
ICS for Interconnection Security Agreement	ICS 503-1 signed 28 Jan 09.
ICS for Security Controls Catalogue	Cancelled (Will use NIST 800-53).
ICS for Security Categorization	Cancelled (Will use NIST 800-60).
ICS for Security Authorization	Cancelled (Will use NIST 800-37).
ICS for Risk Management	(Will be discussed during TGG).

Transition

Transition to the revised C&A (authorization) process will vary in time and method across the national security community. Some organizations have already started to follow the transformed C&A processes and doctrines — even while the documents are still undergoing a final review.

Other agencies have elected to wait until the authoring process is completed, which was originally expected to occur around the end of calendar year 2008. As of this writing, the authoring process is still not complete. However, the participants have indicated that the focus is on "transition" as of late Spring of 2009.

We recommend that the readers of our book refer to their own agency's information system security program for details on their agency's transition timeframe.

For example, the Intelligence Community has initiated their transition through the publication of IC Directive (ICD) 503, *Intelligence Community Information Technology Systems Security Risk Management, Certification and Accreditation.* Additional detail on intelligence community documents in progress is in Table 43.

DOD's transition details are being promulgated in the DOD 8500 series, primarily through the recently issued DOD Instruction (DODI) 8510.01, the online DIACAP Knowledge Service, and the planned revision of DODI 8500.2, *Information Assurance Implementation.* The DIACAP will remain DOD's process and the DOD transition will take place within the existing DIACAP. In the words of the DOD CIO: "DOD C&A is DIACAP" and will be managed as follows:

- Policy: DODI 8510.01 (Nov 2007).
- Governance: PAAs, DISN/GIG Flag Panel, DOD component leadership and staff ... and more.
- Change management: DIACAP Technical Advisory Group.
- Enterprise automation: DIACAP Knowledge Service, eMASS.
- Enterprise training: see DOD IA Portal.

- C&A transformation: DOD transition will be ***inside*** DIACAP.

DOD recently "de-bunked" some existing myths regarding DOD's perspective on the transition. These included:

- DIACAP is going away soon, so don't bother. The truth: DIACAP is here to stay, so learn it now.
- DOD information systems must be C&A'd to both DIACAP and NIST SP 800-37. The truth: DOD information systems will use the DIACAP processes.
- DOD information systems must be C&A'd to both DODI 8500.2 and NIST SP 800-53 – and sometimes to DCID 6/3. The truth: DOD will be adopting the NIST control set. The signed agreement is included on the accompanying CD.
- Only DOD NSS are subject to the 8500 series; other information systems are subject to NIST Special Publications. The truth: All DOD information systems will use a single control set.
- DIACAP requires more paperwork than DITSCAP. The truth: the required documentation is significantly reduced; however, the implementation and validation requirements have been reinforced.
- We need a single DAA for the entire GIG. The truth: DOD components are responsible for the DIACAP process within their organizations.
- Systems with non-compliant IA controls cannot be accredited. The truth: A mitigation plan must be in place and documented in the POA&M.
- C&A is a bureaucracy and practitioners don't have the power to innovate. The truth: There is sufficient flexibility built in to the DIACAP process to allow knowledgeable C&A practitioners to innovate as needed.

The following table provides a summary of the DOD transition plan and alignment to the Risk Management Framework (RMF).

Table 44: DOD transition plan and alignment to RMF

No	RMF step	CNSS issuance	DOD issuance guide	CNSS key concepts	DOD transition
1	Categorize	CNSSI 1199	DOD 8500.1/2	LMH impact levels for confidentiality, integrity & availability	No immediate change. MAC and LC --> LMH impact levels for confidentiality, integrity & availability
2	Select	CNSSI 1253	DODI 8500.2	Graded IA controls in 800-53 format. Includes all 8500.2 controls (different numbers)	8500.2 controls will be cross-mapped & published on DIACAP KS. New 8500.2 will point to NIST 800-53 & CNSSI 1253 controls. Transition will be graceful. Additional DOD and federal profiles will evolve.
3	Implement	None	DIACAP Knowledge Service, STIGs, DOD component issuances		DIACAP KS implementation guides will be mapped to NIST 800-53 & 1253 controls. Alignment of controls, STIGs, and security automation (e.g. SCAP) will be strengthened. Over time, DIACAP

				Knowledge Service will expand to provide implementation guidance for all NIST 800-53 & 1253 controls.
4	Assess	CNSSI 1253A	DIACAP Knowledge Service, STIGs, DOD component issuances	Generally, 1253A provides less detail than Knowledge Service.	DIACAP KS validation procedures will be mapped to NIST SP & 1253 controls. Alignment with STIGs and security automation (e.g. SCAP) will be strengthened. Over time, DIACAP Knowledge Service will expand to provide assessment guidance for all new controls.
5	Authorize	NIST SP 800-37	DODI 8510.01	DIACAP concepts are in new 800-37, which is available now for public review.	Over time, 8510.01 will likely be updated to reflect new terms.
6	Monitor	NIST SP 800-37	DODI 8510.01		

What is the value added by the transformation and transition?

Another motivation for streamlining existing C&A processes is the enormous cost associated with processes that are executed at different levels at every agency. There is a significant benefit to be achieved through standardization and reciprocity. The Office of the Director of National Intelligence (ODNI) is both a sponsor and an early adopter of the standardized processes.

In a recent meeting in Dallas, Texas, ODNI presented the early results of a cost benefit analysis, which revealed significant results:

- Reduction of manpower costs by 30%: Savings in excess of $1 million on one program.
- Reduction in labor hours by 30%: Numbers down from thousands to hundreds of hours.
- Reduction in certification time by 30%: Test activities conducted in 2 to 4 months versus 8 to 12 months.
- Reduction in documentation by 50%: Number of security documents produced down to 2 or 3.

Additional value added prospects which extend beyond the Intelligence Community include:

- Certified system interconnections within and between agencies and departments to share information can be established in less time and with less effort.
- No longer need to rely on costly and time-consuming case-by-case evaluations and judgments.
- Maximize reuse of components and test data across multiple information systems to minimize effort to secure and accredit information systems.
- Consistency and standardization ensure that FISMA reports for department heads and OMB could be generated in half the time.
- Security staff resources can be shifted from 80% administrative to 80% operational.
- Critical new technologies could be deployed in days and weeks instead of months and years.

References

Intelligence Community Directive (ICD) 503, *Intelligence Community Information Technology Systems Security Risk Management, Certification and Accreditation,* 16 September 2008.

National Institute of Standards and Technology (NIST) Special Publication (SP) 800-37 Rev 1, Draft, *Guide for Security of Federal Information Systems*, released for comment 19 August 2008.

The Information Security Automation Program and The Security Content Automation Protocol (SCAP) available at *http://nvd.nist.gov/scap.cfm*.

THE RESOURCE CD

To assist you in all aspects of the authorization process, there is a companion CD to this book. The table below identifies information systems security requirements and guidelines that are found on the accompanying CD, based on selected sources in effect as of January 2009, and indicates templates that will assist in meeting these requirements. It also includes draft regulations and instructions associated with the C&A Transformation.

The table is organized into the following sections:

1. Federal Requirements, such as: 1) Presidential documents; 2) Public Laws; 3) Office of Management and Budget (OMB) documents; and 4) computer security-related Federal Information Processing Standards Publications (FIPS PUBS) issued by the National Institute of Standards and Technology (NIST).

2. Guidelines issued by NIST under the Special Publication 800 series, which may or may not be mandatory; agencies may use them voluntarily unless otherwise specified.

3. Regulations issued by the Department of Defense, which are binding on DOD entities.

4. Standards, Best Practices, and other useful guidelines.

5. Templates for NIST, DOD and general use.

LAW, POLICY, REGULATIONS, AND GUIDELINES

Presidential Documents (Presidential Decision Directives (PDD); National Security Policy Directive (NSPD); Homeland Security Policy Directive (HSPD))
Executive Branch Directive
NSPD 54/HSPD 21, Cyber Security & Monitoring
NSPD 51 /HSPD 20, National Continuity Policy

HSPD 12, Policy for a Common Identification Standard for Federal Employees and Contractors
HSPD 7, Critical Infrastructure Identification, Prioritization, and Protection
PDD 67, Enduring Constitutional Government and Continuity of Government Operations
PDD 63, Protecting America's Critical Infrastructures
Executive Orders
EO 13292, Further Amendment to EO 12958, as Amended, Classified National Security Information
EO 13284, Establishment of the Department of Homeland Security
EO 13231, Critical Infrastructure Protection in the Information Age
EO 13130, National Infrastructure Assurance Council
EO 13103, Computer Software Piracy
EO 13011, Federal Information Technology
EO 12958, Classified National Security Information
EO 12472, Assignment of National Security and Emergency Preparedness Telecommunications Functions
EO 12333, US Intelligence Activities
Presidential Memoranda
Presidential Memorandum, Freedom of Information Act
Presidential Memorandum, Controlled Unclassified Information
Presidential Memorandum, Action by Federal Agencies to Safeguard Against Internet Attacks
Memo from White House Chief of Staff, Security of Federal Information Systems
Presidential Memorandum, Electronic Government
Presidential Memorandum, Privacy and Personal Information and Federal Records
Public Laws
Federal Information Security Management Act of 2002 (FISMA) (Title III of

the E-Gov Act of 2002)
Electronic Government Act of 2002 (E-Gov)
Sec. 639. (A) Prohibition Of Federal Agency Monitoring Of Personal Information On Use Of Internet, Treasury and General Government Appropriations Act of 2002
Section 646, Protection of Citizens' Privacy on Federal Web Sites, Treasury and General Government Appropriations Act, 2001
Electronic Signatures in Global and National Commerce Act
Government Paperwork Elimination Act of 1999 (GPEA)
Health Insurance Portability and Accountability Act of 1996 (HIPAA)
Clinger Cohen Act (formerly the Information Technology Management Reform Act of 1996)
Privacy Act of 1974, as amended
Computer Security Act of 1987
OMB Documents
OMB Memorandum 09-02, Information Technology Management Structure and Governance Framework
OMB Memorandum 08-27, Guidance for Trusted Internet Connection (TIC) Compliance
OMB Memorandum 08-23, Securing the Federal Government's Domain Name System Infrastructure
OMB Memorandum 08-22, Guidance on the Federal Desktop Core Configuration (FDCC)
M-08-21, Reporting Instructions for the Federal Information Security Management Act and Agency Privacy Management
OMB Circular A-11, Preparation and Submission of Budget Estimates, Section 300
OMB Memorandum 08-09, New FISMA Privacy Reporting Requirements for FY 2008
OMB Memorandum 07-18, Ensuring New Acquisitions Include Common Security Configurations
OMB Memorandum 07-16, Safeguarding Against and Responding to the Breach of Personally Identifiable Information

| OMB Memorandum 06-16, Protection of Sensitive Agency Information |
| OMB Memorandum 05-24, Implementation of HSPD-12 |
| OMB Memorandum 04-15, Development of HSPD-7 Critical Infrastructure Protection Plans |
| OMB Memorandum 04-04, e-Authentication Guidance for Federal Agencies |
| M-03-18, Implementation Guidance for the   E-Government Act of 2002 |
| OMB Guidance to Federal Agencies on Data Availability and Encryption |
| Appendix III to OMB Circular A-130, Revised, Security of Federal Automated Information Resources |
| OMB Circular A-130, Revised, Transmittal Memorandum No. 4, Management of Federal Information Resources |
| M-01-05, Guidance on Inter-Agency Sharing of Personal Data-Protecting Personal Privacy |
| M-00-15, OMB Guidance on Implementing the Electronic Signatures in Global and National Commerce Act |
| M-00-13, Privacy Policies and Data Collection on Federal Web Sites |
| M-00-10, OMB Procedures and Guidance on Implementing the Government Paperwork Elimination Act |
| M-00-07, Incorporating and Funding Security in Information Systems Investments |
| **NIST Documents** |
| ***Federal Information Processing Standard Publications (FIPS)*** |
| FIPS 200-01, Change 1, Personal Identity Verification (PIV) of Federal Employees and Contractors |
| FIPS 200, Minimum Security Requirements for Federal Information and Information Systems |
| FIPS 199, Standards for Security Categorization of Federal Information and Information Systems |
| FIPS 198, The Keyed-Hash Message Authentication Code (HMAC) |
| FIPS 197, Advanced Encryption Standard |
| FIPS 196, Entity Authentication Using Public Key Cryptography |

FIPS 191, Guideline for The Analysis of Local Area Network Security
FIPS 190, Guideline for the Use of Advanced Authentication Technology Alternatives
FIPS 188, Standard Security Labels for Information Transfer
FIPS 186-2, Digital Signature Standard (DSS)
FIPS 185, Escrowed Encryption Standard
FIPS 181, Automated Password Generator
FIPS 140-2, Security Requirements for Cryptographic Modules (With Change Notices)
NIST Special Publications (SP)
NIST Guide to the Information Security Documents and Associated Trifold
NIST SP 800-124, Guidelines on Cell Phone and PDA Security
NIST SP 800-123, Guide to General Server Security
DRAFT NIST SP 800-122, Guide to Protecting the Confidentiality of Personally Identifiable Information (PII)
NIST SP 800-121, Guide to Bluetooth Security
NIST SP 800-115, Technical Guide to Information Security Testing and Assessment
NIST SP 800-114, User's Guide to Securing External Devices for Telework and Remote Access
NIST 800-100, Information Security Handbook: A Guide for Managers
NIST SP 800-88, Guidelines for Media Sanitization
NIST SP 800-65, Integrating IT Security Into the Capital Planning and Investment Control Process
NIST SP 800-64, Rev 2, Security Considerations in the System Development Life Cycle
NIST SP 800-61, Computer Security Incident Handling Guide
NIST SP 800-60, Guide for Mapping Types of Information and Information Systems to Security Categories

NIST SP 800-59, Guideline for Identifying an Information System as a National Security System
NIST SP 800-55, Security Metrics Guide for Information Technology Systems
NIST SP 800-53, Rev 2, Recommended Security Controls for Federal Information Systems
NIST SP 800-53A, Guide for Assessing the Security Controls in Federal Information Systems
NIST SP 800-51, Use of the Common Vulnerabilities and Exposures (CVE) Vulnerability Naming Scheme
NIST SP 800-50, Building an Information Technology Security Awareness and Training Program
NIST SP 800-47, Security Guide for Interconnecting Information Technology Systems
DRAFT NIST SP 800-46, Rev 1, Guide to Enterprise Telework and Remote Access Security
NIST SP 800-45, Rev 2, Guidelines on Electronic Mail Security
NIST SP 800-44, Rev 2, Guidelines on Securing Public Web Servers
DRAFT NIST SP 800-41, Guidelines on Firewalls and Firewall Policy
NIST SP 800-40, Procedures for Handling Security Patches
NIST SP 800-37, Guide for the Security Certification and Accreditation of Federal Information Systems
NIST SP 800-36, Guide to Selecting IT Security Products
NIST SP 800-35, Guide to IT Security Services
NIST SP 800-34, Contingency Planning Guide for Information Technology Systems
NIST SP 800-33, Underlying Technical Models for Information Technology Security
NIST SP 800-32, Introduction to Public Key Infrastructure and the Federal PKI Infrastructure
NIST SP 800-30, Risk Management Guide for Information Technology Systems

NIST SP 800-29, A Comparison of the Security Requirements for Cryptographic Modules in FIPS 140-1 and FIPS 140-2
NIST SP 800-28, Rev. 2, Guidelines on Active Content and Mobile Code
NIST SP 800-27, Rev A., Engineering Principles for Information Technology Security
NIST SP 800-23, Guidelines to Federal Organizations on Security Assurance and Acquisition/Use of Tested/Evaluated Products
NIST SP 800-19, Mobile Agent Security
NIST SP 800-18, Guide for Developing Security Plans for Information Technology Systems
NIST SP 800-16, Information Technology Security Training Requirements: A Role- and Performance-Based Model
NIST SP 800-14, Generally Accepted Principles and Practices for Securing Information Technology Systems
NIST SP 800-13, Telecommunications Security Guide for Telecommunications Management Network
NIST SP 800-12, An Introduction to Computer Security: the NIST Handbook
COMMITTEE FOR NATIONAL SECURITY SYSTEMS (CNSS) PUBLICATIONS
CNSSP-6, National Policy on Certification & Accreditation (C&A) of National Security Systems
CNSSSP-22, Information Assurance Risk Management Policy for National Security Systems
NSTISSI 1000, National Certification & Accreditation Process (NIACAP)
DEPARTMENT OF DEFENSE PUBLICATIONS
Department of Defense Directives
DODD 3020.26, Defense Continuity Program
DOD 5200.1-R, Information Security Program
DOD 5400.11, Department of Defense Privacy Program
DODD 8500.01E, Information Assurance
DODD 8570.1, Information Assurance Training, Certification and Workforce

Management

Department of Defense Instructions
DODI 3020.39, Integrated Continuity Program for the Defense Intelligence Enterprise (DIE)
DODI 3020.42, Defense Continuity Plan Development
DODI 5000.02, Operation of the Defense Acquisition System
DODI 8500.2, Information Assurance Implementation
DODI 8510.01, Department of Defense Information Assurance Certification & Accreditation Process (DIACAP)
DODI 8552.01, Use of Mobile Code Technologies in DOD Information Systems
DODI 8580.1, Information Assurance in the Defense Acquisition System

Department of Defense Manuals
DOD 5220.22-M,, National Industrial Security Program Operating Manual (NISPOM)
DOD 8570.1-M, Information Assurance Workforce Improvement Program

Department of Defense Memos
Department of Defense Memo on DOD C&A Reciprocity
Policy on Use of Department of Defense (DoD) Information Systems Standard Consent Banner and User Agreement
Department of Defense Global Information Grid (GIG) Information Assurance
Guidance on Protecting Personally Identifiable Information (PII)
Encryption of Sensitive Unclassified Data on Mobile Computing Devices and Removable Storage Media

Joint Chiefs of Staff Policy
CJCSI 6510.01E, Information Assurance (IA) and Computer Network Defense (CND)

Department of the Air Force Policy
AFI 33-210, Air Force Certification & Accreditation (C&A) Program

Department of the Army Policy
AR 25-1, Army Knowledge Management and Information Technology
AR 25-2, Information Assurance
DA PAM 25-1-2, Information Technology Contingency Planning
DA Best Business Practice(BBP) 002, Certification & Accreditation
BBP 003, Designated Accrediting Authority
BBP 004, Certification Authority
BBP 005, Agent of the Certification Authority
BBP 006, Installation Level Designated Approving Authority
BBP 007, Connection Approval Process
BBP 008, Army Information Assurance Certification and Accreditation Terms for Connectivity to the Installation Service Provider/ICAN
BBP 009, Stand Alone IS and Closed Restricted Networks Information Assurance Certification & Accreditation (IA C&A) Requirements
Department of the Navy Policy (Includes Navy and Marine Corps)
SECNAVINST 5239.3A, Department of the Navy Information Assurance Policy
OPNAV 5239.3C, Navy Information Assurance Program
DON CIO Memo, Platform Information Technology (PIT) C&A Guidance
DON CIO Memo, Senior Information Assurance Officer (SIAO) Alignment And Responsibilities For Information Assurance And Certification And Accreditation Processes
DON DOD Information Assurance C&A Process (DIACAP) Handbook
National Security Agency (NSA) Policy
Security Configuration Guides
Defense Information Systems Agency (DISA) Policy
Security Technical Configuration Guides (STIGS)
Security Checklists
Security Readiness Review (SRR) Scripts

C&A Transformation Documentation
Agreement Between CIOs
CNSS Agreement to Use NIST Documents as Basis for Security Controls and Risk Assessment

TEMPLATES

Federal Required Documentation
NIST System Security Plan – Version 1
NIST System Security Plan – Version 2
NIST Plan of Action & Milestones Guide
NIST Plan of Action & Milestones Guide for System Stewards
NIST Security Assessment Report (SAR) Template
Certification & Authorization Statement Template
Federal Artifacts
Personally Identifiable Information Controls Analysis Template
NIST IT Security Handbook
NIST Configuration Management Plan
NIST Incident Response Plan
NIST IT Contingency Plan
NIST Memorandum of Understanding (MOU) Template
NIST Interconnection Security Agreement Template
Risk Calculation Worksheet Template
Department of Defense Required Documentation
DIACAP Package
DIACAP Artifacts (Evidence of Compliance)
Artifact 1 – Security Concept of Operations (S-CONOPS)
Artifact 2 – Configuration Management Plan
Artifact 3 – Security Design Documentation

Artifact 4 – Contingency Plan/Business Continuity Plan
Artifact 5 – Incident Response Plan
Artifact 6 – Interconnection Memorandum of Agreement
Artifact 7 – Privacy Impact Assessment Determination Checklist
Artifact 8 – Security Test Plan
Artifact 8a – Security Test Plan – Version 2
Artifact 9 – Physical Security Assessment Report
Artifact 10 – Security Education, Training, and Awareness (SETA) Plan
Artifact 11 – Security Assessment Report (SAR)
DOD IA Controls & Validation Procedures
DOD IA Controls Weakness Statements
DOD IA Controls Impact Codes
DIACAP Security Posture Questionnaire
FISMA-CIO Template FY 2008
IA Workforce Training Tracker FY 09
IA Workforce Training Tracker FY09 Guidance
DOD Memorandum of Agreement (MOA) Template
DOD Annual IA Controls Assessment Form
General
Change Request Form
Change Request Status Log
Emergency Change Request Form
Security Impact Assessment Form
HIPAA Analysis Template
C&A Document Tracker Template
Additional Risk Assessment Resources
Sample List of Assets
Sample List of Vulnerabilities

In-Briefing Template
Out-Briefing Template
Threat Identification Workbook
System Life Cycle and Documentation
User Manual Guide

GLOSSARY

Accreditation: Formal declaration by an authorizing official or designated approving authority (DAA) that an information system (IS) is approved to operate at an acceptable level of risk, based on the implementation of an approved set of technical, managerial, and procedural safeguards. (CNSSI 4009)

Acquisition category: A designation for a program of development or acquisition based on cost, determining both the level of review required by law and the level at which the milestone (e.g. progress to the next development or acquisition level) decision authority rests in DOD.

Authorizing official: A senior official or executive with the authority to formally assume responsibility for operating an information system at an acceptable level of risk to organizational operations (including mission, functions, image, or reputation), organizational assets, individuals, other organizations, and the nation.

Assurance: Grounds for confidence that an information technology system or product meets security objectives. (DOD Directive 8500.01E)

Authentication: Security measures designed to establish the validity of a transmission, message, or originator, or a means of verifying an individual's authorization to receive specific categories of information. (DOD Directive 8500.01E)

Authorization: See accreditation.

Availability: Timely, reliable access to date and information services for authorized users. (DOD Directive 8500.01E)

Capital assets: Land, structures, equipment, intellectual property (e.g. software), and information technology including IT service contracts used by the federal government and having an estimated useful life of two years or more.

Certification: Comprehensive evaluation of the technical and non-technical security features of an information system (IS), and other safeguards made in support of the accreditation process, establishing the extent to which a particular design and implementation meets a set of specified security requirements. (CNSSI 4009)

Community of interest (COI): An inclusive term used to describe groups of individuals who share information relative to common goals, interests, missions, or business processes. (DODI 8510.01)

Compusec (computer security): a term used largely by the US military to denote measures required for ensuring secure entry, management and storage of information in computer systems.

Computer network defense (CND): Actions taken to protect, monitor, analyze, detect, and respond to unauthorized activity within DOD information systems and computer networks. The unauthorized activity may include disruption, denial, degradation, destruction, exploitation, or access to computer networks, information systems or their contents, or theft of information. (DOD Directive 8530.1)

Confidentiality: Preserving authorized restrictions on information access and disclosure, including means for protecting personal privacy and proprietary information. Assurance information is not disclosed to unauthorized entities or processes. (DOD Directive 8500.01E)

Configuration: Functional and physical characteristics of hardware or software as set forth in technical documentation or achieved in a product.

Configuration control: The systematic proposal, justification, evaluation, coordination, approval, or disapproval of proposed changes and the implementation of all approved changes in the configuration after the baseline has been established.

Configuration management: Management of security features and assurances through control of changes made to hardware, software, firmware, documentation, test fixtures, and test documentation throughout the life cycle of an IS. (CNSSI 4009)

Control: See information systems security control.

Defense in depth: The DOD approach for establishing an adequate security posture in a shared risk environment that shares mitigation by: integration of people, technology, and operations; layering of security solutions; and the selection of security functions based on their relative level of robustness.

General support system (GSS): An interconnected set of information resources under the same direct management control which shares common (functionality). (OMB A-130)

Global information grid (GIG): Globally interconnected, end-to-end set of DOD information capabilities, associated processes, and personnel for collecting, processing, storing, disseminating and managing information on demand to warfighters, policy makers, and support personnel. It is the organizing and transforming construct for managing information technology throughout the Department of Defense. (DOD Directive 8100.1)

Information: Any communication or representation of knowledge such as facts, data, or opinions in any medium or form, including textual, numerical, graphic, cartographic, narrative, or audiovisual forms. (Defined in OMB Circular A-130, 6(a))

Information assurance (IA): Measures protecting and defending information and information systems by ensuring their availability, integrity, authentication, confidentiality, and non-repudiation. This includes providing for the restoration of information systems by incorporating protection, detection, and reaction capabilities. Used almost exclusively in the US DOD. (DOD Instruction 8500.01E)

Information assurance (IA) control: See information systems security control.

Information system: Any telecommunication or computer-related equipment or interconnected system or subsystems of equipment used in the acquisition, storage, manipulation, management, movement, control, display, transmission of voice and/or data; includes firmware, hardware, and software.

Information systems security: Measures and controls designed to ensure confidentiality, integrity, and availability of information processed and stored by automated information systems (AIS).[119] AIS security considers all hardware and software functions, characteristics and features; operational procedures; accountability procedures; and access controls at the central computer facility, remote computer, and terminal facilities; management constraints; physical structures and devices, such as computers, transmission lines, and power sources; and personnel and communications controls needed to provide an acceptable level of risk for the automated information system and for the data and information contained in the system. AIS security also includes the totality of security safeguards needed to provide an acceptable protection level for an automated information system and for the data handled by an automated information system.

Information systems security control: An objective security condition achieved through the application of specific security safeguards or through the regulation of specific activities. The objective security condition is verifiable, compliance is measurable, and the activities required to achieve the security control are assignable and, consequently, accountable.

Infosec: Defined by the National Security Telecommunications and Information Systems Security Instruction (NSTISSI) 4009 as the protection of information systems against unauthorized access to or modification of information, denial of service to unauthorized users, and provision of service to authorized users. Often used interchangeably with information systems security.

Integrity: Quality of an information system reflecting the logical correctness and reliability of the operating system; the logical completeness of the hardware and software implementing the protection mechanisms; and the consistency of the data structures

---

[119] The unauthorized disclosure, modification, or destruction may be accidental or intentional.

and the stored data; protection against unauthorized modification or destruction of information. (DOD Directive 8500.01E)

Joint accreditation: Occurs when different operational or mission-related components of an information system are under the jurisdiction of different AOs, requiring them to collectively accredit the information system.

Major application (MA): An application that requires special attention to security due to the risk and magnitude of the harm resulting from the loss, misuse, or unauthorized access to or modification of the information in the application. (OMB A-130)

Major investment: A system or acquisition requiring special management attention because of its importance to the mission or function of the agency, a component of the agency or another organization; is for financial management and obligates more than $500,000 annually; has significant program or policy implications; has high executive visibility; has high development, operating, or maintenance costs; is funded through other than direct appropriations; or is defined as major by the agency's capital planning and investment control process. (OMB Circular A-11)

Major system: IT investments that are reported on Capital Asset Plan and Business Case, Exhibit 300. They include projects that fit any of the following criteria:

- Life cycle cost of $35 million or more.
- Annual cost $5 million or more.
- Systems that link to the first two layers of the Federal Enterprise Architecture.
- Financial management systems that cost more than $500,000.
- Projects that were reported on Exhibit 300s in the prior year's budget process.
- Projects that are department-wide;
- Projects that directly support the President's Management Agenda items or are of particular interest to OMB, i.e. meet the criteria of high executive visibility.

Projects that are e-government in nature or use e-business technologies must be identified as major projects regardless of the costs.

Major projects should account for at least 60 percent of the IT investment portfolio for FY 2004 reporting. If you are unsure about what systems to consider as major, consult your CIO.

Mission assurance category (MAC):   The mission assurance category reflects the importance of information in order to achieve DOD goals and objectives, particularly in support of the warfighters' combat mission. Mission assurance categories are based on the determined requirements for information and information system availability and integrity.

Mission critical information system: A system meeting the definition of information system and national security system, the loss of which would stop warfighter operations or the direct mission support to warfighter operations. The designation must be made by a DOD component head.

Mission essential information system: A system meeting the definition of information system and which is basic and necessary for the accomplishment of the organization's mission.   The designation must be made by a DOD component head.

Mission support system: A system handling information important to the support of deployed or contingency forces. It must be accurate, but can sustain minimal delay without seriously affecting operational readiness or mission effectiveness.

National security system (NSS): Any computer system (including any telecommunications system) used or operated by an agency, the function of which involves intelligence activities, cryptologic activities, command and control of military forces, equipment which is an integral part of a weapon or weapons system, or is critical to the direct fulfillment of military or intelligence missions. (Section 5142b, Clinger Cohen Act of 1996)

Non-repudiation: Assurance the sender of data is provided with proof of delivery and the recipient is provided with proof of the sender's identity, so neither can later deny having processed the data. (DOD Directive 8500.01E)

Personally-identifiable information (PII): Information in an information system, online, or otherwise maintained (e.g. documents) that directly or indirectly identifies an individual. NOTE: an individual can be a US citizen, permanent legal resident, visitor to the US, and even an organization.

Plan of action and milestones (POA&M): As defined in OMB Memorandum 02-01, a plan of action and milestones (POA&M), also referred to as a corrective action plan, is a tool that identifies tasks that need to be accomplished. It details resources required to accomplish the elements of the plan, any milestones in meeting the task, and scheduled completion dates for the milestones. The purpose of the POA&M is to assist agencies in identifying, assessing, prioritizing, and monitoring the progress of corrective efforts for security weaknesses found in programs and systems. (OMB Circular A-11)

Portfolio management: The management of selected groupings of IT investments using strategic planning, architectures, and outcome-based performance measures to achieve a mission capability.

Privacy impact assessment (PIA): An analysis of how personally-identifiable information is collected, stored, protected, shared, and managed.

Program: Organized activity that contains any number of basic elements such as conducting risk assessments; conducting IT security training; establishing an incident response capability; writing, establishing, and enforcing policies and procedures; and processes for planning, implementing, evaluating, and implementing remedial action for addressing weaknesses. (Defined in Title III of the E-Government Act)

Program of record (POR): An acquisition program that has been approved through the official DOD budget process and is listed in the Future Years Defense Program (FYDP). These information systems are typically weapons systems, command, control, communications, computers, intelligence, surveillance, and reconnaissance (C4ISR) systems and other systems procured through the processes of DODD 5000.1, Defense Acquisition.

Public information: Official DOD information reviewed and approved for public release by the information owner in accordance with DOD Directive 5230.9. (DOD Directive 8500.1)

Risk assessment: The element of the continuous risk management process that analyzes threat, vulnerabilities, and costs in order to assign relative priorities for mitigation plans and implementation.

Risk management: The ongoing process of identifying these risks and implementing plans to address them. The process by which resources are planned, organized, directed, and controlled to ensure the risk of operating a system remains within acceptable bounds at optimal cost.

Sensitive information: Information in which the loss, misuse, or unauthorized access to or modification of, could adversely affect the national interest or the conduct of a federal program, or the privacy to which individuals are entitled under Section 552a of Title 5, US Code, but which has not been specifically authorized under criteria established by executive order or act of Congress to be kept secret in the interest of national defense or foreign policy. Examples of sensitive information include payroll, finance, and logistics. (DOD Directive 8500.1)

System: A collection of computing and/or communications components and other resources that support one or more functional objectives of an organization. IT system resources include any IT component plus associated manual procedures and physical facilities that are used in the acquisition, storage, manipulation, display, and/or movement of data or to direct or monitor operating procedures. An IT system may consist of one or more computers and their related resources of any size. The resources that comprise a system do not have to be physically connected. (Defined in NIST SP 800-16, Appendix C)

System life cycle (SLC): A formal model of a hardware or software project that depicts the scope of and relationship among activities, products, reviews, approvals, and resources. In addition, the period that begins when a need is identified (initiation) and ends when a system ceases to be available for use (disposal). NOTE: activities associated with a system include the system's initiation, development and acquisition, implementation, operation and maintenance, and ultimately its disposal (that may instigate another system initiation). (Defined in NIST SP 800-34, Appendix E)

Threat agent: An entity that may act to cause a threat event to occur by exploiting the vulnerability(ies) in an information system.

Vulnerability: A flaw or weakness in a system's security procedures, design, implementation, or internal controls that could be exercised (accidentally triggered or intentionally exploited) and result in a security breach or a violation of the system's security policy. (Defined in NIST SP 800-47, Appendix D)

ACRONYMS

ACAT	Acquisition Category
FCA	Air Force Communications Agency
AIS	Automated Information System
AO	Authorizing Official, also known as the Designated Accrediting Authority
APMS	Army Portfolio Management Solution
ARPA	Advanced Research Project Agency
ATD	Authorization Termination Date
BMA	Business Mission Area
BRM	Business Reference Model
C&A	Certification & Accreditation
CA	Certifying Authority, also known as the Certification Agent
CCA	Clinger Cohen Act (of 1996)
CCB	Configuration Control Board
CCI	Configuration Control Item
CCP	Configuration Control Process
CCRB	Configuration Control Review Board; also called the CCB
CERT	Computer Emergency Response Team
CDD	Capabilities Development Document
CDS	Cross Domain Solutions
CIA	Confidentiality, Integrity and Availability
CIAO	Critical Infrastructure Assurance Office

CIO	Chief Information Officer
CISO	Chief Information Security Officer
CISS	Center for Information Systems Security
CM	Configuration Management
CMB	Configuration Management Board
CMP	Configuration Management Plan
CND	Computer Network Defense
CNSSI	Committee on National Security Systems Instruction
COI	Community of Interest
CONOPS	Concept of Operations
COOP	Continuity of Operations Plan
CPD	Capabilities Production Document
CR	Change Request
CSA	Computer Security Act (of 1987)
CSO	Chief Security Officer, often used interchangeably with CISO
DAA	Designated Approving Authority; Designated Accrediting Authority; also known as the Approving Official (AO)
DAA-R	Designated Accrediting Authority Representative
DADMS	Department of the Navy Application Database Management System
DCID	Director of Central Intelligence Directive
DDOS	Distributed Denial of Service
DHS	Department of Homeland Security
DIACAP	Department of Defense Information Assurance Certification &Accreditation Process (2007)
DIMA	Defense Intelligence Mission Area

DIP	DIACAP Implementation Plan
DISA	Defense Information Systems Agency
DISN	Defense Information Systems Network
DITPR	Department of Defense Information Technology Portfolio Repository
DITSCAP	Department of Defense Information Technology Information Technology Security Certification and Accreditation Process (1997)
DNI	Director of National Intelligence
DOD	Department of Defense
DODD	Department of Defense Directive
DODI	Department of Defense Instruction
DSB	Defense Science Board
DOS	Denial of Service
DSAWG	DOD IA Security Accreditation Working Group
EA	Enterprise Architecture
EIEMA	Enterprise Information Environment Mission Area
eMASS	Enterprise Mission Assurance Support Service
EITDR	Enterprise Information Technology Data Repository
EO	Executive Order
EPHI	Electronic Protected Health Information
FDCC	Federal Desktop Core Configuration
FEA	Federal Enterprise Architecture
FEMA	Federal Emergency Management Agency
FIPS	Federal Information Processing Standard
FISMA	Federal Information Security Management Act
ftp	File Transfer Protocol

GAO	Government Accounting Office
GIG	Global Information Grid
GISRA	Government Information Security Reform Act
GSS	General Support System
HSA	Homeland Security Act
IA	Information Assurance
IAM	Information Assurance Manager
IAO	Information Assurance Officer
IASE	Information Assurance Support Environment
IAVA	Information Assurance Vulnerability Alert
IASL	Information Assurance Senior Leadership
IC	Intelligence Community
ICD	Initial Capabilities Document
IG	Inspector General
IIHI	Individually Identifiable Health Information
IPT	Integrated Process Team
IS	Information System
ISA	Interconnection Security Agreement
ISAC	Information Sharing and Analysis Center
ISSE	Information Systems Security Engineering
ISSM	Information Systems Security Manager
IT	Information Technology
KS	Knowledge Service (DIACAP)
LAN	Local Area Network
LOE	Level of Effort
MA	Major Application

MA	Mission Area
MAC	Mission Assurance Category
MIS	Mission Impact Statement
MIT	Massachusetts Institute of Technology
MNS	Mission Needs Statement
NCSD	National Cyber Security Division
NIAC	National Infrastructure Assurance Council
NIPC	National Infrastructure Protection Center
NIST	National Institute of Standards and Technology
NSA	National Security Agency
NSD	National Security Directive
NSS	National Security System
NSTISSI	National Security Telecommunications and Information Systems Security Instruction
O&M	Operations & Maintenance
OMB	Office of Management and Budget
ORD	Operational Requirements Document
OS	Operating System
PAA	Principal Approving Authority; Principal Accrediting Authority; Primary Approving Authority
PC	Personal Computer
PDA	Personal Digital Assistant
PDD	Presidential Decision Directive
PIA	Privacy Impact Assessment
PII	Personally Identifiable Information
PL	Public Law
PM	Program Manager

POR	Program of Record
R&D	Research & Development
ROI	Return on Investment
ROSI	Return on Security Investment
RTM	Requirements Traceability Matrix
SAISO	Senior Agency Information Security Officer
SAR	Security Assessment Report
SC	Security Category
SCA	Security Controls Assessment
SDLC	System Development Life Cycle
SIP	System Identification Profile
SLA	Service Level Agreement
SLC	System Life Cycle
SME	Subject Matter Expert
SORN	System of Records Notice
SOW	Statement of Work
SP	Special Publication
SRS	System Requirements Specification
SRTM	Security Requirements Traceability Matrix
SSAA	System Security Authorization Agreement
SSP	System Security Plan (or Policy)
ST&E	Security Test and Evaluation
STIG	Security Technical Implementation Guide
TAG	Technical Advisory Group
T&E	Test and Evaluation
TCB	Trusted Computer Base

tcp	Transmission Control Protocol
TCSEC	Trusted Computer System Evaluation Criteria
UCDMO	Unified Cross Domain Management Office
UR	User Representative
USC	United States Code
WMA	Warfighting Mission Area

ITG RESOURCES

IT Governance Ltd sources, creates and delivers products and services to meet the real-world, evolving IT governance needs of today's organisations, directors, managers and practitioners. The ITG website (*www.itgovernance.co.uk*) is the international one-stop-shop for corporate and IT governance information, advice, guidance, books, tools, training and consultancy.

Other Websites

Books and tools published by IT Governance Publishing (ITGP) are available from all business booksellers and are also immediately available from the following websites:

www.itgovernance.co.uk/catalog/355 provides information and online purchasing facilities for every currently available book published by ITGP.

www.itgovernanceusa.com is a US$-based website that delivers the full range of IT Governance products to North America, and ships from within the continental USA.

www.itgovernanceasia.com provides a selected range of ITGP products specifically for customers in South Asia.

www.27001.com is the IT Governance Ltd website that deals specifically with information security management, and ships from within the continental USA.

Pocket Guides

For full details of the entire range of pocket guides, simply follow the links at *www.itgovernance.co.uk/publishing.aspx*.

Toolkits

ITG's unique range of toolkits includes the IT Governance Framework Toolkit, which contains all the tools and guidance that you will need in order to develop and implement an appropriate IT governance framework for your organisation. Full details can be found at *www.itgovernance.co.uk/products/519*.

For a free paper on how to use the proprietary Calder Moir IT Governance Framework, and for a free trial version of the toolkit, see *www.itgovernance.co.uk/calder_moir.aspx*.

There is also a wide range of toolkits to simplify implementation of management systems, such as an ISO/IEC 27001 ISMS or a BS25999 BCMS, and these can all be viewed and purchased online at: *http://www.itgovernance.co.uk/catalog/1*

Best Practice Reports

ITG's range of Best Practice Reports is now at *www.itgovernance.co.uk/best-practice-reports.aspx*. These offer you essential, pertinent, expertly researched information on an increasing number of key issues including Web 2.0 and Green IT.

Training and Consultancy

IT Governance also offers training and consultancy services across the entire spectrum of disciplines in the information governance arena. Details of training courses can be accessed at *www.itgovernance.co.uk/training.aspx* and descriptions of our consultancy services can be found at *http://www.itgovernance.co.uk/consulting.aspx*.

Why not contact us to see how we could help you and your organisation?

Newsletter

IT governance is one of the hottest topics in business today, not least because it is also the fastest moving, so what better way to keep up than by subscribing to ITG's free monthly newsletter *Sentinel*? It provides monthly updates and resources across the whole spectrum of IT governance subject matter, including risk management, information security, ITIL and IT service management, project governance, compliance and so much more. Subscribe for your free copy at: *www.itgovernance.co.uk/newsletter.aspx*.

CPSIA information can be obtained at www.ICGtesting.com
Printed in the USA
270550BV00004B/1/P